The Native Trees of New Zealand

*To my son Scott, who accompanied me
on numerous tough trips into the forested
areas of New Zealand during the many
years that this book was in preparation*

The Native Trees
of New Zealand

J.T. Salmon D.Sc., F.R.S.N.Z., F.R.P.S.

Professor Emeritus, Victoria University of Wellington

REED

Botanical consultants

J.W. Dawson M.A., Ph.D.,
Reader in Botany,
Victoria University of Wellington

B.V. Sneddon, M.Sc.,Ph.D.,
Lecturer in Botany,
Victoria University of Wellington

Published by Reed Books, a division of Reed
Publishing (NZ) Ltd, 39 Rawene Road, Birkenhead,
Auckland. Associated companies, branches and
representatives throughout the world.

© 1980 J. T. Salmon

First published 1980
Reprinted 1981, 1986
Revised edition 1986
Reprinted 1989, 1990, 1992, 1993
Revised edition 1996
Reprinted 1997, 2001

ISBN 0 7900 0503 4

Editor: Geoff Walker
Designer: Brian Moss
Illustrator: Jason Carter
Typographer: Bob Henderson
Typesetting by John van Hulst Ltd, Wellington, New Zealand
Fred Witham Ltd, Wellington, New Zealand
Printed by Kyodo Printing Ltd, Singapore.

Contents

Page 6
A small tree of *Urostemon kirkii* in full flower beside the Hokianga Kauri in Omahuta State Forest, January 1980. See also Fig 1, page 335.

Page 8
The almost tropical appearance of a New Zealand rain forest. Trumans Track, Westland.

Foreword

By His Royal Highness,
the Duke of Edinburgh

With patience and diligence it is possible to become an expert in almost any subject, but the truly civilised person is always on the lookout to become more aware of the mystery and wonders of the world. In that sense this book is a must for all civilised people, and particularly for those of New Zealand, for *The Native Trees of New Zealand* reveals the rich diversity of the country's indigenous trees and increases our understanding of their struggle for survival.

The progress of technology and international commerce has made it increasingly difficult to maintain a reasonable balance between development and conservation. This balance cannot be kept by confrontation; it needs a personal sympathy for our natural heritage by those involved in development and personal understanding of the economic facts of life by those involved in conservation.

Someone once said that knowledge is power. I very much hope that knowledge of the native forests of New Zealand will provide the power to conserve them, so that future generations will be able to enjoy their beauty and variety as well as all the creatures which make their homes in them.

Acknowledgements

This book has been many years in preparation. There have, naturally, been difficulties in locating suitable trees of some species to photograph as specimens. It has been a time-consuming process to visit and re-visit selected specimens to secure the necessary detailed photographs, particularly of flowers and fruits.

Over the years I have been indebted to many people for help in locating specimens, and to all these people I am indeed grateful. L should especially like to mention Mr G. C. Weston, Forest Research Institute, Rotorua; many conservators of forests and other Forest Service personnel from Waipoua Forest, Rotorua, Minginui, Nelson and the West Coast; Mr D. H. K. Ross, formerly of the Forest Service head office, Wellington; Mr Geoff Rennison, Abel Tasman National Park, and other national park rangers from Tongariro, Egmont, Abel Tasman, Nelson Lakes and Fiordland national parks; the late Sir Robert Falla; the late Dick Hewitt of Ponatahi Valley, Martinborough; Mrs Audrey Cameron of Hinakura; Mr J. R. Matthews of Waiorongomai Station, Featherston; Mr Dell Purdie of the Nature Conservation Council staff; Mr A. E. Esler, Mt Albert Plant Research Station, Auckland; Dr W. M. Hamilton, Warkworth; Mr Ross Michie, Kaitaia; Mrs Margaret Parsons, Woodside Gorge, Marlborough; Mr John Oswald, Mt Carmel Station, Marlborough; Miss Nancy Adams, National Museum, Wellington; Mr N. G. Cozens, Stoke; Mr Tony Druce, Soil Bureau, DSIR, Lower Hutt; Mrs Katie Reynolds, Whangarei; Mrs Muriel Fisher, Auckland; the late Mr W. M. Brockie and Mr Ray Mole, the two curators of the Otari Native Plant Museum, Wellington, during the course of this work; Mr A. Joliffe, curator of the Christchurch Botanic Gardens; Mr and Mrs W. L. Travers, Taupo; Mr L. H. Metcalf, director, Invercargill City Parks and Reserves; Dr Graeme Ramsay, Entomology Division, DSIR, Auckland.

I would like to acknowledge the help I received from Dr John Dawson and Dr Barry Sneddon of the Botany Department of Victoria University, who acted as botanical consultants, checking and approving the material as it was prepared for the book. Their task was a long and arduous one and I am greatly indebted to them. Needless to say, any errors that remain are mine and mine alone.

I have also received valuable help from the late Prof. Hugh Gordon, Botany Department, Victoria University, from Dr D. R. McQueen and Dr Bruce Sampson, Botany Department, Victoria University, from Sir Charles Fleming and Dr Graeme Stevens of the New Zealand Geological Survey, Lower Hutt, and from Dr Patrick Brownsey, National Museum.

The diagrams in the introductory pages were prepared by myself and executed by members of Bryson Graphics, Wellington, with some assistance from Dr R. B. Pike of Waikanae. All the illustrations are original except for the leaf shapes on pages 24–25 which are taken from those prepared by Miss Nancy Adams of the National Museum for Allan's *Flora*; I am indebted to Nancy for permission to incorporate these into the major diagram.

Finally, I must record my appreciation of the tremendous effort put into the designing of the book by Brian Moss of Bryson Graphics, Wellington. I am indebted, too, to my two editors, Geoff Walker and Graham Wiremu, for their sympathetic approach to the many problems that occurred during the moulding of all this material into a presentable publication.

Introduction

For as long as I can remember I have admired, enjoyed and been interested in trees — at first for their sheer beauty of form, but in later years because of their environmental and ecological importance as stabilisers of climate, purifiers of the atmosphere and controllers of the flow of water over the land's surface.

To be inside a forest and to commune with the trees — reflecting on the grandeur of their solitude, sensing those intangible values that only trees can give towards the spiritual uplifting and refreshment of the soul of Man — gives me great satisfaction. There is something timeless and enduring about a great tree, a sort of immortality, almost a spiritual presence. Perhaps it is not just the trees but all the life that a forest supports, for if you have ears to hear it and eyes to see it, a healthy forest is throbbing with life —birds, insects, ferns, mosses and a myriad of creepy-crawly things — all with a designed purpose on this earth.

I have been in forests in many parts of the world. Perhaps nowhere else beyond New Zealand has this feeling of reverence for a forest struck me so forcibly as when I stood in the tall cathedral-like grove of Mariposa redwoods at Yosemite, in California, one morning at dawn, with only a small deer for company. The majesty of it all; the serenity and deep breathless silence; then the burst of sunlight and the soft sigh of the dawn wind as the forest stirred into an awakening from the night and pulsated with an awareness of life, space and eternity; it remains as one of the great wilderness experiences of my life.

Others before me have experienced these feelings. J. D. Strauss put it this way:

This is their temple, vaulted high,
And here we pause with reverent eye,
With silent tongue and awe-struck soul:
For here we sense life's proper goal.

To be like these, straight, true and fine,
To make our world like theirs, a shrine.
Sink down, Oh, traveller, on your knees,
God stands before you in these trees.

Trees are the most important plants in our environment. They enhance the landscape, dominating it aesthetically and spiritually. Large trees, by their very size and shape, introduce into any scene the three dimensions of vertical lines, volume and pattern, exciting the eye and stimulating a sense of joy and appreciation.Their colours, the glint and glow of sunlight on their shimmering foliage, the rustle of wind through branches and leaves or the patter of raindrops on the spreading canopy and leaf mould beneath, all conjure up in our minds associations of beauty, majesty, admiration and awe. Trees give us a sense of stability and permanence while at the same time providing variety and change as they grow, flower and fruit from season to season, year by year.

Specimen trees, trees in parks, trees in forests all typify the ever-pervading association of living things; both a single tree and a forest form the focal points of communities of life for green plants, birds and animals, insects, fungi and micro-organisms that together make up the web of life.

Trees have grown and evolved into many types and forms over the 400 million years or so that they have been growing on our earth. They are the guardians of the earth's soils and waters, the regulators of its climate and the providers of food and energy. They constitute a great renewable natural resource that can provide us with a multitude of useful things. Trees have provided people with timber for houses, furniture, boats and fuel, but our modern scramble for wealth coupled with our demand for wood products is all too rapidly destroying the world's remaining natural forests. This has already happened in New Zealand. Some tree species in different parts of the world are hovering on extinction and can now only be preserved, like the kauri in New Zealand, by cultivation in man-made forests or by protection in small reserves.

What is a tree?

We can define a tree as a woody perennial plant with a stiff, erect and woody trunk which carries the branches above and clear of the ground. A shrub, on the other hand, does not have a trunk but branches freely from ground level. Under certain conditions some New Zealand shrubs can produce a trunk and grow into a small tree. For the purposes of this book such shrubs are accepted as trees.

Trees that remain in leaf indefinitely are evergreen; those that shed their leaves each autumn are deciduous. Most New Zealand trees are evergreen.

New Zealand trees occur in four distinct shapes: those with a spreading crown such as the kauri, those that are pyramidal or cone-shaped such as *Libocedrus plumosa* or a juvenile kahikatea, those that are palm-shaped such as the nikau or a tree fern, and those that are columnar in form such as the cabbage trees.

Botanically speaking our tree ferns belong to the family Filicales, the true ferns, which reproduce by spores borne on the undersides of the leaves. Our other trees belong to the families Gymnospermae and Angiospermae, reproducing from seeds that arise from strobili in the gymnosperms and from flowers in the angiosperms. The latter include plants whose seeds germinate with two seed leaves, the dicotyledons; those that germinate with one seed leaf are the monocotyledons. Apart from the gymnosperms or pines, which include the New Zealand podocarps, the majority of our seed-forming trees are dicotyledons, only the nikau palm and the cabbage trees being monocotyledons.

The terms *softwoods* and *hardwoods* frequently applied to trees derive from the botanical origin of the timber and not from the physical nature of the wood. Softwoods come from the gymnosperms — in New Zealand the trees with imbricate leaves, and the kauri. Hardwoods come from the angiosperms or broad leaved trees.

J. T. S.
Waikanae
September 1979

Author's note

All photographs reproduced in this book have been taken by the author. For the information of those interested, two 35 mm cameras — a Zeiss Contarex Super and an Olympus OM I — were used for the detailed work. Pictures of whole trees were taken with a Koni Omegaflex camera using Agfachrome 50S 120 size colour film. Kodachrome 25 colour film was used throughout for most 35 mm work, the exception being an occasional roll of Kodachrome 64 when difficult lighting conditions called for greater film speed. All of the close-up photographs of plant details were taken using special Zeiss Luminar lenses in combination with electronic flash as a light source.

Trees in the ecosystem

Trees function in many ways in ecosystems. They help regulate the runoff of water from the land during rain; they regulate climate; they serve as homes for wildlife. But their most important function stems from their ability, as in all green plants, to trap energy from sunlight.

Trees and energy

Trees use energy in the processes of their own living and in manufacturing carbohydrates, oils, hormones, vitamins and other essential substances. These are the basic foods for all living things, including themselves. A tree gets its nourishment from carbon dioxide in the air, absorbed through its leaves, and from salts in the soil, dissolved in water and absorbed through its roots. Carbon dioxide enters the leaves through the stomata; in the presence of chlorophyll, activated by the energy of sunlight and using water absorbed by the roots, the carbon dioxide is converted into food for the tree.

This process of trapping energy from sunlight and building it into chemical compounds is called *photosynthesis* and can be carried out only by green plants. It consists of a series of chemical reactions which are recognised as the most important and the most extensive chemical reaction system taking place on earth. Photosynthesis is the basic life reaction that powers the life processes of all living things. Man is no exception to this rule. When we eat we obtain from our food the energy to live and to work whether we consume plants directly, or indirectly through the body of another animal. The source of that energy is sunlight made available through the photosynthetic green plants. As the photosynthetic reaction proceeds, oxygen is produced as a by-product and it is now recognised that the oxygen of the earth's atmosphere has been largely produced from this source. Trees must have played, and still do play, a most important role in this process.

Trees, water and climate

Water is essential for both the growth and continued existence of a tree. Being capable of dissolving more substances than any other known solvent, it forms the medium in which the chemical reactions of life's processes can be carried on. And as a chemical compound water enters itself into some of these reactions. As a tree grows it uses huge quantities of carbon obtained from the air and enormous quantities of water, most of which must contain in solution the necessary salts for its growth and reproduction. Most of this water comes directly from rain falling on the soil, but some of it is

Rimu-tawa forest canopy. From the summit of Mt Ngamoto, Urewera National Park.

Forest exposure, Mt Ruapehu, 1,400 m, including *Lagarostrobos colensoi*, *Libocedrus bidwillii*, *Podocarpus totara* and *Nothofagus* species.

obtained from the underground water table. Water passes upwards from the roots through the stems and leaves; the metabolic requirements of the tree are drawn off as it goes while the remainder, passing out into the air, raises the moisture content of the atmosphere or condenses on leaves at night as dew.

In this way trees in forests affect the climate, moving water from the underground reservoirs to the atmosphere more rapidly than if that water were allowed to evaporate from the soil surface. Trees growing in tropical rain forests evaporate so much water vapour that the air over large areas above these forests becomes saturated, leading to heavy rain falling, as the temperature drops, almost every night.

Trees and the litter ecosystem

The leaves of deciduous trees are born and die within the space of one year; the leaves of evergreen trees live for several years, often for as long as eight years, before they fall. Falling leaves, twigs and branches together with flaking or peeling bits of bark form a detritus around the base of the tree. This material is attacked by the micro-organisms of decay which, working together, reduce these piles of debris to the simple elements from which they came. Carbon is released as carbon dioxide and returns to the air; the minerals and elements return to the soil so that each and every one may be used again in the living processes of other animals and plants. When the tree itself ages and finally collapses or is blown down, these same processes of decay attack it and return to the air and the soil all the elements from which it was made.

This series of events which recycles the materials of life for re-use over and over again has been going on repeatedly since chlorophyll first appeared on earth about 600 million years ago. Sometimes, through climatic accidents, volanic eruptions, floods and other causes, the processes of decay were halted and whole forests were fossilised and changed to coal or oil. When we burn coal or oil today we are releasing the energy extracted from sunlight by ancient trees and other plants that lived on the earth many millions of years ago. They stored this energy in their own substance which later became preserved as fossil fuels.

Trees and the atmosphere

As a tree grows, producing flowers and seeds, it requires energy. When this energy is obtained from stored food, such as starch, oxygen is required to release the energy from the starch in the normal process of respiration which we observe in all living things. When a tree respires it releases carbon dioxide to the air and uses oxygen from the air. This is a continuous process, whereas photosynthesis takes place only during daylight hours. When it is taking place photosynthesis does, however, mask the release of carbon dioxide in the respiratory process of the tree.

The living forest

Today we grow native trees as specimens in gardens and parks, but in fact these trees evolved in forests over great periods of time. Although large natural forests are rapidly disappearing in New Zealand, as in other parts of the world, being replaced by the artificial monoculture of agriculture and forestry related to our economic system, people still associate New Zealand native trees with those forests in which they grew.

Forests are communities of plants dominated by trees; they are mostly made up of numerous species mixed and growing together to form a living system in equilibrium. Some forests are almost pure stands of a single or of a few species, such as occurs in beech forests and in pockets of lowland podocarp forests. Living within the forest and intimately associated with it are shrubs, ferns, mosses, lichens, fungi and other primitive plants as well as birds, insects and other animals. All these taken together form the community of the forest.

The plant portion of this community is an energy system processing energy from sunlight by photosynthesis, then storing it and making it available, through carbohydrates, to the birds, insects and other forms of life in the forest. In the primordial New Zealand forests insects and related arthropods were the only animals other than birds and two species of bats that were serviced in this way by our forests. Since the advent of Europeans, however, the numerous domestic and sporting animals we have introduced into this country have also been serviced by our forests, often with dramatic and extremely damaging effects.

The forest is generally referred to as a primary producer, processing carbon into carbohydrates. But all green plants, including those outside forests, are primary producers; I prefer to refer to the primary producers of the forest as the *production ecosystem of the forest* — or simply the *production ecosystem* — to distinguish it from the other forest ecosystems.

The litter ecosystem

As leaves and twigs fall to the ground they build up a detritus of leaf mould which is sporadically added to by falling branches and trees, and by the decay of ferns, mosses, lichens, birds, insects and other ground dwellers. Within this detritus there exists another forest community, the soil and litter community of decomposers which forms a distinct but vital ecosystem, the *litter ecosystem,* intimately linked with and supplementary to the production ecosystem itself. These two systems together form the *forest ecosystem,* which can continue to function indefinitely only when these two systems are intact and fully functional. Other systems within the forest — including birds, insects and other forms of wildlife — are supplementary to the production and litter ecosystems.

The litter ecosystem consists of soil and forest detritus together with its inhabitants. This assemblage of mostly tiny living things within the litter layer is vast and counts its populations in hundreds of thousands per hectare, for collembola and mites, and in billions for bacteria. It forms a recycling system returning into circulation the vital substances used by living things as they die so that new life can use these again.

This litter ecosystem is absolutely vital to the health and wellbeing of any forest. When it is destroyed by man or by other causes such as the trampling of animals the forest slowly dies.

The mature forest

As a forest grows and covers a piece of land it shows patterns of development marked by changing successions of plants. From this process there ultimately emerges a mature forest with a defined structure. Such a forest represents a climax in development and is referred to as a *climax forest.* This is a self-sustaining system in equilibrium within itself and

Legumes

with the climate and soil; it will continue to perpetuate itself as long as conditions remain relatively stable.

Its structure is dominated by the great forest trees, mainly timber trees such as the podocarps, whose crowns form the upper canopy. Below this canopy is a further canopy of large trees, usually a close or tight layer which may also carry many lianes and which screens out most direct sunlight from the interior of the forest. Below this second canopy there may be further layers of smaller, less light-demanding trees, tree ferns and lianes, followed closer to the ground by shrubs and ground ferns. The actual ground itself and fallen logs and branches carry growths of mosses, lichens, filmy ferns, fungi and other simple plants.

Along the margins of the forest and along streamsides grow other smaller light-demanding trees whose dense foliage protects the inner forest from cold draughts. This protection helps to maintain the stable microclimates of the ground layer of the forest, which appears to be very necessary for the good health and stability of our native forests.

The breakdown of litter

Very little is known about the litter recycling systems in New Zealand forests, but much research on these topics has taken place in Europe, Japan and America and from this we can get some idea of these processes.

The rate of breakdown of forest litter varies between seasons according to temperature, moisture content and situation. In temperate regions, for instance, an oak leaf may decompose completely in eight to fifteen months, whereas in the tropics a similar leaf may completely disappear in eight weeks after falling.

For several weeks after a leaf has fallen in a temperate region it is not eaten by microfauna. During this time it is invaded mainly by fungi, which tend to break it apart. At the same time it is leached by water that dissolves and removes phenols and other chemical substances into the lower layers of the soil. The leaf then comes under attack from beetles, collembola and other small arthropods, worms and small animals that chew it and pass out its remains as faeces at the same time as they obtain the energy to live from its substance. Their faeces and dead bodies are attacked by microflora to form humus, which is the fertile element of good soil. The role of mites is largely predatory upon springtails and, due to their enormous numbers, they are important in the humification process. It seems clear that decomposition by the microflora (such as bacteria) does not proceed readily until after fragmentation of the litter by fungi and small soil animals has taken place. This fragmentation provides the most suitable substrate for bacteria and micro-organismal growth. Only about one quarter of the litter is converted to humus; the rest disappears by oxidation, leaching and erosion. Sodium, magnesium, phosphorous and potassium are leached and held in the lower soil layers. Sugars and starches are converted to carbon dioxide, water and ammonia. The ammonia is rapidly converted by soil bacteria to nitrates for absorption again into plants.

Woody parts of litter are attacked by beetles and often by termites; these insects have bacteria in their guts that can break down the cellulose of wood. The holes and channels made by insects and their larvae are further attacked and enlarged by fungi. The wood is softened further by water percolating through the channels and gaps, paving the way for attack and decomposition by microbial action. Eventually the softened wood becomes fragmented and the fragments are worked over again until they are finally incorporated into the humic layer. This layer is distributed throughout the upper layers of the soil principally by the activities of earthworms. Complete breakdown is a slow process and generally takes several decades to complete.

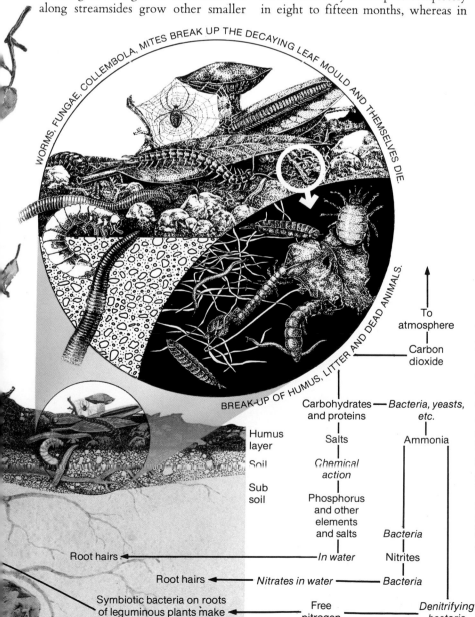

WORMS, FUNGAE, COLLEMBOLA, MITES BREAK UP THE DECAYING LEAF MOULD AND THEMSELVES DIE.

BREAK-UP OF HUMUS, LITTER AND DEAD ANIMALS.

To atmosphere

Carbon dioxide

Carbohydrates — Bacteria, yeasts, and proteins — etc.

Humus layer

Salts — Ammonia

Soil

Chemical action

Sub soil

Phosphorus and other elements and salts

Bacteria

Root hairs ← In water — Nitrites

Root hairs ← Nitrates in water — Bacteria

Symbiotic bacteria on roots of leguminous plants make nitrogen available to plant

Free nitrogen — Denitrifying bacteria

Energy in the forest

When one enters a forest on a fine day it is a serene and tranquil place in which it is difficult to imagine the colossal biological activity that is actually taking place all around. But research in Europe indicates that in a deciduous forest in which the trees have a carbon content of 10,000 tonnes per square kilometre the net primary production of carbon amounts to 1,000 tonnes per square kilometre per year. A temperate zone evergreen forest, such as we have in New Zealand, holds 12,000 to 20,000 tonnes of carbon in every square kilometre and its net primary production of carbon amounts to 1,200-1,500 tonnes per square kilometre per year.

Compared with agricultural land, where the carbon content is 1,000 tonnes per square kilometre and the primary production of carbon is 400 tonnes per square kilometre per year, the forest can be seen as a huge processing laboratory

and storage system. Since all this carbon comes from the carbon dioxide in the air such figures — even allowing for a margin of error in calculations — indicate very clearly the overall value of trees and forests in the maintenance of a healthy biosphere and the conservation of the world environment.

The atmosphere contains about 640 billion tonnes of carbon, of which approximately 16.5 billion tonnes is assimilated by land plants of the world each year. More is used by phytoplankton and other aquatic plants. Almost as much is returned each year through the processes of decay by the litter ecosystems of forests, scrublands and grasslands, so that the turnover of carbon by plants throughout the world is a massive biochemical operation performed largely in forest ecosystems.

The more we destroy these forests and

their ecosystems the more impoverished the world will undoubtedly become.

Ecosystems are bound together by the circulation of water with dissolved mineral substances and by the linkages established through food chains. When an insect eats the leaves of a tree and the insect is in turn eaten by a bird we have a simple food chain. The chain can be further extended if the bird is eaten by a cat and so on. Simple food chains can be interwoven, making for great complexity in feeding relationships within an ecosystem. These food chains are really energy exchange systems. They are explained more precisely as the flow of energy from solar radiation through trees and other organisms, both plant and animal, in successive stages, to emerge finally into the inorganic environment as heat loss from metabolic activity. Less than one tenth of the total solar energy

reaching the surfaces of the earth can be utilised by plants through photosynthesis. For climatic and other reasons only from one to five per cent of this energy is captured by plants. This conversion may appear rather inefficient, but it supplies all the energy used by the biosphere. Our technology has not yet been able to match this by producing raw materials such as carbohydrates directly from sunlight. Thus it should be clear that forest ecosystems, especially the great trees in them, are of immeasurable value to mankind in ways that far transcend their commercial value as timber or wood pulp.

A forest ecosystem can be envisaged, therefore, as a huge energy exchange system in which energy is continually flowing from one organism to another.

Water in the forest

But the functions of a forest ecosystem do not end here. Trees transpire huge quantities of water each day, which can have a profound effect, already mentioned, on climate. When rain drops impinge upon bare earth during a heavy shower they often do so with considerable force and can dislodge soil particles through the resulting mechanical impact upon the soil. These soil particles may be borne away if a stream of surplus water flows across the bare soil because the shower has been too intense for all the water

falling to be absorbed into the ground. Heavy rain can dislodge soil particles from grass pasture in the same way, especially if the sward is poor. This is the beginning of accelerated soil erosion.

However, on land covered by healthy forest this does not normally occur since the trees of the forest protect the soil in two distinct ways:
■ The leaves of the upper canopy intercept rain drops, absorbing the major force of their impact. Those that pass the upper canopy are intercepted by the lower canopies so that by the time the rain water reaches the ground as slow intermittent drips from the trees its major force is spent. The leaves of all the trees, together with their trunks and branches, present a very large area for wetting, and heavy rain is absorbed onto these surfaces before it penetrates to the forest floor. It is usually quite some time after the commencement of rain before it reaches the forest floor, as anyone who has experienced the onset of rain in a forest must know. When rain finally starts to wet the forest floor it does so as more or less gentle drips from the leaf canopies and as trickles of water down the tree trunks into the litter layer. In both cases the force of impact of the rain has been absorbed by the trees and little if any damage is done to the soil surface.
■ The soil surface is further protected from rain drop damage by the litter and

detritus of the litter ecosystem, which can itself absorb the impact of considerable quantities of rain. The litter layer functions as an extensive absorption layer, a giant sponge, as it were, that will absorb vast amounts of water which must wet all the surfaces of every fragment, large and small, in the litter before the water can commence to flow across the actual soil surface beneath. Even when this happens the decayed lower layers of detritus in contact with the soil impose considerable constraints on the movement of free water across the soil surface.

Thus the leafy crowns of trees in the forest canopies and of isolated specimen trees in the open, along with the bark of their trunks and branches and the litter that covers the forest floor or lies beneath a specimen tree, act as a sponge to absorb water during heavy rain and release it slowly by filtering it through litter layers to creeks, streams, rivers and groundwater. The water in streams and rivers flowing through the forest seldom discolours with silt; although it will increase in volume during rain, it remains clean and clear. The forest has imposed a regulatory system on the natural flow of water across the landform on which it grows. In this way forests minimise the effects of erosion of soil by water. Forests reduce the destructive effects of soil erosion to manageable proportions; they do not eliminate them.

Threats to the forest

Much of the New Zealand landscape bears witness to the folly of the wholesale destruction of our forests and the subsequent erosion problems that followed. Behind Gisborne, the country in the Waipaoa River catchment area, inland hill country round Whangamomona in Taranaki, and areas of the West Coast of the South Island are outstanding examples of very severe soil erosion following wholesale uncontrolled forest destruction. As we know so little about the ecology of indigenous forests and how to regenerate them to control erosion, these areas are being re-afforested with exotic pines.

The maximum angle of slope which can safely be cleared of forest in New Zealand varies around 21 degrees. It is dangerous to clear forest in this country from slopes steeper than this — even though in the past many steeper slopes, some almost perpendicular, have been cleared. In an erosion and flood-prone country like New Zealand the impor-

tance of the preservation of forests in perpetuity in the upper watersheds of river systems is only now beginning to be recognised and accepted. The almost equal value of trees in small woodlots along river and stream banks as stabilisers of banks and providers of shelter for wildlife and stock has not yet been recognised. The podsolizing effects of some indigenous forest trees on certain soils is not fully understood and lands cleared, particularly of kahikatea, on the West Coast of the South Island have now become derelict. Similar effects occur with kauri, but fossilised kauri stumps show that several successive kauri forests can grow on old kauri forest land.

As well as functioning as an energy transfer system and as a water regulator a tree also functions as a home and as a source of food for many forms of wildlife. In New Zealand in its primordial condition indigenous trees provided shelter and food for birds, insects and other

small arthropods (jointed segmented animals) as well as fungi and epiphytic plants. Since European occupation our trees have become a source of food for pigs, opossums, deer, goats and feral domestic animals.

The change in ecological emphasis has had a profound effect upon the remaining indigenous forests during the last half century. Species palatable to introduced animals, such as fuchsia, have tended to diminish and even disappear throughout affected forests; unpalatable species have tended to increase and spread. In this way the balance of forest species has been upset and the structure of indigenous forests has been altered more or less permanently. Forests regenerating after the reduction of animal populations show marked changes, with the new forests structurally different from the originals. For example, such changes followed the invasion by deer of the Panikirikiri-Ngamoto forest at Lake Waikaremoana

2

3

Fig 1 Damage by introduced animals. These tree ferns growing at Lake Okataina have had their crowns eaten out and destroyed by opossums. 1971.

Fig 2 A further illustration of opossum damage. Leaves of *Pseudopanax* litter the ground under these trees which have been attacked by opossums at Opepe Bush. 1964.

Fig 3 Erosion fans in the lower Otira Gorge, 1964, resulting from noxious animal damage to the forest.

Fig 4 Sawmilling waste. This is one of the lower limbs of the huge rimu tree shown in Fig 5, page 76, left behind at Opepe Bush after the trunk was removed by a sawmilling company in 1966. These useable limbs are still rotting there today.

Fig 5 Forest on Mt Holdsworth after a herd of deer had passed through. 1966.

Fig 6 Erosion fans, St Arnaud Mountains above Lake Rotoiti, Nelson, brought about by overgrazing by chamois and deer. 1972.

1

4

5

6

in the 1940s and of parts of the Tararua Ranges, as described by Zotov.

With the passing of forests and especially of certain tree species indigenous birds and insects can be seriously affected. A single tree can support a certain number of birds and insects without suffering itself from the effects of their feeding and sheltering. It follows, therefore, that a forested area can support a strictly limited biomass of other life forms depending on the species content of trees and shrubs, the variations in the climate in relation to growth and flowering, and the availability of water. The maximum permanent population of animal life in a forest is not a factor of the apparently booming summer population, but is directly related to the availability and the amount of energy in the form of food it can provide during the winter months. It follows, therefore, that as indigenous forest is cleared, its dependent life forms, mainly birds and insects, are being continually compressed into a

smaller and smaller feeding area which, in all probability, is already carrying its own maximum population.

Not a great deal is known about the support capabilities of New Zealand forests for wildlife, but a study of the Spey River Valley at Lake Manapouri carried out in 1960 indicated that the forest there supported about 144 pairs of birds in each 100 acres (40.47 hectares).

The forest litter community is particularly susceptible to damage by fire, pesticides, trampling by stock, noxious animals and even by man. The destruction of forest undergrowth, of the layers of shrubs and ferns and so on, allows the litter layer to be washed away by successive heavy rains. Throughout New Zealand there are many scenic reserves set aside by farsighted early settlers but which today are in a sorry state indeed, because subsequent land owners have allowed farm animals to wander and feed in these reserves, or because of the depredations of introduced noxious animals.

When these places are fenced and protected it is surprising how quickly, in just a few years, the native vegetation can regenerate itself and reclothe the bare forest floor.

A healthy forest is one in equilibrium, not just within the confines of plant species but in the wider sense of equilibrium between the plants and the other forms of life which the forest supports. This equilibrium fluctuates with the variations in climate as these affect seasonal growth and productivity of the forest trees and associated plants. The interdependence of the forest trees, birds, insects and other life forms is very real; birds, for instance, are very important in the distribution of tree seeds and the combating of insect pests of the forest. It is a tragedy that little if any thought is given to the importance of the environmental values of these ecological facets of forests when decisions are being made to cut deeper into New Zealand's remaining indigenous forests.

The pattern of photosynthesis

Photosynthesis is the most important chemical reaction taking place on earth, the process whereby energy from the sun is transformed by plants into energy in the form of food. It is the very basis of life itself.

Chlorophyll, the green pigment of plants, occurs in several forms, but it is *chlorophyll-a* in the leaf that is the principal catalyst bringing photosynthesis about. Another essential element here is water, containing dissolved mineral salts; it is brought to the leaf from the thousands of root hairs in the soil by the xylem vessels. A leaf will orientate itself towards the sun to obtain maximum light.

Carbon dioxide from the atmosphere enters through the leaf stomata. Water and gas mingle in the central section of the leaf and here, in the presence of chlorophyll located in the *grana* of the chloroplasts in the palisade and spongy mesophyll cells, the photosynthetic reaction takes place.

During the reaction, energy from sunlight excites electrons within the chlorophylla molecule. Trapped on an electron, this energy can be used directly by transferring it to a phosphate compound present in all living cells. From this compound the energy can be used by cells as required in growth, movement, physiological processes and so on. Some energy trapped on an excited electron may be directed along another pathway and used to split a molecule of water into hydrogen and oxygen, the latter being liberated to the atmosphere through the stomata. The hydrogen, through a series of reactions known as the carbon fixation process, is converted to a simple hydrocarbon compound which is then built up to form sugars and other vital compounds.

The carbohydrates formed in photosynthesis are transported in solution, mainly as sugars, from the leaves to the lower trunks, roots and other growing regions. This movement of the sugars in the phloem tubes is called *translocation;* it involves movement from the *source,* the leaf, to a *sink,* for example, the roots, and is brought about by changes in pressure through the movement of water at the

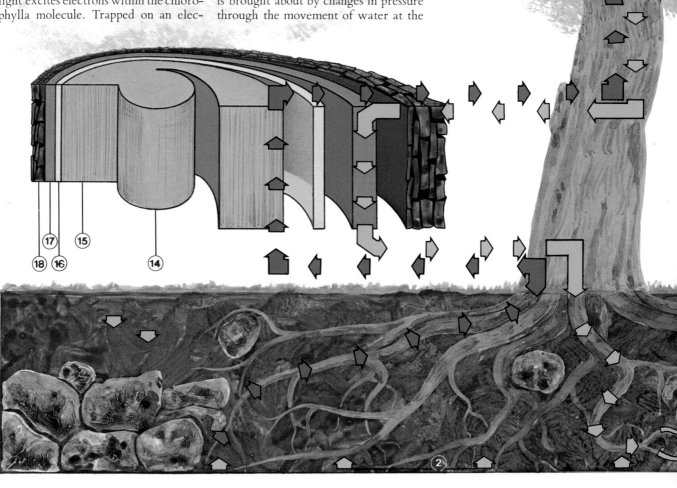

20

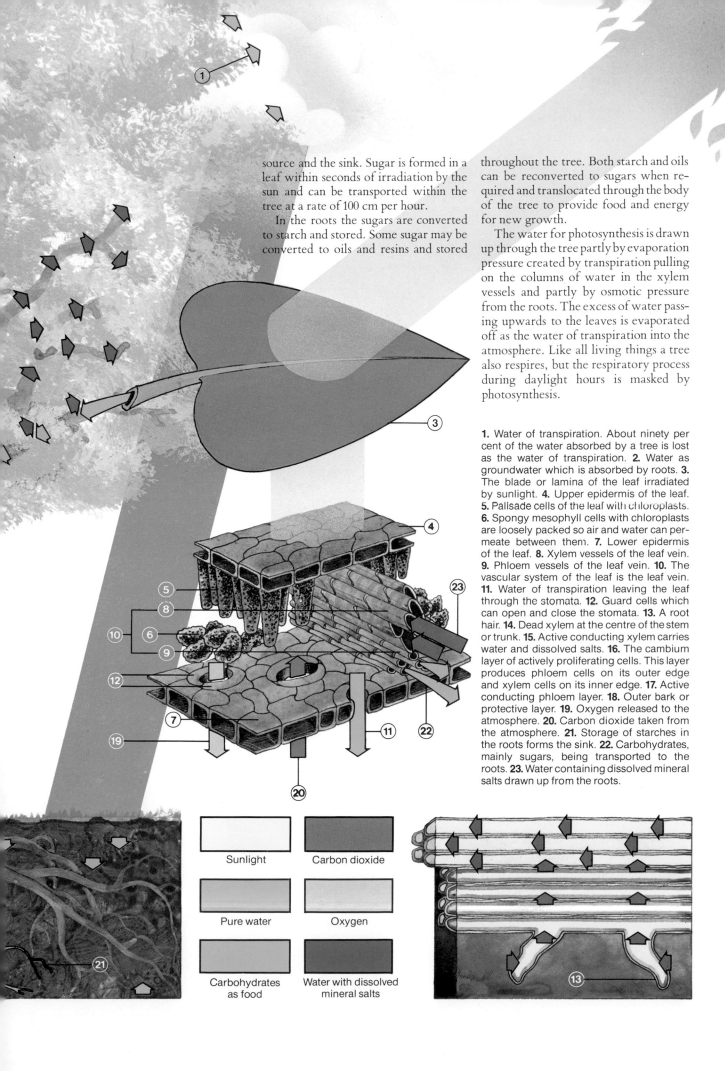

source and the sink. Sugar is formed in a leaf within seconds of irradiation by the sun and can be transported within the tree at a rate of 100 cm per hour.

In the roots the sugars are converted to starch and stored. Some sugar may be converted to oils and resins and stored throughout the tree. Both starch and oils can be reconverted to sugars when required and translocated through the body of the tree to provide food and energy for new growth.

The water for photosynthesis is drawn up through the tree partly by evaporation pressure created by transpiration pulling on the columns of water in the xylem vessels and partly by osmotic pressure from the roots. The excess of water passing upwards to the leaves is evaporated off as the water of transpiration into the atmosphere. Like all living things a tree also respires, but the respiratory process during daylight hours is masked by photosynthesis.

1. Water of transpiration. About ninety per cent of the water absorbed by a tree is lost as the water of transpiration. 2. Water as groundwater which is absorbed by roots. 3. The blade or lamina of the leaf irradiated by sunlight. 4. Upper epidermis of the leaf. 5. Pallsade cells of the leaf with chloroplasts. 6. Spongy mesophyll cells with chloroplasts are loosely packed so air and water can permeate between them. 7. Lower epidermis of the leaf. 8. Xylem vessels of the leaf vein. 9. Phloem vessels of the leaf vein. 10. The vascular system of the leaf is the leaf vein. 11. Water of transpiration leaving the leaf through the stomata. 12. Guard cells which can open and close the stomata. 13. A root hair. 14. Dead xylem at the centre of the stem or trunk. 15. Active conducting xylem carries water and dissolved salts. 16. The cambium layer of actively proliferating cells. This layer produces phloem cells on its outer edge and xylem cells on its inner edge. 17. Active conducting phloem layer. 18. Outer bark or protective layer. 19. Oxygen released to the atmosphere. 20. Carbon dioxide taken from the atmosphere. 21. Storage of starches in the roots forms the sink. 22. Carbohydrates, mainly sugars, being transported to the roots. 23. Water containing dissolved mineral salts drawn up from the roots.

Sunlight

Carbon dioxide

Pure water

Oxygen

Carbohydrates as food

Water with dissolved mineral salts

The structure of a tree

The roots

When the seed of a tree germinates, the first structure to appear outside the seed is the *taproot,* which grows downwards into the soil to anchor and support the seedling tree. According to the species of tree this taproot may extend deep down, to 12 m or more. Some trees, such as lacebark, kowhai and pohutukawa, do not grow extensive taproots but instead develop widely extending systems of fibrous roots that grow laterally from the taproot near the soil surface. Taprooted trees also extend lateral roots to help anchor them more firmly in the ground and to tap water and nutrients.

As the roots extend outwards, always into moist soil, the growing portion of each root is thickly provided with masses of root hairs. By means of the osmotic process, these hairs draw water and dissolved nutrients through their walls and thence into the root. The water passes onwards and upwards through the roots and stems partly by osmosis and partly by the loss of water vapour from the aerial parts, but the complete mechanism by which water can be brought to the top of a tree perhaps 90 m high is not yet properly understood.

Within the root are conducting tubes called *xylem* and *phloem.* Xylem carries water and nutrients and phloem sugars in solution. These tubes form a central core to the root, but in the region where roots combine and pass upwards into the stem of the seedling tree there is a special zone where the xylem and phloem are rearranged to lie near the surface of the stem. This rearrangement permits the stem to grow outwards and enlarge with the growth of the tree. As roots age they lose their root hairs and become covered by a layer of thick corky cells that usually become impregnated with tannins and resins.

The trunk

A tree may be distinguished from all other plants by its woody framework of trunk and branches, which persists above ground for year after year. The familiar tree has a trunk enclosed in a covering of corky cells impregnated with waxes and tannins. This covering is known as the bark. The outer surface of the bark is usually coloured and either smooth or rough through cracking, flaking or peeling. It is these processes which give to the bark of each species its characteristic surface appearance. The bark pattern is largely determined by the manner in which it is formed and later ruptured by growth pressures. As the tree grows and swells the outer bark cracks into flakes or strips that fall or peel away from the inner bark.

The trunk supports the branches and leaves, and, in season, the flowers and fruits. It also carries a system of communicating tubes through which water, nutrients and sugars pass upwards and downwards between the roots and the leaves. A cross-section through the trunk reveals several types of tissue arranged concentrically. Just inside the bark is a ring of vascular tissue made up of an outer ring of thin-walled phloem tubes and an inner ring of larger thick-walled xylem vessels. Between these two rings lies a narrow band of proliferating tissue, the *cambium,* which is the growth tissue of the trunk from which all new phloem and xylem vessels and connecting tissues are formed.

As the tree grows the end walls of the xylem tubes break down leaving long, narrow, continuous water-conducting vessels which traverse the trunk and branches like bundles of water pipes. The phloem tubes do not elongate like xylem. They multiply and retain their end walls as perforated end plates, called *sieve plates.*

B Root hairs developing behind the root tip absorb water and nutrient salts from the soil. Behind the apical portion the hairs atrophy and the root becomes corky.

C Root cross-section. **1.** Xylem cells. **2.** Cortex or outer cellular layers. **3.** Phloem cells.

D Branchlet growing tip. Individual leaves on the branchlets are the seat of photosynthesis and the organs where gases are exchanged between the tree and the atmosphere.

A The young root tip pushes down from the seed into the surrounding soil.

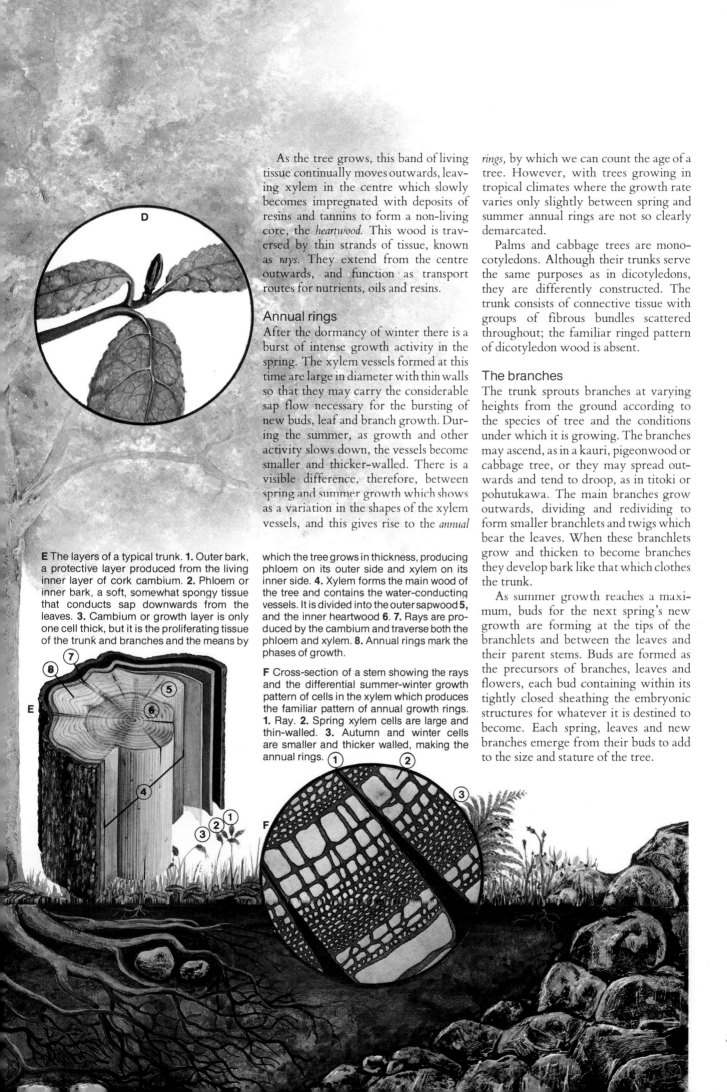

As the tree grows, this band of living tissue continually moves outwards, leaving xylem in the centre which slowly becomes impregnated with deposits of resins and tannins to form a non-living core, the *heartwood*. This wood is traversed by thin strands of tissue, known as *rays*. They extend from the centre outwards, and function · as transport routes for nutrients, oils and resins.

Annual rings

After the dormancy of winter there is a burst of intense growth activity in the spring. The xylem vessels formed at this time are large in diameter with thin walls so that they may carry the considerable sap flow necessary for the bursting of new buds, leaf and branch growth. During the summer, as growth and other activity slows down, the vessels become smaller and thicker-walled. There is a visible difference, therefore, between spring and summer growth which shows as a variation in the shapes of the xylem vessels, and this gives rise to the *annual*

rings, by which we can count the age of a tree. However, with trees growing in tropical climates where the growth rate varies only slightly between spring and summer annual rings are not so clearly demarcated.

Palms and cabbage trees are monocotyledons. Although their trunks serve the same purposes as in dicotyledons, they are differently constructed. The trunk consists of connective tissue with groups of fibrous bundles scattered throughout; the familiar ringed pattern of dicotyledon wood is absent.

The branches

The trunk sprouts branches at varying heights from the ground according to the species of tree and the conditions under which it is growing. The branches may ascend, as in a kauri, pigeonwood or cabbage tree, or they may spread outwards and tend to droop, as in titoki or pohutukawa. The main branches grow outwards, dividing and redividing to form smaller branchlets and twigs which bear the leaves. When these branchlets grow and thicken to become branches they develop bark like that which clothes the trunk.

As summer growth reaches a maximum, buds for the next spring's new growth are forming at the tips of the branchlets and between the leaves and their parent stems. Buds are formed as the precursors of branches, leaves and flowers, each bud containing within its tightly closed sheathing the embryonic structures for whatever it is destined to become. Each spring, leaves and new branches emerge from their buds to add to the size and stature of the tree.

E The layers of a typical trunk. **1.** Outer bark, a protective layer produced from the living inner layer of cork cambium. **2.** Phloem or inner bark, a soft, somewhat spongy tissue that conducts sap downwards from the leaves. **3.** Cambium or growth layer is only one cell thick, but it is the proliferating tissue of the trunk and branches and the means by which the tree grows in thickness, producing phloem on its outer side and xylem on its inner side. **4.** Xylem forms the main wood of the tree and contains the water-conducting vessels. It is divided into the outer sapwood **5**, and the inner heartwood **6**. **7.** Rays are produced by the cambium and traverse both the phloem and xylem. **8.** Annual rings mark the phases of growth.

F Cross-section of a stem showing the rays and the differential summer-winter growth pattern of cells in the xylem which produces the familiar pattern of annual growth rings. **1.** Ray. **2.** Spring xylem cells are large and thin-walled. **3.** Autumn and winter cells are smaller and thicker walled, making the annual rings.

The leaves

Leaves are energy trappers and food factories for the tree, playing a central role in the photosynthesis process. They are also the breathing organs for the tree, which must respire and use oxygen from the air like other living organisms. Water as well, in huge quantities, is transpired from trees through the leaves, passing out from the stomata. The water itself with dissolved salts is drawn up to the leaves to be used in the chemical processing that occurs there.

In deciduous trees the leaves live for one season only, withering and falling from the tree in autumn, their fall often preceded by a magnificent display of colour. Leaves on evergreen trees may live as long as six to eight years before falling; they are continually being lost in small groups from these trees. They usually do so without great displays of colour, but in the New Zealand beeches leaves about to fall often colour up and impart a dispersed gaiety to the tree.

Leaves take on various shapes, sizes and ornamenting structures, according to the species of the parent tree. Botanical works describing trees refer to these shapes for leaves by a series of technical terms such as *elliptic, obovate, pinnate,* and so on. Illustrated on this page are a number of leaf forms, showing the basic shapes and their terminology. Leaves from some trees can combine these shapes, as in, for example, an oblong-obovate specimen; or there can be a combination of these with distinct leaf base and leaf tip shapes.

Some leaves are *wavy,* or have *sinuate* margins, while others are divided or made up of many tiny leaflets. Each tree has its own individual leaf shape and marginal and surface embellishments such as teeth, hairs (*pubescence*), sinuate margins, scales or *tomentum,* which is a dense, matted covering of appressed hairs.

Most leaves are held to the branchlet by a short stalk, the *petiole,* and are known as *petiolate* leaves. Some leaves sit directly on the branchlet without a petiole; these are described as *sessile.* Others which lie between these two extremes are termed *subsessile.*

Leaves are arranged along a branchlet or stem in a definite order peculiar to the parent tree. They may be in *whorls, opposite* each other in pairs or *alternating* as they arise along the branchlet.

The central vein which extends into the leaf from the petiole is known as the main or *midvein,* sometimes as the midrib. The veins extending sideways from the midvein are the *lateral* veins; these usually give rise to a *reticulum* of fine veins pervading the blade or *lamina* of the leaf. The midvein and all lateral veins of a leaf carry the xylem and phloem tubes into every corner of the leaf structure. The pattern which veins form can be useful, together with the leaf shape, in identifying the tree from which a particular leaf has come.

The central illustration shows the upper surface of a typical leaf.
1. Lamina
2. Midvein
3. Lateral or side veins
4. Simple or *entire* margin
5. Petiole
6. Vein reticulum
7. Stipules
8. Apex
9. Base

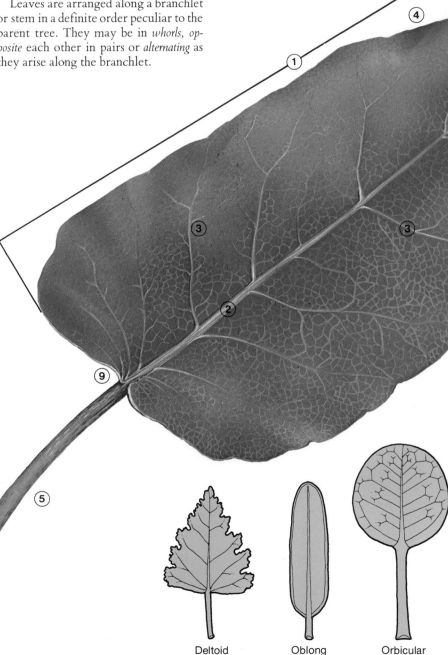

Deltoid　　　　Oblong　　　　Orbicular

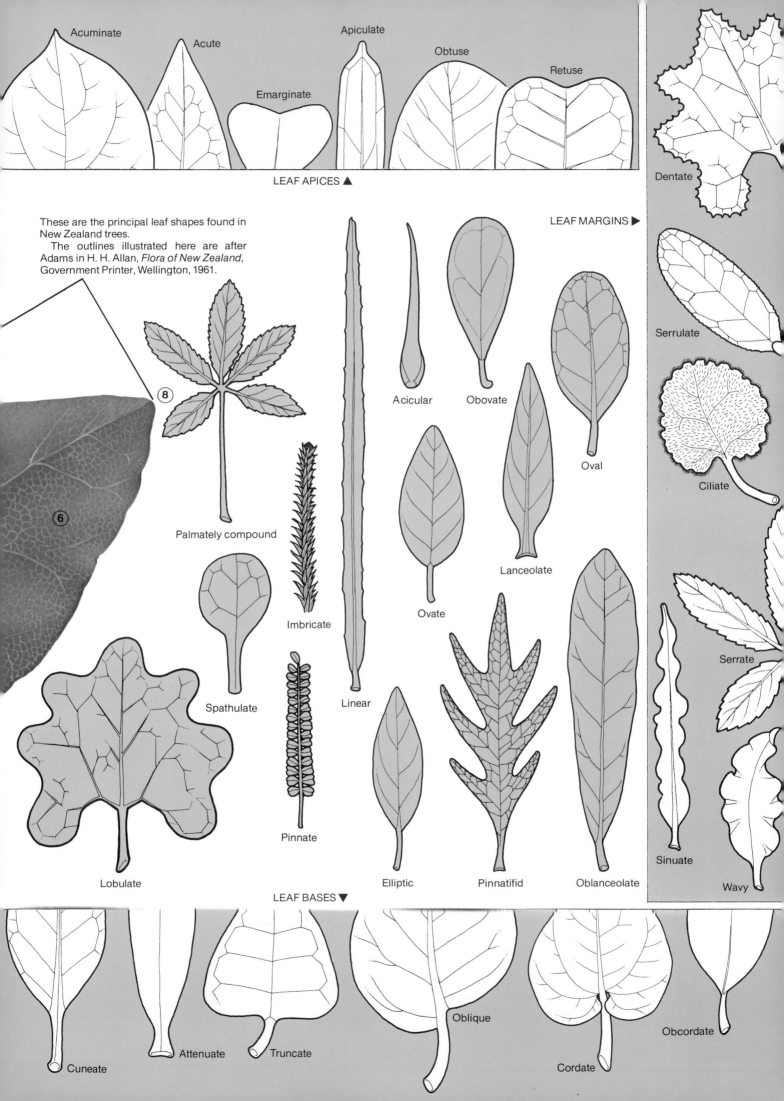

LEAF APICES ▲

Acuminate

Acute

Emarginate

Apiculate

Obtuse

Retuse

These are the principal leaf shapes found in New Zealand trees.

The outlines illustrated here are after Adams in H. H. Allan, *Flora of New Zealand*, Government Printer, Wellington, 1961.

LEAF MARGINS ▶

Dentate

Serrulate

Ciliate

Serrate

Sinuate

Wavy

⑧

⑥

Palmately compound

Spathulate

Imbricate

Pinnate

Acicular

Obovate

Oval

Ovate

Lanceolate

Linear

Ovate

Elliptic

Pinnatifid

Oblanceolate

Lobulate

LEAF BASES ▼

Cuneate

Attenuate

Truncate

Oblique

Cordate

Obcordate

Reproduction

The flowers

The flowers contain the tree's sex organs; their main purpose is to secure cross-pollination from another tree of the same species. In this way the virility and continuity of the species is secured. In gymnosperms, such as the podocarps, reproductive parts are arranged in strobili or cones; in angiosperms they appear in the more familiar flower form with petals arranged in circular fashion around the stamens and ovary.

Some trees have *perfect* flowers, in which both the male and female parts are present together. If the male and female flowers occur on the same tree the tree is termed *monoecious;* if on separate trees it is *dioecious.* Perfect flowers, such as those of manuka or kowhai, have sepals, petals, stamens and ovary all present. Imperfect flowers are unisexual, with either the male or the female parts absent, but the sepals or the petals may also be missing, as in the flowers of coastal maire, *Nestegis apetala.*

Flowers arise *terminally,* at the tips of branchlets, or are *axillary,* arising between a leaf petiole and the branchlet or the parent branch. Flowers adopt many different patterns of shape, form, perfection and arrangement and all these characteristics are of great importance in identifying and classifying trees.

Cross-pollination

To avoid self-pollination several kinds of preventive measures have been evolved by trees. For instance, pollen and ovules on the same tree may mature at different times; or the pollen may be incompatible with the stigma so that if self-pollination should occur the resulting union will be sterile and the ovule will wither away. Cross-pollination is brought about by wind, insects and sometimes by birds.

Pollination by wind is usual among trees of the dense forest, whereas insect pollination is common with trees that naturally grow isolated in the open or along the margins of forests and forest clearings. Pollination by wind is an extravagant method since vast quantities of pollen must be produced in order that one grain floating haphazardly in the air may land on a tiny pistil on another tree. On a windy day pollen can be observed blowing away in dense clouds from a tree like a kahikatea.

When pollen grains settle on a pistil a remarkable series of events takes place. The grains commence to grow downwards as elongating tubes towards the ovary, and the first to reach an ovule penetrates it and brings about the fertilisation of the egg within the ovule. This initiates the development of a seed; in some trees, such as rimu, this proceeds slowly, taking twelve to eighteen months to ripen, while in others, such as kowhai, it is rapid and produces ripe seeds in six to eight months. Flowers pollinated by wind tend to be small, insignificant and unscented; those pollinated by insects or nectar-feeding birds being usually larger, often bright coloured and sometimes scented.

The fruits

The fruit of a tree is formed when the female ovary with the fertilised ovule inside it grows to maturity and is ripened. The ovule is then the seed and the ovary has become the fruit coat. In some fleshy fruits the stalk of the seed has grown up and around the seed to form the fleshy covering or has swollen to form a fleshy base, as occurs in some podocarps.

Once ripe, the seeds are ready for germination and need to be borne away to a suitable place where they can take root and sprout into a seedling tree. Wind is important as a dispersing agent for many seeds. Wind-borne seeds, such as those of kauri, usually have wings or other devices to assist them to drift away from the parent tree. Other seeds—those of miro, for example — are adapted to being eaten by birds and pass unharmed through the bird's digestive tract to be voided in the faeces, often at a considerable distance away from the parent tree.

The ripe seed is in fact a tiny embryonic plant with a minute root and a shoot bearing either one or two seed leaves, the *cotyledons,* that function as food storage organs which nourish the seedling until the first leaves of the new plant are produced.

Right A kowhai with the parts separated. **1.** Pedicel. **2.** Receptacle, the cup-like expansion of the stalk surrounding the ovary. **3.** Sepals, forming the calyx. **4.** Petals, which in the kowhai are named according to their position in the corolla: **S** is the *standard,* **W** the *wings,* **K** the *keel.* **5.** Androecium, the stamens together. **6.** Ovary (in *Sophora* consists of a single carpel). **7.** Ovule. **8.** Anther. **9.** Style. **10.** Stigma. The style, stigma and ovary together form the gynoecium or pistil.

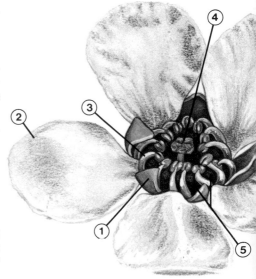

Right A manuka flower is a typical bisexual flower. **1.** Sepal. **2.** Petal. Together these form the perianth. **3.** Stamen with anther. **4.** Style with capitate (head-like) stigma. **5.** Nectary.

Right A kowhai flower. Compare this rather specialised flower form with that of the manuka below on the facing page. **1.** Pedicel, the stalk of the individual flower. **2.** Sepal; the sepals together are called the calyx. **3.** Petal; the petals together are called the corolla. **4.** Stamen. **5.** Anther, which produces the pollen. **6.** Stigma, which receives the pollen. **7.** Style, which bears the stigma.

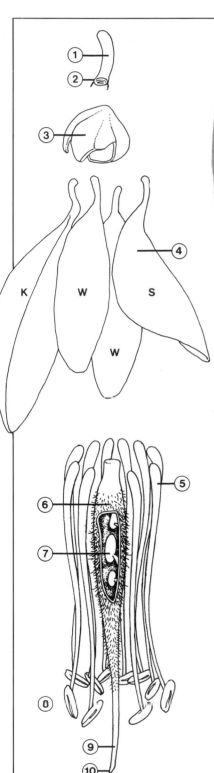

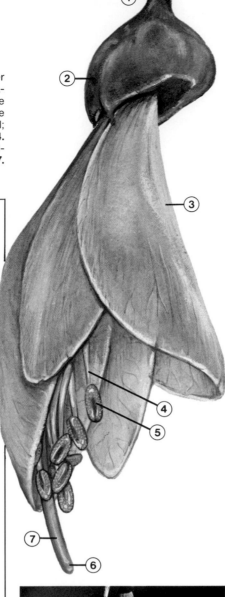

Fruits occur in many different forms. The following principal fruits occur among our native trees. (1) *Fleshy fruits*. A *berry* is a fleshy ovary containing one or more seeds *(Solanum laciniatum)*. A *drupe* differs from a berry in having each seed enveloped by a hard, woody layer, the endocarp (puriri, *Vitex lucens)*. (2) *Dry fruits*. An *achene* is a small, indehiscent fruit consisting of a single seed enveloped in a thin ovarian wall (Compositae). A *nut* is a one-seeded indehiscent fruit enveloped in a hard, woody shell (beech, *Nothofagus)*. A *legume* or *pod* is a one-to-many-seeded fruit formed from a unicarpellate ovary; it may be dehiscent (all *Carmichaelia* tree species) or indehiscent (kowhai, *Sophora)*. A *capsule* is a one-to-many-seeded dehiscent fruit formed from two or more united carpels *(Pittosporum)*. **Above** Coprosma drupes.

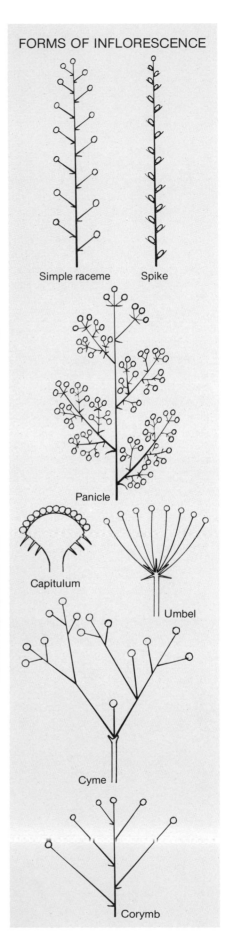

FORMS OF INFLORESCENCE

Simple raceme   Spike

Panicle

Capitulum

Umbel

Cyme

Corymb

How a tree grows

When a tree seed has germinated it must first establish its primary root system to hold it in the ground and to nourish it with water and mineral salts. Once the seedling has established its primary roots it starts the development of its main stem, providing an *apical* or *terminal* bud and one or more lateral branches, each of which terminates in a *lateral* bud.

After growth the development of form is the next requirement; this is attained through the development of *polarity* — its orientation with reference to the three axes of space — and *symmetry*. The vertical trunk-root axis of a tree is the principal guiding line around which a tree is developed and organised. The branches growing from the trunk give the tree spherical, radial or bilateral symmetry; or it may be asymetrical. Thus the tree develops its recognisable shape.

The influences within the body of the tree that control the growth of shape and structure are the hormones produced in the apical and lateral buds of the trunk and branches. The apical bud of the main stem or trunk is the leading bud of the tree. It controls future growth and exerts a profound influence over all the lateral buds, suppressing them, more or less, so that it may grow away from gravity and carry the stem apex upward faster than the lateral branches can grow outward. In this way the ultimate height and form of the tree is organised and controlled.

We make use of this phenomenon when we top a tree to make it spread more; with the apical bud removed, the lateral buds take charge and extend the branches outwards.

In tall trees such as kahikatea the leading bud is very strong so the tree grows tall with minimum lateral spreading. In a pohutukawa tree the growing points of branches abort each year and growth continues from axillary buds so the tree spreads out over a wide area.

The vigour of the apical and lateral buds establishes, each year, the woody tracery of the tree's ultimate frame. The spread of the canopy is determined by the power of the lateral buds to promote outward growth. The height is determined by the apical bud and the ability of the main stem to maintain a column of water in its vessels to the height necessary to service the entire structure of the mature tree. In New Zealand trees such as rimu this can mean an internal water column 40 to 60 m high.

Branchlet growth also reveals the structural pattern of branching and leaf arrangement. The yearly growth of the main stem or a branch can be studied from the growth scars left on branchlets by the bud scales of the terminal buds as they push upward and outward and by the leaf scars left on the branchlet as the leaves fall away.

1

GROWING BRANCH

This diagram incorporates all the different aspects of a growing branch. It is basically modelled on a deciduous plant (to enable all the various points to be illustrated) and is not intended to represent any evergreen New Zealand tree species.

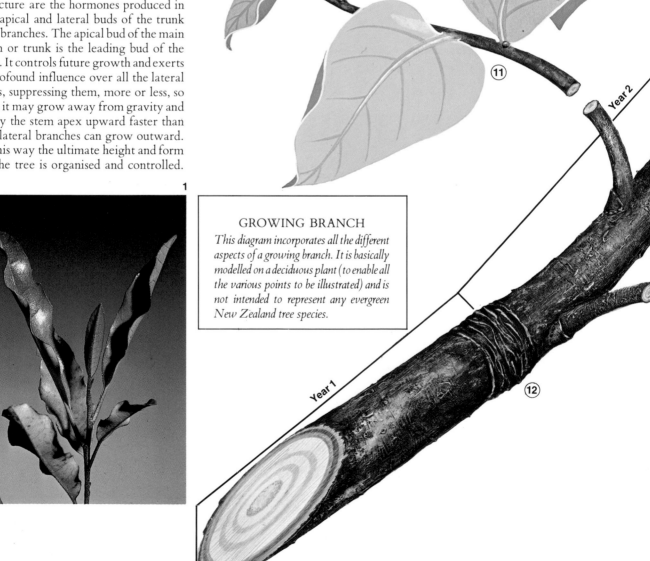

Left: This diagram represents the growth of a branch over a period of about three years. It also depicts the three normal types of leaf arrangement on a twig or branchlet, useful in tree identification. **1.** The terminal bud enclosed in leaf-like scales contains the embryonic structures for the next season's growth. **2.** These leaf scars were left when their leaves withered and fell. **3.** These buds will form the next season's branchlets. **4.** The small pores scattered along the branchlet are lenticels or breathing pores. They perform on the branchlet the same functions undertaken in the leaves by the stomata. **5.** Growth of this branchlet from two seasons before has been partially suppressed by the terminal bud. **6.** These rings are the bud scars left by last season's terminal bud when growth commenced and the branch grew longer. **7.** These two small buds are still suppressed. **8.** This branchlet has developed fully and borne leaves. **9.** These leaves are arranged in *opposite* pairs. **10.** Leaves arranged in *whorls*. **11.** These leaves show *alternate* arrangement on the branchlet. **12.** These rings are the bud scars from growth which took place two years ago.

The new season's growth of buds and leaves is usually fresh and brightly coloured. In some trees it is green, in others yellow-green, in others reddish.

Fig 1 *Quintinia serrata.*

Fig 2 *Melicytus ramiflorus.*

Fig 3 *Nestigis apetala.*

Growth, age and longevity

Some species of trees live to a tremendous age. The oldest living things in the world are trees that grow at altitudes between 2,400 m and 3,300 m in some of the arid regions of the Rocky Mountains in Colorado, Nevada and Utah in North America. Known as bristle cone pines, *Pinus aristata,* these trees are never more than 12 m high. Examination of the growth rings of these trees by the University of Arizona has shown some of them to be over 5,000 years old. But great age in trees is not uncommon: the giant sequoias of California, which include the most massive of all living things, have some trees over 4,000 years old.

In New Zealand, too, we have had our veterans amongst the kauris, some of which have been estimated, by counting growth rings, to be over 2,000 years old. The massive kauri at Mercury Bay could have been over 4,000 years old. Amongst our New Zealand podocarps, trees up to 800 years old were not uncommon in the great lowland forests of the North Island. A huge totara slab at Victoria University came from a tree that was little more than a seedling when Columbus discovered America. It was felled at Taihape in 1906, when it was 435 years old.

In general, slow-growing trees live longer than fast-growing trees. They are tougher, their wood is more durable and they are more securely anchored by their roots than rapid growers whose wood is often brittle and more prone to decay when exposed to the elements. Fast-growing trees are more likely than slow growers to suffer damage during storms.

Growth rates

The rate of growth in trees varies between species and is also greatly influenced by the place in which an individual tree is growing. Such factors as climate (especially the rainfall and mean temperature), the porosity and the fertility of the soil, the availability of nutrients and of sunlight, all affect the rate of growth. Most trees have characteristic patterns of growth and these, along with growth rates, are fairly well established for most of the important European and North American trees. The rates and patterns of growth for New Zealand trees are, unfortunately, not so well known.

Most large New Zealand forest trees are regarded as slow growing but, from my observations, in their early stages at least this is not entirely correct. Under good conditions a kauri grows at about 30 cm per year in the young stage, but after reaching a height of about 5 m slows down considerably and takes hundreds of years to produce its fully developed spreading crown. A rimu seedling can grow at up to 22.5 cm per year until it reaches the conical stage at about 6 m high, when its growth rate becomes very much slower. The same applies with most of our other podocarps. A puriri can reach a sizable small tree in about twelve years but takes some hundreds of years to attain the height and spread of some of the giant puriri trees seen in the north.

More perhaps is known about the growth of our native beeches. Silver beech, *N. fusca,* can grow at 25 cm per year and become a sizeable, millable tree in sixty to eighty years. Small trees such as lacebarks (*Hoheria* spp.) and *Pittosporum* can grow at up to 75-100 cm per year, reaching maximum height in about ten years. Ngaio is also a fast-growing tree, spreading outwards and upwards at about the same rate. Many trees grow quickly to near maximum height after which growth slows and the tree spreads laterally.

Fig 1 Juvenile stages of some New Zealand species are strikingly different from adult trees. The most unusual of these is lancewood, *Pseudopanax crassifolius.* Shown here are long, drooping juvenile leaves and the shorter, more upright adult leaves.

Fig 2 The various shapes through which the kahikatea, *Dacrycarpus dacrydioides,* passes, from the straggly seedling on the forest floor to the mature forest giant. **a.** A very young seedling. **b.** The pyramidal structure at about eight to ten years old. **c.** This conical shape persists for many years. **d.** The adult begins to emerge as the mature crown starts to form. **e.** A mature adult kahikatea with its stout trunk and tight crown. **f.** The final stage: a very old tree.

Fig 3 Te Matua Ngahere, the Father of the Forest, is the largest tree in the Waipoua Kauri Forest and the second largest tree in New Zealand. It is 16.15 m in girth at about 1 m from the ground. The height to the first branch is 10.6 m. Its age is estimated at about 2,127 years.

1

2

Fig 3 ▶

The character of the New Zealand forest

The New Zealand forest is evergreen and characterised by the density of its undergrowth of shrubs, lianes and ferns. On the forest floor the detritus and its associated mosses and lichens forms a soft, thick litter layer. Small creeks and seepages clothed with mosses, lichens, liverworts and filmy ferns impart a softness, a stillness and a dampness to our forests that is almost unique. Some of these characteristics are illustrated on this page.

Fig 1 Dense epiphytes belonging to *Astelia* and *Freycinettia* on Truman's Track near the Paparoa Range. 1978.

Fig 2 Fungus, mosses and lichens typically clothing the base of a large tree growing in the forest interior on Mt Egmont. 1965.

Fig 3 A rain forest near the Fox Glacier, a forest which is full of lianes, ferns, mosses and lichens, 1973.

Fig 4 Another rain forest interior, this one on the McKinnon Pass. With 900–1,000 cm of rain each year, everything is clothed with mosses and lichens. 1975.

1

2

Fig 5 The interior of a mixed podocarp-hardwood forest is less dense. These are typical understoreys of seedlings, shrubs and ferns in a rimu-matai-mahoe forest. Opepe Bush. 1973.

Fig 6 A typical feature of our forests. The sound of water falling from this tiny waterfall is completely absorbed by the surrounding mosses and small plants. Waiho River. 1966.

3

4

5

6

Types of New Zealand forest

New Zealand's indigenous forests fall primarily into two main forest types: (1) the conifer-hardwood, dominated by gymnosperms, mainly podocarp trees, but also by kauri and sometimes by cedar (*Libocedrus*); (2) the beech forests, dominated by one or more of the four indigenous species of *Nothofagus*. Most of these forests are dense, intimate associations of species. Only occasionally do pure stands of any one species occur; when they do, they are generally small in area.

Dense conifer-hardwood forests are very luxuriant, with understoreys of small trees, shrubs and ferns. Mosses and lichens are common, and lianes and epiphytes plentiful. This forest type is generally subdivided into three subtypes: (a) the kauri-podocarp-hardwood forest which covered much of the northern part of the North Island; (b) the podocarp-hardwood forests that constituted the so-called lowland rain forests of the North Island and the West Coast of the South Island; (c) podocarp-hardwood-beech forests found extensively along the mountain ranges of both islands, particularly the South Island.

Before introduced noxious animals arrived the podocarp-hardwood forests of the North Island were in many places almost impenetrable without the aid of a slasher to clear the track. From my boyhood I recall forest of this nature in the Urewera around Lake Waikaremoana, now largely altered by noxious animals. I remember my father telling me of a climb of Mt Hauhungatahi near Erua, probably around 1909. His party intended to go through the bush encircling the lower and middle slopes of the mountain out to the clear top and return in one day. However, the forest was so dense that a track had to be slashed all the way through the bush from Erua to the upper bush line. The party set out early on a Saturday morning but did not break through to the clear summit area until about mid-day on the Sunday, after spending the night in the bush. Today that podocarp-hardwood forest is largely opened out, though still a reserve.

Most of this wonderful lowland forest of the North Island has been cut out or burned since that time. All that remain these days are the remnants of the West Taupo and Urewera forests; there are also scattered pockets of scenic reserves.

In fact the only really extensive areas of indigenous New Zealand forests that still remain intact are growing at Whirinaki and Pureora in the North Island, as beech forests along the South Island mountain ranges, podocarp-hardwood forests in South Westland, and as podocarp-hardwood-beech forests in Fiordland and along the south coast of the South Island. The forests of Stewart Island have not been extensively interfered with, apart from damage by deer.

At the beginning of European settlement the podocarp-hardwood type of forest covered much of the lowland North Island from sea level to 900 m, starting from Wellington northwards

1

2

Fig 1 A dense pure podocarp stand growing near Minginui in the Whirinaki State Forest. 1974.

Fig 2 The massive, straight trunks of rimu, matai and miro trees rise high above the undergrowth like Grecian columns in the podocarp-hardwood forest at Opepe Bush. 1975.

Fig 3 Interior of a stand of podocarp-hardwood-beech forest in Pelorus Valley. There is beech regeneration in the middle distance. 1972.

Fig 4 The more open floor of a beech forest interior. This southern beech forest in the Eglinton Valley contains *Nothofagus fusca* and *N. menziesii*.

Fig 5 A typical North Island beech forest in the Kaimanawa Forest Park. Note the characteristic undergrowth of ferns and shrubs. 1975. The beech forest of the North Island is frequently less open than the South Island, as the interiors in these two photographs show.

3

4

5

through the Manawatu and the Wairarapa and round west of Lake Taupo to the Waikato River mouth. There were additional extensive areas to the east in the Bay of Plenty, Urewera and western Hawke's Bay. It also covered the Mahia Peninsula. Intermingled with these areas, up to elevations of 700 m, were areas of podocarp-hardwood-beech forests; they were usually dominated by beech trees, but there were podocarp-softwoods scattered throughout with hardwoods as an understorey. The largest block of this type of forest covered the East Cape region from Mahia northwards, with another block in the west stretching from the Mokau River south to Patea and Wanganui.

North of the Raglan-Whakatane line these forests gave way to the kauri-podocarp-hardwood forests dominated by kauri trees, often in pure stands. The associated hardwood trees were mainly tawari and taraire; the podocarp species included rimu, miro, totara, toatoa and tanekaha.

Beech forests, as pure beech types, occurred in the North Island mountain ranges from the Raukumara Range along the Huirau Range in the Urewera south to the Tararua Range. Beech forests occur on Mt Ruapehu but not Mt Egmont. In the South Island, beech dominated the forests along all the main ranges from north-west Nelson to southern Fiordland and Te Waewae Bay, but beeches have never grown on Stewart Island. From D'Urville Island southwards the podocarp-hardwood-beech type of forest grew at the lower levels below about 650–700 m; there were extensive forests in the Marlborough Sounds, Nelson to Golden Bay, and Karamea to Reefton regions. It also grew in south Westland, in Fiordland and around the coast to Te Waewae Bay. Beech forests are generally more open, with less undergrowth than podocarp-dominated forests.

Forests are often referred to as coastal, lowland and montane. Of these, coastal forests are narrow strips of forest, seldom more than two or three kilometres deep, extending inland from the coast itself. Podocarp-hardwood-beech forests in the Marlborough Sounds are a good example of this type of forest; so are the kohekohe-dominant forests that used to exist along the Horowhenua and Manawatu coasts. Examples of the latter are preserved in remnant scenic reserves round Waikanae and Paraparaumu.

Lowland forests are the once extensive forests that covered the rolling lowland country of the North Island and along the west and south coasts of the South Island.

Montane forests commence at about 610–900 m and continue to the upper bush line; this varies from about 1,200 m in the north to around 860 m in the far south.

The nikau palm dominated small areas

of coastal forest around the North Island and the north-west of the South Island. Small reserves of this type of forest have been set aside in the Bay of Islands, at Piha and Morere, and on the coast north of Greymouth.

Pure mangrove forests are common in the estuaries of North Auckland.

Fig 1 The dense, luxuriant undergrowth of a North Auckland kauri forest. 1979.

Fig 2 Section of the edge of the Whirinaki State Forest near Minginui exposing a dense stand of huge podocarps. 1974.

Fig 3 The edge of a South Island beech forest near Lake Rotoroa showing the typical growth of large trees on the edge. 1972.

6

7

8

9

Fig 4 Podocarp-hardwood forest with a canopy of many large rimus (yellow-green). Near Erua, 1970.

Fig 5 An exposure along the edge of a dense stand of kauris. Waitakere Ranges, 1966.

Fig 6 in the Hihitahi State Forest near Taihape. An almost pure stand of mountain cedar, *Libocedrus bidwillii*. 1969.

Fig 7 A typical swamp-bog association of trees on Mt Ruapehu. Those illustrated here include *Halocarpus bidwillii*, bog pine, and *Lagarostrobos colensoi* and *Dracophyllum* species. 1974.

Fig 8 A fine exposure of southern rata, *Metrosideros umbellata*. These trees are from a pure stand growing near Tautuku Beach, Chaslands. 1964.

Fig 9 The characteristic canopy of a North Island beech forest; the olive-green trees are *Nothofagus menziesii*. A superb view from the Renata Ridge, Tararua Forest Park, 1970.

Fig 10 The grandeur of the South Island beech forest. Almost pure forest of southern beech clothes the slopes and floor of the Hollyford Valley. 1976.

10

8

Fig 1 A rimu-tawa forest canopy, looking down on Lake Waikaremoana from Mt Ngamoto. 1966.

Fig 2 Podocarp-hardwood-beech forest, Mt Ruapehu, containing *Lagarostrobos colensoi*, *Libocedrus bidwillii*, *Phyllocladus trichomanoides* and *Nothofagus* species. 1972.

Fig 3 The canopy of a pure stand of tawa near the Kaimai summit. 1976.

Fig 4 A striking exposure of pure kahikatea on the banks of the Poerua River, South Westland. 1978.

Fig 5 *Eugenia maire* trees growing in a swamp surrounded by beech forest at Lake Pounui. 1968.

Fig 6 North Auckland forest interior with taraire, puriri, nikau and coprosma. On the slopes of Mt Taumatamahoe, 1979. Growing in a sub-tropical climate, the North Auckland native forest has a quite distinctive character all of its own.

Fig 7 Distinctive trunks of a small stand of kamahi trees growing in Opepe Bush. 1975.

Fig 8 Second-growth forest near Lake Rotoma consisting of almost pure rewarewa. 1976. Much cut-over forest has regenerated in rewarewa. But although this native tree has a beautifully figured wood, in recent years large areas of this new growth have been destroyed and replaced with exotic pine plantations.

Fig 9 Tall, spindly trunks in the interior of a kanuka forest near Opepe Bush, 1963. This forest has acted as a nursery bed in the intervening years for regenerating podocarps, which are now beginning to grow towards the light.

Fig 10 Kohekohe trees. Extensive stands of pure kohekohe forest once grew from North Cape to Nelson, but have now largely disappeared. This photograph from a reserve near Ohau shows the typical smooth trunks characteristic of these attractive trees. 1979.

Fig 11 Interior of a typical Fiordland rain forest in the Clinton River area. 1975. Similar rain forest occurs in the North Island on Mt Egmont.

9

10

11

Antiquity of the New Zealand forest

The principal tree species of the New Zealand forest have an ancestry which goes back far into antiquity. Our podocarp rain forests contain more species with ancient lineages than similar forests elsewhere and are therefore among the most ancient forests in the world. These tree species have an unbroken ancestry stretching back without much modification to the ancient continent of Gondwanaland for as long as 190 million years or more.

About 190–135 million years ago, in the Jurassic period of geological time, trees belonging to the Podocarpaceae were evolving and spreading over the east and south-east regions of Gondwana. By about 135–100 million years ago, in the Lower Cretaceous period, these podocarps had covered a large area of Gondwana; the pollen grains of two genera of these early trees have been identified from the Lower Cretaceous deposits of New Zealand, found in Fiordland and in the southern Nelson district. One of these genera, *Microcachryidites*, became extinct in New Zealand, but a living representative, *Microcachrys*, is now found in Tasmania; as a fossil it is known from Australia and Kerguelen Island as well as from New Zealand.

The other genus of the two, *Dacrycarpus*, has a living representative in this country in the kahikatea or white pine, *Dacrycarpus dacrydioides*, and others living in New Guinea, New Caledonia, Indonesia and Burma. The ancestor of kahikatea was probably a species, *Podocarpidites ohikaensis*, the pollen of which is found in New Zealand in deposits dating back into the Eocene period 54-37 million years ago. So kahikatea, it seems, has a line of descent extending back in time for about 110 million years, perhaps even longer.

The podocarps apparently reached their peak during the Oligocene period, 37–25 million years ago, after which a number of their species disappeared. These are now found only as fossils, mainly as fossil pollens. But some persisted to modern times and are found today as living species in New Zealand, Tasmania, Australia, India, East Africa, the Malaysian Archipelago, Borneo, Papua and New Guinea, the West Indies, and Central and South America.

The ancient continent of Gondwana apparently remained intact with only minor rifting and marine transgressions throughout the Jurassic and Lower Cretaceous periods. This enabled a fairly wide dispersal of podocarps over the land surface. When in later Cretaceous and Tertiary times the continental land mass eventually started to break up and the sections to drift apart, the podocarps were widely distributed over the original land mass. This has contributed to the associations and distribution patterns shown by present-day survivors.

Amongst these survivors is the New Zealand rimu, *Dacrydium cupressinum;* the pollen grains of its ancestor can be identified in deposits as far back as the early Oligocene, about 37 million years ago. These fossil grains are identical to those of the present-day tree. Like that of the kahikatea, the evolution of rimu can be traced, through fossil pollen grains of trees which must have been very similar to rimu, as far back as Upper Cretaceous time. This is the Haumurian period in New Zealand geological history, about 70 million years ago.

Similar stories of ancient lineages can be traced for all our New Zealand podocarp species. The species *Halocarpus kirkii, H. biformis* and *H. bidwillii* together form a group of closely related forms with almost identical pollen grain structures whose ancestors can be traced through fossil pollen grains back to Upper Oligocene time, 30–25 million years ago. Miro and totara appear to be more recent arrivals; their fossil pollens can be traced back only as far as Upper Miocene times, about 15–7 million years ago. Matai is more recent still, with its earliest recorded fossil pollen grains occurring in the Wanganui and Hawera series of New Zealand deposits which belong to the Pliocene and Pleistocene periods, 7 million to 10,000 years ago. For *Phylloadus,* the remaining New Zealand genus of the Podocarpaceae, known fossil pollens indicate an ancestry extending far back to Upper Cretaceous times about 100–65 million years ago. However, related extinct species of the genus *Phyllocladidites* carry this line of descent of *Phyllocladus* as far back as early Cretaceous time, 135–100 million years ago.

Although that part of the Gondwanaland mass which was to become New Zealand was affected by climatic cooling and glaciation these podocarp genera and species have survived to the present day without much modification. It is this unbroken ancestry that makes the New Zealand podocarp forests such a priceless heritage.

Our beech forests, too, have an ancestry as ancient and as fascinating as that of the podocarps — while our kauri forests surpass them both in terms of antiquity. If we accept the fossil araucariacean *Araucariacites australis* as the evolutionary precursor of the kauri, *Agathis australis,* this ancient tree first appeared in the Jurassic period, 190–135 million years ago, and persisted to Oligocene times. The genus *Agathis,* the kauri, appears as fossils in mid-Cretaceous times about 100 million years ago but did not completely displace its araucarian ancestor until the Oligocene period, about 30 million years ago.

The Swedish botanist R. Florin considers that ancestors of the New Zealand podocarp and kauri trees of today were living in the Jurassic or possibly even as early as the Permian period, over 230 million years ago, but at that time were distinct from the Northern Hemisphere conifers.

Beech trees first appear as fossils in the Gondwanaland deposits of early Cretaceous times, 135–100 million years ago. These, the first of three groups of beeches, are known as the *brassi* group; they persisted in the New Zealand region until the Upper Pliocene period when they became extinct here but continued to grow in South America, New Guinea and New Caledonia. In New Zealand the *brassi* beeches were superseded by the

---

FOSSIL POLLEN

The pollen of a tree species is specific to that tree, differing in structure, shape and sculpturing from the pollen of any other tree. Collections of fossil pollen grains are almost indestructible, being preserved in silts, mudstones and sandstones and in swamps. By the use of special techniques, they can be removed from these deposits and studied. The evolutionary history of genera and families of plants together with information about past climatic periods in which they lived can be pieced together from these studies.

Geologic periods with known evolutionary geological time scale of some common *New Zealand* tree genera.

THE EVOLUTION OF TREE GENERA

Nothofagus brassi group

ERA	PERIOD	EPOCH	STARTING TIME IN MILLIONS OF YEARS	NEW ZEALAND SERIES EQUIVALENTS	DOMINANT LIFE FORMS	GENERA
Cenozoic	Quaternary	Holocene	1	Hawera		
Cenozoic	Quaternary	Pleistocene	2			Dodonea
Cenozoic	Tertiary	Pliocene	7	Wanganui		
Cenozoic	Tertiary	Miocene	25	Taranaki / Southland / Pareora	Angiosperm plants / Mammals / Birds	Cyathea, Ixerba; Macropiper, Aristotelia, Coriaria, Griselina; Alectryon, Fuchsia, Weinmania, Libocedrus; Beilsmiedia, Cordyline, Avicennia
Cenozoic	Tertiary	Oligocene	37	Landon		Coprosma, Senecio, Olearia; Myrsine, Pseudowintera, Brachyglottis
Cenozoic	Tertiary	Eocene	54	Arnold		Hoheria, Dracophyllum, Rhopalostylis; Dysoxylum, Laurelia
Cenozoic	Tertiary	Paleocene	65	Dannevirke		Metros deros, Leptospermum, Nothofagus fusca group; Dicksonia
Mesozoic	Cretaceous	Upper	100	Mata / Raukumara		Agathis, Dacrydium, Knightia; Nothofagus menziesii group, Phyllocladus, Podocarpus
Mesozoic	Cretaceous	Lower	135	Clarence	Dinosaurs / Gymnosperm plants	
Mesozoic	Jurassic	Upper	158	Taitai		Podocarpus (Dacrycarpus)
Mesozoic	Jurassic	Middle	175	Oteke		
Mesozoic	Jurassic	Lower	190	Kawhia		
Mesozoic	Triassic	Upper	205	Herangi	Reptiles / Ferns / Araucarian plants	Early podocarps e.g. Microcachryidites
Mesozoic	Triassic	Middle	215	Balfour		
Mesozoic	Triassic	Lower	230	Gore		
Palaeozoic	Permian	Upper	255	D'Urville		Araucariacites
Palaeozoic	Permian	Lower	280	Aparima		

Each genus can be followed in its colour band from the lower left of the diagram where the time of its first appearance can be read off. Where a genus does not remain to the present time its colour band terminates opposite the geologic time of its extinction in New Zealand. The Holocene epoch occupies only about 10,000 years.

41

fusca group and paralleled by the *menziesii* group. This latter group appears first in Upper Cretaceous times, and these fossils are the direct ancestors of the present-day New Zealand silver beech, *Nothofagus menziesii*. In fact the fossil pollen grains of Upper Cretaceous specimens are indistinguishable from the pollen grains of the familiar silver beech trees of our times. This gives silver beech a direct ancestry of about 70–100 million years. The *fusca* group of beeches evolved a little later in the Paleocene period, 65–54 million years ago, and have persisted to the present day. The beech trees of New Zealand and their forests represent, therefore, the culmination of an evolution process that has been going on for about 135 million years.

Although today beech forests are characteristic of the South Island, during the glaciations of Tertiary times beech trees were largely removed from the south and driven north. Fossil pollen grains found in these northern areas indicate beech-dominant or kauri-dominant forests alternating with climatic changes over North Auckland during the Pleistocene period 2 million to 10,000 years ago.

The species I have mentioned form the core, the most ancient part of New Zealand's forests. The remaining tree species include tree ferns of great antiquity, dating back to Jurassic or possibly even Triassic times, some 230–190 million years ago, along with many species of Angiospermae which evolved in the period from Paleocene to Upper Oligocene, followed in Miocene times by a great outburst of evolutionary speciation.

In New Zealand glacial periods never completely exterminated all forests, as happened in some other parts of the world. There always existed some refuges from which the land became reforrested during milder climatic times. We live today in one of these milder interglacial periods; when *Homo sapiens* first came to New Zealand they found a land clothed with unique luxuriant forests of great antiquity.

But Europeans regarded, and still regard, these forests as a resource for uncontrolled exploitation, ignoring the great scientific and cultural value of even the remnants of these forests that still exist. As I write, only 3,000 hectares of our podocarp forests remain in the central North Island, and even these are being felled. The kauri has fared even worse. The real scientific value and the great antiquity of these primordial New Zealand forests surely support claims made by biologists and geologists for the creation of more reserves from what little remains.

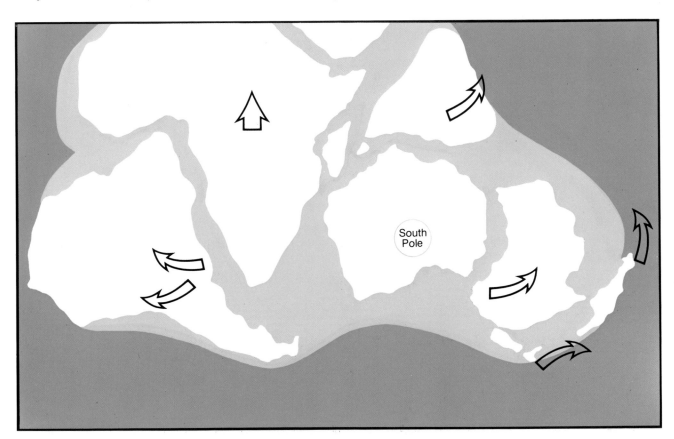

South Pole

THE BREAK-UP OF GONDWANALAND

The ancient southern continent of Gondwanaland straddled the South Pole during Carboniferous and Permian times. In the Triassic and Jurassic, between 230 and 135 million years ago, the New Zealand and Tasmanian section started to move slowly away, while still retaining a connection with the eastern region. As the Cretaceous period dawned, Gondwanaland began to break apart, with India and Africa drifting to the north and South America to the west; Australia, with its marginal lands of Tasmania, New Zealand and New Guinea, revolved slowly clockwise and drifted to the east, leaving Antarctica over the South Pole. During the late Jurassic and early Cretaceous period the Tasman Sea began to open up between Australia and the future New Zealand. The ancestors of plants such as the podocarps, ferns and araucarians — unique to New Zealand — were established on the New Zealand land mass before this time. The relationships that exist between these plants in New Zealand today and related plants in Australia, Tasmania, New Guinea and Indo-Malaysia can be generally explained by the theory of continental drift.

A primordial podocarp stand surviving from our ancient lowland podocarp forest. These trees growing near Minginui are several hundred years old. ▶

Botanical discovery in New Zealand

Most people are probably only vaguely aware of how our plants came to be discovered and named. It is a fascinating story.

The part played by Captain James Cook during his three voyages of discovery to New Zealand is probably the best known. Cook's first expedition in the *Endeavour* (1768-71) was primarily for the purpose of observing the transit of Venus. The expedition left England with ninety-four persons aboard, amongst whom were an astronomer and ten scientists who would carry out botanical and zoological work. Sir Joseph Banks, a distinguished scientist who was to be president of the Royal Society for over forty years, financed the botanical side of the expedition, spending £10,000 providing stores and equipment. He engaged Dr Daniel C. Solander, a Swede from the University of Uppsala and a pupil of Linnaeus, to accompany him, as well as three artists, John Reynolds, Sydney Parkinson and Alexander Buchan.

The *Endeavour* anchored on 8 October 1769 at Teoneroa, now called Poverty Bay. Here, over three days, Banks and Solander collected about sixty species of plants. They included the karaka, ngaio, the large-leaved kowhai, rangiora, koromiko and a species of *Carmichaelia*. It is probable that the karaka, *Corynocarpus laevigatus*, was the first species collected.

While at Teoneroa Cook's crew gathered large quantities of two coastal herbaceous plants, *Lepidium oleraceum*, Cook's scurvy grass, and *Apium australe* (*prostratum*) or Cook's celery, both of which he used to combat scurvy among his men. These were probably the first New Zealand plants to be used for medicinal purposes by Europeans.

On 21 October the *Endeavour* arrived at Tigadu, now called Anaura Bay, where Banks and Solander accumulated at least ninety species. These included, among the trees, the fuchsia and the karamu, *Coprosma lucida*, along with the kaka beak, *Clianthus puniceus*.

At Uawa, probably Tolaga Bay, about 160 different species were collected. Recorded for the first time were the tree species kohekohe, puriri, rewarewa, karamu, *Coprosma robusta*, the nikau palm and probably mahoe, *Melicytus ramiflorus*. Observed Cook: "The country abounds with a great number of plants and the woods with a great variety of beautiful birds, many of them unknown to us."

At Opurangi, now called Mercury Bay, the transit of the planet Mercury was observed on 9 November 1769. Here Banks and Solander collected over 200 different kinds of plants, including for the first time pohutukawa, mangrove, akepiro, *Olearia furfuracea*, the silver tree fern, *Cyathea dealbata*, and the grass tree, *Dracophyllum sinclairii*. Although kauris were common in this area neither Banks nor Solander noticed this species.

The *Endeavour* now sailed down the Firth of Thames and up the Waihou River, which Cook called the Thames, where a landing was made to examine a kahikatea forest. Banks wrote: "The banks were completely clothed with the finest timber my eyes ever beheld, of a tree we had before seen, but only at a distance, in Poverty Bay and Hawke's Bay. Thick woods of it were everywhere upon the banks, every tree as straight as a pine, and of immense size, and the higher we went the more numerous they were." In this area they saw for the first time the two forest trees tawa and matai.

Further collections were made in the Bay of Islands before Cook headed south to Queen Charlotte Sound where the *Endeavour* anchored on 16 January 1770. Here Banks and Solander made a huge collection amounting to about 220 different species, mostly from around Totaranui. They included the grass tree, *Dracophyllum filifolium*, southern rata, heketara, horoeka, rimu, beech and kanono. By this time the collection had grown to such size that Banks was experiencing difficulty in preserving it adequately and had to devote some time ashore drying out paper and specimens.

On the expedition's return to England in 1771 Solander's descriptions of some 360 species of New Zealand plants illustrated by over 200 plates were prepared for publication. Unfortunately, Solander died suddenly in 1782, and this important manuscript has remained unpublished.

Banks was not included in Cook's second expedition. His place was taken by Johan R. Forster, who joined the expedition as naturalist and took his son George with him as artist. At the Cape of Good Hope Dr A. Parrman, a botanist and a pupil of Linnaeus, was taken on board. The ships *Resolution* and *Adventure* reached Dusky Bay, now Dusky Sound, in March 1773. Here the Forsters collected many new plant species, including the broad-leaved cabbage tree, *Cordyline indivisa*, inanga or the grass tree, *Dracophyllum longifolium*, the mutton-bird shrub or raumakaroa, and several mountain daisies, including *Celmisia coriacea*.

Ever concerned about scurvy, Cook prepared in Dusky Sound a liquor which he called spruce beer. It was made from young shoots of rimu fermented with treacle or molasses and was later improved by the addition of a tea brewed from manuka leaves.

Further collecting in Queen Charlotte Sound resulted in the discovery of many notable plants, among them flax, *Phormium tenax*, the wild spaniard, *Aciphylla squarrosa*, the nikau palm, the stinking coprosma, karamu, and manuka.

On the return of Cook's second expedition to England, J. R. Forster was banned from writing any account of the voyage. He was informed that he had been employed purely as a collector, a statement that was unjust and incorrect. Highly offended, both the Forsters re-

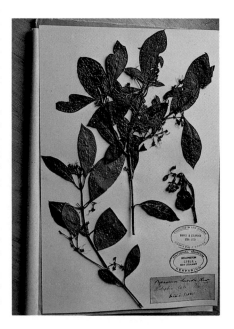

A herbarium specimen of *Coprosma lucida* from the Banks and Solander collection, now in the National Museum in Wellington. The red handwriting is Solander's. Collected plant specimens are pressed and dried and usually treated against insect attack. They are then mounted on sheets of stiff paper as herbarium specimens. *National Museum*

turned to Germany, where they published seven books dealing with New Zealand plants and with the expedition.

The first was *Characteres Generum Plantarum* by J. R. and G. Forster, published in 1776 and containing descriptions of new genera of plants discovered during the voyage. Included in this publication are such genera as *Brachyglottis, Coprosma, Leptospermum, Corynocarpus, Melicytus, Rhipogonum, Aciphylla* and *Phormium. Florulae Insularum Australium Prodromus* by G. Forster, 1786, contains descriptions of the plants collected during the voyage, many species being described here for the first time. *De Plantis Esculentis* by G. Forster, also published in 1786, gives descriptions and uses of fifty-one edible plants from the voyage. G. Forster's *A Voyage Round the World*, 1777, contains further information on useful plants.

The Forsters' descriptions of many of our plants are not very full and detailed, but their contribution to our botany is recognised in the generic name *Forstera* and the specific name *forsteri* given to a number of our plant species.

In a similar way both Banks and Solander are commemorated by the specific names *banksii* and *solandri*, as in the cabbage tree, *Cordyline banksii*, and the beech, *Nothofagus solandri*.

Cook's third expedition of 1776-80 added little to the botanical knowledge of New Zealand.

The Banks and Solander collections

from Cook's first voyage were the property of Sir Joseph Banks, who bequeathed them to a Mr Robert Brown. He, in turn, and on condition he was made Keeper of the Department of Botany in the British Museum, made them over to the Museum in 1828. Two duplicate sets of Banks and Solander's plants, each of them about 200 species, have been placed in New Zealand, one in the Auckland Institute and Museum and the other in the National Museum at Wellington. Although Solander prepared full detailed descriptions of the species collected and over 200 copper engravings were made, these descriptions remain as an unpublished manuscript, preserved in the British Museum to this day and entitled *Primitiae Florae Novae Zelandiae*. Solanders manuscript and the Banks and Solander collections have been used by many botanists. There is a copy of the manuscript in both the New Zealand museums that hold the duplicate collections, and sets of the illustrations are in both these museums and in the Alexander Turnbull Library.

Many of the names proposed for the plants in Solander's manuscript have been adopted by subsequent botanists in their publications about New Zealand plants. Amongst those so adopted may be mentioned *Dacrydium cupressinum* (rimu), *Metrosideros excelsa* (pohutukawa), *Myrtus bullata* (ramarama) and, among specific names only, the horoeka, named *Aralia crassifolia* by Solander and now known as *Pseudopanax crassifolius*.

In 1822 the French corvette *Cocquille* sailed from Toulon on a voyage of discovery in the south seas. The expedition was commanded by Duperrey, with Dumont d'Urville as executive officer and botanist, assisted by P. A. Lesson, an assiduous collector. The *Cocquille* anchored for four weeks in the Bay of Islands, where collections of plants were made. On its return to France, the *Cocquille* was refitted and renamed the *Astrolabe* before setting out on a second expedition. In January 1827 the *Astrolabe* anchored on the west shore of Tasman Bay in a shelter now known as Astrolabe Bay. There an island was named Adele Island after d'Urville's wife. A large collection of

A herbarium specimen of *Sophora microphylla* collected by Banks and Solander. *National Museum*

plants included the new species kanuka, kahikatea, taupata and aka, *Metrosideros perforata*. Also among the collection were rimu, mahoe, karamu, kamahi, manuka, pate and toetoe. A further collection was made from Currents Bay on the opposite side of Tasman Bay and from D'Urville Island. At Bream Head near Whangarei the species *Pseudopanax lessonii* was discovered. D'Urville explored the Waitemata Harbour and the Bay of Islands before returning to France.

The plant collections were deposited with the Museum National d'Histoire Naturelle in Paris. In 1832 A. Richard, a French botanist, published descriptions of 379 species of New Zealand plants in *Essai d'une Flore de la Nouvelle-Zelande*. This was part of a fine publication sponsored by the French Government entitled *Voyage de Decouvertes de l'Astrolabe: Botanique*. Richard's work was based on the collections from the *Cocquille* and *Astrolabe* as well as those of the Forsters. Some of the species described had been previously found and named by Banks and Solander, but Richard was the first person to publish scientific names for these plants in a recognised publication. The *Flore* contains descriptions of 210 flowering plants and 169 species of other plants such as ferns and mosses, and was the first publication to deal with the plants of New Zealand as a whole. It includes descriptions copied from Forster's original work but made much more comprehensive.

Both d'Urville's and Lesson's names are commemorated in the names of several New Zealand plants. D'Urville is recalled in the genus of seaweeds known as *Durvillea* and also in the grass tree, *Dracophyllum urvilleanum*. Lesson is remembered in the tree *Pseudopanax lessonii*.

In 1837 d'Urville commanded an expedition in the *Astrolabe* and the *Zelee*, visiting Hobart in 1840, from where they sailed to the Antarctic, the Auckland Islands, Campbell Island and Stewart Island. Specimens were collected from the Auckland and Campbell Islands and these were described in volumes twelve and thirteen of *Le Voyage au Pole Sud, 1853*. All had been previously named and described by other botanists.

The pioneering stage of botanical discovery in New Zealand had now drawn to a close. A period of consolidation began, along with extensive inland exploration and discovery as European settlers arrived.

In 1834 William Colenso, a missionary printer with a keen interest in natural history, arrived at the Bay of Islands. With great enthusiasm he began to devote his spare time to botanical exploration in the north. He became famous for his long walks through the country, observing and collecting many plant specimens, the bulk of which he sent to Sir William Hooker, Professor of Botany at Glasgow University.

In 1838 Colenso travelled to the Bay of Plenty and East Coast districts, and in 1839 he walked overland to Cape Reinga. In 1841–42 he travelled by schooner to Hicks Bay; after walking down the coast to Kaupapa he turned inland to Lake Waikaremoana. He then traversed the mountains of the Urewera country to Rotorua, and walked across the Waikato district to the Manukau and Kaipara Harbours and back to Paihia. On this walk Colenso collected almost 1,000 botanical specimens new to science.

The ships of the British Antarctic Expedition arrived in the Bay of Islands in 1841. Assistant surgeon on the ship *Erebus* was J. D. Hooker, one of the world's great botanists. On the other ship, the *Terror,* the assistant surgeon was a Dr D. Lyall, whose name is linked with the giant *Ranunculus lyallii* and other species. Thus a friendship between Colenso and Hooker began which lasted for over half a century. Colenso went with Hooker on many botanical excursions and sent him much botanical material.

Colenso's name is commemorated in the nomenclature of a number of New Zealand plants. One is the generic name *Colensoa,* established by Hooker for the plant now classified as *Pratia physaloides* (the name *Pratia* was established prior to Hooker's name, *Colensoa*). Others are specific names, such as those of the trees *Lagarostrobos colensoi*, *Pittosporum colensoi* and *Pseudopanax colensoi*, and the fern *Cyathea colensoi*.

During his visit in 1841 Hooker also made the acquaintance of Andrew Sinclair, later to become Colonial Secretary under Sir George Grey. He was also a keen naturalist; his name is perpetuated in the grass tree, *Dracophyllum sinclairii*.

Hooker collected assiduously around Paihia, along the Kerikeri River and the Waikare Inlet, and around Waimate and Waitangi. On the return of the *Erebus* and *Terror* to England, he set about publishing his findings. The publication of his *Flora Novae-Zelandiae* in two volumes in 1852 and 1855 marked the first consolidation of knowledge of the botany of New Zealand. These two volumes contained descriptions of 1,767 species of New Zealand plants as well as 130 coloured plates and an essay on plant geography. Colenso and other collectors continued to send specimens to Hooker, and in 1864 Hooker published part one of the *Handbook of the Flora of New Zealand,* with the second part following in 1867. This was an entirely new publication which included many new species not previously described.

The publication of Hooker's *Handbook* closed the pioneering stage of botanical discovery, but mention must be made of several further naturalist-explorers who contributed a great deal to this period.

Ernst Dieffenbach came to New Zealand as the ship's surgeon on the *Tory* in 1839 and did much exploring and collecting of plants around Wellington, Taupo, the Tongariro mountains, the Waikato and on Mt Egmont. A Supreme Court judge, W. T. L. Travers, with his son Henry, came to New Zealand in 1849 and together explored the Nelson, West Coast and Spenser Mountains districts; the grass tree, *Dracophyllum traversii,* is named after him. Henry Travers went to the Chatham Islands, where he found the giant forget-me-not, *Myosotidium nobile.* John C. Bidwill, a merchant, visited New Zealand in 1839, when he became the first European to climb Mt Ngauruhoe; from here he made the first collection of New Zealand alpine plants, sending them to Kew. In 1848 he returned, collecting plants around Nelson and in the Nelson Lakes area. The bog pine, *Halocarpus bidwillii,* is named after him.

Between 1840 and 1843 the French ships *L'Aube* and *L'Allier* were stationed at Akaroa; their surgeon was E. Raoul, who spent much time collecting plants on Banks Peninsula. His descriptions, first published in Ser. 3, Vol 2 of the *Ann. Sci. Nat.,* were later included in a book entitled *Choix de Plantes de la Nouvelle-Zelande,* published in 1846. Raoul is commemorated in the genus *Raoulia* and several other plants.

In 1826 and again in 1838 the superintendent of the Sydney Botanical Gardens, Allan Cunningham, visited the Bay of Islands. He became acquainted with Colenso and made extensive plant collections. His brother, Richard Cunningham, visited New Zealand in 1833 and made further collections, all of which were sent to Kew. The name is commemorated in the specific names of several plants, for example the orchid *Dendrobium cunninghamii.*

David Monro, who came to New Zealand in 1842 and settled in Nelson, later becoming Speaker of the House of Representatives, was yet another enthusiastic collector. He explored the northern part of the Southern Alps, sending specimens to Hooker. The Kaikoura mountain senecio, *Senecio monroi,* was named after him by Hooker.

Between 1858 and 1860 Julius von Haast and James Hector arrived in New Zealand. Both were explorers and geologists, but in their travels they also discovered a number of plants. Their names are attached to species such as *Senecio hectori, Raoulia haastii* and the celmisias *C. hectori* and *C. haastii.* Along with John Buchanan, an artist and collector, Hector explored the central and west Otago districts, and later the Kaikoura Mountains and Mt Egmont. Buchanan's name is preserved in *Pittosporum buchananii.* Sir Julius von Haast later founded and

Thomas Kirk (1828-98), botanist, naturalist and teacher, noteworthy for over sixty publications on New Zealand plants including *The Forest Flora of New Zealand,* published in 1889.

became director of the Canterbury Museum. Sir James Hector started the New Zealand Geological Survey and the Colonial Museum, now the National Museum in Wellington, and also became its first director.

In 1865 F. W. Hutton arrived in New Zealand from England. With Hector and Haast he became one of a select trio which contributed much to the biology and geology of New Zealand during the nineteenth century. Hutton is commemorated in the specific names of several plants, for example *Pittosporum huttonii.*

Almost contemporary with Hutton were Donald Petrie and Thomas Kirk. Petrie, an avid collector, established an extensive herbarium. Kirk, who arrived in 1863, feared that New Zealand's indigenous forests could be facing ultimate destruction, and published a paper expressing this fear entitled *The Utilisation of New Zealand Timbers.* His *The Forest Flora of New Zealand* was published in 1889. Kirk's name is attached to many of our plants, such as the tree *Dacrydium kirkii* and the genus *Kirkianella.* He published over sixty papers on New Zealand plants, more than any other botanist up to the turn of the century.

G. M. Thomson, a naturalist, schoolteacher and later a Member of Parliament, became concerned about the damage caused in our forests by introduced animals. His book *The Naturalisation of Animals and Plants in New Zealand* was published in 1922.

A further important early naturalist was Thomas F. Cheeseman. He organised one of the first naturalists clubs, in Auckland, and in 1887 visited the Kermadec Islands and the Three Kings Islands. In 1895 he toured the northern part of Northland with J. Adams, another keen botanist. Cheeseman visited the Cook Islands in 1896. On all his travels he collected botanical specimens which formed the basis of his extensive herbarium at his Auckland home; it was bequeathed to the Auckland Museum.

Cheeseman's *Manual of the New Zealand Flora,* published in 1906, was the first attempt at a complete *Flora* for this country. It was edited and revised by W. R. B. Oliver in 1925, and remained the principal reference work on New Zealand plants until publication of H. H. Allan's *Flora of New Zealand* in 1960. Oliver, a

This large boulder marks the grave of Leonard Cockayne at Otari.

former director of the National Museum, is most noted for his studies of the genera *Coprosma* and *Dracophyllum.*

In 1880 there arrived a person who was to have considerable influence on botany in this country. Leonard Cockayne was first a schoolteacher, then a farmer, and later a plant ecologist of world fame. He established a garden at Brighton near Christchurch, where he grew and studied native plants for about twelve years, exchanging plants and seeds all over the world. After 1903 he began exploring the country and the outlying islands. He visited Chatham Island in 1901, and the Auckland, Campbell, Antipodes and Bounty Islands in 1903. He made reports for the Department of Lands on Kapiti Island in 1907, Tongariro National Park and Waipoua Kauri Forest in 1908, and Stewart Island in 1909.

His first book, *New Zealand Plants and Their Story,* appeared in 1910. His *Observations Concerning Evolution Derived from Ecological Studies in New Zealand,* published in 1912, contained much detailed information about the growth of native plants. With E. P. Turner, first Director of Forestry, Cockayne co-authored the popular book *The Trees of New Zealand,* which first appeared in 1928 and has since run to many printings. Cockayne's most important book, *The Vegetation of New Zealand,* which is Part XIV of Engler and Drude's *Die Vegetation der Erde,* was published in Leipzig in 1921.

As a result of a suggestion by Cockayne, the Otari Open-air Native Plant Museum was set up in 1927 by the Wellington City Council and has been maintained and expanded ever since. A large boulder from the Belmont Hills marks the grave of Leonard Cockayne and his wife Maude in the Otari rock garden. The inscription on the tablet reads: "Will our descendants prize this unique heritage from the dim past, and preserve these sanctuaries intact?"

H. H. Allan, author of our present *Flora,* was a disciple of Cockayne. Cockayne looked at our plants not as specimens but as living things, to be grown, nurtured and observed. His ideas are stimulating the new generation of professional botanists at work in New Zealand today.

Amateur botanists have also responded to Cockayne's ideas at Otari and have established gardens of native plants in their districts and around their homes. Amongst the many could be mentioned that of John Anderson at "Glendonald", Albury, and of Muriel Fisher at Birkenhead, Auckland. Notable amongst the reserves is the fine domain created by Norman Potts at Opotiki and known as Hukutaia Domain, the Cockayne Memorial Garden in the Botanic Gardens in Christchurch and, more recently, the outstanding Waipahihi Botanical Reserve at Taupo, established by the Waipahihi Botanical Society.

Introduction to the species

A guide to identification

The average person strolling in the forest sees usually only the bark and leaves of a tree; the flowers and fruits are seldom seen because they are often high out of reach and only available for limited periods during the year. Unfortunately because leaves are so variable in form and structure even within a single species of tree, it has not been possible to construct a simple key or guide to enable quick identification of specimens. To assist with identification, however, the illustrations of full tree specimens in this book have been enlarged as far as practicable within the limits of space available and the illustrations of leaves have as often as possible been reproduced at natural size.

Any systematic study of living things necessitates the use of classificatory systems and the Linnaean system of nomenclature. Each species in this book has two latinised names given it by the botanist who first described it. This is in accordance with the binomial system of naming living things devised and published by the Swedish botanist Carl von Linnaeus in 1758 and employed in scientific literature throughout the world ever since.

Plants are often given common names. Such names are often apt and descriptive and, in New Zealand, frequently involve the Maori names of our trees. Both common names and Maori names are included alongside the scientific names throughout the book and can be found in the index of common names on page 378.

The system of classification followed in this book is that used by H. H. Allan in *Flora of New Zealand* Vol. 1, 1961 and by L. B. Moore and E. Edgar in Vol. 2, 1970. In some places, however, Allan's classification and nomenclatural priorities have been departed from to achieve an acceptable page design. Such departures in this book are minor and do not seriously affect the overall classification of our plants as it is generally accepted.

Throughout the book some of the major groupings of New Zealand trees are introduced on special pages, identified by their background colour. It should be pointed out that while some of these groupings are based on major family classifications (such as Podocarpaceae and Myrtaceae), others are based on the more minor genus groups (such as *Pseudopanax, Dracophyllum* and *Olearia*). In the context of New Zealand's native trees the genus groups, rather than the wider family groupings, are often more significant.

Occasionally advances in botanical knowledge have created problems. A recent Swedish publication has revised the genus *Senecio* and removed some New Zealand species of *Senecio* from that genus. As this book was going into final production, copies of this paper had not become available for general study in this country. It is understood that *S. elaeagnifolius* is transferred to the genus *Brachyglottis* as *B. elaeagnifolia; S. reinoldii* becomes *B. rotundifolia,* while *S. kirkii* is removed to a new genus, *Urostemon*. These changes are noted here for future reference if and when they are accepted into New Zealand botany.

The book was at first envisaged as a comprehensive photographic study of each New Zealand tree showing each tree as a specimen, its leaves, flowers, fruits and bark together with any other features of interest and importance in its identification. Early in the design of the book it became evident that where possible some form of condensation was, for reasons of space, a necessity. Therefore, amongst genera that include similar trees the photographic portrayal has been reduced to the essentials for identification and such genera treated more on a comparative basis. This has been done with *Carmichaelia, Coprosma, Dracophyllum* and *Olearia.*

The species

This page provides a guide to species contained in *The Native Trees of New Zealand*. Although a general index and an index of common names can be found at the end of the book, this table will enable the reader to locate each tree species quickly.

Family Podocarpaceae

This is a predominantly Southern Hemisphere family of plants which includes twelve genera covering 100 known species. Eight genera with seventeen species occur in New Zealand: *Dacrycarpus, Podocarpus, Dacrydium, Halocarpus, Lagarostrobos, Lepidothamnus, Prumnopitys* and *Phyllocladus.* Most are forest trees, although a few are erect or low, sprawling shrubs; two of the latter occur in New Zealand.

Podocarps are conifers. Belonging to the Gymnospermae, they do not bear flowers in the normally accepted sense but produce cones, also called *strobili,* which may be quite small. Podocarps are evergreen trees, mostly with linear or awl-shaped leaves which may be replaced with phylloclads (as in *Phyllocladus*).

Podocarpus is the most extensive genus with seventy-two species distributed through New Zealand, Australia, Malaysia, India, Japan, East Africa, the West Indies, and Central and South America. *Dacrydium* has twenty species in New Zealand,

Tasmania, Malaysia and Chile including rimu, *Dacrydium cupressinum,* below. The six species of *Phyllocladus* are found in New Zealand, Tasmania, Borneo and New Guinea. The subgenus *Dacrycarpus* grows only in New Zealand and includes but one species *D. dacrydiodes,* the kahikatea. The remaining four genera contain five species, of which four are found in Tasmania and one in Southern Chile.

The Podocarpaceae are a very ancient family, appearing first in geological time during the Jurassic period, about 190—135 million years ago.

At the time of European settlement of New Zealand our podocarps were best seen in the lowland podocarp-mixed-hardwood forests of the central North Island (the so-called North Island rain forests) and on the West Coast of the South Island. According to Holloway and others, these podocarps may be slowly declining, being slowly replaced by beeches. This may be due to a slow cooling in the New Zealand climate interfering with their ability to set seeds.

Family *Podocarpaceae:* Some seventy species of podocarps occur widely from tropical to temperate regions of the world. Eight genera containing nine species of forest trees and one shrub occur in New Zealand.

Genus *Dacrycarpus:* A New Zealand genus with one endemic species of forest tree.

Dacrycarpus dacrydioides
Kahikatea/White pine

The kahikatea is our tallest native tree, mature specimens as high as 60 m being recorded. It is found throughout New Zealand in forests up to 600 m altitude, where it is often the dominant tree in swampy areas. The kahikatea will also grow well on drier sites. It is still fairly common as scattered trees, but only a few stands of pure kahikatea forest remain today, mainly on the West Coast. Where swampy places are left alone, kahikatea groves are regenerating in both the North and South Islands.

The kahikatea seedling bears juvenile foliage until 1−2 m high, when semi-adult or adult foliage may appear. The tree then passes through several distinctive stages, one of which is seen in the magnificent specimen growing near Ross on the West Coast in **Fig 2**. The trunk may be up to 1.6 m through, sometimes with buttresses around the base, the smooth bark scaling off in large, ovoid flakes.

The juvenile, semi-adult and adult foliage stages may occur together on the same tree. Juvenile leaves are long and narrow, slightly curved with acute tips; they are arranged more or less in two rows along the stems, up to 7 mm long and 1 mm wide. Semi-adult leaves are similar in shape but shorter, only up to 4 mm long, arranged more around the stems but not so closely appressed to the stems as the adult. The adult leaves are scale-like, up to 2 mm long and closely appressed to the stems. The foliage spray in **Fig 1** shows adult leaves on the main stem with semi-adult leaves and juvenile leaves on subsidiary stems.

The male cones and female ovules are borne at the tips of the branchlets on separate trees. A male tree glows a faint orange when the cones are mature, a female red when its berry-like receptacles are ripe.

1

2

Fig 3 The developing kahikatea passes through a series of distinctive stages before becoming the fine old specimen in Fig 5. After appearing as the straggly seedling on the forest floor illustrated in Fig 8 the young kahikatea adopts a characteristic conical form which persists for many years. The tree illustrated here has semi-adult foliage and smooth bark which is horizontally striped. Cascades, May 1966.

Fig 4 This young tree is beginning to change from the juvenile conical form to the mature stage, showing foliage in semi-adult stages below and adult stages on top. Others of similar habit can be seen in the background. Weheka, Westland, December 1971.

Fig 5 After passing through the mature stage illustrated by the specimen in Fig 2 the aging tree adopts its final form. The crown opens, with the branches becoming stouter and more ascending. This very old kahikatea growing at Waiorongomai was severely damaged during the *Wahine* storm of 1968. I have seen another tree of similar vintage nearby and a further specimen near Lake Pounui on the lower slopes of Mt Matthews. These three trees are the largest and finest kahikateas I have seen. November 1968.

Fig 6 Male kahikatea trees show a faint orange glow when their cones are mature. This group was growing at Lake Rotoiti, Rotorua, November 1968.

Fig 7 The crown of the specimen on the left is opening out and its branches becoming more ascending as the tree passes into its final stage. Several specimens still in the younger, conical form are growing on the right, and a flowering kaikomako can be seen at left. Waiorongomai, December 1964.

3

4

5

6

7

8 **9** **10**

11
14 **12** **13**

Fig 8 Typically straggly kahikatea seedling with juvenile foliage growing on the forest floor at Opepe Bush. It was photographed in November 1978.

Fig 9 Spray of the long, narrow, juvenile leaves showing how they arise more or less in two rows along the stems. Twice natural size.

Fig 10 The trunk of the aging kahikatea depicted in Fig 5. Note the way in which the branches ''swell'' from the trunk and the large, ovoid-flaked area of bark. The wood is straight-grained, tough and easy to work, although it is not durable if exposed to weather. It is prone to attack by wood-boring insects.

Fig 11 The bark of a young tree. Note the pimpled surface and horizontal banding.

Fig 12 Characteristic flaking on the bark of a mature tree.

Fig 13 The mature trunk is often buttressed at the base. Awakeri Springs, January 1977.

Fig 14 A typical profusion of male cones on a semi-adult tree. This was growing at Waiorongomai, October 1965.

16

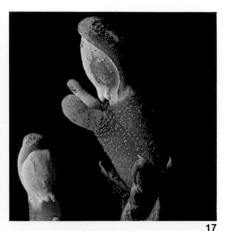

17

15

Fig 15 Ripe male cone that has shed most of its pollen. October. Five times natural size.

Fig 16 At pollination the ovule is a tiny white structure attached to its bract at the tip of the branchlet. The right-hand structure in this photograph shows a side view, the left a rear view. October. Four times natural size.

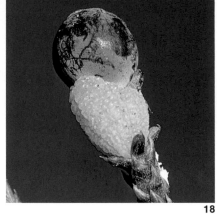

18

19

The photographs in Figs 17– 21 illustrate the various stages a developing kahikatea seed and its receptacle pass through in the six months following pollination.

Fig 17 After pollination. The developing egg-shaped seed is half enveloped by its bract and has its micropyle facing down so as to be almost level with the base of the bract. To the left of the seed are two white, finger-shaped processes which are undeveloped ovules. Below these is the developing receptacle which is green at this stage. The structures in this photograph show a front view (left) and a side view (right). The developing seed partly enclosed by its bract can be clearly seen. Late November. Three times natural size.

Fig 18 As the seed matures the receptacle changes colour, from green to yellow and finally to the bright orange-red colour of that illustrated in Fig 19. The specimen in this photograph clearly shows the bluish bloom which covers the mature seed of kahikatea. Late April. Five times natural size.

Fig 19 A ripe seed atop its ripe, fleshy, orange-red receptacle with two undeveloped ovules in front. The edge of the fused bract becomes much less prominent at maturity, but can still usually be seen as a faint ridge extending vertically over the seed. Early May. Five times natural size.

21

Fig 20 A group of mostly ripe seeds and receptacles. Those illustrated here are borne on semi-adult to adult foliage. Lake Pounui, April 1969.

Fig 21 Six months later than Fig 16 with seeds and receptacles at various stages of maturation. April. At three times natural size.

20

Genus *Prumnopitys:* A Southern Hemisphere genus with three species found in New Caledonia and New Zealand. The two New Zealand species are endemic forest trees.

Prumnopitys taxifolia
Matai/Black pine

1(a)　　　　　　　　　　　　　　　　　1(b)

A robust tree up to 25 m high, with a trunk up to 1.3 m across and a broad crown held on stout, erect, spreading branches. It forms a round-headed tree when mature which becomes more open and spreading as it ages. The young shoots are lush and colourful, imparting a fresh appearance to the tree in spring. In the forest, matai trees can be recognised quite easily from their bark. Characteristically greybrown and punctate, it flakes off in thick rounded or ovoid chunks which leave reddish blotches on the trunk. On young trees the flakes are larger and more irregular. Matai trees can live to a great age. One specimen near Lake Ianthe, in Westland, is reputedly more than 1,000 years old.

The wood is brown in colour, heavy, very hard and brittle with a close, rather handsome grain. It is exceptionally strong and durable, much used for flooring and weatherboarding. It is also used, to a lesser extent, in the manufacture of furniture.

The matai seedling has long, flexuous, drooping branchlets with yellowish or brownish-green leaves. It slowly grows into a shrub of intertwining, divaricating branchlets bearing rather scattered brown leaves. These are 5—10 mm long and 1—2 mm wide, with sharply pointed tips. After a number of years the adult tree grows out from the top of this shrub and then the divaricating branchlets atrophy and fall away. Adult leaves are up to 15 mm long and 10—20 mm wide. Straight or slightly curved in shape, they have obtuse, often apiculate tips and the undersurface is silvery-blue in colour, though tending to become darker as the leaves age.

Matai is dioecious, with sexes on separate trees. The male cones arise on spikes from the axils of the leaves, and are often borne in great profusion. The female ovules are tiny, and occur in groups of three to ten on an axillary spike up to 40 mm long. Most ovules do not develop to seeds, but usually atrophy.

Fig 1 Matai leaves from new spring growth.
(a) Underside, showing silvery-blue.
(b) Upperside. Note the apiculate tips.
About natural size.

Fig 2 Seedling showing drooping, flexuous habit. Opepe Bush, September 1978.

Fig 3 Grove of matai, with spring growth. Female trees on left have tighter habit of growth with more compact foliage than male tree on right. This open habit suggests freer carrying away of pollen by wind. Woodside Gorge, November 1968.

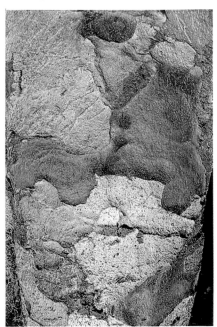

Fig 4 A mature matai at Woodside Gorge, March 1973.

Fig 5 Bark of an old matai. Note the vertical ridging and marks of previous scaling. From a tree at Lake Manapouri. November 1963.

Fig 6 Bark of an old matai, showing flaking. From a tree at Opepe Bush, August 1976.

Fig 7 Bark of a young matai, showing relatively large scaling and flaking areas. Photographed here at Woodside Gorge, March 1973.

Fig 8 Bark from a young but mature matai, showing large flakes and typical reddish flaked areas. Woodside Gorge, March 1973.

Fig 9 A very old matai with its upright and spreading branches. Waiorongomai, November 1969.

Fig 10 Ripe male cones are carried on spikes that arise from the leaf axils. Lake Pounui, November 1968. Here about natural size.

Fig 11 Male cones showing the mature microsporangia filled with pollen. The pollen will be released when the green scales open. Lake Pounui, November 1968. Four times natural size.

Fig 12 Developing buds of new matai foliage. Waiorongomai, October 1968. This photograph is slightly over natural size.

Fig 13 New leaves developing along a sprouting branchlet. Late October. About natural size.

Fig 14 Spray of old matai leaves showing strong mid-rib and grooved branchlets. March. This spray photographed at about natural size.

4

5

6

7

8

9

10

11

12

13

14

15

16

17

18

Fig 15 Last season's mature seeds and foliage growth bearing this season's spike of ovules. This shows that the seeds take about eighteen months to mature and ripen. Lake Pounui. January 1969. Just over natural size.

Fig 16 A young matai at the shrub stage. Woodside Gorge, March 1973.

Fig 17 A young spring shoot of matai leaves. About natural size.

Fig 18 Ovules enlarging after pollination. Each has a small bract that is shed as the ovule grows.

Fig 19 Developing female spike with six ovules. Lake Pounui, November 1968. Twice natural size.

Fig 20 Matai seeds, full-sized but not yet ripe. During ripening most will drop off, leaving only one or two per spike. Lake Pounui, January 1969. About natural size.

Fig 21 Ripe matai seeds with their typical purplish bloom. Hinakura, February 1971. Three times natural size.

19

20

21

THE MATAI SEED

The ripe seed of matai, which takes twelve to eighteen months to mature, is up to 9 mm across and a deep blue-black with a pale purplish bloom. Its stalk never swells to form a fleshy receptacle as in most other New Zealand podocarps.

Many seeds are produced by one tree, but few seem to germinate. In Opepe Bush, for instance, there was only one matai seedling in an area where dozens of kahikatea, rimu and miro seedlings occurred.

Prumnopitys ferruginea
Miro/Brown pine

Miro forms a fine, tall, round-headed forest tree up to 25 m high, with a trunk up to 1 m across. The bark is finely punctate, scaling and falling off in thick flakes. Miro is a slow-growing tree, preferring shady situations, and is found all over New Zealand in lowland forest to an altitude of 1,000 m. It can grow into a very fine specimen tree. The juvenile, 6 – 8 m high, with its longer leaves and drooping habit, can be very graceful indeed.

The wood is hard and durable, straight-grained and sometimes beautifully figured. It is exploited increasingly as a substitute for matai in weatherboarding and flooring.

Adult miro leaves have less acute tips than juvenile leaves, and are usually 15 – 20 mm long and 2 – 3 mm wide. Juvenile leaves are a lighter green or brownish-red, and up to 30 mm long. Male cones are almost sessile, always solitary, and arise in the axils of the leaves. They are not borne in profusion, as with matai, and do not seem to occur regularly every year.

Ovules appear during June, or early July in central districts. They are usually borne singly at the end of a short axillary branchlet which is covered in small scales. Normally seeds from the previous season are still green at this time. They take more than twelve months to ripen and become purplish coloured.

Fig 1 A cluster of ripe miro seeds. When very fresh, they are often covered with a bluish bloom, giving them more of a purple colour. Waiorongomai, late November 1970. Reproduced at slightly over natural size.

Fig 2 A miro seedling. Opepe Bush, June 1973.

Fig 3 A grove of miro trees. This fine stand was exposed by sawmilling, and is located on the northern edge of what now constitutes Opepe Scenic Reserve. June 1973. The miro in its natural state prefers shady forest conditions.

5

Fig 4 A fine tall miro tree with rounded, elongated head. Exposed by sawmilling at Opepe Bush. April 1965.

Fig 5 Lower surface of adult miro leaves. They lie in one plane on either side of the branchlet, and show distinct mid-ribs and stomata, or breathing pores. Natural size.

Fig 6 Spray of juvenile leaves, upper surface. Natural size.

Fig 7 Buds of female flower branchlets arising from leaf axils. Waiorongomai, mid July 1970. Four times natural size.

Fig 8 A stalked female branchlet at pollination. Note single ovule at apex with scales below. October 1970. Four times natural size.

Fig 9 Last season's seed, mature but still unripe, with the new season's ovule developing. Waiorongomai, late November 1970. Twice natural size.

4

MIRO AND THE NATIVE WOOD PIGEON

*The fruit of miro is a favourite food of the native wood pigeon (*Hemiphaga novaeseelandiae*). Its brilliant colouring enables it to be seen from a considerable distance, and it smells strongly of turpentine, which the birds find attractive. They will often come long distances to gorge themselves when the drupes are ripe, and because miro seeds figure so prominently in their diet, wood pigeons have an important part to play in the tree's dissemination. They are also attracted to the fruit of other trees such as pigeonwood, thus playing an important role in the ecology of native forests.*

6

7

8

9

Fig 10 Miro bark showing characteristic punctate (dotted) surface and scaling. Opepe Bush.

Fig 11 This ripe male cone is just starting to shed its pollen. Some pollen grain can be seen on the surrounding leaves. Late October. Five times natural size.

Fig 12 A good crop of male miro cones. They stand erect from the branchlets to release their pollen. Waiorongomai, October 1966.

Fig 13 Mature but unripe male cones. These do not yet stand erect. Waiorongomai, September 1966.

11

12

10

13

Podocarpus totara/Totara
P. cunninghamii/montane totara
(formerly P. hallii, Hall's totara)
P. nivalis   P. lawrencii

The name totara is commonly applied to the two tall, slow-growing forest trees *Podocarpus totara* and *P. cunninghamii*. They are best distinguished from one another by their bark: thick, stringy and usually deeply furrowed on *P. totara*, but thin, flaky and rather paperlike on *P. cunninghamii*. *P. totara* is the taller, to 30 m with a straight trunk up to 20 m and diameter 2 m; *P. cunninghamii* reaches a height of 20 m with a trunk up to 1.25 m through. Both are found often growing together in lowland forests from sea level to 600 m, but *P. totara* usually gives way to *P. cunninghamii* above 480 m.

A totara tree may live to a great age, often as much as 800 years. The great totaras at Mangitawhai may be 1,000 years old, and the biggest specimen in New Zealand, near Mangapehi in the King Country (see Fig 9), is believed to be 1,800 years old. In its early stages a totara forms a spreading, bushy and attractive tree. As it gains height it acquires a massive trunk and branches that bear dense foliage. Older trees become more open in habit and the top tends to die back. Enormous roots spread out over the ground at the base of the trunk.

The leaves of *P. totara* are sessile, 1.3–3 cm long and 3–4 mm wide; juvenile leaves are narrower, only 1–2 mm wide. On *P. cunninghamii*, juvenile leaves may reach 5 cm long and 4–5 mm wide; the adult leaves are smaller, 2–3 cm long by 3–4 mm wide.

Two other species of totara occur in New Zealand. They are *P. lawrencii*, a shrub or small tree up to 9m high, and *P. nivalis*, a prostrate or semi-prostrate shrub, sometimes almost a miniature tree, found in alpine regions. *P. lawrencii* grows from the Marlborough Sounds to South Westland, being common in the Nelson Lakes area. It has pungent, needle-sharp leaves and slender branchlets; its leaves are 1.5–2.5 cm long and 0.75–3.5 mm wide. The males may bear up to four cones on a single peduncle.

Fig 1 All totaras have branchlets with a distinctive groove. This is a leaf spray of *P. totara*. From a tree growing at Waikanae, February 1980.

Fig 2 A fine specimen of *P. cunninghamii* growing above the Moawhango River. Alongside on the right is a specimen of *Plagianthus regius*. April 1969,

Fig 3 *P. totara* tends to cast its bark in long strips, which shroud the trunk like long, narrow curtains until they fall away. Pohangina Valley, August 1970.

Fig 4 Upper surface of *P. totara* leaves showing their sessile habit, indistinct midvein and pungent tips. Twice natural size.

Fig 5 The lower surface of a *P. totara* leaf showing the sessile habit and the distinct, broad, stomatal striping. The broad, indistinct midvein can also be seen. Compare this leaf underside with that of *P. cunninghamii* in Fig 8. Twice natural size.

Fig 6 Underside of *P. lawrencii* leaf showing the subsessile habit, midvein, the distinct, regular, stomatal striping and the sharp, pointed apex. This illustration twice natural size.

Fig 7 *P. cunninghamii* leaves are subsessile to very shortly petiolate with a broad, distinct midvein. Upper surface. Two and a half times natural size.

Fig 8 *P. cunninghamii* leaf lower surface showing regular, pale, narrow stomatal striping. Twice natural size.

Fig 9 This tree known as the Pouakani Totara grows near Mangapehi in the King Country and is reputed to be the oldest (1,800 years) and largest (39.62 m high) still in existence. Note the huge trunk, 3.63 m in diameter at a point 1.4 m above the ground, and the more open-branched habit that is characteristic of older totaras.

P. nivalis has thick, leathery leaves with thickened margins.

All totaras are dioecious, with male strobili and female ovules on separate trees. Male strobili appear as small swellings on stalks in the axils of leaves of the previous year's branchlets during August and September, ripening and shedding pollen in November and December. The strobili occur singly or in groups on a single peduncle; males of *P. totara* may have as many as four strobili on a single peduncle and those of *P. cunninghamii*, five. Ovules occur singly or in pairs at the tip of short pedunculate branchlets which arise in the leaf axils near the base of the new season's shoots. They grow quickly after pollination. Although often produced in profusion, only a few ovules appear to develop into seeds.

Today totaras can be found in most remaining podocarp forests of the North Island, in Peel Forest, Canterbury, and throughout the Westland and Fiordland forests. Fine specimens of montane totara occur on the Wilmot Pass and on Mt Egmont.

10

Fig 10 *P. totara* 'Aurea' is a very fine cultivar of totara, with rich, golden-coloured foliage, and makes a beautiful specimen tree for parks and gardens. This fine specimen of golden totara was growing in Otari, April 1973.

Fig 11 The typical thick, stringy and furrowed bark of *P. totara*.

Fig 12 The bark of *P. cunninghamii* is markedly different to that of *P. totara*. Its thin, paperlike appearance is clearly shown here. The foliage at the bottom of this photograph belongs to a climbing fern, *Blechnum filiforme*.

Fig 13 The base of the trunk of an old totara. These distinctive, large, swollen roots spread out from the large trunk and are typical of older trees. Peel Forest, Canterbury, January 1966.

Fig 14 A spray of *P. nivalis* showing ripe male cones, leaf arrangement and thick leaves. Note the typical further thickened leaves and midvein. This specimen twice natural size.

11

12

13

14

15

16

17

18

Fig 15 Totara is a very hardy and slow-growing tree. The spreading habit of this well-shaped tree growing on a farm near Whangarei makes an excellent shade for stock and shows how well *P. totara* grows as a specimen tree in the open. Such trees are often an attractive feature of open farmlands in the Wairarapa, parts of North Auckland, the Marlborough-Nelson district, the Kaikoura coast and also Canterbury. January 1970.

Fig 16 *P. totara* branchlet showing the terminal and lateral developing shoots of new branchlets. Below these can be seen two immature green male cones borne singly in the axils of the leaves. Akatarawa, late October 1968. Twice natural size.

Fig 17 After appearing on the previous year's branchlets in August and September the male cones ripen and shed pollen during November and December. In this close view of a male cone of *P. totara* shedding pollen it can be seen that some microsporangia are already empty. Four times natural size.

Fig 18 Ripe male cones of *P. totara*. These are not as far advanced as those illustrated in Fig 17. Three and a half times natural size.

Fig 19 Ripe male cones of *P. cunninghamii*. As with *P. totara*, these occur singly in clusters of two to five on a single stalk. Akatarawa Saddle, November 1969.

DURABLE WOOD WAS WIDELY USED

Totara wood is red, straight-grained and easy to work; although rather brittle, it is one of the most durable timbers known. In the early days of European settlement totara was used extensively for house piles, house frames and for fence posts, telegraph poles, railway sleepers and bridges. Being resistant to teredo worm, it was also used in the piling of many early wharves.

To the Maori people the totara was a symbol of strength and goodness. From these trees they made their canoes and their carved whare-whakairo, pataka and food boxes. The bark was used for thatching and for making storage vessels.

19

21

22

20

25

23

24

26

Fig 20 Spray of *P. totara* showing the positions of ripe seeds and receptacles at the bases of the shoots after these have been extended during the spring/summer growing season. Hinakura, April 1961.

Fig 21 Ovule-bearing branchlets of *P. totara* shortly after pollination. Note the axillary position of these branchlets, which each bear a peduncle and an oblong yellowish-green receptacle with two small ovules at the tip. Six times natural size.

Fig 22 Maturing seeds and receptacles of *P. cunninghamii*. Three times natural size.

Fig 23 Ripe female branchlet of *P. cunninghamii*. The seed is relatively longer and narrower than that of *P. totara*. Four times natural size.

Fig 24 Ripe seeds and receptacles of *P. nivalis*. Twice natural size.

Fig 25 A ripening female branchlet of *P. totara* with swollen fleshy receptacle and ovoid seed. When fully ripe the receptacle is bright red (as in Fig 23). Four times natural size.

Fig 26 The massive trunk and zone of new branch growth halfway up this old *P. totara* contrast with the open habit of the older branches at its summit. This fine old tree was growing in the Pohangina Valley reserve, once an extensive pure stand. August 1970.

Genus *Halocarpus:* An endemic New Zealand genus containing three species of forest trees.

Halocarpus bidwillii
Bog pine/Mountain pine

Bog pine normally grows as a spreading or erect, closely branching shrub, but occasionally as a small tree reaching 3.5 m in height, with a short trunk up to 38 cm through. Sometimes the horizontal branches form roots as they grow, giving rise to a ring of "shrubs" around the parent. Thus develops an extensive mini forest with the appearance of a huge, low-spreading tree or shrub. The parent tree may die, leaving its circlet of outliers intact and flourishing.

Bog pine is a hardy plant, growing in both bogs and dry, stony ground from Cape Colville, on the Coromandel Peninsula, to Stewart Island — usually between 600 m and 1,500 m in the north but coming nearer to sea level in the south. A scientific reserve at "The Wilderness" near Lake Te Anau has excellent examples growing in stony ground. Bog pine Is also common around Mt Ruapehu bogs as well as in open stony ground, often in association with *H. biformis.*

The juvenile leaves are thick and leathery, rather narrow and elongated, without petioles but with pronounced mid-ribs below. They spread all round the branchlet. The adult leaves are scale-like, closely appressed to the branchlets: Stomata are clearly visible in both stages. The wood is brittle and of little value.

Fig 1 This spray of bog pine shows thick juvenile leaves, up to 10 mm long and 1.5 mm wide, clustered around the stem while lower down the scale-like appressed adult leaves can be seen. Note the thin reddish bark which is beginning to form on the main stem as the branchlets mature. This specimen shown at about three times natural size.

Fig 2 This huge plant of bog pine has spread over a large area as its horizontal branches have formed new roots, so that it has become a multiple shrub or "mini forest". "The Wilderness", Te Anau, December 1975.

Fig 3 A single plant of bog pine only 75 cm high, growing beside a bog at the Lewis Pass. Even plants of this small size may bear cones. January 1973.

Fig 4 A growing stem showing the transition between juvenile and adult leaves. The mid-rib of the juveniles can be clearly traced in the sequence of the leaves to the keel of the adults. Taupo, May 1970. Four times natural size.

Fig 5 Branchlets of bog pine, with thick leathery adult leaves 1 – 2 mm long. Note the characteristic scale-like form of the leaves, with keels, thickened margins and clear, prominent stomata (white spots). The keels give the stems a four-sided look. Barryville, May 1972. Four times natural size.

Fig 6 As the stem grows and ages, this thin, red-coloured bark forms between the leaves. Six times natural size.

Fig 7 The outer bark of the mature tree is grey, loose and flaky. As it peels it reveals the reddish inner bark. Like the majority of bog pine trees, this one carries a good deal of moss and lichen on its trunk and lower branches. Mt Ruapehu, April 1973.

9

10

Fig 8 Male cones, 3−5 mm long, occur at the tips of the branchlets, often in profusion, during October and November. The exact time depends upon the location, those in the north of the North Island appearing in early October and those in the south following later. These were photographed at "The Wilderness", November 1969.

Fig 9 Ripe male cones of bog pine shedding pollen. The pollen sac at the apex ruptures first, and rupturing proceeds in a spiral fashion around the cone. Some pollen adheres to the cones and stems. "The Wilderness", November 1969. Three times natural size.

Fig 10 Seeds are produced in large numbers, as this spray with ripe fruits shows. From a tree at the Lewis Pass, March 1965.

Fig 11 Young ovules emerging from axils of carpidia. Ovules appear at the tips of the branchlets in November as the male cones produce pollen. After fertilisation the ovule grows rapidly and develops a white or yellowish fleshy aril from its base. Mt Ruapehu, early November 1969. Four times natural size.

Fig 12 Twin seeds developing with the thick fleshy arils between them. Such paired seeds are quite common in *H. bidwillii*. Each seed is enclosed in an integument and an outer covering, the epimatium, which is sculptured in parallel ridges. Mt Ruapehu, late January 1969. Four times natural size.

Fig 13 By early February the fruit is mature but not yet ripe, with the green-coloured seed sitting on the white aril. February 1969. Reproduced at twelve times natural size.

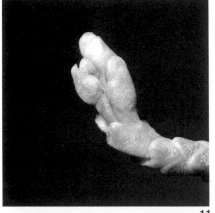

11

12

13

14

Fig 14 Ripening is rapid, and by mid February or early March the aril has swollen considerably and the seed has darkened to a deep purple-black. The fruit is now ripe. Mid February 1970. Twelve times natural size.

Halocarpus biformis
Yellow pine

In the forest yellow pine occurs as a small tree reaching 10 m in height, with a trunk 60 cm through, spreading branches and a rounded crown. In exposed positions it forms a tight, rounded, cypress-like shrub or small tree, perhaps only 1 m high. It is found from the volcanic plateau of the North Island to Stewart Island, from sea level to 1,400 m. Rare in the north, it is more plentiful in the south, often occurring in small local stands on rich soils in high-rainfall areas. On the southern slopes of Mt Ruapehu it is found occasionally in the forests and, above the bush line, around bogs with *H. bidwillii*.

The sweet-perfumed wood is pink-coloured, tight-grained and extremely durable — possibly the most durable of New Zealand native woods.

The sexes of yellow pine are on separate trees. The seed appears to form at very irregular intervals and takes about twelve months to reach maturity.

1

2

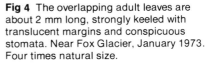

Fig 1 This small yellow pine was photographed at the edge of the forest on Mt Ruapehu. May 1972.

Fig 2 The silver-grey outer bark of yellow pine peels away in small thick flakes to reveal a reddish-brown inner layer, as on this tree growing on Mt Ruapehu, May 1972.

Fig 3 Branchlets of mature yellow pine trees sometimes revert to the juvenile form, as here, with juvenile leaves at the top, irregular, elongated and appressed scale-like intermediate leaves in the centre, and adult leaves at bottom left and right. Also from a tree at Mt Ruapehu, December 1973.

Fig 4 The overlapping adult leaves are about 2 mm long, strongly keeled with translucent margins and conspicuous stomata. Near Fox Glacier, January 1973. Four times natural size.

Fig 5 Growing stems of yellow pine, with adult leaves. The growing tips are often tinged with red. Mt Ruapehu, May 1972. Six times natural size.

Fig 6 Another yellow pine, growing in a more exposed position above the bushline on Mt Ruapehu. May 1972.

Yellow pines growing in the open tend to be more compact than those growing in the forest. These examples illustrate the marked differences of size and shape.

3

4

5

Fig 7 Developing seeds. Immature seeds are difficult to detect as they are very small and hidden among the tiny leaves forming at the tips of the branchlets. Seeds and cones appear irregularly on yellow pine. Those photographed here were the first to appear in a survey begun on Mt Ruapehu in 1968. The seeds appeared in December 1973, on a tree directly in line and downwind from a male tree which had borne cones the previous January (see Fig 11). January 1974. Three times natural size.

Fig 8 A ripe seed. Mt Ruapehu, late February 1974. Eight times natural size.

Figs 9, 10 Double and triple seeds, common on female trees. Late February 1974. Six times natural size.

Fig 11 Single or twinned, male cones occur in great profusion at the tips of the branchlets during late January and February. They form during October and grow slowly until January, when they mature rapidly in the hotter weather. January 1973.

Fig 12 Ripe male cones are small, only 2 – 5 mm long, like this one shedding pollen. January 1973. Five times natural size.

Fig 13 As the pollen is shed, the cone quickly collapses, losing its bright colour to become drab fawn. Occasionally male cones occur in triplets, as here. February 1973. Five times natural size.

6

7   8   9   10

11   12   13

Halocarpus kirkii
Monoao

Monoao is a rather handsome tree which, when seen at a distance, is not unlike a small kauri in its general appearance. It can usually be recognised by its attractive juvenile foliage, which often persists on the lower branches until the tree is about 10 m high. The tree reaches a height of 25 m, with a trunk up to 1 m through and flaking grey-brown bark that has a pustular or pimply texture. The pale reddish-brown wood is tight-grained, strong and very durable.

Monoao is not a common tree, being found occasionally in lowland forests to an altitude of 700 m from Hokianga Harbour in the north to the southern end of the Coromandel Peninsula and on Great Barrier Island.

The leaves of juveniles and of the lower branches of adult trees are narrow and leathery, up to 4 cm long and 3 mm wide. The adult leaves are thick, scale-like and much smaller; the leaves overlap and lie appressed to the branchlets in four rows.

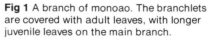

Fig 1 A branch of monoao. The branchlets are covered with adult leaves, with longer juvenile leaves on the main branch.

Fig 2 Juvenile leaves. These may persist on mature trees up to 10 m high, and appear to be more common and to persist longer on female trees. Natural size.

Fig 3 The adult leaves of monoao are 2 – 3 mm long, thick and leathery with faint keels, translucent margins and many irregularly arranged stomata. Three times natural size.

Fig 4 The bark of the young tree is relatively smooth and does not flake. Hukutaia Domain, Opotiki, April 1973.

Fig 5 A fine specimen of monoao. This is a female tree, with a tall juvenile growing to the right. Young trees taper upwards and are very graceful in habit. Photographed on the main ridge above the Kauaeranga Valley, Coromandel Range, April 1971.

Fig 6 Mature trees have a thick pustular bark that peels in large irregular flakes. From the tree shown in Fig 5.

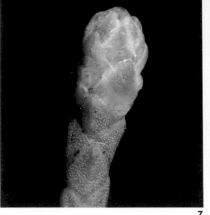

7 8

Figs 7, 8, 9 Development of the male cone. Above: beginning, early November 1973. Above right: mid-November. Right: maturity with ripe pollen sacs, early December. Four and a half times natural size.

Figs 10, 11, 12 Development of the seed. Left: twin seeds at a very early stage of development, March 1970. Centre: near maturity, changing from green to black, April 1971. Right: maturity, late April, Coromandel. Four times natural size.

Fig 13 Seeds occur mostly on upper branches, often as twins and triplets, and always at the tips of branchlets. Male cones also arise at the tips, but are spread over the tree. Quite young male and female trees bear cones abundantly, but in the juvenile, seeds always appear to fall before maturity. Even on old female trees, few seeds appear to reach the ripe stage of that in Fig 12. Development of the seed takes about eighteen months, from October to April of the second year following. Otari, February 1970.

5   6   9

10   11   12

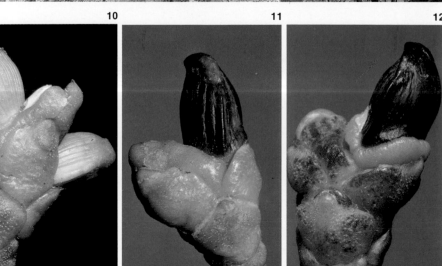

13

73

Dacrydium cupressinum
Rimu/Red pine

Rimu forms a very tall forest canopy tree, usually 20–35 m high but sometimes reaching 60 m. The straight trunk is generally up to 1.5 m through but may be larger in very old or taller specimens. The bark peels off in elongated thick flakes. Next to kauri, rimu is the best known of New Zealand timber trees. With its pendulous branchlets, it is a very graceful and beautiful tree at all stages of its growth.

The open-branched juvenile tree has attractive light-green foliage and is most unusual and elegant. As it grows it forms a small pyramidal tree. This semi-adult form persists for many years, and may even bear seeds. It finally produces strong lateral branches at its apex to form the tall, straight-trunked adult with a spreading crown bearing pendulous foliage. The lower branches of the semi-adult tree atrophy and fall away as the adult grows and matures.

Rimu's narrow, elongate, keeled leaves overlap around the branchlets, and on juvenile trees they are soft and pliable, up to 7 mm long and 1 mm wide; the leaves of semi-adult trees are up to 4 mm long, while those of the adult are only 2–3 mm long, more rigid, somewhat triangular in cross-section and more closely set together than those of juvenile trees. As the tree ages the leaves become more scale-like. During the winter the leaves of juveniles may turn bronze in colour but become green again in spring. The adult leaf growing tips are also often bronze-coloured.

Though naturally a tree of the rain forests, rimu will form a fine specimen tree when growing in the open space of a forest clearing, sheltered field or lawn.

As we have seen, rimu is one of our most ancient trees; fossil pollen grains of trees very similar to *D. cupressinium* have been traced back 70 million years. Rimu was very common in the podocarp forests that once covered New Zealand. In these forests it was often the dominant tree, sometimes occurring in almost pure stands over small areas. Some huge specimens exist today in some remnants of the

1

Fig 1 An exposure of a pure stand of rimu at Opepe Bush, April 1965.

Fig 2 Branchlets of semi-adult rimu leaves. Coromandel, January 1965. Four times natural size.

Fig 3 A beautiful semi-adult tree growing alongside the Coromandel to Whitianga road in January 1965.

Fig 4 A fine specimen of rimu exposed on the edge of Opepe Bush by sawmilling, October 1973. Once such a tree has been exposed to the weather it usually falls within a few years unless quickly protected by new growth. It needs the protection of surrounding trees, as well as of the undergrowth, to remain strong and healthy.

once extensive West Taupo forests and in a few North Island reserves such as the margins of the Urewera forests near Minginui and at Opepe Bush near Taupo. Very large trees still standing today can be from 700 to 800 or even 1,000 years old. The original Opepe Bush contained many fine rimu and other podocarp species, but the greater part was cut out in the late 1960s to leave the small reserve that stands today.

Rimu still has a very widespread distribution, occurring throughout the North, South and Stewart Islands, from sea level to 600 m. In most forests the distinctive crowns of the mature rimus emerge above the level of the surrounding mixed podocarp-broadleaf forest. Rimu usually occurs in mixed forests in association with other podocarps, hinau or pokaka, tawa and beech. A forest type usually referred to as rimu pole forest occurs on flat, wet terraces on the West Coast of the South Island and on

Stewart Island. There are extensive rimu stands from North Okarito Forest southwards.

The heavy wood of rimu is deep red in colour, strong, hard and durable — though not so durable as kauri or totara. The heartwood is nearly always beautifully figured, as a result of the grain being twisted during growth. Heart rimu is one of the most beautifully figured woods in the world, and for this reason has always been highly prized in New Zealand as a finishing timber for doors, door frames, panelling and furniture.

The timber has also been extensively used in the past for house framing and weatherboarding, but with growing scarcity and diminishing cut its use is becoming more restricted. In future the use of rimu will undoubtedly be confined to plywood veneers and other decorative purposes. The wall panelling, floor and furniture of floors 5 – 8 in the Beehive Building, Wellington, have been completed entirely from rimu.

5

6

Fig 5 The trunk of a huge rimu tree that grew at Opepe Bush until it was cut down by sawmillers in 1966. At 1.2 m from the ground the trunk measured 6.09 m in girth.

Fig 6 Rimu bark peels in long, thick flakes. The bark is stringy and is usually pimpled. North Auckland, February 1965.

Fig 7 The graceful drooping habit of young rimus is well illustrated by this group near Pelorus Bridge, January 1972.

Fig 8 Branchlets with mature leaves from an old tree. The leaves may be thick and close-set, or thinner and more open depending on age and sex. Four times natural size.

Fig 9 Branchlets with juvenile leaves from a young tree. Four times natural size.

Fig 10 Adult female foliage with immature (green) cones and ripe (red) cones. Rimu sets seeds only at irregular intervals, usually of five to six years. The sexes are on separate trees. Whangarei, April 1970. Four times natural size.

7

8

9

GREAT RAETIHI FOREST FIRE OF 1918

The great rimus in the old podocarp forests that once covered New Zealand were truly massive trees. During my boyhood my father, who worked as a civil engineer and surveyor on the construction of the railway line between Mangaweka and Taumarunui, often talked about the great forest that existed along the route of the railway. He spoke of the huge rimu trees that stood between Horopito and Raurimu, some of which he claimed to have measured by his theodolite as being 200 ft (61 m) high. Such trees were also very old. Whereas much of the old rimu forest was felled by the axe, the remainder of this great forest was wasted in the great Raetihi bush fire of 19-20 March 1918. It was generally thought (although never finally confirmed) that the forest was set alight by coals dropped from a railway engine.

The great fire itself was a major catastrophe. It burned for two days, devastating vast areas of forest and almost destroying the townships of Raetihi and Ohakune. Along with the great podocarps, 150 houses and nine sawmills were lost in the conflagration and a family of three lost their lives when their farmhouse was burned. In Palmerston North where I lived, 100 kilometres away, day turned to night as the skies darkened with smoke; schools were forced to close. The loss of resources to the timber industry was considerable.

10

11   12   13

14

When rimu male cones occur (only every five to six years) they are borne in great profusion from mid to late October. The precise time at which they appear depends on the tree's locality. The male cones develop to maturity quite quickly (unlike the female cones, which take up to eighteen months) and shed pollen within six to eight weeks of the time when they first become noticeable. 1972 was a good year for rimu male cones; the photographs on this page were taken during that year near Wanganui and also at Longwoods in the Wairarapa. It is of interest to note that the next good seed year was not until 1978.

Fig 11 An early stage in the development of a *D. cupressinum* male cone. Bushy Park, Wanganui, late November 1972. This specimen at three times natural size.

Fig 12 Male rimu cones more mature than those illustrated in Fig 11. By now, as this photograph shows, the pollen sacs (microsporangia) are clearly visible through the translucent envelope formed from the microsporophylls (the leaf-like organs bearing the pollen sacs). This specimen was photographed at Bushy Park in late November 1972. Here at three times natural size.

Fig 13 By now the male cone is fully mature and is beginning to shed pollen. The pollen grains can be clearly seen as pale dots adhering to the leaves above the base of the cone and also to the outside of the microsporophylls. This specimen from Bushy Park, photographed in late November 1972. Three times natural size.

Fig 14 A wider view of rimu male cones showing how each cone appears at the tip of a drooping branchlet. From a tree at Longwoods, Wairarapa, photographed in November 1972.

The female cone develops over a period of about eighteen months. Although many cones reach the green stage, there seems to be considerable loss between this and the ripe red stage. The Whangarei tree from which Fig 20 was photographed was smothered with green cones in November 1969 but by February 1970 only nine were ripe and about a hundred in the process of ripening. After seed fall rimu appears to rest for at least two years before the cycle starts again.

15

Fig 15 The female cone is a single ovule nestling in a cup-like arrangement of leaves at the tips of a branchlet; this curves upwards to expose the micropyle at the top of the ovule to pollen drifting on the wind. The stage shown here is just after pollination when the seed starts to develop. Opepe Bush, mid-November 1968. Four times natural size.

Fig 16 The developing ovule sits inside a cup-like scale, the epimatium. As the seed grows it extends well beyond the epimatium. Opepe Bush, late November 1968. Four times natural size.

Fig 17 A ripening seed with the micropyle still visible at its tip. Opepe Bush, November 1969. Four times natural size.

Fig 18 Sometimes these brown seeds occur, persisting without any swollen receptacle. They are apparently infertile. Opepe Bush, May 1965. Four times natural size.

Fig 19 Ripening female cones with the green epimatium showing clearly at the base of the seed. At this stage the leaves at the tip of the branchlet often become swollen (as shown here); they ultimately form a succulent structure, the receptacle, that colours red as the seed ripens. Opepe Bush, December 1969. Four times natural size.

Fig 20 A mature female cone. The epimatium and its subtending bract scale (both red) and the receptacle leaves (orange) have now changed colour and the seed has become a deep blue-black. Whangarei, January 1970. Eight times natural size.

16

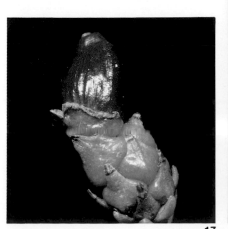

17

18

HOW HARDY IS A RIMU SEEDLING?

After a good seed year seedlings can occur in great numbers over a small area of forest floor. The survival rate is, however, very low.

I have successfully transplanted seedlings from such areas; one of these, 8 cm high, was taken from an exposure where a rimu had seeded near Thames to my garden in Wellington in January 1972. By January 1974 it had grown to 35 cm. It was then again transplanted and by January 1978 it had grown to a height of 1.5 m. This suggests that rimu seedlings can be transplanted fairly readily and may be hardier than is generally thought.

19

20

Lepidothamnus intermedius
Yellow silver pine

This small spreading tree is up to 15 m high with a generally straight trunk up to 60 cm through. It is scattered in the North Island, but it is more common on the West Coast and it is the principal tree in the swamp forests of Stewart Island. It is a hardy, slow-growing tree, found from sea level to about 900 m in regions of very wet climate. Shown here are trees by a bog on Mt Kaitarakihi in the Coromandel Range.

There are juvenile, semi-adult and adult stages, which are reflected in the leaves. Juvenile leaves are 9 — 15 cm long, spreading and limp, rather narrow and faintly keeled; semi-adult leaves are scale-like, thick and leathery, rather blunt and rounded apically, 1.5 — 3 mm long and appressed to the stem in four rows.

The tree is dioecious, and seeds can be produced each year. The ovule of the female appears in November among the leaves at the tip of the branchlet, maturing over the next sixteen to eighteen months. Male cones are ripe by late November and pollinate in early December.

The wood is reddish-yellow and full of a resin which oozes out in droplets and is, presumably, responsible for the highly inflammable nature of the timber. The wood is very strong and durable, and has been used for telegraph poles and railway sleepers.

4 **5** **6**

Fig 1 Branchlets with semi-adult and adult leaves, both of which are keeled, faintly margined and provided with several irregular rows of stomata. Twice natural size. All these photographs were taken at Mt Kaitarakihi.

Fig 2 A fine spreading adult tree growing out from the ridge of Mt Kaitarakihi. This tree had a trunk only about 1.5 m from the ground to the lowest branches. In the foreground are some neinei trees.

Fig 3 A semi-adult tree with typical spreading habit. A neinei tree is growing in the foreground, November 1971.

Fig 4 Early development of the ovule; scale leaves protect the red ovule surrounded by the white epimatium. November 1970. Five times natural size.

Fig 5 About one year later the green seed is almost mature and the epimatium forms a low collar that supports the seed. November 1971. Ten times natural size.

Fig 6 In a few more weeks the seed turns to a deep purplish-black colour and the epimatium with the apical leaves turns yellow; the seed is now ripe. April 1972. Ten times natural size

Fig 7 A ripe male cone beginning to shed pollen; some grains are adhering to the surface. Male cones are up to 6 mm long. November 1970. Ten times natural size.

Fig 8 A spray from a semi-adult tree with male cones, which are borne singly at the tips of the branchlets. November 1970.

Fig 9 A spray of juvenile leaves showing their spreading habit and arrangement in four rows. About natural size.

7 **8**

Fig 10 A branchlet with adult leaves at apices, semi-adult leaves below these and juvenile leaves at bottom. This specimen is reproduced at about natural size. Taupo, May 1970.

Fig 11 A branch with leaves giving way to bark and branchlets bearing semi-adult and adult leaves. Coromandel, April 1977. About natural size.

Fig 12 The finely pitted bark is mottled with patches of browns and greys. It does not peel as in many species of podocarps.

9 **10** **11** **12**

Lagarostrobos colensoi
Silver pine

1

In its younger stages the silver pine is a cone-shaped tree but later develops a tall, moderately spreading crown and reaches a height of 15 m with a trunk up to 1 m through. The trunk is usually straight and clear of branches for some distance from the ground. Found from sea level to an altitude of about 950 m, silver pine occurs in the North Island from Mangonui in Northland to Mt Ruapehu, and in the South Island it grows throughout the West Coast. Shady situations with rich soil in a wet climate are its favourite growing conditions.

There are three distinct growth stages, each defined by the foliage. In the juvenile tree the leaves are up to 12 mm long, narrow, pointed, rather limp and spreading, and with distinct bands of stomata on their undersurfaces. As the plant reaches the semi-adult stage, the leaves are smaller, 4 – 5 mm long, flattened and arranged in two opposite rows in the same plane. The leaves of the adult tree are thick, keeled and scale-like, appressed to the branchlets in four rows.

Silver pine grows very slowly and is very hardy. The wood is light in colour, hard and durable, and is often used by farmers for fence and gate posts.

Fig 1 A branch bearing branchlets with juvenile leaves and, lower down, adult leaves. October 1970. About natural size.

Fig 2 Adult leaves are up to 2.5 mm long, with subacute tips and sparse, irregularly arranged stomata. Four times natural size.

Fig 3 A fine old specimen of silver pine on Mt Ruapehu (1,000 m), May 1972. Silver pine is common in the forests on the Ohakune side of the mountain.

2

3

4

5

6 7

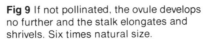

8 9

Fig 4 A typically cone-shaped juvenile tree of *L. colensoi*. Note how it differs in shape from the mature tree in Fig 3. This specimen grows at the uppermost end of its altitude range, at a height of 950 m on Mt Ruapehu. It was photographed in October 1972.

Fig 5 Male cones occur in great numbers. They appear singly at the tips of the branchlets. Otari, October 1970. Three times natural size.

Fig 6 A tiny translucent swelling at the tip of a branchlet marks the beginning of the male cone. The process begins in early September. This photograph is four times natural size.

Fig 7 The growth of male cones is rapid. By mid-October the ripe male cone is already starting to shed pollen. Also four times natural size.

Fig 8 At this early stage in development of the female cone, the fleshy ovule is hidden by the carpidium (left), epimatium (right) and two bracts at the tip of the branchlet. Mt Ruapehu, October 1970. Six times natural size.

Fig 9 If not pollinated, the ovule develops no further and the stalk elongates and shrivels. Six times natural size.

Fig 10 The bark of a young tree, showing the irregular longitudinal ridging and pimpling characteristic of young silver pine. Taurewa, March 1970.

Fig 11 By comparison, the bark of this older tree is thicker, and peeling in chunky flakes to reveal an inner layer which still bears some ridging and pimpling characteristics of the young tree. Mt Ruapehu, March 1970.

Figs 12, 13 As the seed grows it becomes surrounded and supported by the epimatium, which forms a keeled cup-like structure. This remains green while the seed turns a deep blue-black. Otari, early April 1970. Four times natural size.

The fruiting of *L. colensoi* seems to occur irregularly, and the period from pollination to ripe seed is about eighteen months. Both male and female cones are borne at the tips of the branchlets and semi-adult trees can bear cones. Female cones are generally borne singly, but twins sometimes occur.

10 11

12 13

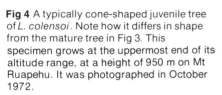

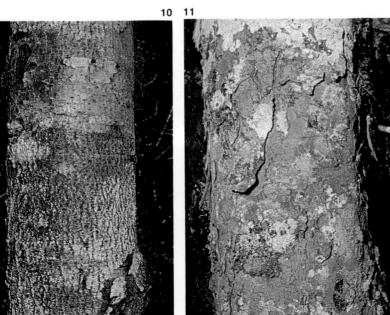

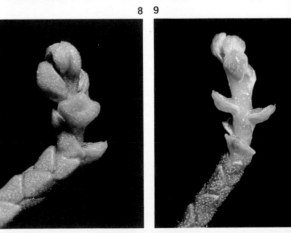

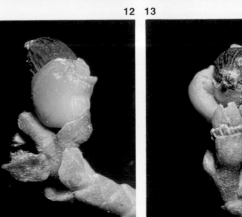

Family *Podocarpaceae*

Genus *Phyllocladus:* Includes six species of evergreen trees and shrubs found in New Zealand, Tasmania, Borneo and the Philippines. Three species are found only in New Zealand. These plants have no true leaves; their flattened branchlets, called cladodes, perform the function of leaves and bear, along their margins, the female flowers and fruits. Phylloclads are ancient plants.

Phyllocladus aspleniifolius var. alpinus
Mountain toatoa

1

3

Mountain toatoa is a small, strongly aromatic tree up to 9 m high with a short trunk up to 40 cm through. The wood is elastic, making the plant very wind-resistant. It is found on the Coromandel Peninsula between Cape Colville and Te Aroha and from the volcanic plateau southwards between 900 m and 1,600 m to Mt Cargill, Fiordland and Southland. In South Westland and Southland it occurs down to sea level.

True leaves occur only on seedlings and occasionally on young plants. They are narrow and pointed, up to 1.5 cm long. In juvenile and adult plants the function of the leaves is taken over by the phylloclades, flattened branchlets which in juveniles are up to 2 cm long, thin and of various and irregular shapes, either deeply or shallowly lobed with toothed margins and narrowing at the base into a short stalk. On older trees the thick and leathery phylloclades become relatively shorter, with thickened margins often deeply cut into narrow lobes and bearing irregularly spaced "teeth"; or denticles.

Sexes are separate but on the same tree, the male cones arising in clusters of two to five (single ones are rare) at the tips of branches. Female cones arise along the margins or on the stalks of the phylloclades as rounded lumps (cupules), each with two or more greenish cracks which may bear seeds in their axils.

At least three forms of mountain toatoa are known. A recent revision (1980) by A. P. Druce of his *Checklist of the Trees, Shrubs and Lianes of New Zealand* lists this tree as essentially a subspecies of the Tasmanian species *P. aspleniifolius.* So *P. alpinus* now becomes *P. aspleniifolius* var. *alpinus.*

4

5

Fig 1 The upper surface of a phylloclade, showing its marginal denticles, deep lobes and sparse, irregularly arranged stomata. Volcanic plateau. Twice natural size.

Fig 2 The lower surface of the same phylloclade showing typical bluish colour and crowded stomata. Twice natural size.

Fig 3 A mountain toatoa tree growing on the volcanic plateau. April 1973.

Fig 4 A growing stem with new phylloclades forming in which the thickened margins are clearly visible. From a plant at Otari, mid November 1969. Twice natural size.

Fig 5 The bark of a mature tree at Taurewa. March 1970.

2

7

Fig 6 This photograph shows an association of mountain toatoa with silver pine (*Lagarostrobos colensoi*), near Taurewa in March 1970. The *L. colensoi* are the smaller conical yellow-green trees, with toatoa at right and centre (the tall tree). The spreading tree in the left foreground is a putaputaweta *(Carpodetus serratus)*. The forest in this photograph is clearly regenerating.

6

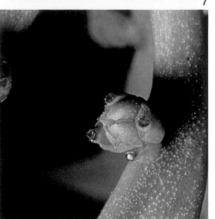

8

9

11

10

Fig 7 Female cones on phylloclade stalks. Otari, November 1969. About natural size.

Fig 8 A female cone ready to receive pollen, showing the crimson-margined micropyles, Otari, November 1969. Three times natural size.

Fig 9 Female cones with ripe seeds. The seeds appear to take three to four months to mature and ripen. Note the white arils. Mt Ruapehu, February 1974.

Fig 10 Large numbers of female cones. At Mt Ruapehu, February 1974.

Fig 11 Male cones shedding pollen. Red at first, they can grow to 6 mm in length. Mt Ruapehu, December 1972. Ten times natural size.

Phyllocladus glaucus
Toatoa

1

A handsome tapering tree up to 15 m high with a trunk up to 60 cm in diameter, toatoa is found growing in forests from sea level to 600 m, from as far north as Mangonui south to Rotorua. It is easily recognised by its phylloclades, so distinct from the pinnately arranged phylloclades of *P. trichomanoides* or the single, thick, cut and lobed phylloclades of *P. aspleniifolius* var *alpinus*.

Toatoa's phylloclades are wedge-shaped, large, thick and leathery, 4 – 6 cm long by 2 – 4 cm wide, and have finely toothed margins; eight to twelve occur in two rows along each rachis, which may be up to 40 cm long. The phylloclades are sea-green when young but become bronze-coloured when they mature. Narrow leaves, up to 1.5 cm long with blunt tips, occur on seedlings and, intermittently, at the base of older plants.

Sexes may be separate on the same tree or on different trees. The male cones arise in clusters of ten to twenty on thick stalks at the tips of branches. Female cones arise as clusters of four to seven ovules, each cluster on a short pedicel, each ovule partly enclosed by a greenish-coloured bract. Cones are arranged in groups of four to nine in two rows.

Fig 1 A rachis showing the upper surface of the phylloclades, which are in two rows lying in one plane. This photograph half natural size.

Fig 2 The lower surfaces of the toatoa phylloclades shown in Fig 1. Half natural size.

Fig 3 A small tree of toatoa growing near Hikuai, on the Coromandel Peninsula, January 1965. The branches in toatoa grow upwards more steeply than in tanekaha *(P. trichomanoides)*, whose branches are not only more horizontal but are sometimes drooping towards their tips.

Fig 4 The apex of a branch bearing a whorl of rachides, each bearing a number of female cones towards the base. Opotiki, November 1968. Half natural size.

3

4

2

Fig 5 Female cones with their ovules ready for pollination. The thick margin of the phylloclade behind the flowers has typically fine serrations. Opotiki, November 1968. Four times natural size.

Fig 6 After pollination the cones form into an angular mass with the immature red or purple seeds protruding out from the fleshy green bracts. Taupo, July 1969. Half natural size.

Fig 7 Mature cones showing seeds in their bracts. The seed takes twelve months to mature and each is surrounded at the base by a white fleshy aril, one being visible in the cone at lower left. The seeds are 3 mm long. Taupo, July 1969. Twice natural size.

Fig 8 The bark of toatoa, from a tree at Whangarei, February 1965. Like other species of *Phyllocladus*, the bark can often be heavily coated by growths of lichens and mosses.

Fig 9 A cluster of ripe male cones showing their stout stalks and pollen sacs (microsporangia). Otari, November 1973. About natural size.

Fig 10 The microsporangia in this photograph have folded open and the pollen has all been released. Otari, November 1973. About natural size.

Fig 11 A single male cone. Note the scales (microsporophylls) and the pollen sacs (microsporangia). Otari, November 1973. Three times natural size.

5

6

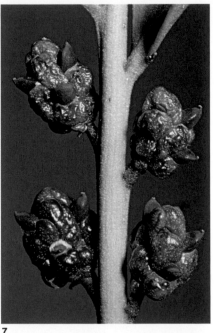

7

8

9   10   11

Phyllocladus trichomanoides
Tanekaha/Celery pine

1

A tall, graceful, pyramidal forest tree up to 20 m high with a smooth trunk up to 1 m through, around which slender spreading branches arise in circles. Tanekaha is found in lowland forest up to 800 m above sea level from North Cape to a line between Wanganui and Waipukurau in the North Island; and in northern Marlborough and western Nelson in the South Island. It is a hardy tree that grows equally well in shade or in the open. Some fine stands occur near Tihoi, west Taupo, and in the Waipari Valley near the headwaters of the Waihou River.

The phylloclades are arranged in two rows and pinnately on rachides arising in whorls from the branches. The rachides are up to 30 cm long and the phylloclades, with their minutely toothed margins, are up to 2.5 cm long. There are nine to fifteen phylloclades to each rachis, giving it the appearance of a celery leaf — hence its common name. True leaves are narrow, reddish-brown, up to 2 cm long and deciduous; they occur on seedlings only but are represented on the adult tree by a tiny scale at the base of each phylloclade.

The sexes are separate but on the same tree. The male cones arise in clusters of five to ten at the tips of the branches; at first they are deep purple but change to crimson as they mature and ripen. The reduced female cones comprising normally one or two ovules within cup-like bracts arise on modified phylloclades at the tips of the branches.

The close-grained wood is yellowish-white and is one of the most elastic timbers known in the world. Strong, durable and readily worked to a smooth finish, the wood of the tanekaha tree has been used for making fishing rods and even bridge building.

2   3   4

Fig 1 A tanekaha branch showing the arrangement of phylloclades and the whorls of its rachides. Waitakere Ranges, May 1966.

Fig 2 The bark of a young tanekaha tree in west Taupo. April 1966.

Fig 3 The mature bark of the tree shown in Fig 4. The bark contains a high proportion of tannins, and a red dye was extracted by the Maoris for dyeing their cloaks.

Fig 4 This fine specimen of tanekaha is growing in the Kauaeranga Valley, near Thames. The tree's straight trunk, rising without any branches for 6 m or more from the ground, is characteristic of the species. January 1974.

Fig 5 A cluster of ripe male cones showing the habit at the tips of the branches. It is surrounded by whorls of phylloclades. Otari, October 1968. One and a half times natural size.

Fig 6 An early stage in the development of the male cones. The bud has recently opened and the male cones are growing outwards. Rotorua, August 1976. Five times natural size.

Fig 7 Immature male cones of tanekaha, showing the structure of the microsporophylls and the typical purplish bloom of this stage of their growth. Otari, September 1970. Four times natural size.

Fig 8 These cones are ripe, and the yellow pollen sacs are showing between the red microsporophylls. Otari, October 1970. About natural size.

Fig 9 A ripe cone shedding pollen. The microsporophylls open outwards to release the pollen from the ruptured pollen sacs. Otari, late October 1970. Four times natural size.

5

6

7

8

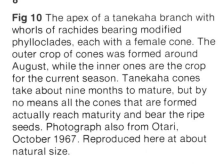

9

Fig 10 The apex of a tanekaha branch with whorls of rachides bearing modified phylloclades, each with a female cone. The outer crop of cones was formed around August, while the inner ones are the crop for the current season. Tanekaha cones take about nine months to mature, but by no means all the cones that are formed actually reach maturity and bear the ripe seeds. Photograph also from Otari, October 1967. Reproduced here at about natural size.

Fig 11 Female cones showing the cupules, inside which are the ovules. Wind-blown pollen enters through the reddish-margined micropyles of the erect ovules. Otari, September 1970. Four times natural size.

Fig 12 A mature cone with a ripe seed in front. After pollination the seed grows within the margined cup-like bract, and the micropyle becomes less obvious. The seed takes four to six months to mature. Otari, March 1971. Four times natural size.

10

11

12

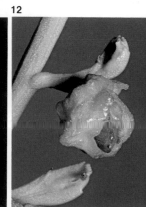

Family *Cupressaceae:* A family of some 19 genera of forest trees and shrubs with a world wide distribution.

Genus *Libocedrus:* A genus with three species in New Caledonia and two endemic species in New Zealand.

Libocedrus plumosa/Kawaka
L. bidwillii/Pahautea

These two New Zealand cedars are very similar in general appearance. Pahautea forms a tree 20 m high with a trunk 1 m through, while the slightly larger kawaka is a tree up to 25 m high with a trunk 1.2 m through. Both have a cone-shaped head of heavy, almost horizontally spreading branches.

The branchlets arise from the branch to lie in one plane and bear four rows of closely set leaves. In the juveniles of both species the leaves of the two lateral rows are closely set. There are separate male and female cones, which occur on the same tree. The trunk of both species is normally without branches for some distance above the ground and both have a thin parchment-like bark which falls in long strips.

Pahautea wood is red, soft and straight-grained but splits easily. That of kawaka is a darker red with dark streaks running through the even grain.

Pahautea occurs between 250 m and 1,200 m, mainly in wet, mountainous forests from Te Aroha Mountain in the Coromandel Range southwards; it is also found at lower levels on the West Coast of the South Island, where it is a common forest tree, and in Southland. A fine, almost pure stand occurs in Hihitahi State Forest east of Waiouru Military Camp. Kawaka occurs from sea level to 600 m, from Mangonui southwards to about Rotorua in the North Island; in the South Island it grows in the north-west Nelson area between Collingwood and Westhaven.

1

3

4

6

5

7

8

9

2

Fig 1 A group of pahautea trees, part of an almost pure stand in the Hihitahi State Forest. Note the trunks bare of lower branches and the cone-shaped crowns typical of the tree. April 1969.

Fig 2 A fine specimen of pahautea growing in a gorge on Mt Ruapehu. Although commonly found in moist soils, pahautea will grow in dry, rocky situations equally well. May 1972.

Fig 3 Bark of pahautea showing its typical long, thin strips.

Fig 4 Closer view of pahautea bark showing its parchment-like nature.

Fig 5 Spray of kawaka from a tree in the Canaan, north-west Nelson, showing the branching habit and dead leaves on the main stem preceding bark formation. November 1965.

Fig 6 Pahautea foliage showing triangular, acute-tipped, appressed adult leaves, about 2 mm long, and immature male cones at the tips starting to grow. Twice natural size.

Fig 7 Kawaka foliage showing compressed adult leaves arranged in four rows around the branchlets. Lateral leaves are elongate, spreading, up to 5 mm long; the dorsal (not visible here) and ventral leaves are up to 2.5 mm long. Twice natural size.

Fig 8 Foliage spray of kawaka showing predominantly juvenile leaves up to 7 mm long and shorter leaves near the growing tips. About natural size.

Fig 9 Spray of juvenile pahautea foliage.

Fig 10 A newly formed female cone of pahautea. It consists of four large dark-green scales arranged in opposite pairs. Otari, October 1969. This small cone is magnified here at ten times natural size.

Fig 11 The mature female cone of pahautea showing the four scales, each with the distinctive large green spine. The lower pair of scales are always sterile while the upper pair bear the seeds. In this photograph the seeds are about to be released. Otari, November 1969. These specimens at three times natural size.

Fig 12 The final stage. Two ripe pahautea cones opened to release the seeds, one of which still remains in the cone on the right. Otari, Nobember 1969. One and a half times natural size.

Fig 13 Pahautea's male cones are borne in great numbers. They are each 6 − 11 mm long, at the tips of the branchlets. Each cone is four-sided with three scales (microsporophylls) on each side, ten to twelve to each cone. Male and female cones of pahautea like kawaka appear on the same tree. From a tree at Otari, September 1969.

Fig 14 Close view of the mature male cone of pahautea. Otari, September 1966. The mature forms of the cones of kawaka arise in the same way and are basically of very similar appearance.

Fig 15 The immature male cones of kawaka. Kawaka's male cones are borne singly on the tips of the branchlets but usually are not as prolific as those of pahautea. Kawaka's cones are more angular, 4 − 6 mm long, and have eight to fourteen microsporophylls. From a tree at Otari, August 1979.

Fig 16 Close view of the immature male cones of kawaka at a later stage. Otari, September 1979. The immature cones of pahautea arise in the same way and are of very similar appearance.

10

11

12

13

14

15

16

Family Araucariaceae
Genus *Agathis*

This family consists of two genera, *Araucaria* and *Agathis*. All its representatives are evergreen trees found only in the Southern Hemisphere. The family evolved far back in geological time, in the Jurassic era about 150 million years ago, and contains today sixteen species of *Araucaria* and twenty species of *Agathis*. *Araucaria* has no native species in New Zealand today, though fossil Araucarians are known from the Middle Jurassic deposits in parts of New Zealand.

The genus *Araucaria* contains such notables as the monkey puzzle tree, *A. araucana,* from Chile, the candelabra tree, *A. angustifolia,* from Brazil, the Australian hoop pine, *A. cunninghamii,* and the Norfolk Island pine, *A. heterophylla.*

Like the species of *Agathis,* trees belonging to the genus *Araucaria* produce excellent timber.

Agathis is a genus of twenty very large trees found around the West Pacific in New Zealand and in Australia, Malaysia, Celebes, Indonesia, the Philippines, New Caledonia and Fiji. Members of this genus are in fact some of the largest trees found anywhere in the world and grow to a great age. They all have massive, columnar trunks covered by scaling bark which exudes a sticky gum.

The only New Zealand species is the well-known kauri, *Agathis australis.* It grows nowhere else. Female cones found high on the kauri are illustrated below. The South Queensland kauri, *A. robusta,* is very similar to the New Zealand kauri, however, and two other similar species grow further north in the state of Queensland. A tropical species of huge proportions, *A. alba,* the mountain agathis, grows in Malaysia and Indonesia; like the New Zealand kauri it is valued for its fine timber and gum.

Because of its huge trunk, free of branches to a great height, and the huge branches of its crown, more timber can be cut from a kauri tree than from any other tree of a comparable size. The tree has formed the basis of timber-logging industries in many places.

Agathis australis
Kauri

Kauri is the most famous of New Zealand native trees and one of the largest trees found anywhere in the world. Those remaining today average 30 m high, with a columnar trunk up to 3 m in diameter. It is free of branches for up to 18 m above the ground. Tane Mahuta, the famous tree in Waipoua Forest, is 51.2 m high with a girth of 17.2 m, and has been calculated to be over 2,100 years old. Another large kauri growing on the south-east spur of Mt Tutamoe near Whangarei is recorded as 20.12 m in circumference and 30.48 m to the first branch above the ground. But even larger trees, up to 60 m high and 7 m through the trunk, have been known. The largest kauri on record, known as the "Father of the Forests", grew at Mill Creek, Mercury Bay. Measured around 1850, its height was 21.8 m, apparently to the first branch, and its girth was 23.43 m.

Kauri once covered much of the area of North Auckland and the Coromandel Peninsula with dense forests from sea level to 600 m; the southern limit was bounded by a line from Raglan Harbour through Hamilton to a little south of Tauranga. Although confined in its natural state to this region, kauri can be grown almost anywhere in New Zealand. Some fine specimens have been grown as far south as Dunedin. No reason can be given for its confinement to the north, and no fossil evidence has been found of any earlier existence of kauri forests south of their present-day occurrence.

Rich deposits of kauri gum in layers in the ground, separated by silt deposits, have been found in a number of places in Northland, indicating the previous existence of ancient forests. Drilling for wells and examination of swamp deposits where there are successive layers of logs also show that in some areas of Northland three, sometimes four, kauri forests have

1

2

3

grown up, lived and decayed. Their remains have been found to a depth of 100 m. A piece of kauri wood taken from a gumfield near Whangarei has been shown by carbon dating to be over 34,000 years old.

The spreading crown of the kauri is, relative to the trunk, immense; it is rather open as the tree ages and is supported on huge branches that appear simply to swell out of the upper trunk. The first or lower of these branches can be up to 2 m through where they leave the trunk. Kauri trees are rather slow growing over their life span although young trees have been recorded as growing at the rate of 0.35 m per year. The juvenile tree is pyramidal in shape, with a slender trunk extending from the ground to the apex of the tree, and it persists in this form for fifty years or more before shedding its lower branches and expanding its trunk and crown.

In even the oldest trees the trunk is kept clean and free of epiphytes by the continuous shedding of small and large flakes of bark which build up in a large

Fig 1 A spray of juvenile kauri foliage. About half natural size.

Fig 2 This perfect kauri specimen grows at Parry Kauri Park, near Warkworth. It is estimated to be about 800 years old, its girth is 7.81 m and the height from the ground to the first branch 12.2 m. It is known as the McKinney Kauri. December 1977.

Fig 3 The leaves of seedlings and the juvenile leaves of small trees are often bronze coloured. Half natural size.

mound, 2 m or more in height, around the base of the tree. This, in time, decays to rich humus and is densely penetrated by the roots of the tree, giving the impression that the tree is growing from it. Kauri bark is fairly thick and exudes gum, which also flows copiously from any wound to the tree as well as from cones and even, at times, from branchlets and the bases of leaves.

Kauri timber is light and very durable, of a yellow-brown colour, straight-grained, amazingly free from knots and other defects, and easily worked. It has been used for ship masts and spars, boat building, railway carriages, road paving, house and office building and furniture making. Today it is a scarce resource reserved for specialist purposes.

To the ancient Maoris the kauri ranked second only to the totara in importance. Some of the greatest northern war canoes were constructed out of single massive kauri trunks, felled in the forest after elaborate tapu ceremonies, then hollowed out with the use of fire and stone tools. The hulls of canoes made from single trunks in this way were known to reach 25 m. Burning kauri gum was used for heating and lighting, and a powder from the soot was used in tattooing.

Of the estimated 1,215,000 hectares in the original kauri forests, only about 142 hectares remain. Much of what has gone was wasted by poor sawmilling technology and through forest fires such as those at Puhipuhi in 1881 and 1887. Some idea of the extent of the milling can be gleaned from the operations of the Kauri Timber Company in 1896-1903, when 267 million super feet of timber were produced.

As well as the timber the gum of the kauri was greatly prized as an ingredient for the manufacture of high quality paints and varnishes. It was obtained by digging over areas where kauri forests had been felled, and later by "bleeding" kauri trees.

The thick leathery leaves, with their parallel veins, are sessile and arise on the branchlets either alternately or oppose one another. Leaves of young trees are lanceolate, 5−10 cm long and 5−12 mm wide; adult leaves are blunter and only 2−3.5 cm long.

Both male and female cones are borne on the same tree and a tree twenty-five to thirty years old may begin to bear fertile seeds. When the female cone is ripe the scales open, releasing the winged seeds which are borne away by the wind. Seeds remain viable for only a short period, and usually germinate when they settle in an open situation where light can penetrate readily.

The proportion of seeds that germinate is low, but kauri is now being grown for afforrestation purposes.

Fig 4 Young kauri trees such as these fine examples photographed in the Omahuta Forest, January 1980, are known as "rickers". They persist in this juvenile form for many years and can attain a considerable height with their tall thin trunks and narrow pyramid shaped crowns. Eventually these rickers will shed their lower branches, and as their slender trunks and narrow crowns expand they will assume the shape of the mature tree.

Fig 5 The healthy bark of this mature kauri shows thick flakes before peeling, and yellow gum exuding in small trickles. The bark keeps the tree free of epiphytes by continuously shedding flakes. Waipoua Kauri Forest, February 1965.

Fig 6 The bark of a young kauri tree is quite different from that of the mature tree and persists like this for anything from forty to eighty years. Otari, June 1973.

Fig 7 The huge kauri illustrated here has become celebrated for the unusual formation of its trunk. While most kauris have a trunk circular in cross-section, this one is distinctly square-shaped. The tree nevertheless displays to advantage the general characteristics of the mature kauri — a massive trunk and a heavy spreading crown. It can be seen from the Coroglen Road, which crosses the Coromandel Peninsula. November 1971.

4　　5　6

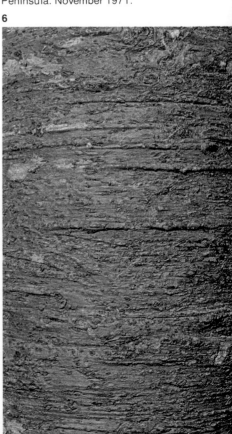

8 9 10

12

FIRST AXEMAN WAS A FRENCH EXPLORER

The first written records of the New Zealand kauri were made in May 1772 by members of Marion du Fresne's French expedition to the Pacific when his ships anchored in the Bay of Islands. The Frenchmen felled a kauri at Manawaraora Bay on 29 May 1772, shaping it into a new foremast for one of their vessels. They also watched a massive Maori war canoe built of a single piece of kauri and holding a hundred men. It is curious that these great trees were not recorded by anyone on Cook's earlier voyage. Cook's expedition did discover a quantity of kauri gum but thought it was a product of the mangroves where it was found.

Fig 8 Kauri has its sexes separate but they do arise on the same tree, and cones of varying ages can occur together on any one tree. Both male and female cones are produced at about the same time, usually annually. Here we see a group of globular female cones with their scales starting to open to receive pollen, and, behind them, a group of finger-like young male cones. Gum is exuding from the two female cones at the top. Notice also the pale thin bark of the branchlets and the branch, as well as the apical and lateral buds at the tips of the branch. Waipoua Kauri Forest, October 1966. One and a half times natural size.

Fig 9 Male and female cones often occur in close association on the same branch, as the female and the males in this photograph. The female cone has its scales opened back in readiness to receive pollen carried by the wind from the ripe male cones elsewhere on the same tree or from other trees. Waipoua Kauri Forest, October 1966. About natural size.

Fig 10 Both male and female cones are formed of overlapping spirally arranged scales. As a male cone develops it grows to a maximum length of 5 cm, becoming yellowish-green when mature. This cone exuding gum has been scattered with pollen from another cone. Waipoua Kauri Forest, October 1966. Natural size.

Fig 11 After about twelve months of development the male cone turns dark brown as it becomes ripe. The pale orange-coloured pollen sacs show through as the microsporophylls begin to open to release their pollen. Waipoua Kauri Forest, early November 1966. About natural size.

Fig 12 Two female cones open for pollination have pollen grains adhering to them, especially the lower of the two. The underside of the leaf in the centre also has pollen grains adhering to it. Pollen is produced in prodigous quantities and carried from male cones by the wind. Waipoua Kauri Forest, early November 1966. About natural size.

Fig 13 This year-old female cone has been pollinated and is partially covered by a bluish (glaucous) bloom. This bloom gives the cones an attractive appearance, but as they normally occur near the top of the tree they are usually difficult to see. Waipoua Kauri Forest, September 1960. About natural size.

Fig 14 As they mature the female cones become darker, with the scales tinged yellow or brownish-red. When mature they are 5 – 7.5 cm in diameter. The cones shown here are in their second year of growth and it is not until their third year that they will ripen and shed their brown winged seeds. Waipoua Kauri Forest, September 1960. About half natural size.

Fig 15 These mature kauri cones, 7 cm in diameter, are exuding gum and their scales are starting to open to expose the winged seeds. When fully ripe the scales drop off, releasing the seeds to be borne away by the wind. The seeds remain viable for a short period only. Waipoua Forest, September 1960. Natural size.

11

ANCIENT REMNANTS OF ONCE-GREAT COROMANDEL FOREST

An idea of the size of the great kauri giants can be obtained by climbing the Billy Goat Track above the Kauaeranga Valley in Coromandel Forest Park and passing beyond the waterfall and tarns at the top into a wide amphitheatre in the hills. Here amongst regenerating scrub are a number of huge kauri stumps, 6 m across and more; they must have been enormous trees, part of a once-great forest in the area. The trunks were brought down on a railway, some remains of which still exist, to the river below. Some dams constructed to float the logs to Thames are still preserved in the bush and are quite easily seen.

13

14

15

Family *Winteraceae:* A Southern Hemisphere family of shrubs and small trees occurring in tropical South-east Asia, South America and New Zealand.

Genus *Pseudowintera:* An endemic New Zealand genus of three species, two of which may be small trees or shrubs and the third is a shrub.

Pseudowintera colorata
Horopito/Pepper tree

Horopito is a small tree up to 10 m tall or, more commonly, a shrub 1 − 2.5 m high. Sometimes called red pepper tree, it is found in forests and scrublands from sea level to 1,200 m throughout most areas of New Zealand.

The leaves are yellow-brown to green above, and blue-green to glaucous below and usually extensively blotched with red. The new shoots in the spring are a brilliant red and the plant, when growing in the open, along forest margins or in clearings, makes a gorgeous display of colour. In shade, deep in the forest, it does not colour up so brilliantly. The leaves are elliptic to obovate-elliptic, and leathery. They are not shiny, the lower surface especially having a dull, almost matt appearance. They vary in size and can be 2 − 8 cm long by 1 − 3 cm wide, with petioles about 1 cm long.

It has been suggested that hybrid species between *P. colorata* and *P. axillaris* are fairly common, but apparent hybrids are usually *P. colorata* plants growing in deep shade and lacking the reddish coloration of the leaves. Horopito, in Maori terminology, includes both these species, as does the name pepper tree. I prefer to call *P. colorata* horopito and *P. axillaris* pepper tree, though the leaves of both species are aromatic when crushed and pungent to the taste.

1

2

3

Fig 1 A fairly large tree of horopito, growing in the bush on the south side of Mt Ruapehu, March 1970.

Fig 2 An elliptic-obovate leaf of horopito showing the yellow-green upper surface with slight red edging. About natural size.

Fig 3 An elliptic leaf showing the bluish underside and the dots of the sunken stomata. Note the strong midvein. About natural size.

Fig 4 A red horopito on the edge of Chaslands Bush, photographed in February 1964.

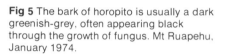

Fig 5 The bark of horopito is usually a dark greenish-grey, often appearing black through the growth of fungus. Mt Ruapehu, January 1974.

Fig 6 The dainty flowers of horopito arise singly or in clusters of up to five or more along the stems, usually axillary, from September until December. They are about 1—1.5 cm across. Opepe Bush, October 1969. Four times natural size.

Fig 7 A flower and a bud. The flowers are faintly aromatic. Opepe Bush, October 1969. Four times natural size.

Fig 8 The ripe berries are black in horopito, sometimes a deep reddish-black, and 3—5 mm in diameter. Waipunga Gorge, April 1974. Three times natural size.

Fig 9 Brilliant spring foliage of horopito, from a tree in Hihitahi State Forest. About natural size.

Fig 10 An elliptic leaf, highly coloured and with a fungus growth common on horopito. Taurewa, November 1974. One and a half times natural size.

Pseudowintera axillaris
Pepper tree/Horopito

Pepper tree is a shrub or a small tree growing up to 8 m tall. It is found on the edges of forests and in clearings, as well as inside the forest, from sea level to 2,750 m. It occurs from Mangonui in North Auckland south to Westport in the west and Banks Peninsula in the east. It is not met with as frequently as *P. colorata.*

The green leaves are shiny on both surfaces. They are not blotched, but have numerous pin-like aromatic glands and, like those of horopito, are pungent to the taste. The tree was used by the Maoris for its medical properties: the leaves produced a decoction used as a stimulant and for skin diseases, venereal diseases and stomach ache; chewed leaves relieved toothache. Early Europeans also used the bark as a quinine substitute and the sap for skin diseases. Its dark-red wood is tough, and has been used by woodworkers for ornamental work such as inlaying.

Figs 1, 2 Undersides and uppersides of the leaves, which may be elliptic, elliptic-oblong or obovate. They are 6 – 10 cm long by 3 – 6 cm wide. About half natural size.

Fig 3 Flowers arise as axillary fascicles of two to ten along the stems. They are 1 – 1.5 cm across, faintly aromatic. Stokes Valley, October 1970. Half natural size.

Fig 4 The flowers and buds magnified at twice natural size. Otari, October 1970.

Fig 5 Almost ripe fruit. They become a darker orange-red when fully ripe. Notice also the buds for next year's flowers and the leaf undersides. Maungatukutuku Valley, April 1975. About natural size.

Fig 6 A pepper tree growing in Opepe Bush, October 1973.

Fig 7 The bark. Hukutaia Domain. January 1974.

Beilschmiedia tarairi
Taraire

Family *Lauraceae:* A large family with mainly tropical and subtropical distribution. It contains about thirty-two genera and some 2,500 species of trees, shrubs and lianes. It includes the bay laurel, Californian laurel, sassafras tree of North America, China and Taiwan, the avocado pear, and the cinnamon and camphor trees. Except for the sassafras all are evergreens and most are aromatic. Three genera are found in New Zealand.

Genus *Beilschmiedia:* Contains about forty species of shrubs and trees found in tropical Asia and Africa, tropical America, Australia and New Zealand. The two New Zealand species are endemic.

Up to 22 m in height, with a straight slender trunk up to 1 m across and a crown of stout, spreading branches bearing large distinctive leaves, taraire is a very handsome tree. It is found from near North Cape south to a line from Raglan through the Bay of Plenty to Mt Hikurangi. It occurs from sea level to 350 m, mostly along stream sides or in situations where the soil is of good quality. It was the most common medium-sized understorey tree of our kauri forests.

The leaves are on petioles about 1.5 cm long, and are arranged alternately or almost opposite along the branchlets. Branchlets, flower stalks, petioles, undersides of young leaves and leaf veins are all clothed with a dense reddish-brown tomentum, or velvety covering.

The wood of the taraire tree is close-grained, light and easily worked; however it is not very durable.

Fig 1 A typical taraire growing at the forest edge near Kerikeri, February 1965.

Fig 2 Taraire bark is dark brown in colour, but it is often obscured by the growth of light coloured lichens. Here the bark shows through this lichen growth which, at a distance especially, gives the trunk a light, almost grey-white appearance. Kerikeri, February 1965.

Fig 3 Leaves of taraire are up to 15 cm long by 6 cm wide, and elliptic to obovate-oblong in shape. The veins are marked by a cladding of reddish-brown tomentum, which sometimes extends thinly over the upper surface and along the margins. About half natural size.

Fig 4 The underside of the mature leaf is pale bluish-green and dull. The midvein and main laterals are raised and clad with tomentum. About half natural size.

1

3 4

Fig 5 Taraire can make a fine shade tree, as this specimen, growing in a field near Whangarei, shows. December 1970.

Fig 6 The juvenile trees of taraire are slender, having tall, thin trunks and sparse, slim branches. Waipoua Forest, February 1965.

Fig 7 This close-up of the leaf bases, petioles and flower stalks shows taraire's distinctively thick, velvety tomentum. Coromandel, December 1978. About natural size.

Fig 8 The flowers at five times natural size, showing the tomentose hairs on the outer surface of the perianth. Colville, December 1969.

Fig 9 A spray of flowers arising from the axils of leaves. The sexes occur together on the same flower, and taraire's small flowers grow on short axillary panicles among the leaves. Whangarei, December 1970.

Fig 10 The large oval fruits are up to 3.5 cm long with a bluish bloom. As they ripen the bloom wears off to reveal the shining dark purple of the drupes. The Maori people boiled these in water to prepare them for food. The fruit of taraire is much favoured by the native pigeon. Auckland, May 1961. About half natural size.

5

6

7 8

9 10

Beilschmiedia tawa
Tawa

Tawa is a tall erect forest tree reaching 25 m in height with a spreading crown and a trunk up to 1.2 m through covered by a smooth, even-textured and rather nondescript bark. The tree is found throughout the North Island and in the South Island as far south as Westport in the west and the Clarence River in the east. It occurs from sea level to 800 m, and in the North Island tawa is the most common tree in many forests, where its light yellow-green foliage adds a pleasing brightness to the forest interior.

The long, narrow, willow-like leaves, up to 10 cm long and 2 cm wide, are aromatic, and the undersurfaces are often bluish-coloured with the midvein and other principal veins distinct. The leaves are on slender petioles about 1 cm long, and young leaves and branchlets are usually covered with silky hairs.

Tawa's small flowers are borne on panicles, up to 8 cm long, arising between the axils of the branchlets towards the tips of the branches. The fruit is a large dark oval drupe, up to 3 cm long, which has a distinctive bloom when fresh.

The white wood is straight-grained but soft and not very durable. It was used by the Maori people for making their long bird spears. It is extensively used today for papermaking and, with the advent of preservative treatments, is now coming into more general use. The floor, wall panelling and furnishings of floors 1 – 4 of the Beehive Building in Wellington are all made from the attractive wood of this tree.

3

Fig 1 The upper surface of a tawa leaf, showing its covering of silky hairs. Hutt Valley, July 1973. About natural size.

Fig 2 The undersurface of the same leaf shown in Fig 1. Note its blue colouring. About natural size.

Fig 3 This fine specimen of tawa was photographed growing on the edge of the forest near Barryville in May 1972. Tawa trees growing inside the forest (as in Fig 6) have a much greater height between the ground and the first branches.

Fig 4 Tawa trees develop stout buttressed roots when they grow old, as seen in these two trees from Barton's Bush, Hutt Valley. November 1964.

Fig 5 The bark of tawa is smooth and dark coloured. On older trees it is nearly always partially covered with growths of light coloured lichens and mosses, as shown here. Hutt Valley, July 1973.

4

5

THE MEDICINAL PROPERTIES OF TAWA

Along with many other members of the laurel family, including the well-known bay tree, the tawa possesses medicinal properties. The Maori people and European settlers were able to cleanse wounds with a decoction made from the bark. Relief from stomach aches and colds was provided from another decoction.

Fig 6 The interior of a tawa forest can often be very beautiful, especially when sunlight shines through the foliage. Mt Ngamoto, Waikaremoana. January 1974.

Fig 7 Young foliage of tawa is very colourful and, together with the branchlets, is silky with hairs. Flower buds are just appearing low down in this photograph. Hutt Valley, November 1968.

Fig 8 Tawa foliage with flower panicles, which arise between the axils on the branchlets. Hutt Valley, December 1968.

Fig 9 A tawa flower fully open and releasing pollen. Hutt Valley, December 1968. Eleven times natural size.

Fig 10 Tawa drupes, often called "plums", ripe and ready to fall. The drupes are frequently produced in tremendous numbers, varying from year to year. In a good year they will fall and thickly litter the ground. The autumn of 1978 was an especially good season in the Wellington district, the branches of the trees being bent down by the weight of the fruit they bore. The drupes were soaked in water, dried and pulped for food by the Maori people. They are also a favourite food of the native pigeon. Waikanae, March 1978. Twice natural size.

1

2

Litsea calicaris
Mangeao

Family *Lauraceae*

Genus *Litsea:* A tropical genus of about 180 species of trees and shrubs with the sexes on separate plants. The single New Zealand species is indigenous.

A much-branched small tree up to 12 m tall with a trunk up to 80 cm through, mangeao forms a spreading, rounded crown in the open, but is more confined and erect in the forest. It is found from sea level to 600 m, from North Cape south to Mokau and East Cape. It is fairly common in forests in this region, but is slow-growing and favours rich soils.

Mangeao is dioecious, its sweet-scented flowers borne profusely on umbels arising from axils towards the branch tips. The drupe, 1.5 – 2 cm long, sits on a pedicel produced from the flower tube.

The light-coloured wood is strong, tough, elastic and durable; it has been used for cooperage and wheel-making. It was used for floor 9 of the Beehive.

4   5   6

3

7

Figs 1, 2 Upper (left) and lower mangeao leaf surfaces. Half natural size. Leaves are 5 – 12 cm long, up to 5 cm wide and leathery. They are ovate to ovate-elliptic.

Fig 3 A lovely mangeao growing at Hamurama Springs, March 1966.

Figs 4, 5, 6 Mangeao flowers. In Fig 5 male flowers are shedding pollen; Fig 6 shows bud opening. Rotorua, September 1975. Three times natural size.

Fig 7 Lichens often grow on the dark-brown bark. Hamurama Springs, December 1970.

Fig 8 Mangeao drupes, from a tree near Te Puke, February 1963. Half natural size.

8

Hedycarya arborea
Pigeonwood/Porokaiwhiri

Family *Monimiaceae:* A small family of tropical to subtropical trees and shrubs, mostly fragrant. There are about thirty genera with 450 species found in the tropics and temperate regions of the Southern Hemisphere. Two genera occur in New Zealand.

Genus *Hedycarya:* A genus of about twenty species of trees and shrubs, all with opposite leaves, found in New Caledonia, Polynesia, Australia and New Zealand. The single New Zealand species is endemic.

A rather erect, small, aromatic tree up to 12 m high with ascending branches and a trunk up to 50 cm through. The thick leathery leaves, on petioles 2 cm long, are up to 12 cm long by 5 cm wide, shining above, duller and paler below, with margins saw-toothed, serrate or plain, and a distinct vein pattern.

The sexes of pigeonwood are on separate trees with the flowers borne on many-flowered branching racemes. There are no sepals or petals as such but rather undifferentiated perianths of tepals forming the visible flower, which has a strong aromatic scent. Midveins, petioles and margins are usually hairy. The fruit of the pigeonwood is a juicy drupe, 1.5 cm long, occurring in clusters. When ripe the drupes are bright reddish-orange and are a favourite food of the native pigeon. Pigeons seem to be able to eat large numbers of drupes at a time, and will become very sleepy and slow-moving when indulging.

Occurring from sea level to 800 m, pigeonwood prefers a wet climate and a rich soil. It is found throughout the North Island and as far south as Banks Peninsula in the east. Pigeonwood also grows offshore in the north on the Three Kings Islands.

1

2

Fig 1 Ripening drupes. Lake Pounui, in November 1968. Two-thirds natural size.

Fig 2 A fine specimen of pigeonwood. Waiorongomai, March 1975.

Fig 3 The leave undersurface. Natural size.

Fig 4 Leaves can be elliptic (as here) to obovate or lanceolate to oblanceolate. This leaf upper surface is natural size.

Fig 5 Male flower racemes. Waiorongomai, October 1965.

Fig 6 The male flower is up to 1 cm across and consists of a perianth with pubescent tepals around a cluster of stamens. Lake Pounui, December 1968. Four times natural size.

Figs 7, 8 Female flowers are smaller than males, only up to 6 mm across: a ring of pubescent tepals around a cluster of carpels. Lake Pounui, December 1969. Four times natural size.

Fig 9 Bark with moss and lichen growths. Coromandel Peninsula, January 1974.

Fig 10 The young leaves, young branchlets and leaf petioles are light to moderately densely pubescent. Coromandel, January 1974.

Fig 11 A branchlet showing pubescence, faint grooving and densely pubescent new buds between moderately pubescent leaf petioles. Kauaeranga Valley, January 1974. Twice natural size.

Fig 12 The undersurface of an oblanceolate shaped leaf. Two-thirds natural size.

Family *Monimiaceae*

Genus *Laurelia:* A genus of three species of aromatic trees, two in Chile and the other in New Zealand. It is perhaps a little unusual in having the sexes separate, on the same tree or, occasionally, together in the same flower.

Laurelia novae-zelandiae
Pukatea

A tall forest tree up to 36 m high with a trunk up to 2 m through, pukatea grows best in damp and wet places. In the forest it grows tall with a clean, straight trunk, free of branches for some distance from the ground. After exposure by clearing, the trunk often grows new branches lower down, as shown in Fig 1. The branches are erect and fairly open, carrying a crown of very attractive foliage. In mature trees the trunk is always supported at its base by large flange-like buttresses. The branchlets are four-sided and sparsely hairy when young.

The thick, leathery leaves are elliptic to elliptic-obovate, the margins coarsely and bluntly serrate, glossy above, less shining and paler-coloured below, up to 8 cm long and 5 cm wide, borne on petioles grooved on the upper side and up to 1 cm long. The flowers may be perfect, or male and female on the same tree, and arise as axillary racemes, up to 3 cm long, with peduncles hairy. The false fruits are urn-shaped, green, turning brown when ripe. The wood is a pale brown tinged with yellow, sometimes clouded with darker brown. It is tough and strong.

Pukatea grows from sea level to 610 m in swampy forests, damp gullies and creek beds. It occurs all over the North Island and in Marlborough on the east to as far south as Fiordland in the west.

1

2

Fig 1 A fine specimen near Lake Rotoma. The lower branches have grown since the nearby forest was cleared. May 1972.

Fig 2 Pukatea's pale, rather blistery bark. Near Ohura, December 1965.

Fig 3 A four-sided branchlet with young (lighter green) and old (darker) leaves. A small section of the paler leaf underside shows near bottom right. Lake Pounui, December 1968. About two-thirds natural size.

Fig 4 This tall pukatea growing on a forest edge near Waikanae shows the clean trunk and open vertical branching of the species. April 1969.

Fig 5 Pukatea trunk buttresses. The tree can sometimes be found with its roots growing in water.

Fig 6 Flower buds and male flowers, Kaitoke, October 1966. There are anthers but no style or stigma. Natural size.

Fig 7 A perfect or bisexual flower showing stamens (red), staminodes (abortive stamens) (yellow, wedge-shaped) and hairy styles with stigmas and hairy perianth. Kaitoke, November 1970. Four times natural size.

Fig 8 A female flower. There are no stamens, but a ring of staminodes surround

the hairy style with its stigma. Kaitoke, November 1970. Four times natural size.

Fig 9 The urn-shaped seed cases, about 2.5 cm long. In both the female and bisexual flowers after fertilisation the tubular receptacle elongates to form this structure, which splits into sections to release the hair-covered fruits, each of which has a single seed inside it. Lake Pounui, March 1974. About half natural size.

Fig 10 Pukatea seedcases splitting open and releasing the plumed fruits, which are borne away on the wind. Waikanae, May 1979. About natural size.

Family *Chloranthaceae:* A family of mainly tropical or subtropical herbs, shrubs and trees with minutely stipulate leaves arranged in opposite pairs. The flowers are small and the sexes are on the same or separate trees. Five genera containing sixty-five species are known.

Genus *Ascarina:* A small genus of about ten species found in Malaysia, Polynesia and New Zealand. The single New Zealand species is endemic.

Ascarina lucida
Hutu

A small aromatic tree up to 8 m high. The thin, red-coloured branchlets bear towards their tips groups of coarsely serrated leaves, the tips of their serrations sharp and dark coloured. The flower spikes, about 3.5 cm long, are at the ends of the branchlets. Each inflorescence spike contains male flowers which possess one or rarely two stamens and female flowers which have a single carpel. Found from sea level to 760 m, sparingly in the North Island, common on the West Coast, Stewart Island and the Kermadecs.

1

2

3

4

5

6

7

Fig 1 Hutu trees made attractive by the sunlight shining through their foliage. Lake Matheson, January 1973.

Fig 2 A typically pendulous flower spike showing male flowers. Hukutaia Domain, September 1969. About natural size.

Fig 3 Male flowers with anthers opening to shed pollen. Photographed from the same spike as Fig 2, but a week later. Four times natural size.

Fig 4 Hutu berries. Taupo, April 1979.

Fig 5 A group of leaves showing the red branchlet, leaf upper surfaces and petioles, which can be up to 1 cm long. Near Opotiki, November 1968.

Fig 6 The leaf undersides are paler and less shining with their midveins strongly raised. About half natural size.

Fig 7 The bark of hutu.

Macropiper excelsum
Kawakawa/Pepper tree

Family *Piperaceae:* A small family of herbs, shrubs and small trees found mainly in tropical and subtropical regions of the Southern Hemisphere. The flowers are minute and clustered together in bracted spikes. About five genera and 2,000 species are known, one of which occurs in New Zealand.

Genus *Macropiper:* A genus of nine species of small trees and shrubs found throughout the Pacific eastward from the Bonin, Marianas and New Hebrides Islands, Lord Howe Island and New Zealand to the Marquesas, Society and Austral Islands. The single New Zealand species is endemic.

Kawakawa is a small, densely-branched, aromatic tree which grows up to 6 m tall. It is also commonly found as a shrub. It is found throughout the North Island and south to Okarito and Banks Peninsula in the South Island. This widespread tree is often abundant in the forest, in shady gullies and on shaded rocky outcrops.

The round, red or black zig-zagging branches are swollen and jointed at the nodes. The large, fleshy though rather leathery leaves are more or less heart-shaped, 5—10 cm long by 6—12 cm wide. They have chordate bases and pointed tips. A feature of this tree's leaves is that they are almost always badly holed by chewing insects, which makes it difficult to locate a plant in good condition. The leaves are opposite and on petioles up to 4 cm long which often have the stipules joined on. The sexes are on separate trees and are closely packed on tall erect spikes up to 8 cm high. The fruits, which develop on the female spike, are small drupes, 2—3 mm in diameter, closely packed together, green at first but turning orange when ripe.

A variety *psittacorum* has larger leaves and longer spikes. It occurs on offshore islands of the northern North Island such as Three Kings, Poor Knights, Little Barrier and Mayor.

The fruit, bark and leaves of kawakawa all have medicinal properties. The bitter root extract is useful for treating urinary troubles; the leaves and bark can be used for treating cuts and stomach aches. A pulp from the leaves relieves rheumatic pain when applied to affected joints. A hot poultice can be used to treat bad bruises. The leaves when burned near crops give off an acrid smoke which can deter most insect pests.

1

2

Fig 1 A kawakawa tree growing in sunlight among bush near Levin, April 1965. The tree's densely-branched habit is clearly shown.

Fig 2 Kawakawa's large, fleshy, heart-shaped leaves are 5—10 cm by 6—12 cm, shiny above but duller and paler green on the undersurfaces. The leaf structure is unusual. There is no main vein, rather a series of veins radiating from the base of the petiole. Photograph from Karaka Bay, September 1968. About half natural size.

4   5   6

Fig 4 Section of a male spike showing male flower with two stamens terminating in two anthers full of pollen. Karaka Bay, September 1968. About twice natural size.

Fig 5 A section of a male spike with ripe anthers still intact and others that have opened and are shedding pollen. Karaka Bay, September 1968. Here about natural size.

Fig 6 A section of a female spike showing minute female flowers, each with three to four stigmas, on top of each ovary. Waikanae, November 1978. Three times natural size.

Fig 7 A female spike with ripe drupes, much prized by birds for food. Karaka Bay, in February 1969. About natural size.

3

Fig 3 A cluster of male spikes. On the right the ripe anthers are ready to release pollen; the next to the left is shedding pollen, while the two spikes on the left have released all their pollen. Karaka Bay, September 1968. This specimen reproduced at about natural size.

Fig 8 Leaves of the variety *psittacorum* are larger (10 - 16 cm long and 11-20 wide), more glossy and rather yellowish-green.

Fig 9 Bark of the main species. Swellings represent the earlier nodes of the original stem. Near Opotiki, April 1973.

7

8   9

Melicytus lanceolatus
Mahoe wao

Family *Violaceae:* A large world-wide family of trees, shrubs and herbs having stipulate, mostly alternately arranged leaves and regular or irregularly shaped flowers. About sixteen genera covering some 900 species are known. Three genera occur in New Zealand and one of these includes three species of trees.

Genus *Melicytus:* Three New Zealand small trees and a shrub species, one of which extends to Norfolk Island, Tonga and Fiji. The flowers are unisexual with males and females on separate trees.

A rather slender, erectly-branching small tree up to 6 m tall with a trunk up to 30 cm through. Mahoe wao has rather brittle branches bearing long lance-like alternate leaves that have finely saw-toothed margins. The open-branched habit with the leaves borne towards the outer extremities of the branches gives the tree an attractive appearance.

The small flowers arise in clusters of two to five, either from the axils of the leaves or lower down from the bare branchlets; in the latter case they are often in such great profusion as to clothe almost completely the branchlets with blossom. Flowers can vary greatly in colour, even on the same tree, though this appears to occur more with male flowers than with female, which are mostly yellow. The fruit is a dark-purple berry, also borne in great profusion. The flowers are delicately fragrant. The bark varies from brown to almost white.

Mahoe wao is found from sea level to 915 m through the North, South and Stewart Islands, commonly in forests and along forest margins. In the South Island it is more commonly found west of the main mountains. In its juvenile form it is a slender, open-branched tree with slightly drooping foliage; this is clearly illustrated by the juvenile trees in **Fig 1** growing in Ball's Clearing, Hawke's Bay, January 1973. When grown in the open out of the forest, mahoe wao forms a spreading round-headed tree.

1

2

3

4

Fig 2 Mahoe wao spray showing typical leaf, upper surface and axillary flowers. Leaves are 5 – 16 cm long by 1 – 2 cm wide on petioles up to 1.5 cm long. Here about natural size.

Fig 3 Leaf underside, with its prominent midvein. Also about natural size.

Fig 4 The bark is faintly wrinkled and varies from brown to almost white. From West Taupo, December 1973.

Fig 5 The rounded crown produced when the tree grows in the open. From edge of Ball's Clearing, January 1972.

Fig 6 A typical mahoe wao tree with its distinctive white bark growing on the edge of forest. This specimen at West Taupo, December 1973.

Fig 7 Ripening berries 4 – 6 mm in diameter covering a branch of a tree in the Waipunga Gorge, April 1974. When ripe the berries are dark purple, much sought after by native birds. One and a half times natural size.

Fig 8 The five-petalled flowers have the petals folded back and measure 5 mm across. These female flowers have a long style with a trilobed stigma. Otari, September 1970. Photographed here at four times natural size.

Fig 9 Dark-coloured variation of the flower, also female. Mt Ruapehu, October 1972. Four times natural size.

Figs 10,11 Two further variations in the flower colour. Both show rudimentary non-functional anthers. Mt Ruapehu, October 1972. This photograph is four times natural size.

Fig 12 These flowers clothing a mahoe wao branch show the great profusion in which they can occur. From a tree at Otari, in September 1965.

5

1

Melicytus ramiflorus
Mahoe/Whiteywood

A small tree, usually spreading, growing to 10 m tall, sometimes more, with a trunk up to 60 cm through. The bark is whitish and usually more or less covered with fine white lichens. The trunk is usually short, with branching starting close to the ground. Young leaves are a bright yellow-green, giving the tree a pleasantly fresh appearance in early spring. The flowers are produced in abundance in clusters of two to ten on slender pedicels up to 5 mm long, in the axils of the leaves and along the branchlets.

The branchlets are brittle and the soft wood is of little use. It can, however, be made into a special charcoal for the making of gunpowder. The Maoris used a flat piece of the wood rubbed vigorously with a pointed piece of kaikomako to produce fire.

Mahoe is one of the most common native trees found in forests and scrublands all over the country; it is often predominant on partially cleared land. It is hardy and can withstand wind but will often become mis-shapen and gnarled in windy places. This tree is apparently able to live to a considerable age.

3

4 5 6 7

Fig 1 Mahoe leaf about natural size. Leaves are 5– 15 cm long by 3– 5 cm wide.

Fig 2 Underside of mahoe leaf. This is also about natural size.

Fig 3 An old gnarled mahoe. Note epiphyte of *Astelia* on the tree's lower right. Maungatukutuku Valley, March 1976.

Fig 4 Male flowers along a branchlet. Karaka Bay, December 1967. The main crop of flowers occurs during November-December, but in mild districts a second, lighter crop occurs during April-May. About one and a half times natural size.

Fig 5 Male flowers arising from the axils of the leaves. Karaka Bay, December 1968.

Fig 6 Male flowers enlarged to three times natural size. Karaka Bay, December 1968.

Fig 7 Female flowers arc smaller than males and have a four to six-lobed stigma clearly visible in the open flower by the berry one quarter of the way up from the bottom. Poahau Valley, November 1970. One and a half times natural size.

Fig 8 Mahoe tree growing in the Poahau Valley, November 1970.

Fig 9 Bark with lichens from a medium-sized tree. Woodside Gorge, December 1969.

Fig 10 Bark from an old tree, carrying a lot of lichens. Waiorongomai, September 1965.

Fig 11 Berries are often borne profusely. Karaka Bay, February 1970. Natural size.

Fig 12 Ripe berries are deep purple. Karaka Bay, March 1970. Natural size.

Fig 13 Growing shoot showing the serrated leaf margins and petioles up to 2 cm long.

8   9   10

11   12   13

Melicytus macrophyllus
Large-leaved whiteywood

The main difference between this tree and mahoe, the most common of the whiteywoods, lies in leaf shape. *M. macrophyllus* has a larger, leathery leaf, the obovate leaves sometimes growing up to 20 cm long by 10 cm wide, on petioles 2 cm long. The flowers of the large-leaved whiteywood are bigger.

M. macrophyllus is a small tree, sometimes a shrub, growing up to 6 m tall with a trunk up to 40 cm through. It is found in lowland and hilly forests from sea level to 600 m from North Auckland down to the Waikato. The tree has also been found growing locally at Waikari, near Dunedin. It can make an attractive spreading specimen when grown in the open.

Fig 1 The leaf underside showing the paler lower surface and distinct venation. About natural size.

Fig 2 Leaf spray, upper surfaces. The leaves of *M. macrophyllus* are coarsely and bluntly serrate, obovate to oblong, with their apices acute or rounded. The apices here are more acute than those illustrated in Fig 1. Hukutaia Domain, November 1968.

Fig 3 The white berry is spotted with purple and is up to 6 mm in diameter. Waipoua Forest, March 1979.

Fig 4 *M. macrophyllus* flowers are up to 7 mm across in clusters of three to twelve on pedicels 1.5 cm long that curve downwards. From a tree growing at Taupo, December 1978. This specimen about two-thirds natural size. The flowers of *M. macrophyllus* are larger than those of *M. ramiflorus*.

Fig 5 The light-coloured bark of the large-leaved whiteywood.

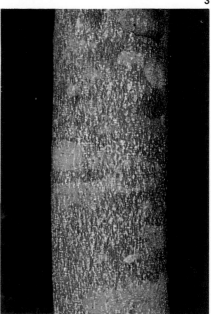

Fuchsia excorticata
Kotukutuku

Family *Onagraceae:* The fuchsia family consists of twenty-one genera embracing 640 species and is distributed throughout the montane tropical and temperate regions of the world. Only two genera are found in New Zealand; they are *Epilobium,* with thirty-seven species, all of which are herbs, and *Fuchsia,* with four species.

Genus *Fuchsia:* A genus of small trees and shrubs containing about 100 species ranging from Mexico through Central and South America to Tahiti and New Zealand. The four New Zealand species are endemic; one is a tree, one a liane, one a trailing shrub and the fourth an upright shrub.

A small tree up to 14 m high, or sometimes a shrub. Fuchsia trees can be recognised by their red, papery, outer bark which is normally peeling to reveal a satiny-smooth, pale yellowish-brown or yellowish-green inner bark. The trunk is usually 60 – 80 cm through, sometimes up to 1 m in very old trees. These points are clearly illustrated in the tree from Opepe Bush, Taupo, in **Fig 1.**

The pointed ovate-lanceolate or ovate-oblong leaves are on petioles up to 4 cm long, and fall in winter. The flowers hang downwards, each on a slender pedicel up to 15 mm long that arises from the axil of a leaf or directly from a branch before the leaves appear. The fruit is an elongated berry, black and juicy when ripe (when it is delicious to eat). The Maori name for the berry is konini, the name by which the tree itself is known in Westland. The wood, which is gnarled and twisted, dark brown in colour with paler streaks and wavy markings, is strong and very durable. It is sometimes used for inlaying and other ornamental work.

Kotukutuku is the largest fuchsia in the world. It is common all over New Zealand from sea level to 1,060 m and is also found on the Auckland Islands. It is common in second-growth areas, where it may even be the dominant tree, or along stream banks.

1

Fig 2 Leaf upper surface. Natural size.

Fig 3 Leaf underside. About natural size.

Fig 4 A spray showing leaves, new shoots and two flowers. Akatarawa, November 1965.

Fig 5 The flowers occur in two forms. The first is a hermaphrodite flower in which the pollen is deep blue — a very rare colour for the pollen of any flower — and the style is of varying length. The second is a female in which stamens are short and the style is at least twice as long as the flower tube. Both occur together in the same vicinity but not on the same tree. The opening flower is green shaded with purple; it turns purple then deep red. Akatarawa, November 1965. Natural size.

Fig 6 Red hermaphrodite flower and opening buds. Otari, October 1969. Natural size.

Fig 7 Buds and flowers arising from leaf axils and the bare branchlet. Akatarawa, November 1969. Photographed here at about natural size.

Fig 8 Berries at varying stages of maturity. Mt Kaukau, Wellington, January 1968. About twice natural size.

Fig 9 A typical very old kotukutuku trunk, from Peel Forest, Canterbury, December 1964.

Fig 10 Hermaphrodite flowers. Lewis Pass, November 1964. Here about half natural size.

Fig 11 Kotukutuku trees often grow along roadsides and on banks. A small tree from near Lake Rotoroa, Nelson, January 1972.

Fig 12 A fine specimen of kotukutuku with its typical spreading canopy. From Thundering Creek, Haast Pass, January 1973.

9

10

11 12

Toronia toru
Toru

Family *Proteaceae:* A large family of sixty-two genera with 1,050 species of trees and shrubs mainly growing in regions where there is an annual long dry season. They are found in tropical Asia, Malaysia, Australia, New Caledonia, New Zealand, tropical South America, Chile, the mountains of tropical Africa, South Africa and Madagascar. The family includes such well-known plants as proteas, leucodendrons, grevilleas, hakeas and banksias.

Genus *Toronia:* An endemic New Zealand genus containing one species of forest tree.

An erect, much-branching small tree up to 12 m high with the branches upwardly directed and the trunk about 20 cm or more in diameter. The long, narrow, linear-lanceolate leaves are up to 20 cm long and up to 15 mm wide, thick, leathery and shining on both surfaces. The branchlets are smooth, but new growth, buds and flower stalks are clothed with short brownish-red appressed hairs. The leaves are arranged alternately or in more or less erect whorls along the branchlets. They may turn a bright red colour as they die.

The flowers, which arise in erect six to sixteen-flowered racemes, are very fragrant; their sweet honey-like scent fills the surrounding air on a still day. The fruit is a drupe usually about 12 mm long but often up to 18 mm; it has a fine velvety texture and is pale olive-green at first, turning reddish as it ripens.

The wood of the toru is a dark red and is used for inlaying and similar work. The tree occurs from sea level to 850 m amongst scrublands and forest in the north of the North Island from Mangonui south to about Tokomaru Bay. It is abundant in some areas.

1

Fig 1 A well-grown toru tree at Kaitoke, July 1973.

Fig 2 The bark is light grey, wrinkled and pimply (the black marks in this picture are due to a fungal growth). Photographed here in the Kauaeranga Valley, December 1972.

Fig 3 Young branchlet showing the alternate leaf arrangement, the long, narrow, linear-lanceolate, apiculate leaves narrowing gradually to the petiole, which is short, not more than 2 mm long. This photograph shows the leaf uppersurfaces and the red-brown appressed hairs of the growing bud and apex. Hinakura, November 1970.

Fig 4 The same branchlet, turned to show the paler leaf undersurfaces.

2

3

4

5

Fig 5 The flower racemes, each about 5 cm long, arise from the axils of the leaves towards the tips of the branches. The stalks are also clothed with reddish-brown hairs. Otari, October 1969.

Fig 6 The flowers, 10 — 18 mm in diameter, are shown here about one and a half times natural size. Photographed on a tree at Otari, October 1968.

Fig 7 Young branchlets showing appressed hairs and erect axillary racemes with flower buds. Otari, August 1970.

Fig 8 This toru from the Kauaeranga Valley shows clearly the upright, much-branched habit of the tree. December 1970.

Fig 9 Toru drupes ripen during April-May. Taupo, April 1971. Almost natural size.

6

7

8

9

1

Family *Proteaceae*

Genus *Knightia:* A genus of three species of trees and shrubs. One is endemic to New Zealand and the other two are found only in New Caledonia. Flowers have the perianth cylindrical with the segments curled spirally, a manner characteristic for the genus.

Knightia excelsa
Rewarewa
New Zealand honeysuckle

A tall upright branching tree up to 30 m high with a trunk up to 1 m through. Rewarewa is one of the most distinctive looking of our native trees and specimens in the forest often reach 12—15 m before the first branch arises (Fig 2). In the open the tree retains its distinctive appearance.

The young branchlets are angular and covered by a dark-brown tomentum extending along the midvein and lower surfaces of the leaf. The leaves of young trees are long and linear-lanceolate. Adult leaves are linear-oblong, usually acute pointed, thick, leathery, sometimes almost woody. They have bluntly serrate margins and are 10—15 or even 20 cm long by 2.5—4 cm wide. The flowers have spirally-coiled perianth segments. They are arranged in axillary or terminal racemes, either in pairs or singly. The pale reddish wood is beautifully grained and figured and much prized for furnishings and for inlay work. The heartwood produces a fine finish when worked, but it is not durable if used outside.

Rewarewa grows from sea level to 850 m and is found throughout the North Island and in the South Island in the Marlborough Sounds. Large areas of second-growth rewarewa occur in the central districts of the North Island and in pockets of the Kaimai Ranges between Rotorua, Tauranga and Whakatane.

2

3

4

Fig 1 The pale underside of a leaf showing tomentum on the branchlet, petiole and midvein. Photographed here at about half natural size.

Fig 2 A typical rewarewa in forest beside Lake Rotoma, August 1972. The trunk is tall and straight before the first branching occurs.

Fig 3 Rewarewa's characteristic upright habit is shown by this tree growing in the Otaki Gorge, March 1965.

Fig 4 Looking down on a leaf spray showing the upper surfaces with distinct midvein and the brown tomentum on the buds, petioles and branchlet. Photographed here at about two-thirds natural size.

Fig 5 Rewarewa's inflorescence (the flower cluster) is pollinated by birds and is made up of a number of individual flowers which are crowded into a raceme. The perianth segments of each flower form a tube swollen at the base. When this is ready to open it splits into four at the top, revealing the club-shaped stigma of the female carpel at the apex of the style. Similar splits then commence at the base of the tube to join up with those at the top. The segments of the tube coil in a spiral fashion around the base of the flower. Together the many individual flowers produce this peculiar structure which appears to be a flower but which is really a raceme of many flowers. The flowers are borne high on the tree and exude an objectionable smell. Ngaio Gorge, Wellington, November 1965. About half natural size.

Fig 6 The finely textured bark is usually fairly clean and free of lichens and other superficial growths.

Fig 7 The tomentose fruits up to 4 cm long take a year to open, splitting into two halves and releasing the winged seeds. The terminal projections are the persistent styles of the flowers. Specimen from a tree at Otari, June 1974. Photographed at about half natural size.

5

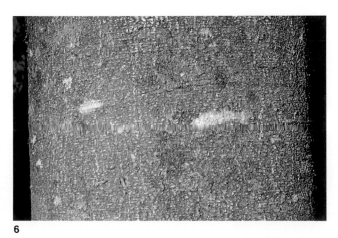

6

7

Coriaria arborea
Tutu

Family *Coriariaceae:* A family containing only a single genus with some fifteen species found in southern Europe, eastern Asia, Central and South America and New Zealand. The reason for the unusual discontinuous world distribution of these plants is thought to arise from their being a very ancient group with a once world-wide distribution. Many of these species have since disappeared from the places where they originally grew.

Genus *Coriaria:* The fifteen species of shrubs and small trees in this genus are characterised by four-sided branches. Many of the species are poisonous if eaten. There are eight species in New Zealand, only one of which is a small tree; all the others are shrubs or subshrubs. All these species hybridise and all are poisonous.

Tutu is a tree with poisonous properties. In spring the sap of the plant is poisonous, as are the seeds in autumn. There are many cases on record of people becoming extremely ill and even dying from the tree's effects. Many cases of animal deaths from the effect of the poisonous glucoside in the sap and seeds are recorded, particularly in the early days of European settlement. The glucoside, called "tutin", was isolated and described by Prof. T. H. Easterfield and Mr B. C. Aston in 1900. In a healthy person as little as 1 milligram produces nausea, vomiting and general incapacity over a period of twenty-four hours. No antidote is known. The Maoris prepared an intoxicating beverage from the berries after the seeds had been removed. Early European settlers are recorded as having prepared this drink, but the effects of imbibing it were not always predictable.

Tutu is usually a stout shrub but often a small tree up to 8 m high with a trunk up to 30 cm through. It occurs all over New Zealand and the Chathams from sea level to 1,060 m. It is found in scrubland, along forest margins, in gullies and on alluvial ground. Tutu is one of the first plants to appear after a forest fire and it is recorded as being the first plant to grow on the pumice deposits thrown out from the eruption of Mt Tarawera in the late nineteenth century.

1

2

Fig 1 A small tutu tree photographed at Waipahihi Reserve, Taupo, October 1969.

Fig 2 The bark of an old tree. At Taupo, October 1969.

Fig 3 The dark-green shining leaves are opposite all along the branch in two rows, giving the appearance of a fern. The leaves are 5—10 cm long by 4—5 cm wide, with distinct venation and pointed tips, on short stout petioles about 2—3 mm long. This specimen is photographed at about one-third natural size.

Fig 4 The dull underside of the leaves. About natural size.

3

4

5

6

7

Fig 5 The young growth is lush, and it is the sap from this spring foliage that is very poisonous. Taupo, October 1970.

Fig 6 The bark of a young branch. Taupo, October 1970.

Fig 7 The tiny flowers hang in long racemes from the branches. Taupo, December 1973.

Fig 8 The protogynous flowers hang from pedicels up to 5 mm long. Karaka Bay, November 1968. This specimen about natural size.

Fig 9 The stigmas shrivel and the large anthers of the stamens extend on slender filaments. The pollen is wind-borne. Karaka Bay, December 1968. Also photographed at natural size.

Fig 10 After pollination the five sepals persist while the five petals of each flower grow large, thick and fleshy. Turning black, they form the fruit that encloses the several seeds. Jacks Pass, Hanmer, January 1971.

9

8

10

Family *Nyctaginaceae:* A family of small trees, shrubs and herbs comprising thirty genera and 290 species found mainly in the tropics, especially America. *Bougainvillea* is probably the best-known genus in this family.

Genus *Pisonia:* A tropical and sub-tropical genus of about fifty species of trees and shrubs found on many Pacific Islands and tropical America with one species in New Zealand.

Pisonia brunoniana
Parapara

This is an unusual tree, the sole representative in New Zealand of a group of tropical and sub-tropical plants producing glandular aggregations of sticky fruits that can capture and kill quite large birds and even small reptiles. *P. brunoniana* itself will ensnare small birds. It is a small tree 4 – 6 m high with a trunk up to 60 m through and brittle branches bearing large, shining, dark-green leaves. It occurs on the Three Kings Islands and along the northern North Island to East Cape from sea level to about 150 m.

1

2

3

4

5

6

Fig 1 Tree at Opotiki, December 1974.

Figs 2, 3 The greenish flowers, each up to 10 mm long, are borne in many-flowered panicles. Fig 3 about three times natural size. Dr W. M. Hamilton's property at Warkworth, January 1979.

Fig 4 The elongated fruits each have five ribs and an apical "mouth", and form large tangled masses. At first green, they become black and very sticky when ripe. Small birds are caught by the sticky mass and held until they die. Seeds actually germinate on their remains, later falling to the ground to take root. Here about one-fifth natural size. Warkworth, January 1979.

Fig 5 Bark of the tree in Fig 1.

Fig 6 Leaf underside. The leaves are 10 – 40 cm long and 5 – 15 cm wide. About one-sixth natural size. Warkworth, January 1979.

Family Pittosporaceae
Genus *Pittosporum*

Except for the American continent, where it does not occur, the Pittosporaceae is a widespread family of trees, shrubs and vines growing in warmer latitudes. It includes nine genera with about 249 species. Eight of these genera occur in New Zealand; one, *Pittosporum*, is found in New Zealand as well as in Australia.

The genus *Pittosporum* is a sub-tropical and tropical genus found in Africa, Asia, Australia, some Pacific islands and New Zealand. The genus includes 150 species, of which twenty-six are endemic to New Zealand. Of these, eight are small trees and six grow either as small trees or shrubs; one, described from a single tree, later destroyed, on Kawau Island, has not been found elsewhere — it is possibly extinct. Amongst the remaining eleven species two are epiphytes and the other nine are small shrubs.

Though some New Zealand species of *Pittosporum* have only limited distributions, a number are commonly found in forest clearings, along forest margins, streamsides, lake and river banks, and amongst scrub in most parts of the country. Their attractive and variable foliage, along with their bell-like flowers, has brought many of them into garden cultivation. Some, such as *P. tenuifolium* and *P. crassifolium,* are grown as hedges. The bright-green, undulate leaves of *P. tenuifolium,* the yellow-green leaves of *P. eugenioides*, the darker-green, rather leathery leaves of *P. crassifolium* with their silvery-white to buff tomentum

on the undersurfaces, the bronze tomentum of the growing tip and young leaves of *P. ellipticum* — these variations make these species especially attractive as specimen trees. The large umbels of deep-pink flowers carried in profusion by *P. umbellatum,* for example, together with the pleasant, compact, rounded, columnar shape of this tree, make it one of the more outstanding of the New Zealand species.

Pittosporum flowers are bell-like with a tube formed from the petals' basal portion; their upper portion curves backwards along the tube. They are usually perfect, but some species have perfect and female flowers or male and female flowers, usually on separate trees but sometimes on the same tree (for example, *P. tenuifolium*, below). The flowers are borne in terminal umbels or fascicles or singly between the leaf axils.

The fruits are usually two to three-valved. They are dark-brown or black capsules which when split open reveal a highly coloured interior with the small, black, highly polished seeds adhering together in a sticky mass of glutin.

Following the *Flora P. colensoi, P. fasciculatum* and *P. buchananii* are shown in this book as separate species. Recent taxonomic opinion, however, tends towards regarding *P. colensoi* as a subspecies of *P. tenuifolium* and the other two species as being of doubtful status; these trees may possibly be only variations in a *P. tenuifolium — P. colensoi* complex.

Pittosporum eugenioides
Tarata/Lemonwood

A tree up to 12 m tall with a trunk up to 60 cm through, this is the largest New Zealand pittosporum. If crushed, its leaves emit a strong lemon-like smell, hence the common name of lemonwood.

As a young tree tarata grows as a compact, yellow-green-leaved pyramidal tree. It later forms a rounded crown from which is produced the more open, stoutly branched, beautiful mature tree. The leaves have undulating margins and are 10 — 15 cm long by 2 — 4 cm wide with slender petioles up to 2 cm long.

Tarata's flowers arise in large terminal clusters, their peduncles hairy and each flower 1 — 1.5 cm across. The flowers are sweet scented with a heavy honey-like scent that can be rather overpowering. Their sex type varies; some are purely female, while others with anthers and smaller but probably functional pistils can be regarded as perfect. The fruit is a small, egg-shaped, two to three-valved capsule.

The tree is found all over New Zealand in forest clearings, and along forest margins and stream banks from sea level to 600 m. It occurs frequently in cut-over forest that is regenerating. The flowers occur from October to December and the fruits ripen in twelve to fourteen months. The Maori people mixed the flowers with fat for annointing their bodies. They frequently extracted the sap for use as a scent.

2

3

Fig 1 Leaf upper surface. One and a half times natural size. Note the undulating margins and yellowish midvein.

Fig 2 A beautiful mature tarata tree in Waipahihi Reserve, Taupo, May 1973.

Fig 3 The bark of a mature tarata. Otari, September 1965.

Fig 4 A lovely example of the young conical form. Mair Park, Whangarei. December 1970.

Fig 5 Undersurface of the leaf in Fig 1.

Fig 6 Yellow tarata flowers. These are the perfect form. Otari, October 1968.

Fig 7 Bark from a young tree in the conical stage of development.

Fig 8 Perfect flowers with the anthers just beginning to shed pollen. Otari, October 1968. Reproduced here at three times natural size.

Fig 9 Female flowers showing rudimentary anthers and large swollen ovaries. From Otari, October 1968. Three times natural size. The female flowers of *P. eugenioides* are generally a little smaller than the perfect forms.

Fig 10 A branch bearing new season's green fruits on the right and last season's ripe fruits at left. Otari, March 1970.

133

Pittosporum huttonianum

This pittosporum has a restricted habitat; it is found only on the Great and Little Barrier Islands and the Coromandel Peninsula.

It is a small, sparingly-branched tree growing up to 8 m tall, with a trunk up to 20 cm through. *P. huttonianum* also grows as a shrub. The leaves are large, faintly wavy, elliptic to obovate-oblong and leathery; they are up to 12 cm long and 5 cm wide, arranged alternately to subwhorled.

The dark-red flowers arise in the axils of the leaves singly or in two to five-flowered clusters. The two-valved seed capsules on pedicels 1—2 cm long are clothed with downy tomentum when they are young.

Fig 1 Mature leaves, upper surfaces. Two-thirds natural size.

Fig 2 A spray of new foliage. Coromandel, November 1968.

Fig 3 Underside of a leaf in Fig 1.

Fig 4 A fine specimen; note the open branching habit. Coromandel, December 1965.

Fig 5 The dark-flecked and wrinkled bark of *P. huttonianum*.

Fig 6 A branchlet and leaf petiole. Hukutaia Domain, April 1973. Three times natural size. This photograph clearly illustrates a feature of this tree: the growing buds, young branchlets and undersurfaces of immature leaves and their petioles are clothed with a loose, tangled tomentum.

Pittosporum dallii
Dall's pittosporum

This is a pittosporum found only in a few isolated localities in the north-west Nelson district. Two fine specimens were grown at Otari by W. B. Brockie. These trees provided all these photographs, but they have since been cut down.

P. dallii is a small, spreading, glabrous tree up to 6 m high with a trunk up to 20 cm through. The bark on the trunk is grey, that on the branchlets a deep purplish-red. The thick elliptic to elliptic-oblong, coarsely serrate, acute leaves are 5−10 cm long by 2−3.5 cm wide, on reddish petioles 2 cm long. The tree's yellowish-white flowers are strongly sweet scented. P. dallii seed capsules are two-valved.

1

2

3

4

5

Fig 1 A spray showing the opposite leaf arrangement, dark-coloured branchlet and reddish petioles.

Figs 2, 3 Leaf upper (Fig 2) and undersurface (Fig 3), showing prominent midvein and fine venation. About natural size.

Fig 4 The distinctive bark of the trunk.

Fig 5 These P. dallii flowers from two trees at Otari, photographed in November 1960, were yellowish-white, but P. dallii flowers are also recorded as being white. Each petal is about 2 cm long, the flower about 5 cm across when freshly opened.

Pittosporum umbellatum
Haekaro

Haekaro occurs sparingly in lowland forests and in scrublands down the east coast of the North Island from North Cape to about Wairoa. In the forest it will grow upwards with a slender trunk, spreading out when it reaches the light. It has become fairly popular as a garden tree, and in such situations it becomes bushy (Fig 4), bearing many umbels of pink to reddish flowers in season.

The tree grows up to 8 m tall; the branches grow upwards with a tendency to form whorls (Fig 1). The young branchlets, peduncles, leaf petioles and the midveins are thinly clothed with white or reddish-coloured; silky, erect hairs. The large leathery leaves are alternately arranged, except at the tips of the branches where they tend to be subwhorled; they are 5 – 10 cm long and 2 cm wide, with petioles up to 2 cm long. The flowers of this tree are perfect and occur over a long flowering period from September to January. Haekaro's two-valved seed capsule is woody, either rounded or almost four-angled.

1

2

Fig 1 A rather fine specimen growing at Hukutaia Domain, Opotiki, April 1973. The upward-growing, whorled branches of the tree are clearly displayed.

Fig 2 The distinctive bark, from the tree pictured in Fig 1.

Fig 3 Leaf spray showing the large, leathery, subwhorled leaves above those alternately arranged, also hairy branchlet and petioles.

Fig 4 A haekaro tree in full flower, growing in the garden of Dick Hewitt's farm at Ponatahi, Wairarapa. It was photographed in September 1968.

Fig 5 A branchlet and two leaf petioles, showing the distinctive silky, erect hairs. This specimen at about four times natural size.

Fig 6 Leaf upper surface, showing hairy petiole and midvein and prominent mid and side veins. About three-quarters natural size.

Fig 7 Underside of the leaves in Fig 6. This specimen also at about three-quarters natural size.

Fig 8 The new season's growth commences while the tree is in flower. The young branchlet is clothed with erect, silky hairs. Ponatahi, September 1968.

Fig 9 The flowers occur in many-flowered umbels, each flower about 2 cm across and bearing both male and female parts. The silky, erect hairs can be seen on the few exposed peduncles in each umbel here. Ponatahi, September 1968. Pictured at about half natural size.

Pittosporum ellipticum

This pittosporum is a small tree with open, spreading branches, growing up to 8 m high. This species is confined to the northern parts of the North Island where it is found in lowland forests from Mangonui south to Tairua on the Coromandel Peninsula. It is rare and local in distribution.

P. ellipticum is distinguished by its large elliptic leaves and dense brown to golden-coloured tomentum covering the young leaves, leaf undersides, petioles, branchlets and peduncles. Leaves may also be elliptic-ovate to obovate in shape and are 5–10 cm long by up to 5 cm wide. Unlike *P. virgatum* (facing page), *P. ellipticum* does not have a juvenile form.

Fig 1 *P. ellipticum* leaf upper surface. About natural size.

Fig 2 Flowers occur in terminal umbels. Notice the tomentum on the peduncles and sepals. Piha, September 1964. Almost twice natural size.

Fig 3 A leaf spray of *P. ellipticum* showing the tomentum, leaf arrangement and the silky-white hairs on the upper surfaces. Hukutaia, November 1968.

Fig 4 Thick tomentum covering a branchlet, leaf buds and leaf petioles. Three times natural size.

Fig 5 A leaf spray showing the tomentum and white hairs on the upper surfaces.

Fig 6 Leaf lower surface and tomentum. About natural size.

Fig 7 The bark of *P. ellipticum*.

Fig 8 The seed capsule is 17 mm In diameter and two or three-valved. Hukutaia, January 1974. About natural size.

Pittosporum virgatum

Like *P. ellipticum,* this is rare and local in its distribution. *P. virgatum* is a small slender tree found in lowland forests of the North Auckland and Coromandel Peninsulas and on Great Barrier Island. The tree reaches 6 – 8 m high, with erect, slender, springy branches. It has a dense brown tomentum covering the young leaves, branchlets, petioles and peduncles. A juvenile form occurs; it has sinuate, toothed or lobed leaves 1 – 2 cm long by 2 – 4 cm wide, or ovate, small, serrated leaves up to 1 cm long by 3 – 5 mm wide. This uncommon pittosporum may be slowly dying out in the forests around Kaitaia where I have seen more dead trees than living ones.

1

2

Fig 1 Adult leaves are 2 – 6 cm long by 1 – 2 cm wide. One and a third times natural size. All the photographs on this page are from trees at Pukepota, Kaitaia, April 1979.

Fig 2 Leaf lower surface and seed capsule showing the tomentum. One and a third times natural size.

Fig 3 Branchlet, petioles and leaf lower surfaces. The tomentum is not quite as dense as that of *P. ellipticum.* Four times natural size.

Fig 4 A leaf spray of *P. virgatum* clearly showing the tomentum.

Fig 5 The bark of *P. virgatum.*

Fig 6 A spray of juvenile foliage. Some varying leaf forms are clearly visible in this photograph.

Fig 7 A spray of *P. virgatum's* adult foliage showing the distinctive hairy midveins and the brown tomentum on the branchlets and seed capsules.

3

7

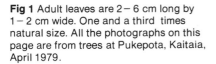
4

5

6

Pittosporum tenuifolium
subsp. colensoi/Black mapou
P. ralphii/Karo

Both these pittosporums have large leaves, those of black mapou 4–10 cm long and 2–5 cm wide and those of karo 7–12.5 cm long by 2–2.5 cm wide. Both grow as small trees with spreading branches, the larger black mapou growing up to 10 m tall and the smaller karo up to 4 m.

The leaves of black mapou are without tomentum; those of karo are densely clad on the lower surfaces with white or buff-coloured tomentum, as also are the branchlets, petioles and peduncles. Flowers in black mapou are axillary, either single or in small cymes; karo flowers occur as terminal umbels.

Karo grows along stream sides and forest margins only in the North Island, from Thames south to Wanganui and Dannevirke in the east. Black mapou is more widespread; it occurs in the North, South and Stewart Islands from Bay of Plenty southwards, from sea level to 900 m, but only west of the Alps in the South Island. Black mapou is common in patches over the central volcanic plateau in the North Island.

1

2

3

4

Fig 1 A specimen of black mapou left after forest clearing. From the Taurewa Intake, August 1974.

Fig 2 A spray of black mapou showing the alternate, thick, leathery leaves and the flower buds arising in the leaf axils.

This fine specimen was photographed at Erua near National Park, October 1969. It is reproduced here at about natural size.

Black mapou is very variable in form.

Fig 3 The upper surface of a leaf of black mapou. The leaves are elliptic to obovate-oblong, sometimes elliptic-lanceolate and usually acute apically. Those shown here are approximately natural size.

Fig 4 The undersurface of a black mapou leaf. This example is somewhat more obovate-shaped. Slightly smaller than natural size.

Fig 5 Black mapou flowers. From the Kaimanawa Ranges, September 1964. About natural size.

Fig 6 Newly opened black mapou flowers. Erua, November 1968. Three times natural size.

Fig 7 Three-valved seed capsules of black mapou from this season's flowers (above) and from last season's (below). Taurewa, November 1974. About twice natural size.

5

6

7

Fig 8 A tree of *P. ralphii* grown by Norman Potts at Opotiki, November 1968.

Fig 9 Spray of *P. ralphii* leaves showing elliptic shape, alternate arrangement and tomentum on petioles and branchlets. From Waipahihi Reserve, June 1979.

Fig 10 Branchlet, leaf petiole and bud of *P. ralphii* showing the white tomentum. About four times natural size.

Fig 11 The fresh bark of *P. ralphii*.

Fig 12 Upper surface of a *P. ralphii* leaf on a branchlet bearing seed capsules as well. About three-quarters natural size.

Fig 13 *P. ralphii* tomentose lower leaf surface and opened three-valved seed capsules with seeds. Taupo, June 1979.

Fig 14 The flowers of *P. ralphii* arise in terminal umbels each of three to ten flowers. Taupo, November 1968. Half natural size.

Fig 15 *P. ralphii* seed capsules. Taupo, January 1974. Three times natural size.

Pittosporum obcordatum
Heart-leaved kohuhu

The distribution of this tree is discontinuous. Trees were described from Akaroa (1844), Kaitaia (1901) and the Wairoa River (1920) but can no longer be found there. The tree is now best known from garden specimens, but I have been told by Norman Potts that it grows in the East Coast area. The tree in **Fig 1** grows in the Hukutaia Domain, Opotiki (photographed in April 1973), planted there by Mr Potts.

This is a narrow, erect, upward-branching small tree which reaches around 3−4 m high, perhaps more.

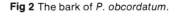

Fig 2 The bark of *P. obcordatum*.

Fig 3 Flowers arise along the branches in groups of one to five from the axils of the leaves. They are on short pedicels 1−2 mm long, with the petals forming a tube about 6 mm long. They vary in colour from creamy yellow to pale purple or creamy white. The flowers are perfect. From a plant grown by Mrs Audrey Cameron at Hinakura. November 1964. Natural size.

Fig 4 A group of five flowers from a tree at Hukutaia Domain, November 1966. Three times natural size.

Fig 5 *P. obcordatum* branchlet. Adult leaves are 4−8 mm long by 2−7 mm wide. Leaves of juvenile plants are more elongated, being suborbicular to broadly ovate and up to 2 cm long. Hukutaia Domain, January 1974. Three and a half times natural size.

Pittosporum crassifolium
Karo

1

Karo is one of the most notable of New Zealand's scented plants. It is widely cultivated, especially for hedges and shelter, and several most attractive horticultural varieties have been developed. They are particularly popular in North Island gardens.

First described from Flat Island in the Cavelle Islands, karo is now known to occur naturally on the Kermadec Islands and in the North Island from North Cape to Poverty Bay. It favours streamsides and forest margins, mainly near the coast from sea level to 950 m. It has spread in the wild as far south as Wellington.

The shrub or small tree grows up to 9 m high with ascending branches. The lower surfaces of the branchlets, petioles and peduncles are covered with a very dense white or pale buff-coloured tomentum. The alternate, thick, leathery leaves are 5–7 cm long, sometimes up to 10 cm, and up to 2.5 cm wide. The red to dark-red scented flowers are functionally unisexual and are heavily scented; during the flowering season the evening air near karo trees is filled with a delightful fragrance. The tree's large three to four-valved seed capsules, which grow up to 3 cm long, are covered by a white or yellowish tomentum.

3

Fig 3 A karo tree growing on the shore of Wellington Harbour at Karaka Bay, April 1965. This tree is bearing the distinctive seed capsules.

Fig 4 Karo's distinctive seed capsules grow up to 3 cm long. These specimens are four-valved, but the tree will also grow three-valved capsules. In this photograph some of the tomentum which usually clothes the capsules has been rubbed off by the weather. Karaka Bay, April 1975. At about natural size.

Fig 5 A terminal umbel of karo flowers; although perfect, these flowers are probably functionally male. Female umbels of this tree have one to two flowers and male umbels five to ten. The peduncles bearing the flowers usually droop slightly. This photograph illustrates clearly how the flowers sit neatly amongst the leaves; the pilose sepals and the tomentum on the peduncles, leaf lower surfaces and margins are all clearly visible. Karaka Bay, September 1968. This specimen also at about natural size.

4

2

Figs 1, 2 Upper (Fig 1) and lower leaf surfaces. Karo leaves have a distinct "crackled" appearance on the shining upper surface, a dense whitish or buff-coloured tomentum on the leaf undersides and stout petioles. The thick, leathery leaves are obovate-elliptic to narrow obovate or obovate-cuneate in shape. The margins of the leaves are rolled down.

5

6

Fig 6 A grey-green variegated form of this tree, displaying its attractively figured leaves and darker female flowers. From a plant at Otari, photographed in September 1970. About natural size.

Fig 7 A single flower from the umbel shown in Fig 6, showing the pilose sepals and peduncles. *Pittosporum* flowers fold back their petals shortly after opening. This specimen is at three times natural size.

Fig 8 Karo and kohuhu, *P. tenuifolium*, form natural hybrids in the wild. A typical *P. crassifolium* x *P. tenuifolium* hybrid is illustrated here; its female flowers are probably sterile. From a plant grown by Audrey Cameron at Hinakura, October 1965. Reproduced here at about natural size.

Fig 9 Karo seed capsules splitting open to reveal the shining black seeds set in a golden-yellow mass of glutin. Karaka Bay, May 1970. About one and half times natural size. The seed capsules are held on stout peduncles about 1.5 cm long.

7

8

9

Pittosporum tenuifolium
Kohuhu

A small tree some 9 m in height with wavy, margined, silvery-green, glossy leaves. Inside the forest it grows with a slender, straight trunk, but along the margins of forests and in the open it forms a tight, much-branched tree from the ground upwards.

Kohuhu is a very hardy tree and has become very popular in gardens for hedges and shelter belts. With its light-green, shining leaves it can grow into quite an attractive specimen tree. A number of pleasing cultivars with variegated foliage have been de-

veloped. Kohuhu grows naturally from near North Cape southwards, from sea level to 920 m. It is not found west of the main ranges in the South Island.

The flowers occur singly or as small cymes, in the axils of the leaves near the branch tips. The flowers are either male or female on separate trees or together on the same tree. Occasionally they are perfect. The reddish-purple flowers turn black as they age and are sweet scented at dusk. *P. tenuifolium's* branchlets are shining deep red or reddish-black.

Fig 1 Glossy green upper side of a kohuhu leaf. The leaves are 3 –7 cm long by 1 –2 cm wide, oblong to oblong-ovate or elliptic-obovate in shape, with obtuse or acute tips. About natural size.

Fig 2 The paler, glabrous leaf underside. Young leaves and their petioles are sometimes slightly hairy, the older leaves never so. About natural size.

Fig 3 The forest form of kohuhu, exposed by clearing at Taupo. February 1970.

Fig 4 Grey, blistered bark of an old tree.

Fig 5 The form of a tree growing in the open. Mission Bay, Taupo, January 1965.

Fig 6 An unusually shaped kohuhu growing in a valley above Lake Wakatipu in January 1966.

5

6

7

8

9

10

Fig 7 The perfect form of kohuhu's flower. Taupo, November 1978. About natural size. The sepals are hairy only when young.

Fig 8 The female flower form, photographed at Taupo in November 1978. The sepals are present and hairy in a newly opened flower but they soon atrophy. This photograph about two and a half times natural size.

Fig 9 The seed capsules are three-valved, woody and rough-surfaced, their glossy black seeds held in a sticky yellow glutin. Here about one and a half times natural size. Waipahihi Reserve, May 1970.

Fig 10 A kohuhu spray, clearly showing the elliptic-obovate and oblong-ovate leaves, their alternate arrangement and the dark-red, shining branchlets. Photographed at Karaka Bay, November 1965.

147

Pittosporum fairchildii
Three Kings pittosporum

This pittosporum is found naturally only on Great Island of the Three Kings Islands but is now grown as a specimen tree in parks and gardens.

It is a small, compact tree growing to 5 m high with slender spreading and ascending branches. Branchlets, undersides of leaves and petioles are clothed with white woolly hairs when young. The leaves are 5–7.5 cm long and 2–3.5 cm wide, on petioles about 6 mm long; they are thick and leathery with thickened margins, arranged alternately in sub-whorled groups of three to four. The dark-red terminal flowers are solitary or in two to four-flowered umbels, on slender hairy pedicels. The woody seed capsules, 2.5 cm across, are three to four-valved.

Fig 1 *P. fairchildii's* shining, dark-green, mature leaves, showing the alternate and subwhorled arrangements. About two-thirds natural size.

Fig 2 Hairy undersurface of a young leaf. Leaves vary from this obovate-cuneate shape to elliptic-oblong, with either obtuse or subacute tips.

Fig 3 Young branchlets and leaves showing very hairy clothing of stems and leaf undersurfaces with scattered woolly hairs on leaf upper surfaces and a glossy, hairless seed capsule. Warkworth, December 1977. Note the hairy thickened leaf margins.

Fig 4 A tree growing at Hukutaia Domain, Opotiki, April 1973.

Fig 5 *P. fairchildii's* grey, rugose bark.

Fig 6 A young branchlet showing the clothing of woolly hairs covering the branchlet, petioles and terminal bud. From the tree in Fig 4. This specimen at three times natural size.

Pittosporum patulum
P. fasciculatum
P. buchananii

1

P. patulum grows only in the upper reaches of the Cobb, Buller, Wairau and Clarence Rivers, along stream banks or forest margins. It is a small tree up to 5 m high, found mainly as the juvenile form. In the adult tree leaves are crowded towards the tips of the spreading to ascending branches and are 4—5 cm long by 1.5 cm wide, oblanceolate to narrow-obovate in shape. The fragrant, dark-red flowers occur in terminal umbels.

P. fasciculatum grows only around Lake Taupo and on Mts Ruapehu and Tongariro. It grows to 5m with flowers in dense terminal or axillary clusters on the branches, and is now generally regarded as co-specific with *P. tenuifolium* subsp. *colensoi*.

P. buchananii grows naturally on Mt Egmont and near Wellington and Mangonui. Of doubtful specific validity, it is a small tree, up to 6 m tall, with spreading ascending branches and dark red flowers arising singly or as pairs in the leaf axils.

2

3

Fig 1 Branchlet from a juvenile *P. patulum* showing clothing of tangled, woolly hairs and some juvenile leaves. One and a half times natural size. The juvenile form persists for many years and adult trees are in fact rarely found. Adult branches are marked by conspicuous leaf scars.

Fig 2 *P. patulum* juvenile foliage. The juvenile leaves are thick, glossy and linear, up to 5 cm long and 5 mm wide, coarsely and bluntly toothed or lobed, sometimes pinnatifid. Young shoots and flower stalks are sparsely hairy.

Fig 3 Spreading branchlets of *P. patulum* with juvenile leaves showing the undersides with prominent midveins.

Fig 4 *P. fasciculatum* leaf lower surface. The leaves are 4—10 cm long and 1—2 cm wide. They are obovate-oblong to elliptic or lanceolate in shape, with obtuse or acute tips and distinct midvein and venation. About natural size.

Fig 5 Spray of *P. fasciculatum* showing leaf upper surfaces.

Fig 6 *P. buchananii* branchlets and leaves bear a silky pubescence. The petiolate leaves are 6—13 cm long and 3—5 cm wide, dark green and shining above, paler below and alternately arranged. They vary from oblong to obovate in shape.

Fig 7 Branchlet of *P. buchananii* showing the silky pubescence and a seed capsule.

4

5

6

7

Family Myrtaceae

This large family includes 100 genera and 3,000 species of trees, shrubs and lianes found mainly in tropical and South America, the West Indies, Indo-Malaysia, China, New Guinea, New Caledonia, Borneo, Australia, New Zealand, Fiji and some Pacific Islands. New Zealand shares with Australia the distinction of possessing some of the largest and most beautiful trees belonging to this family.

The Myrtaceae are recognised by their attractive, fluffy flowers. The numerous long anthers are conspicuous and often highly coloured, and hide the sepals and petals (for example *Metrosideros parkinsonii,* below). Their leaves are simple, entire and leathery, arranged in opposite pairs and dotted with aromatic oil glands. Many species have edible fruits and most produce valuable timber.

For convenience, the family is usually divided into two major subfamilies: the Myrtoideae, in which the fruit is a berry, and the Leptospermoideae, in which the fruit is a dry capsule. A third, smaller group of heath-like shrubs found only in north and west Australia is also recognised.

The Myrtoideae includes, among other genera, the genus *Myrtus,* which includes the European myrtle, and the related genera *Neomyrtus* and *Lophomyrtus* of New Zealand. It also includes *Psidium,* which contains *P. guajava,* the guava of tropical America, now grown all over the world, and *Syzygium*, which has a species in New Zealand but is best known from the clove tree, *S. aromatica,* of Indonesia. The cloves of commerce are the unopened, dried flower buds.

The Leptospermoideae includes the genus *Leptospermum,* containing the manuka and kanuka of New Zealand and the tea-trees of Australia, the genus *Metrosideros,* containing the beautiful New Zealand pohutukawa and the ratas, and the genus *Eucalyptus,* which has 500 species in Australia and Tasmania and three species in Indo-Malaysia, containing some of the largest trees in the world. The Australian mountain ash, *Eucalyptus regnans,* grows normally to 75 m high; specimens are known that have reached 106 m in height, making this the second tallest tree in the world.

Eucalypt trees have been introduced and grown with success in many parts of the world, notably South Africa and Ethiopia. They are common in New Zealand. But for beauty they do not match the pohutukawa, *Metrosideros excelsa,* which although a much smaller type of tree adorns our northern coasts during December with lasting displays of bright-red or crimson flowers that place it high on the list of the world's most spectacular trees. In full bloom the northern and southern ratas, *M. robusta* and *M. umbellata,* also provide a never-to-be-forgotten sight.

Fig 1 Pohutukawa in flower, Coromandel coast, December 1969.

Family *Myrtaceae*

Genus *Metrosideros:* A genus containing some sixty species of trees, shrubs and lianes found in South Africa (one species), the Philippines, New Guinea, north-east Australia, New Caledonia, New Zealand and some Polynesian islands. Eleven species occur in New Zealand and of these five are trees and the remainder lianes. All the New Zealand species are endemic.

Metrosideros excelsa/Pohutukawa
M. kermadecensis/Kermadec pohutukawa

At the time of European settlement of New Zealand pohutukawa trees were confined to the coastal areas of the North Island, from the Three Kings Islands southwards to Poverty Bay on the east coast and around the mouth of the Urenui River, a little north of Waitara, on the west coast. They also grew along the shores of some of the lakes in the Rotorua district. The Kermadec pohutukawa occurred mainly on Sunday Island of the Kermadec Islands group and is closely related to *M. collina* var. *villosa,* which is found in some of the Polynesian islands.

Since then many species have been extensively planted in many parts of New Zealand, both inland and on the coasts. *M. kermadecensis* has been used as a street tree in a number of places, including streets in Wellington, and *M. excelsa* has been extensively planted in parks and gardens. This has taken place particularly in the North Island, but the tree has also been planted successfully around Nelson, on Banks Peninsula and as far south as Dunedin in the east and Jacksons Bay in the west.

Pohutukawa grows best close to the sea, where it often produces massive spreading trees that overhang the water, the huge branches growing out almost horizontally in many specimens. Its deep roots enable the tree to cling to steep banks and rocks and remain there. Normally, however, the tree has a short stout trunk up to 2 m in diameter and stout, often huge, spreading branches producing a broad crown reaching up to a height of 20 m. The branches are often twisted, bent or gnarled, sometimes quite grotesque in appearance.

The largest pohutukawa in New Zealand, Te Wahoa Rerekohu, grows at Te Araroa and has a height of 19.81 m and a spread of 38.4 m. It is reputed to be over 300 years old. On the small promontory at the tip of Cape Reinga, in northernmost New Zealand, grows a pohutukawa tree reputed to have been there for about 800 years; it is sacred to the Maori people, who regard it as the departure point of the spirit from this world.

The finest and oldest pohutukawa trees can now be viewed around the Coromandel Peninsula, especially north of Colville on the western side, and in isolated pockets around the eastern coasts. There are also fine trees near Opotiki and Ohope Beach in the Bay of Plenty and around the East Cape route. Some fine trees can be found in the Bay of Islands, and there are outstanding specimens on the northern outlying islands from the Three Kings to the Little and Great Barrier Islands.

When in flower during December and January the tree presents a brilliant spectacle, being often completely smothered with its crimson to brilliant-red flowers. But even with the tree not in flower, pohutukawa's fresh, deep-green foliage makes it an

2

Fig 1 (previous page) A pohutukawa in flower clings to a cliff face at Oamaru Bay on the Coromandel coast, photographed in December 1969. It can be seen that new aerial roots have formed in an attempt by the tree to hold on to the cliff in the face of erosion.

Fig 2 A spray of pohutukawa showing the branchlet and stout petiole 10 – 12 mm long, both tomentose, and the acute elliptic leaf with glossy upper surface and tomentose lower surface. In the young leaf shown here the upper surface is also hairy and the midvein very prominent. Adjacent leaf pairs are aligned at right angles to each other. This specimen reproduced at about natural size.

Fig 3 A fine grove of pohutukawa in full flower at Waitoitoi on the Coromandel coast, photographed in December 1969. The picture shows clearly the short, stout trunk, broad crown and huge spreading branches typical of the tree.

Fig 4 "A brilliant spectacle." A magnificent section of flowers from a tree in full bloom at Paekakariki, photographed in December 1964.

3

4

attractive tree. When young it is bushy and tight to the ground, and it may persist in this form, up to about 7 m high, for a long time before developing the large spreading branches that are typical of the mature older trees. In this young stage the tree will flower profusely and set seed.

The paired leaves on short petioles are arranged in four rows on the stem, a pattern shared by all species of the genus. The leaves are up to 10 cm long by 5 cm wide, varying in shape from elliptic to oblong, usually acute but sometimes, particularly in older trees, obtuse. Fairly thick and leathery when mature, they are softer and more pliable when young, glossy above and covered by a dense white tomentum below, as are the young branchlets and petioles. The leaves of young plants are hairless.

The inflorescences (flower clusters) are in pairs at the tips of the branchlets. The many flowers have the pedicels, peduncles and calyces clothed with a dense white tomentum. Although it is the red stamens which are the conspicuous part of the flower, there are also small red petals, tomentose sepals and a nectar cup surrounding the style. A great many birds are attracted to pohutukawa's flowers because of the copious nectar carried in the flower cups.

Pohutukawa trees are often encountered with many aerial roots coming from low branches or the trunk. These are frequently tangled and joined around the trunk or branch from which they arise. This creates a sort of netting effect, from which only the larger reach the ground.

The Kermadec pohutukawa (Figs 7 and 8) can be distinguished from *M. excelsa* by its smaller size, up to 16 m high with a trunk up to 1 m through. Its branchlets are round but sometimes angled, and it has shorter petioles, usually about 5 mm long. The broader, shorter leaves are up to 5 cm long by 2 cm wide, broadly ovate to elliptic-oblong, with their margins somewhat recurved. Leaf undersides, flower stalks and sepals are clothed with a dense white tomentum as in *M. excelsa*. The flowers are smaller and occur intermittently almost all the year with a major flowering round November-December, usually a little earlier than *M. excelsa*.

Pohutukawa varieties have become very popular among many home gardeners. Yellow-flowering pohutukawa trees were discovered in about 1940 on Motiti Island in the Bay of Plenty, and a range of cultivars has been developed from these. A variegated form has also been developed as a cultivar grown in some gardens for its handsome foliage.

5

6

Fig 5 A massive pohutukawa overhangs the stony coast of the Coromandel Peninsula, photographed in December 1969. This area, particularly north of Colville on the western side, now contains some of the finest specimens of old pohutukawas.

Fig 6 The spectacular pohutukawa flowers, showing the distinctive red stamens tipped with yellow anthers carrying pollen. The cups surrounding the styles are full of nectar; the copious supply usually attracts many birds to the tree during the December-January flowering period. In this photograph some tomentose sepals are visible but the small red petals, which are not a distinctive part of the flower, are hidden by the stamens. Pictured also at Coromandel, January 1965. This specimen is about half natural size. The flowers of *M. excelsa* are larger than those of the Kermadec pohutukawa, pictured in Fig 8.

7

8

Fig 7 The broadly ovate leaves of the Kermadec pohutukawa, showing the glossy upper surface with clear veins, tomentose lower surface and tomentose branchlet and petioles. Very often the young branchlets of *M. kermadecensis* are coloured red, as shown in this photograph. The recurved leaf margins are here clearly illustrated. About natural size.

Fig 8 A spray of the Kermadec pohutukawa showing flowers, leaves and leaf arrangement. From a plant in Wellington, November 1967. About natural size.

Fig 9 Seed capsules beginning to open to reveal the reddish-brown seeds. Most capsules are three-valved, but a few are four-valved. Wellington, early April 1970. These specimens are pictured at about half natural size.

Fig 10 Pohutukawa's thick, stringy bark hangs and peels in long, narrow flakes. Old tree on the Coromandel coast, January 1965.

Fig 11 Aerial roots arising from a trunk. Cape Brett, January 1978.

9

10

11

Metrosideros robusta
Rata

The rata usually begins life as an epiphyte perched high on another tree. It germinates from a wind-borne seed that settles in a fork of the host or in a clump of epiphytes already perched upon the host tree. From here it sends down aerial roots and also side roots, which grow horizontally around the host's trunk to join the original aerial root or another. In this way the epiphyte gradually encloses the host trunk and finally becomes a tall, often massive tree with a hollow trunk and huge spreading branches. Some claim that the rata kills the host, but this has been questioned. It is probable that a rata can germinate only on an aging host: vigorous trees can resist its growth.

A rata tree can be up to 25 m high with a trunk up to 2.5 m through. A mature rata becomes itself heavily burdened during its life with lianes and epiphytes such as *Freycinetia* and *Astelia*. The weight of these, together with the ferns and mosses that grow upon it, finally brings about its collapse during storms.

The tree's close-grained, tough wood is very hard and strong. It has been used for shipbuilding.

Rata is today seen at its best throughout the Urewera forests, but it occurs from the Three Kings Islands throughout the North Island and in the north-west part of the South Island south to about Westport, from sea level to a maximum of 900 m.

Fig 1 Rata leaves are thick and leathery, up to 5 cm long and 2 cm wide, on petioles about 2 mm long. The branchlets, which are clothed with hairs, are red-coloured when young. About natural size.

Fig 2 In flower during December and January, the rata is one of the great sights of our North Island forests. Lake Waikaremoana, January 1966.

Fig 3 A very old rata in flower towers above the forest at Lake Waikaremoana in January 1965.

Fig 4 Leaf lower surface. Natural size.

Fig 5 The base of the trunk of the ancient tree in Fig 9, showing the typically huge roots. Trampling on these roots is actually very damaging to the tree and can kill it.

Fig 6 A magnificent rata in flower at Lake Okataina, December 1971.

DIFFERENT FORM GROWING ON GROUND

A rata tree usually arises from a germinating seed high among the branches of a forest host. But if a rata seed should germinate on the ground a rather different looking tree can result. A rata growing on the ground has a short, usually crooked trunk and a quite different form. Trees like this can be seen on limestone rocks in the Takaka district in north-west Nelson, where their huge roots sprawl over the rocks, clinging to the ground like enormous epiphytes.

2

3

Fig 7 The base of an enormous rata at Lake Waikaremoana, showing fused aerial roots and the hollow left by the decay of the original host tree. The size of this tree can be judged from the figure standing in the cavity. October 1965.

Fig 8 Rata's bark is thin and falls in small rectangular flakes. Photographed at Lake Waikaremoana, January 1965.

Fig 9 A very old rata heavily festooned in typical fashion with *Astelia, Collospermum,* ferns and other epiphytes. Lake Pounui, in December 1969.

Fig 10 Rata flowers are similar to those of pohutukawa but are smaller and usually of a more intense red. Twice natural size.

Metrosideros umbellata
Southern rata

Unlike rata, *M. umbellata* grows from the ground to a tree up to 15 m high with a trunk up to 1 m through. In exposed situations it becomes gnarled and twisted and reduced in size. Flowers are borne in profusion, making the tree a brilliant spectacle visible some distance away from November to January, depending on location. The thick, leathery, acute, lanceolate leaves are up to 5 cm long and up to 2 cm wide, on petioles 5 mm long and dotted with many oil glands. The heavy, tough, strong wood has been used for ship-building.

Southern rata occurs from sea level to 760 m. It grows from Whangarei south, but is rare and local in the North Island. It is especially common on the West Coast of the South Island and is found mainly in higher rainfall regions, including Stewart Island.

Fig 1 Sprays of southern rata showing the branchlets and the leaves dotted with oil glands. Tiny flower buds can be seen to be forming at the tips of the branchlets. From the Dun Mountain Track, Nelson, November 1969.

Fig 2 A southern rata in bloom on the banks of the Haast River in January 1973. The tree's flowering is relatively spasmodic, most trees flowering well only once every few years. It favours the high rainfall conditions of the West Coast.

Fig 3 Flowers on a small tree at Tautuku Beach, Southland, in December 1964. Massed displays of these brilliant red flowers provide one of the most colourful sights in the New Zealand bush.

Fig 4 A spray of flowers and flower buds about to open. This specimen from Chaslands, Southland, December 1964. It is here about two-thirds natural size.

4

5

6

THE NORTHERN AND SOUTHERN RATAS

The southern rata differs from its northern cousin in significant ways. The southern rata's flowers, for example, are a more brilliant red. It does not begin life as an epiphyte but grows from a seed on the ground like most other forest trees. It is a somewhat smaller tree, growing to only 15 m high compared with the northern rata's giant 25 m. The leaf structure is also different, the northern tree's leaf tending to be shorter and rounder. Whereas the northern M. robusta is found mainly in the North Island and the north-west of the South, the southern rata is primarily a tree with a South Island habitat. It grows rarely north of Cook Strait.

7

Fig 5 Several unusual yellow-flowering forms of southern rata are known. This flower is from a tree at Denniston on the West Coast of the South Island, photographed in January 1975.

Fig 6 Southern rata's leaf upper surface, with flower buds at the branchlet tip. Note the thick and leathery nature of the leaf and the many oil glands dotted all over it. Natural size.

Fig 7 The paler leaf lower surface, showing the petiole and oil glands. Also natural size.

Fig 8 Bark on a southern rata trunk, complete with a shoot of young leaves growing from it. The young leaves are soft and silky to touch and have this lovely reddish-orange colouring. Southern rata's branchlets and petioles are always hairless. Photographed at Tautuku Beach, December 1964.

8

Metrosideros parkinsonii
North-west Nelson rata/Shrubby rata

1

This uncommon rata species is a straggling or semi-prostrate plant in the forest, but in the open it becomes a slender tree up to 7 m high with a trunk up to 4 cm through. It is found on the Great Barrier Islands and in the South Island in the north-west Nelson area and the Paparoa Ranges, south to near Greymouth. The tree grows from sea level to 920 m.

This rata's thick and leathery leaves are elliptic-ovate to ovate-lanceolate, acute or obtuse and up to 5 cm long by 2 cm wide. The leaves are often red or golden coloured above, paler below. The north-west Nelson rata is notable for its beautifully symmetrical cymes of very attractive deep-red flowers.

2

3

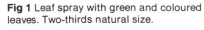

4 5

Fig 1 Leaf spray with green and coloured leaves. Two-thirds natural size.

Fig 2 Clusters of flowers arising from the forks of branches. Note the scaly bark. All these photographs are from a private garden in Karaka Bay, Wellington, in September 1970. Here about half natural size.

Fig 3 The small tree from which these photographs were taken.

Fig 4 The flower buds are covered by the incurving stamens, which curl back as the flower opens. Half natural size.

Fig 5 The flowers in the compound cymes are arranged to give this striking symmetry. About half natural size.

Fig 6 Leaf underside, showing the stout petioles about 2 mm long. Half natural size. The leaves of *M. parkinsonii* are sub-opposite on the four-sided branchlets.

6

160

Family *Myrtaceae*

Genus *Leptospermum:* A genus of fifty species of shrubs and small trees found in Malaysia, Australia and New Zealand. The three New Zealand species are endemic, one being a prostrate shrub and the other two growing either as shrubs or small trees.

Leptospermum ericoides
Kanuka

Known in Northland as manuka but elsewhere as kanuka, *L. ericoides* forms an aromatic shrub of varying form or a spreading tree. It grows up to 15 m high, with a trunk up to 60 cm through.

The leaves are aromatic and up to 12 — 15 mm long and 2 mm wide. They are linear to narrow-lanceolate, acute but not pungent, and arise singly or in groups of three to five. The small flowers about 5 mm across smother the tree in great profusion. They arise as two or five-flowered cymes, or sometimes singly from the axils of the leaves.

Kanuka occurs throughout the North and South Islands from sea level to 900 m, in forest and scrub.

1

4

2 3

5

Fig 1 A kanuka tree so smothered with flowers that the branches are weighted down. Lake Rotoiti, Nelson, January 1972.

Fig 2 A fine spreading kanuka at Ponatahi, September 1968. Kanuka does not form as good a shelter or nurse bed for other plants as manuka. Its red wood is hard and durable and was used by the Maori people to make weapons. European settlers used the wood for wharf piles, tool handles, wheel spokes and fencing. Kanuka provides excellent firewood, burning with great heat.

Fig 3 Kanuka bark.

Fig 4 Branch showing the leaves and flowers. Hinakura, December 1969.

Fig 5 Close-up of the flowers and leaves in Fig 4. Note the thickness of the leaves. Three times natural size.

Leptospermum scoparium
Manuka/Tea tree

Manuka is found all over New Zealand, from sea level to about 1,000 m, and on the Chatham Islands. It often forms extensive areas of scrub that protect regenerating forest seedlings and form a shelter for native orchids and other small plants. Known north of Auckland as kahikatoa, *L. scoparium* grows either as a shrub of varying form and habit or as a tree up to 4 m high with spreading ascending branches.

The branchlets and young leaves are clothed with whitish silky hairs and when crushed or broken are strongly aromatic. The flowers usually arise singly in the axils of the leaves and are about 12 mm across. Manuka bark is stringy, peeling in long flakes very similar to that of kanuka, *L. ericoides* (shown in Fig 3 on page 161).

Manuka wood is red-coloured, hard and durable. It has been used for fencing and for tool handles, and it is much prized as a firewood, burning with a fierce heat.

L. scoparium is often called the tea tree. A "tea" drink was made from manuka leaves by Captain Cook's men and by the early settlers; the name tea tree was given to the tree by Cook. The Maori people used it as a medicinal plant. Decoctions made of the leaves were used to reduce fever and treat colds; preparations of the bark were used as sedatives.

2

3

Fig 1 A very tall manuka tree in flower. Photographed at Woodside Gorge, December 1969.

Fig 2 Branchlets showing leaf arrangement and the fine silky pubescence on the young stems and buds.

Fig 3 Underside of leaves showing aromatic glands and pungent tips. The small subsessile leaves are 4—12 mm long and up to 4 mm wide. They are narrowly lanceolate or ovate in shape and are fairly thick and leathery.

Fig 4 A spreading manuka tree near Awakeri Springs, September 1976.

Fig 5 A spray of manuka in flower. Flowers are borne in great profusion, smothering the tree with white so that a hillside of manuka in flower can look as if it is covered by a thin coating of snow during some summer months.

Fig 6 This close-up photograph of flowers and buds shows the delicate nature of the flower, its whiteness and the ring of coloured anthers surrounding the green pistil. The silky hairs of the young leaves show clearly on those immediately above the large open flower. Lake Pounui, December 1968. This specimen has been photographed at about two and a half times its natural size.

1

4

5

Fig 7 Manuka seed capsules showing their five-valved structure. Seeds take at least one year to mature and are liberated by rupture of the hard woody capsule along the sutures between the valves. After the release of the seeds the capsule may remain on the tree for several years before falling. Hinakura, July 1973. Twice natural size.

Fig 8 A popular horticultural variety, "Martini", photographed at Otari, September 1968. Four and a half times natural size. Horticulturally-raised manuka varieties include a wide range of flower colours ranging from deep red to crimson and purple. Flower forms are both single and double. Wild manuka flowers from October to April but many horticultural varieties flower most of the year.

Fig 9 Close-up of a pink-coloured flower from a wild tree. Hinakura, December 1969. It was from pink forms such as this that the beautiful garden varieties were developed. Three and a half times natural size.

6

7

8

9

Lophomyrtus bullata
Ramarama

Family *Myrtaceae*

Genus *Lophomyrtus:* A small genus endemic to New Zealand. It contains two species of small trees.

A shrub or a small tree up to 6 m high found in coastal and lowland forests up to 600 m above sea level throughout the North Island and in the Nelson and Marlborough districts of the South Island. The plant grows in shade or full sunlight, preferring open parts of the forest and forest margins, where its leaves colour up more strongly. The ramarama tree is readily recognised by its blistered, reddish-coloured leaves, which are usually broadly ovate in shape and oppositely arranged. The small leaves are thick and leathery, up to 30 mm long by 15 mm wide, on petioles 2 – 5 mm long. The single white or very pale pink flowers arise singly on woolly peduncles in the axils of the leaves. Their sepals and petals are dotted with very small glands and hairs.

A decoction made from the leaves of ramarama was used by the Maori people for the treatment of bruises on the body.

Ramarama will grow into a handsome shrub if it is treated as a specimen and grown in the open. It hybridises freely with rohutu *(L. obcordata* — see following page), producing attractive natural hybrids that have been developed by nurserymen into striking horticultural varieties. *L. ralphii* var. *purpurea,* for example, one of the most common of these hybrids, has leaves of a deep bronze-purple and is a fine shrub.

1

2

Fig 1 The underside of the leaf showing the tomentum along the midvein and along some of the side veins. Natural size.

Fig 2 Upper side of a leaf showing the blistered appearance, shining surface and petiole. Twice natural size.

Fig 3 A spray showing the typical red-blotched leaves and their arrangement. Young stems and petioles are hairy. Taupo, October 1965.

3

4

Fig 4 Spray of foliage from inside a dense forest; the green and yellow-green leaves show very little red blotching. The berries are at various stages. Taupo, June 1964.

Fig 5 A small tree in a gleam of sunlight inside the Maungatukutuku Valley forest, March 1976. The leaves of this tree were almost entirely yellow-green with very little red blotching.

Fig 6 Ramarama flower buds starting to open. Taupo, January 1974. This photograph shows clearly the hairs on the peduncles, receptacles and sepals, and the glands in the petals. Pictured here at about two and a half times natural size.

Fig 7 A close-up of a flower showing the style, the characteristic cluster of stamens and the hairy fringe to the petals. Taupo, January 1974. Three times natural size.

Fig 8 After pollination most parts of the flower fall off, leaving these strange looking structures which grow into berries during the following twelve months. The ripe berry is ovoid in shape and dark red to black in colour. Also photographed at Taupo in January 1971.

5

6

7

8

Lophomyrtus obcordata
Rohutu

A forest and scrubland shrub or tree with thin, often upright, clustered branches. This tree will hybridise spontaneously with *L. bullata* (previous page) whenever the two species grow together; some interesting natural hybrids result.

The small obcordate leaves, 5−10 mm long and wide, are dotted with glands and arranged in opposite pairs or in clusters. The perfect flowers arise singly in the axils of the leaves. The young branchlets, leaf midveins and leaf undersides are hairy.

Rohutu is found throughout the North and South Islands, growing from Mangonui southwards from sea level to 1,050 m in coastal and lowland forests.

1

2

3

5

4

6

Fig 1 Two trees growing together at Ponatahi, September 1968.

Fig 2 Leaf upper surface. Two and a half times natural size.

Fig 3 Ripe berry and thick, leathery leaves. Two and a half times natural size.

Fig 4 Leaf undersides. Two and a half times natural size.

Fig 5 The bark of *L. obcordata*.

Fig 6 The flowers, 6 mm across, are borne on slender hairy pedicels up to 20 mm long. Rotorua, December, 1965. Slightly above natural size.

Family *Myrtaceae*

Genus *Neomyrtus:* An endemic New Zealand genus which contains only one species, *N. pedunculata.*

Neomyrtus pedunculata
Rohutu

A shrub or small tree up to 6 m high. *N. pedunculata* has four-angled branchlets which are hairy only when young. The perfect flowers, about 6 mm across, are on long pedicels up to 15 mm long from which the berries later hang. The leaves are of two shapes: obovate-oblong and 15–20 mm long by 10–15 mm, or obovate and 6–15 mm long by 4–10 mm wide. They are all thick and leathery, with rolled or thickened margins, dotted with glands. The petioles are without hairs and are up to 4 mm long.

N. pedunculata occurs all over New Zealand from Kaitaia to Stewart Island, growing from sea level to 1,050 m, mostly along forest margins and in scrub.

2

3

4

5

6

Fig 1 Small tree on the edge of forest in the Waipunga Gorge, December 1974.

Fig 2 The flowers of *N. pedunculata* occur in profusion, arising from the axils of the leaves. Makarora Valley, January 1973. Four times natural size.

Figs 3, 4 Berries with upper (Fig 3) and lower (Fig 4) leaf surfaces. Waipunga Gorge, April 1974. Twice natural size.

Fig 5 The bark of *N. pedunculata.*

Fig 6 Branchlet showing the four-angled form and rather unusual rounded leaf undersides. Makarora Valley, January 1973. Three times natural size.

Family *Myrtaceae*

Genus *Syzygium:* A very large genus of 1,000 species of trees and shrubs found mainly in tropical and subtropical parts of the world. It is best known for the clove tree, *S. caryophyllus.* There is one endemic species in New Zealand.

1

Syzygium maire
Maire tawaki

A handsome tree up to 15 m high with a spreading canopy formed from many branches. Maire tawaki occurs in lowland swampy and boggy forests from sea level to 450 m throughout the North Island. It is also found on the northern tip of the South Island. A characteristic of this tree is that it can grow in very wet ground, even with free water around it, and if the swamp or bog is drained the tree dies within one or two years.

The smooth-barked trunk is up to 60 cm in diameter. The leaves arise opposite in pairs and are elliptic-oblong, somewhat sinuate and undulate, on slender petioles about 8 – 10 mm long. They are often marked by small blisters and dark patches, and taper at each end. The sexes are usually together on the same tree. The flowers, each about 12 mm across, are borne in many-flowered cymes which may be 8 – 10 mm across. A true myrtle always bears its flowers singly on separate stalks, and its fruit contains several seeds, but *Syzygium* flowers are in clusters on single stalks with one seed in each fruit.

The fruit is a berry about 12 mm in diameter with a single seed and a hard outer coating. The flowers occur during autumn and the berry is ripe twelve months later in the following autumn. The brittle wood of the tree makes excellent firewood.

3

4

Fig 1 A typical leaf of *S. maire* showing the upper surface. This specimen at twice natural size.

Fig 2 Lower surface of a typical leaf, showing the stout petiole and midvein. Twice natural size.

Fig 3 A fine maire tawaki in flower growing in typical fashion on the edge of a swamp near Lake Pounui. Photographed in March 1975.

Fig 4 A branchlet showing the four-angled form and arrangement of the leaves. Some of these leaves show the blisters and dark blotching which often occurs on the leaves of this tree.

2

5

Fig 5 A small grove of *S. maire* trees in a swamp near Waikanae, March 1978.

Fig 6 Close-up of a flower showing the stamens ringing the nectar cup with the style in the centre. This flower is one of seven in the cyme borne on a single stalk. The flower at the top is opening and the petals are falling off. Both the sepals and the petals of these flowers fall off before the flower is fully open. Lake Pounui, March 1971. This specimen reproduced at about natural size.

Fig 7 Spring growth of young leaves. Note the olive-green shoot with tiny new leaves. Lake Pounui, November 1973. About natural size.

6

7

8

Fig 8 A cyme with many flowers showing how the flowers make a more or less flat spray across their tops. The small pink petals and green sepals still remain on some of the buds in this cyme. Lake Pounui, March 1974. The specimen in this photograph is reproduced here at about half natural size.

Fig 9 The characteristically smooth bark of *S. maire*.

Fig 10 The tree's brilliant berries each hold one seed. The structure at the apex of each berry is the remains of the calyx. Lake Pounui, March 1977. This photograph is one and three-quarters natural size.

9

10

Entelea arborescens
Whau

Family *Tiliaceae:* A family of tropical and temperate zone trees and shrubs containing forty-one genera and about 400 species. They are found mainly in South America, Africa and South-east Asia with a few species in Australasia. The best-known species are the limes and lindens of the genus *Tilia,* the African rumslind tree, *Sparmannia africana,* and the jute trees, *Corchorus capsularis* of India and *C. olitorius* of Africa, producers of commercial fibres.

Genus *Entelea:* An endemic New Zealand genus containing one species, *E. arborescens.*

With its large, bright-green, soft leaves, large white flowers and extraordinary fruits, whau is an attractive New Zealand tree with an unusual, almost tropical appearance.

Whau forms a canopy tree up to 6 m high but also grows as a shrub. It has a trunk up to 25 cm in diameter and a soft, pitted bark. In warmer districts the tree will grow with great luxuriance, and on off-shore islands such as the Three Kings and Cuvier can produce leaves up to 60 cm long. Normally the leaves are 15−25 cm long by 15−20 cm wide on petioles about 20 cm long. Whau occurs in coastal and lowland forest, from sea level to 250 m, from the Three Kings Islands south to Raglan and the Bay of Plenty, and then spasmodically south to Queen Charlotte Sound, Nelson and Golden Bay. It is usually found in coastal areas in sheltered gullies and along the bases of cliffs.

The branchlets, young leaves and flower sprays are clothed with soft, branched hairs. The large white flowers, which are bisexual, arise in large, flat clusters from the leaf axils towards the tips of the branchlets.

The distinctive fruit is a large capsule covered with spines rather like bidibid burrs. Whau is the only New Zealand tree to have its fruits thus encapsulated.

Fig 1 A whau tree growing out from the base of a cliff near the Mokau River mouth. December 1973.

Fig 2 The leaf upper surface, showing the prominent venation, serrated margins and long petiole. About one quarter natural size.

Fig 3 Leaf lower surface with its prominent raised veins. Whau leaves always droop. Also about one quarter natural size.

Fig 4 A whau tree in full flower near the Mokau River mouth in October 1965.

Fig 5 The mature seed capsules occur as broad, flat clusters raised upright above the leaves at the branch tips. Mokau River, December 1965. Each capsule is about 2 cm across.

Fig 6 The distinctive seed capsules, opening to show their seeds. Lake Pounui, February 1961. A little less than natural size.

Fig 7 Whau's soft, pustulate (blistered) bark.

4

Fig 8 The large white flowers are about 2.5 cm across; their petals nearly always have the crinkled appearance shown here. From a tree at Otari, November 1965.

Fig 9 A closer view. Lake Pounui, November 1972. Twice natural size.

5

7

6

8

9

Family *Elaeocarpaceae:* A tropical and subtropical family containing twelve genera and 350 species of trees and shrubs mainly from tropical Asia and America. Of the two genera appearing in New Zealand *Elaeocarpus* contains 200 species and *Aristotelia* five.

Genus *Aristotelia:* A genus of five species of shrubs or small trees with one species found in each of Chile, Peru, eastern Australia and Tasmania, with two in New Zealand. The New Zealand species are both endemic, one being a tree and the other a shrub.

Aristotelia serrata
Wineberry/Makomako

One of the graceful small trees of our forests, forest margins and roadsides, occurring throughout New Zealand from sea level to 1,050 m. Wineberry is usually the first tree to appear in clearings after slips or tree felling, when it forms dense thickets. In cold districts it is deciduous but in warmer areas it often retains some foliage during winter.

The tree reaches 10 m high with a trunk 30 cm through. The bark of young branchlets is red; that of old wood is black. The deeply serrated leaves are membranous and translucent and often reddish in colour below. They are up to 12 cm long and 8 cm wide on slender pubescent petioles up to 5 cm long.

3

1

2

Fig 1 A wineberry tree at the side of the road at Haast Pass, January 1971.

Fig 2 Tall wineberry trees reaching for the light on the Akatarawa Road, November 1970. Wineberry trees lining roadsides often have this tall, slender form.

Fig 3 The upperside of a leaf showing the long petiole, broad ovate-cordate shape and prominent veins. A feature of wineberry leaves is that leaf shapes can vary between trees and even on the same tree.

Fig 4 Underside of an ovate leaf showing pubescent petiole and veins.

4 5

Fig 5 Male flowers showing their pubescent pedicels; female flowers are similar but without stamens. Otari, October 1970. Three times natural size. Wineberry's male and female flowers occur on separate trees and are borne on panicles up to 10 cm long.

Fig 6 Bark of the trunk. Wineberry bark has medicinal qualities; soaked in water it makes an infusion that relieves sore eyes.

Fig 7 A branch with panicles of male flowers showing the variation in colour that occurs. The flowers, pale on first opening, darken steadily with age. The flower colour can vary on different trees. Photographed at Akatarawa, November 1965.

Fig 8 A wineberry spray with female flowers showing the opposite arrangement of the leaves. Also photographed at Akatarawa, November 1965.

Fig 9 Panicles of ripe berries. Waima Ure River Gorge, March 1969. The berries are deep red to almost black and about 5 mm in diameter.

6 7

8 9

Family *Elaeocarpaceae*

Genus *Elaeocarpus:* This genus has two species endemic to New Zealand, with a further 198 species distributed over eastern Asia, Indomalaysia, Australia and some Pacific islands.

Elaeocarpus hookerianus
Pokaka

A canopy-forming tree which passes through very distinctive juvenile stages during its growth from a seedling. The juvenile is characterised by twisting, interlacing branches which bear scattered obovate to narrow-linear leaves with coarse, saw-like teeth along their margins. The juvenile tends to be rather sprawling, but after a few years the main stem of the future tree grows out from the top and gives rise to adult leaves. The juvenile stage often persists on the lower part of the tree for many years. The lower adult leaves may be toothed and lobed for years before the tree assumes its full adult form.

The mature tree grows up to 12 m tall with greyish-white bark and a trunk up to 1 m through. It occurs from Mangonui southwards to Stewart Island in forest and scrub from sea level to 1,050 m. The leaves are alternate on stout petioles; they have a prominent midvein and crenate or bluntly serrate margins. The perfect flowers are borne on slender racemes, each on a peduncle about 1 cm long. The fruit is an ovoid drupe about 18 mm long. The wood of the pokaka tree is tough and strong.

Pokaka seedlings often appear in quite large numbers after virgin bush has been cut over for timber.

1

2

Fig 1 The interlacing branches of pokaka's juvenile stage clearly showing the saw-toothed leaves of varying shapes and sizes.

Fig 2 Branchlet of pokaka showing the leaf arrangement and crenate to serrate leaves.

Fig 3 The mature tree. A pokaka in flower at Hinakura, November 1970.

3

Fig 4 Underside of a pokaka leaf, showing strong midvein and the narrow-oblong leaf shape. Pokaka leaves are leathery, lanceolate in shape and acute or obtuse. They are 3 – 11 cm long and 1 – 3 cm wide. Natural size.

Fig 5 Upper surface of a broad-lanceolate leaf. Pokaka leaves are grouped mostly towards the tips of branches. Natural size.

Fig 6 The juvenile tree. This is a small, sprawling seedling with one layer of interlacing branches near the ground and a second layer developing near the top of the stem. As the seedling grows it becomes more tangled but it tends to preserve this layered effect. Opepe Bush, September 1976.

7

8

9

10

Fig 7 The bark of an old pokaka tree growing in Peel Forest. It was photographed in January 1966.

Fig 8 Looking upwards at a raceme of pokaka flowers, which hang downwards from their stalks. Photographed at Hinakura in November 1970. Pokaka flowers are perfect.

Fig 9 The purplish ripe drupe of pokaka, at Hinakura, March 1966. The drupe takes about five to six months to ripen fully. Reproduced at slightly over three times natural size.

Fig 10 A close view of some of the flowers illustrated in Fig 8. This photograph shows clearly the pokaka flower's greenish sepals and creamy-yellow lobed petals; the anthers have terminal pores for shedding pollen. The flower at top left is displaying a green ovary. Hinakura, November 1970. Four times natural size.

175

Elaeocarpus dentatus
Hinau

A fine canopy tree up to 18 m high with a trunk up to 1 m through. Hinau occurs all over both the North and South Islands in lowland forest from sea level to 600 m. It passes through a juvenile stage which has narrow leaves 10—15 cm long with wavy margins.

The leaves are about 12 cm long and 2—3 cm wide. They arise on stout petioles 25 mm long borne at the tips of the branchlets. The glorious flowers droop from long racemes arising from the leaf axils or direct from the branches. Hinau's fruit is a purple, ovoid drupe, up to 18 mm long; it has a kernel like an olive which was used by the Maori people to make a floury meal which was baked and eaten as a bread.

1

Fig 1 This lovely hinau tree in full flower grows at the head of the Reikorangi Valley. December 1977.

Fig 2 Racemes of hinau flowers arising from leaf axils on the branchlet. Each flower is borne on a silky-hairy peduncle about 1 cm long; the flowers vary between 8 and 15 mm across. From a tree at Karaka Bay, November 1965.

Fig 3 The hairy sepals of hinau flowers can just be seen in this close view. Otari, November 1969. Almost twice natural size.

Fig 4 The upper surface of a hinau leaf with its long petiole. Natural size.

Fig 5 The leaf lower surface. Two pits (domatia) are visible just above the centre. Also natural size.

Fig 6 Hinau bark.

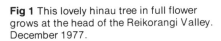

2

3

4

5

6

Hoheria populnea
Lacebark/Houhere

Family *Malvaceae:* An extensive family of herbs, shrubs and trees comprising about eighty genera and 1,000 species spread over the tropical and subtropical parts of the world. It includes such well-known plants as *Abutilon* and *Hibiscus*, the marsh mallow *(Althea officinalis)*, the tree mallow *(Lavatera arborea)* and several important economic plants such as cotton *(Gossypium)* and *Abutilon avicennae*, Chinese jute. Three genera, *Hibiscus, Hoheria* and *Plagianthus*, occur in New Zealand.

Genus *Hoheria:* A genus of five species endemic to New Zealand. They are commonly referred to as lacebarks or ribbonwoods.

A graceful, erect, much-branched, rather poplar-like tree which grows up to 11 m high and is one of our most attractive native specimens. In the autumn, so smothered with its white flowers that its leaves are almost concealed, it is a beautiful sight.

The common name of lacebark derives from the pattern of the bark. The tree's bark is tough and made up of several layers, the inner ones being pierced by outgrowths from the inner wood which form a lace-like pattern. In pioneering days the inner bark of *Hoheria* species was much used for ornamental trimming on baskets, women's hats and so on. Because of its strength it was also used for cordage by some early settlers.

H. populnea branchlets are slender, clothed with a pale bark and grooved. The serrate-margined leaves, up to 14 cm long by 6 cm wide, are on slender petioles up to 2 cm long. The somewhat leathery leaves vary in shape from broad ovate or ovate-lanceolate to elliptic. Juvenile plants of this tree display divaricating, more or less entangled branchlets which bear smaller leaves up to 3 cm long on delicate petioles up to 1 cm long. *H. populnea* is sometimes semi-deciduous, becoming nearly bare in late winter.

The flowers are perfect and are borne in great profusion either singly or in cymose clusters in the axils of the leaves. They are strongly and quite delightfully scented. The odd-looking winged fruits consist of five seed cases each with a single seed arranged as wings around a central axis.

H. populnea is found as a natural wild plant only in the North Island, from North Cape to the Waikato and Bay of Plenty, growing from sea level to 450 m. It is the only species of *Hoheria* which grows wild from Kaitaia to North Cape. It has become one of the most popular of our native trees and so many beautiful cultivars have been developed from it that the tree can now be found almost anywhere in the country.

1

Fig 1 (previous page) The beautiful flowers of *H. populnea*. From a tree at Karaka Bay, March 1966. Slightly less than natural size.

Fig 2 A fine specimen tree of *H. populnea* growing in the Waipahihi Reserve, Taupo. May 1973.

Fig 3 Section of branchlet and leaf petiole; note the groove in the side of the branchlet. This specimen at one and a half times natural size.

Fig 4 Bark from a young tree.

Fig 5 Bark from an old tree.

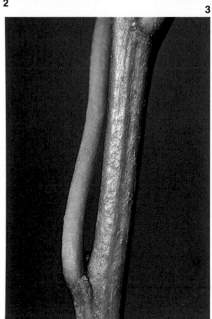

Fig 6 *H. populnea* flowers with distinctive purple-coloured stamens and styles are known to occur occasionally on certain trees. These were from a tree at Otari in March 1961. About natural size.

Fig 7 The leaf upper surface, showing the vein pattern and the shiny surface. From a tree at Kaitaia. About natural size.

Fig 8 Lower leaf surface, displaying the vein pattern more closely. The leaves are usually acuminate at the apex and either rounded, truncate or subcordate at the base. Also from Kaitaia. About natural size.

Fig 9 Close view of the beautiful flower of this tree. Kaitaia, April 1979. Here at about twice natural size. The peduncles and sepals are clothed with star-like hairs which are normal and also occur on young new growth. There are five carpels.

Fig 10 Branch bearing the unusually shaped ripe fruits. The seeds are encased in the wings. The fruits of some other *Hoheria* species are similar, but in others the wings are obscure or absent. This photograph is about natural size.

Fig 11 Branchlet showing the alternate leaf arrangement and flower buds arising from the leaf axils. Karaka Bay, 1966.

Fig 12 One of the many variegated foliage cultivars developed from this tree. This variety is *H. populnea* 'Variegata'. Some ten cultivars have been developed, many of which make outstanding garden specimens and have become very popular.

ATTRACTIVE NEW GARDEN FORMS

Among the beautiful new garden varieties of this tree are H. populnea 'Alba Variegata', which has creamy-white margins to its dark-green leaves, and 'Purpurea', whose leaves have deep-purplish lower surfaces. Stamen colours also vary in these cultivars.

179

Hoheria sexstylosa
Long-leaved lacebark/Houhere

The long-leaved lacebark is readily distinguished from *H. populnea* by its longer, very deeply toothed, lanceolate leaves and denser clothing of star-like hairs on the younger stems and the flower heads. This persists, although more sparsely, on the older stems of the plant. *H. sexstylosa* itself is an erect, much-branching canopy tree, up to 6 m tall; the tree's foliage has a tendency to droop.

The sweet-scented, abundant flowers are bisexual, either single or in cymose clusters from leaf axils. There are six to seven carpels in each flower; this distinguishes them from *populnea* flowers, which usually have only five carpels.

A variety of *H. sexstylosa,* var. *ovata,* is quite common. The leaves are rather like those of *populnea,* but there are from five to eight carpellate flowers. There is a juvenile stage of tangled branches which are yellowish in colour with small leaves.

H. sexstylosa grows in forests and forest margins from Whangarei south to Nelson; it is also known from Banks Peninsula and near Gore. The variety *ovata* occurs from north-west Nelson to Greymouth.

2

3

4

5

6

7

8

9

Fig 1 Branchlet showing the alternate leaf arrangement and pubescent tip. Notice the irregularly serrate leaf margins.

Fig 2 Specimen tree growing at Flat Point, Wairarapa. March 1973.

Fig 3 A large dome-shaped specimen of *H. sexstylosa* var. *ovata* growing above Karaka Bay, Wellington, March 1965. The tree is in flower.

Fig 4 This is a very fine old specimen of *H. sexstylosa,* growing on a forest margin near the Moawhango River, April 1969.

Fig 5 Characteristic star-like hairs on a young branchlet. About one and a half times natural size.

Fig 6 Upper surface of fresh leaves and the tip of their branchlet showing occasional hairs on the leaves and a heavy clothing of star-like hairs on the branchlet and petioles. Leaves are up to 15 cm long and 5 cm wide; illustrated here at about half natural size.

Fig 7 Leaf lower surface, showing the vein pattern and the star-like hairs on petioles and midveins. This specimen also at about half natural size.

Fig 8 Juvenile leaves, at about natural size. They reach a length of 15 mm, rarely 25 mm.

Fig 9 *H. sexstylosa* flowers, photographed at Mt Holdsworth, March 1966. Here about natural size. The flowers are produced in great abundance along the branchlets.

Fig 10 Close view of the sweetly scented flower, clearly showing the six styles. Hukutaia Domain, January 1974. Three times natural size.

Fig 11 Close view of the flowers and buds of the variety *ovata,* showing the six styles with their typical pink colouration. Note the hairs on the pedicels and sepals. Karaka Bay, Wellington, March 1970. Three times natural size.

The fruits of *H. sexstylosa* are similar to those of *H. populnea.*

10

11

Hoheria lyalli
H. glabrata
Mountain ribbonwoods

1 ——————————————————————————————————— 2

Two small, spreading, deciduous trees, *H. lyalli* growing up to 6 m tall and *H. glabrata* to 10 m. They are found on forest margins, stream terraces and shrubland between 600 m and 1,050 m in the mountains of the South Island. *H. lyalli* occurs mainly on the dry eastern slopes of the divide and *H. glabrata* generally on the wetter western slopes. Some recent opinion seems to identify only one species, *H. lyalli*, but this tree differs in having its parts rather more densely clothed with star-like hairs than *H. glabrata*.

3
5

4
6
7

Fig 1 *H. glabrata* leaf upper surface. The leaf petiole of this species is longer than that of *H. lyalli*. About natural size.

Fig 2 *H. lyalli* leaf lower surface. The leaves of both species are alternate, though almost opposite. This specimen also about natural size.

Fig 3 The flowers of *H. glabrata* are each 4 cm across. Franz Josef, January 1969.

Fig 4 A specimen of *H. lyalli* growing at Arthurs Pass, January 1967.

Fig 5 A fine tree of *H. glabrata* in flower. It was growing on the west side of Lewis Pass in 1970.

Fig 6 A close view of a flower of *H. lyalli* showing how the branchlets and flower stalks of this tree are densely clothed with star-like hairs. There is a paucity of such hairs on *H. glabrata*, suggesting a clear point of difference between the two species. One and a half times natural size.

Fig 7 The distinctive bark of *H. glabrata*. That of *H. lyalli* is very similar.

Hoheria angustifolia
Narrow-leaved lacebark

1

A slender, spreading tree up to 10 m tall, growing from sea level to 900 m along forest margins, sometimes forming groves, from Taranaki southwards through the South Island. *H. angustifolia* passes through a juvenile stage when it is a bushy shrub with interlacing, flexible branchlets with small leaves up to 8 mm long by 7 mm wide on slender petioles 1– 2 mm long. Adult leaves are up to 3 cm long by 1 cm wide with petioles up to 5 mm long. *H. angustifolia* is smothered in white flowers when in full bloom.

Fig 1 A specimen of *H. angustifolia* growing at Peel Forest, Canterbury, in January 1967. The tree is in flower.

Fig 2 Leaf spray showing the paler leaf lower surfaces and the leaf petioles. Notice the prominent serrations.

Fig 3 A leaf spray from *H. angustifolia* juvenile stage illustrating the different shapes of the juvenile leaves.

Fig 4 The attractive white flowers. Flower buds and the darker-green, more shining leaf upper surfaces are also shown. Peel Forest, January 1966.

Fig 5 Close view of a flower at three and a half times natural size. There are five styles to each flower, and the pedicels and sepals are hairy. From Hukutaia Domain, January 1974.

Fig 6 Fruits in the early stages of their formation with the wings just apparent. From a tree at Hukutaia Domain, December 1973.

2

3

4

5

6

Family *Malvaceae*

Genus *Plagianthus:* A genus of fifteen species of trees and shrubs confined to Australia and New Zealand. The two New Zealand species, one a shrub and the other a tree, are both endemic.

Plagianthus regius
Manatu/Ribbonwood

Manatu is the largest of the New Zealand deciduous trees. When it is in flower its large inflorescences give the tree an attractive lime-green appearance. The male tree is the more spectacular.

It is a medium-to-large, heavy-branched tree up to 15 m tall with a trunk up to 1 m through. The young growing tree passes through a bushy juvenile stage of tough, interlacing, springy branches with small, irregularly lobed or crenate-serrate, soft, broadly ovate, ovate-lanceolate or rounded leaves, up to 20 cm long by 15 mm wide, on petioles 5 mm long. Adult trees can often show reversion shoots towards the juvenile stage, and generally the juvenile stage persists near ground level after the tree has become adult.

The adult leaves are on petioles up to 3 cm long and are up to 7.5 cm long by 5 cm wide. They vary in shape from ovate to ovate-lanceolate or broadly ovate; they have an acuminate tip and coarsely but not sharply serrate-crenate margins. They are not unlike *Hoheria sextylosa* in overall appearance, but they are softer and not as shining.

The flowers, which are usually unisexual, tend to be on separate trees but may be together. Only 3—4 mm in diameter, they occur in large, drooping, paniculate cymes. Male flowers are yellowish, the females green and smaller. Manatu flowers from October to January.

The wood has no commercial use. Manatu was known by the Tuhoe Maori people as houhi onga onga, or simply houhi, since they believed it grew out of the tree nettle, ongaonga. The tree's bark is similar to that of the *Hoherias*.

The tree is found somewhat locally from Mangonui southwards throughout the North and South Islands, Stewart Island and the Chatham Islands. It grows on riverbanks and on alluvial terraces in coastal and lowland forest margins from sea level to 450 m.

Fig 1 Lower surface of a manatu leaf. About natural size.

Fig 2 Leaf upper surface, showing the blunt marginal serrations. Also about natural size.

5

6

7

Fig 3 A beautiful specimen of manatu with new spring foliage at Waiorongomai, November 1969. This tree's heavy-branching habit is clearly illustrated.

Fig 4 A tree changing to the adult form. In this photograph the remains of the juvenile stage can be clearly seen clinging around the centre of the trunk and at its base at ground level. This tree was growing in the Waipahihi Reserve, Taupo. Photographed in November 1978.

Fig 5 The bark of manatu is very rough. On old trees it is often discoloured by lichens and a sooty fungus. The tough, strong, inner layers were used by the Maori people to make a rope from which they fashioned nets for fishing.

Fig 6 Male flowers close up to show the arrangement of the sepals, petals and stamens. Barton's Bush, Hutt Valley, October 1968. Manatu flowers are small, only 3 — 4 mm across; these specimens are at six times natural size.

Fig 7 The abundant flowers are borne on long, paniculate cymes that hang down from the branches. Trentham, October 1965. These are male flowers, which are more yellowish in colour than the female. Male cymes are up to 25 cm long, but female cymes are shorter.

Fig 8 Female flowers after pollination, with the carpels swelling to form the fruit. Lake Pounui, December 1974. Seven times natural size.

8

Fig 9 Sprays of female flowers with fruits forming. The ovoid, pointed fruit of this tree is 3 — 5 mm long and sits in a persistant cup formed by the sepals. The seed contained in each carpel is solitary. In male flowers of the ribbonwood the ovary is vestigal; in female flowers the anthers are abortive. This specimen was photographed at Trentham Park in November 1965.

9

Family *Cunoniaceae:* A family of trees and shrubs containing twenty-six genera and 250 species found mainly in the Southern Hemisphere temperate zone.

Genus *Weinmannia:* Contains 170 species found in Madagascar, Malaysia, the Philippines, Mexico, the West Indies, Chile and New Zealand. With species in Mexico, the West Indies and the Philippines, *Weinmannia* is the only genus of the Cunoniaceae that extends into the Northern Hemisphere. The two New Zealand species are endemic.

Weinmannia racemosa/Kamahi
W. silvicola/Tawhero/Towhai

These are two closely related trees. Kamahi forms a spreading tree up to 25 m high with a trunk up to 1.2 m through; it grows in lowland forests from sea level to 900 m, from Auckland to Stewart Island. Tawhero forms a canopy tree up to 15 m high with a trunk 1 m through; it grows in forest and along forest margins from Mangonui to the Waikato and Bay of Plenty.

Adult kamahi leaves are simple, 3—10 cm long by 2—4 cm wide, on petioles up to 2 cm long; they are leathery, elliptic to broad-ovate in shape and bluntly serrate. Adult leaves of tawhero are compound, three to five-foliate but occasionally simple, the leaflets thick and leathery; the leaves are 4—7 cm long by 2—3 cm wide, elliptic to obovate-oblong in shape.

Both trees produce racemes of flowers in profusion, the trees appearing smothered in bloom during late spring, summer and autumn. Kamahi passes through a juvenile stage which can last for years; this stage, which even flowers, has compound leaves of three leaflets. Tawhero also has a juvenile stage; the leaves consist of up to ten pairs of leaflets.

The wood is light coloured and although strong is not very durable if exposed to the weather. Kamahi timber has, however, been used for sleepers and piles, for house construction and for fence posts.

Fig 1 Racemes of kamahi flower buds. Their red stalks and pedicels impart a warm glow to the tree in late spring. At Kauaeranga Valley, December 1979.

Fig 2 Close view of kamahi flowers. From Akatarawa, November 1970. At three times natural size.

Fig 3 The undersurface of a kamahi leaf is light coloured with a distinct vein pattern. Natural size.

Fig 4 Branchlet showing the opposite leaf arrangement. Young new leaves are reddish-coloured and popular for floral art.

Fig 5 Kamahi bark is greyish, blotched with white, and is relatively smooth.

Fig 6 This fine specimen of a kamahi tree just coming into flower was growing on top of the Waitaanga Saddle, near Ohura, in December 1973.

Fig 7 Upper surface of a kamahi leaf showing its rather thick and leathery texture. At natural size.

7

6

Fig 8 Racemes of kamahi flowers obscure the leaves when in full bloom. Akatarawa, in November 1970. Each raceme is up to 12 cm long.

Fig 9 Kamahi flowers and fruits forming on older racemes. Pahiatua, December 1965. One quarter natural size. Like the flower buds, the fruits are reddish-coloured and when ripe impart a pleasant red glow to the tree.

Fig 10 A tree of tawhero in full flower at Mangamaku Gorge, January 1970. Not all tawhero trees form such a fine rounded canopy; many are more erect with ascending branches.

Fig 11 Branchlet of tawhero showing three, four and five foliolate leaves. The young branchlets, petioles, peduncles and pedicels are pubescent.

Fig 12 Racemes of tawhero flowers. Kauaeranga Valley, January 1974. The racemes are 8 – 12 cm long.

Fig 13 Close view of the flowers in Fig 12; in this photograph they are magnified to six times natural size.

8

9

10

11

12   13

Family *Cunoniaceae*

Genus *Caldcluvia:* A genus of 12 species found in South America, Australia, Malaysia, New Guinea and New Zealand where one species is endemic.

Caldcluvia rosaefolia
Makamaka

Makamaka is found in lowland forest only between Kaitaia and Whangarei and is best seen today in the Waipoua Forest Sanctuary.

It is a small spreading tree growing up to 12 m tall with a trunk up to 60 cm through. With its light-green leaves, *C. rosaefolia* is quite a handsome tree, especially when grown as an isolated specimen. The branchlets, petioles, young leaves and panicle stalks are coated with short light-brown or whitish hairs. The pinnate leaves are similar to those of *Weinmannia sylvicola*, especially its juvenile form, but with sharper teeth. *C. rosaefolia* passes through a juvenile stage in which the leaves have six to ten pairs of leaflets and are up to 25 cm long.

The small flowers, which are crowded together on much-branched panicles, are either female or bisexual with both forms of flower sometimes occurring together on the same tree. In flower it is so smothered with flowers that the leaves can scarcely be seen.

1

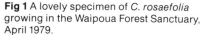

Fig 1 A lovely specimen of *C. rosaefolia* growing in the Waipoua Forest Sanctuary, April 1979.

Fig 2 Panicles of flowers and buds. From a tree growing at Otari, October 1965.

Fig 3 The leaf upper surface. Adult makamaka leaves have three to five pairs of leaflets and a terminal leaflet larger than the lateral ones. The terminal leaflet is 4 – 7 cm long. Note the small foliaceous stipules at the base of the petiole. This specimen at half natural size.

Fig 4 Undersurface of a leaf showing the venation, hairy rachis and midveins. The leaves of makamaka are sharply serrate, in contrast to the bluntly serrate leaves of the closely related *Weinmannia sylvicola*. A further difference in the leaf forms of the two trees is that makamaka leaflets tend to diminish in size from the leaf tip towards the leaf base. Half natural size.

Fig 5 A fine young makamaka tree pushes towards the light in the bush at Hukutaia Domain, January 1974.

Fig 6 The dark, pustulate (blistered) bark of *C. rosaefolia.*

Fig 7 Makamaka flowers in great abundance. As this photograph clearly shows, in full flower the tree presents such a mass of white to pinkish-coloured flowers that the leaves are concealed. Otari, October 1963.

2

Fig 8 Close-up of the flowers, also showing the hairs of the panicle stalk. The flowers here, most if not all of which are perfect, are at different stages of opening. Sometimes female and perfect flowers of this tree actually occur on the same panicle, which is unusual. Otari, August 1970. Four times natural size.

Fig 9 Panicles of seed capsules. These bear persistent sepals and styles. Otari, April 1973.

Fig 10 A close view of some seed capsules showing the persistent sepals and styles and hairs on the capsules and panicle stalks. Also from Otari, April 1973. At four times natural size.

Carpodetus serratus
Putaputaweta

Family *Escalloniaceae:* A family of seven genera and 150 species of trees and shrubs found in tropical and temperate regions in South America, Eastern Himalayas, the Philippine Islands, New Guinea, New Caledonia, Australia and New Zealand.

Genus *Carpodetus:* A genus of ten species found in New Guinea and New Zealand. The solitary New Zealand species is endemic.

A small tree up to 10 m high with a trunk up to 30 m through and branches that spread outward in flattened tiers. It is found throughout both North and South Islands and Stewart Island along forest margins and stream banks from sea level to 1,050 m.

Putaputaweta's leaves are thin but leathery, often mottled, ovate-elliptic to broad-elliptic in shape. They have finely serrated margins and are up to 6 cm long by 3 cm wide. The young branchlets, petioles, peduncles and pedicels are pubescent. The small white flowers are clustered on broad flat panicles up to 5 cm across; there are perfect and functionally female flowers, each on separate trees.

The juvenile form has zigzag, spreading, interlacing branchlets with smaller leaves and can bear flowers. Mature plants often occur with reversion shoots of the juvenile form; remains of the juvenile form may persist after the tree becomes adult.

The tree has a very sappy wood and is therefore difficult to burn. Putaputaweta wood itself is strong and tough but not very durable when exposed to the weather. It has been used for making tool handles.

1

2　　　　　　　**3**　　　　　　　**4 5**

Fig 1 The form of a typical putaputaweta tree with its spreading, flattened branches. This tree in the Reikorangi Valley is in flower. December 1976.

Fig 2 The broad-elliptic form of the leaf showing the upper side and petiole. Natural size.

Fig 3 Underside of the same leaf. Notice the distinct vein pattern and sharp serrations. Also natural size.

Fig 4 A new broad-ovate leaf showing the upper side and pubescent petiole and branchlet. Natural size.

Fig 5 Underside of the same leaf showing hairs on the leaf, petiole and branchlet. The reddish tinge is typical of new leaves. Natural size.

Fig 6 Panicles of ripening fruits, which turn black when ripe. On many of the fruits here a prominent girdle above the middle is clearly visible. This is the rim of a cup-like receptacle which is part of the flower (see Fig 8). Lake Pounui, March 1961.

Fig 7 The bark of putaputaweta.

Fig 8 The individual flowers are perfect, about 5 mm across. In bud the petals meet edge to edge, not overlapping one another as in many flowers. The sepals, petals and stamens are attached to a cup-like receptacle, the rim of which marks the fruit. Lake Pounui, December 1968. Six times natural size.

Fig 9 A flat panicle of flowers amongst the leaves at the end of a branchlet. Lake Pounui, December 1968.

6

7

8

9

Family *Escalloniaceae*

Genus *Ixerba:* An endemic New Zealand genus with only one species, *I. brexioides.*

Ixerba brexioides
Tawari

Tawari is a tree of the forest interior often found growing in dark shady places in hilly and mountain forests, from sea level to 900 m. When met in flower it is one of the most graceful and beautiful of our native trees. Even when the tree is not in flower its unusual long narrow leaves give it a most distinctive appearance.

Tawari is a bushy or canopy tree up to 15 m high with a trunk which sometimes reaches 60 cm across. The branchlets, petioles, peduncles and pedicels are hairy when young. The narrow, thick, leathery, shining leaves are up to 16 cm long and 4 cm wide; they have widely separated blunt teeth, each tooth being tipped by a gland. In seedling plants the leaves are blunt and rounded at the apex.

The conspicuous, unusual-looking flowers are perfect, 2.5 − 3.5 cm across, and borne in panicles at the tips of the branchlets. The five stamens of the flower stand erect from the five petals; the ovary, which has copious nectar at its base, is five-celled and tapers into a twisted five-furrowed style. As the seed capsules grow the styles remain on their apices. When the capsule is ripe it splits into five valves; the splits extend up the style and divide it into narrow strips. The capsule takes about six months to ripen and bursts when the flower buds of the next season are well formed (Fig 5). Tawari's dense wood is very hard.

1

2

Fig 1 A tree exposed by forest clearing on the Mamaku Plateau. October 1965.

Fig 2 The bark from an old tree.

Fig 3 Spray of leaves showing undersides and the distinctive teeth, each tipped by a gland. About half natural size.

Fig 4 Ripening seed capsules with their tapering styles at the apices. Mamaku Plateau, April 1971. Here at almost natural size.

Fig 5 Ripe seed capsules six months after pollination, alongside the buds of the new season's flowers. The buds remain at this stage for several months and then enlarge rapidly and open. Mamaku Plateau, May 1972.

Fig 6 Open and unopen seed capsules. The right-hand capsule shows five valves, which are connected by strips to the now-divided style. In the upper capsule the style is being divided. Mamaku Plateau, April 1971.

3

4

5

6

7

8

Fig 7 An open seed capsule. As the capsule opens, two black seeds, each attached to a red fleshy aril, are held in each of the five valves. At this stage the seed capsule is most attractive. Mamaku Plateau, April 1971. About three times natural size.

Fig 8 A panicle of flowers nestles among the leaves at the end of a branchlet. Notice the five stamens standing erect from the petals of each flower. Mamaku Plateau, December, 1965. Twice natural size.

Fig 9 Leaf upper side. Natural size.

9

Family *Escalloniaceae*

Genus *Quintinia:* **A** genus containing twenty species found in the Philippine Islands, New Guinea, Australia and New Zealand. The three New Zealand species are endemic.

Quintinia acutifolia
Westland quintinia

Despite its name, the Westland quintinia occurs in the North Island on the Great and Little Barrier Islands, the Coromandel Peninsula and from Waimarino to Taranaki. In the South Island it is common from north-west Nelson south to the Fox Glacier. The tree has very attractive foliage; the young leaves are yellow-green, while the adult leaves are a light green which often turns bronze coloured when the tree is exposed to sunlight.

Q. acutifolia is a bushy forest tree up to 12 m tall with a trunk up to 50 cm through, found in forest or in small forest clearings from sea level to 760 m. The leaves are up to 16 cm long by 5 cm wide; they are broadly elliptic-obovate to obovate-cuneate, either wavy or flat. The leaf undersides are a pale, creamy, olive-green. The stout petioles are up to 2 cm long. The young branchlets, young leaves, petioles, peduncles and pedicels are sticky to touch and are sparsely clad with flaky scales.

The flowers are functionally either male or female, each found on separate trees. They are borne on long, narrow, rather open racemes up to 7 cm long. The petals are about 3 mm long and bend back, leaving the stamens and style projecting and fully exposed. As with the tawari, the styles persist on the seed capsules, which are oblong or ovoid in shape.

1

2

Fig 3 The lower surface of a Westland quintinia leaf showing the typical pale, creamy surface and the sparse, flaky scales along the midrib, petiole and tip of the branchlet. The leaves of *Q. acutifolia* have occasional small teeth along the margins towards the apex, which is either acute or obtuse. This specimen reproduced at natural size.

Fig 4 Upper surface of an adult quintinia leaf. The leaves are quite large, growing up to 16 cm long. This specimen reproduced here at half natural size.

Fig 5 Long, narrow racemes of flowers arise towards the tips of the branchlets from the axils of the leaves. Photographed at Hokitika, November 1963.

Fig 6 Close view showing the structure of the flowers; those pictured here are functionally male. The tendency of this tree's petals to bend right back is clearly illustrated. Hokitika, November 1963. At twice natural size.

Fig 1 A group of Westland quintinias growing in Gillespie's Bush, Fox Glacier, showing the bushy, rather columnar shape typical of the tree. January 1973.

Fig 2 A more open, more conical form of the tree, also at Gillespie's Bush, Fox Glacier, January 1973.

Fig 7 A branchlet showing the alternate leaf arrangement and a raceme of seed capsules arising from a leaf axil. The styles are persisting on the capsules.

Fig 8 The fairly smooth bark is reflective and tends to shine.

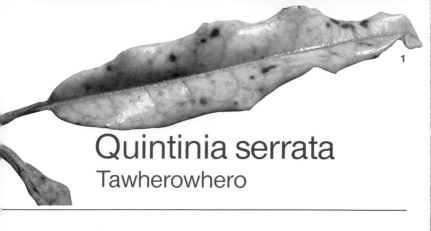

Quintinia serrata
Tawherowhero

A small, open-branching tree which grows up to 9 m high. It is closely related to the Westland quintinia, *Q. acutifolia,* but is restricted in distribution to the northern part of the country. *Q. serrata* is found only from Mangonui in the north to northern Taranaki and Poverty Bay, growing from sea level to 1,050 m. It tends to favour shady places, steep slopes and banks.

It differs further from the Westland quintinia in its narrower, rather more coarsely serrate leaves that are often blotchy. The leaves are 6–12.5 cm long by 2.5 cm wide, on petioles 2 cm long. The flowers of this tree are very similar to those of *Q. acutifolia.*

Fig 1 The upper surface of a typical leaf showing the wavy margin and blotches on the leaf surface. About natural size.

Fig 2 A group of *Q. serrata* trees growing in Waipoua Forest, April 1979.

Fig 3 Undersurface of a narrow-lanceolate leaf. About natural size. Leaves can vary in shape from this to oblanceolate or narrow-oblong, depending on the locality.

Fig 4 A close view of a *Q. serrata* flower panicle. From a tree on the Billy Goat Track, Kauaeranga Valley, Coromandel Peninsula. Three times natural size. The racemes are about 8 cm long, similar to those of *Q. acutifolia.*

Fig 5 A spray showing the alternate leaf arrangement. The reddish-brown leaves are about to fall. Otari, May 1979.

Fig 6 Unripe woody seed capsules of *Q. serrata* are about 5 mm long, obovoid in shape. Three times natural size. Kauaeranga Valley, December 1970.

Sophora tetraptera
Kowhai

Family *Papilionaceae:* Plants of this family have bacterial nodules on their roots that fix nitrogen. The Papilionaceae includes trees, shrubs, herbs and lianes that are found mainly in temperate regions of the world. There are about 375 genera and about 10,000 species, of which eight genera and forty-nine species are found in New Zealand. Four of the New Zealand genera include trees.

Genus *Sophora:* A genus containing fifty species of trees and shrubs found in subtropical and temperate parts of North and South America, Asia, Australia and New Zealand. Two of the three New Zealand species are endemic and all are known locally as kowhai.

The kowhai is undoubtedly New Zealand's most beautiful tree. Its feathery leaves and pendulous flowers borne in great profusion make any tree in full flower a sight never to be forgotten. The kowhai has a delicate beauty quite different from the striking and overwhelming beauty of a rata or a pohutukawa. The flower colour ranges from a pale lemon-yellow *(S. prostrata)* through strong yellow *(S. microphylla)* to a golden yellow *(S. tetraptera),* depending on the location and probably the genetic content of individual trees.

Kowhais are plentiful and can be seen in flower to advantage in parts of North Auckland, around Lake Taupo (where they are usually at their best for a week before until a week after Labour Weekend) or in the vicinity of Taihape, the Rangitikei River gorges and Hawke's Bay. They are also common near Ponatahi in the Wairarapa. In the South Island there are many kowhais along the Kaikoura Coast and in the river valleys leading from there, at Peel Forest in Canterbury and in the Matai Valley near Nelson.

S. tetraptera is the North Island kowhai, found originally growing wild along streamsides and lowland forest margins from East Cape to the Ruahine mountains, from sea level to 450 m. It has, of course, been extensively planted and is now one of the commonest of our native trees, found far and wide throughout the country. The kowhai flower has even been adopted as our national flower.

S. tetraptera forms a small spreading tree up to 12 m high **(Fig 1)** with a trunk up to 60 cm in diameter; the branchlets are clothed with a pale-brownish tomentum when young, but lack hairs when mature. The leaves are up to 15 cm long, pinnately compound with ten to twenty pairs of leaflets. The leaflets are 15 – 35 mm long, subsessile or with very short petioles. They are ovate to elliptic-oblong in shape and clad with appressed silky hairs.

1

The yellow to golden-yellow flowers are carried in four to ten-flowered racemes, each flower about 5 cm long. The raceme stalks, calyx and flower pedicels are clothed with a silky-brown tomentum. The flower has five unequal petals: the *standard* (the outermost covering petal), the *wings* (the two side petals) and the *keel* (composed of two laterally fused petals which form a trough in which the stamens and style lie). In *S. tetraptera* the wings are shorter than the keel and longer than the standard. The base of the flower is filled with nectar which is a favourite food for many native birds.

The seed pods are up to 20 cm long, usually with six or more seeds; these are at first yellow but become brown as they age. *S. tetraptera* germinates and grows into a mature tree directly, with no juvenile stage, and flowers within a few years. The wood of *S. tetraptera* has been found to be very tough, hard and durable.

The kowhai trees have medicinal properties and were used by the Maori people for this purpose. Poultices were made from the bark for applying to wounds and tumours, and an infusion of the barks of kowhai and manuka was used to treat internal pains, bruises and broken limbs. Even the ashes of the tree were put to use, in the treatment of ringworm.

2

3

4

Fig 2 A plant of the *S. tetraptera* cultivar 'Gnome', which grows as a shrub up to 2 m high and flowers prolifically with larger flowers. It is popular as a garden plant. Otari, October 1969.

Fig 3 The bark from an old tree.

Fig 4 A tree heavy with flowers on farmland in the Ponatahi Valley, Wairarapa. September 1968.

Fig 5 A section of the upper surface of a leaf of *S. tetraptera* showing elliptic-oblong leaflets and appressed hairs on the rachis and leaflets. Natural size.

Fig 6 The lower surface of the same leaf. Also natural size.

Fig 7 Leaves of *S. tetraptera* with the leaflets more ovate in shape than those in Figs 5 and 6. Waikanae, July 1979.

Fig 8 The flowers occur in cascades of racemes along the drooping branches. The flowering time is spring, but the actual time varies, being earlier further north and later further south and in more elevated places. Ponatahi Valley, September 1968.

Fig 9 The ovary is at the base of the long style. After pollination it grows downwards to form a long "pod" carrying the fertile seeds. Waikanae, July 1979.

Fig 10 Close view of the flowers, showing the long keel, shorter wings and the still shorter standard. Waikanae, September 1979. About natural size.

5

6

WHICH KOWHAI?

Which of the three species of the kowhai should be regarded as the national flower of New Zealand? The species S. microphylla *is the more widespread tree. But* S. tetraptera *is more popular as a garden plant, suggesting, therefore, that the flower of* S. tetraptera *(illustrated on this page) should be designated as our national flower.*

7

8

9

10

Sophora microphylla/Kowhai
S. prostrata/Prostrate kowhai

S. microphylla is a smaller, more feathery looking tree than *S. tetraptera,* reaching a height of 10 m with a trunk 60 cm through. The branches are more spreading and drooping, although there is pale brown tomentum on the branchlets, leaves and flower stalks as in *S. tetraptera. S. microphylla* differs distinctly in its flower, which has wings equal to the standard in length and the keel only a little longer than the wings or standard.

S. microphylla is the most widespread of the New Zealand kowhais. It grows also in Chile and on Gough Island in the South Atlantic. It grows naturally on riverbanks and forest margins and in open places throughout the North and South Islands and the Chatham Islands, but like *S. tetraptera* it has now become widespread through cultivation.

The pinnate leaves, up to 15 cm long with twenty to forty pairs of obovate-oblong leaflets, are each 5 – 7 mm long. Sometimes these are almost orbicular and they usually lose their appressed hairs as they become older. Unlike *S. tetraptera* this tree passes through a juvenile stage; this is a twiggy shrub with yellow, flexible, rather wiry interlacing branchlets bearing a few leaves. It lasts for many years with the branches often persisting around the base of the adult trunk for some time. Two varieties of the tree known as *fulvida* and *longicarinata* are recognised.

1

2

3

Fig 1 The leaves of *S. microphylla*. Leaves with some leaflets missing are not uncommon.

Fig 2 The leaves of *S. microphylla* var. *fulvida* differ in having a dense golden-brown tomentum covering the leaf rachis, plus hairier leaflets which are close set as shown here. The leaves are 8 – 10 cm long and there are up to fifty pairs of leaflets. From a tree at Hukutaia Domain. Four times natural size. This variety is found wild in coastal scrub and forest west of Auckland.

Fig 3 Lower surface of the leaf in Fig 2.

Figs 4, 5 Flowers and leaves of *S. microphylla*. Both from Woodside Gorge, October 1969. Flowers at natural size.

Fig 6 A leaf of the variety *longicarinata* grows up to 20 cm long and has twenty to forty pairs of leaflets, each on a short petiole. The tree is up to 5 m high and is found near Takaka. The flower of this variety is lemon-yellow, 5 cm long, with the keel longer than the standard. The leaflets are hairy only on the lower surface.

4

5

7

6

Fig 7 A tree of *S. microphylla* clearly showing the characteristic drooping foliage. This specimen was growing on the Kaikoura coast, December 1964.

Fig 8 This is the third species of kowhai, *S. prostrata*. It grows normally as a bushy or a prostrate shrub, although occasionally it becomes a small tree around 2 m high. The leaves, pictured here, are up to 2.5 cm long with eight pairs of subsessile leaflets 4 mm long; they are hairless except for the midrib below.

Fig 9 The flowers of *S. prostrata*. Woodside Gorge, September 1969. They occur singly or two or three together, on slender, silky-haired peduncles. They are up to 3 cm long with the keel noticeably longer than the wings and standard. These specimens at about natural size.

8

9

Family *Papilionaceae*

Genus *Chordospartium:* A genus endemic to New Zealand with only one species.

Chordospartium stevensonii
Weeping broom/Tree broom

The weeping broom is a distinctive tree up to 9 m high with ascending, ultimately drooping branches and an umbrella-like canopy of slender, drooping branchlets. The latter are almost cylindrical and grooved, and bear racemes of pale lavender flowers at their nodes. The trunk can be up to 36 cm in diameter and covered by a green, smooth or, on older trees, a greyish, rough bark.

This unusual tree is found only in Marlborough between 450 and 750 m, growing on silty flats in the Clarence River Basin and in the valleys of the Jordan River, Avon River, Swale and Jam Streams and Grey River. In 1971 I visited the Jordan Valley and took the photographs on these pages. The tree grows easily from seed and a number of small trees and seedlings were scattered about, along with growing and mature trees and the remains of the trunks of trees that had fallen. Some of these measured up to 112 cm in girth at 30 cm from the ground. A few young plants were also growing on a loamy slope in a shady curve of the creek.

The young weeping broom seedling looks more or less like a piece of straw; it shows no green at all and has no leaves. Judging from the seedling I have grown in my own garden, this "stick" grows slowly, branches looking more or less dead for at least six to seven years. After this the new branchlets start to grow green, with the characteristic round, grooved appearance. The development of the trunk and branches is illustrated in Figs 6 to 9. I would think that a tree such as that in Fig 1 would be sixty to eighty years old, quite an age for a broom.

The delicate flowers of the weeping broom, in racemes up to 9 cm long, are produced in great profusion, usually every second year on older trees. Quite young trees, often barely 1 m high, will flower.

1

Fig 1 A weeping broom growing in the Jordan Valley. It is about 9 m high and in flower. January 1971.

Fig 2 A raceme of flowers arising from a node on a branchlet; the curling upwards of the tip is typical. Each flower is up to 9 mm long. From a plant growing at Otari, December 1973. Slightly over natural size.

Fig 3 Close view of the flowers: note the hairy sepals. Otari, December 1973. Six times natural size.

Fig 4 A young weeping broom, probably about twelve years old; trees of this size can sometimes flower. Jordan Valley, January 1971.

Fig 5 The flowers of *C. stevensonii* are borne in great profusion from mid-December to January. These are branchlets from a tree in full flower growing in the Jordan Valley, January 1971.

Fig 6 The bark of a seedling tree at seven years of age. Green branchlets have begun to appear at both right and left of the main stem.

Fig 7 The bark of an older seedling with its typical green, cylindrical, grooved branchlets and some brown juvenile bark still persisting at the top left.

Fig 8 The greenish bark of the mature tree still shows the wavy pattern of the bark of younger stages of growth.

Fig 9 In older trees the bark cracks and becomes rough.

2

3

4

REDISCOVERED

The weeping broom has a unique story. William Martin records that a Mr Weld obtained some seed from C. G. Teschemaker probably at the turn of the last century and grew the plant in England some years before it was known to New Zealand botanists. The tree was found again here in 1904 by George Stevenson in the Clarence Valley and described by Cheeseman in 1910.

5

6

7

8 9

Family *Papilionaceae*

Genus *Notospartium:* An endemic New Zealand genus of three species, two of which are shrubs and the third a small tree. All are leafless or nearly so.

Notospartium glabrescens
Pink tree broom

In full flower this is one of our most spectacular native plants. The pink tree broom is found only in Marlborough, growing in rocky situations from sea level to 1,200 m. It is recorded from the Woodside Gorge, the Clarence and Waima Ure river valleys and occasionally on the slopes of the Seaward Kaikouras between the Awatere and Clarence rivers.

It is a shrub or small tree up to 10 m high with erect or spreading branches; the many branchlets are mostly leafless, green, somewhat compressed or flattened; they are upright on the upper part of the tree but tend to droop on the middle and lower sections.

The attractive flowers occur on slender, rather open racemes up to 5 cm long and vary in intensity of colour from tree to tree, as these photographs show. Quite young plants appear able to bear flowers. Flowering varies in intensity from year to year, the flowers appearing from early December to early January. The photographs here from the Woodside Gorge were taken in December 1969 and I am told by Mrs Margaret Parsons, who lives by the entrance to the gorge, that it was an exceptionally good year.

The spotted seeds occur in indehiscent pods two or more to each pod and will germinate reasonably easily. As in *Chordospartium* there are striking differences in the barks of young and old plants.

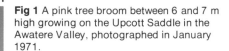
1

Fig 1 A pink tree broom between 6 and 7 m high growing on the Upcott Saddle in the Awatere Valley, photographed in January 1971.

Fig 2 The flowers from the tree in Fig 1. These flowers are much more strongly and deeply coloured than those from the trees in the Woodside Gorge shown in Figs 3, 4 and 5.

Fig 3 A superb tree in full flower near the top of the Woodside Gorge. It was photographed in early December 1969, a good year for pink tree broom flowers.

Fig 4 Paler flowers on a Woodside Gorge specimen showing the great profusion of the flowers and the flattened branchlets that bear them. Also photographed in December 1969.

Fig 5 A close view of the paler-pink flowers of a tree from the Woodside Gorge. Compare this colour with that of the flower in Fig 2. Each flower is about 12 mm long. December 1969. Twice natural size.

2

Fig 6 A quite small plant of *N. glabrescens*, so small that it is really a shrub. It is laden with flowers and also illustrates the tree's capacity to grow on rocky places. Growing in Woodside Gorge, early December 1969.

Fig 7 Seed pods vary from 8 — 25 mm in length and contain several spotted seeds each about 2 mm long. Woodside Gorge, March 1969.

Fig 8 The bark on growing stems is "ropey" at first but later becomes smoother and grey. Woodside Gorge, December 1969.

Fig 9 Bark from an old tree on the Upcot Saddle, January 1971. The growth nodes show as distinct circular rings.

Carmichaelia williamsii/Giant-flowered broom
C. arborea/South Island broom
C. odorata/Scented broom
C. aligera/North Island broom
C. angustata/Leafy broom

In these native tree brooms the green branchlets perform the functions of the leaves; they are rounded, compressed or flattened in shape, often grooved and distinctly notched at the nodes. The plants are usually much branched, the branchlets spreading and often intertwining. Most are leafless, or nearly so when mature, but when leaves are produced they are one-foliolate or pinnately three to seven-foliolate, normally with a terminal leaflet. Leaves occur more on seedlings or on plants in the shade. The flowers of all species except *C. williamsii* are small and similar, mostly pale pink or whitish with varying degrees of deeper pink or purplish streaking.

The most distinctive feature of the tree brooms is their seed pods, which consist of two valves attached to a thick framework that terminates in a protruding pointed structure called the beak and to which the seeds inside are attached. After the pods are ripe the valves eventually fall away, leaving the exposed seeds hanging inside the framework. The seeds are usually mottled, and some, such as those of *C. aligera,* are brightly coloured.

All *Carmichaelia* species are rather difficult to identify and there is certainly an urgent need for further intensive study by cultivation, but these photographs should assist in the indentification of the tree forms.

Fig 1 Flattened branchlets of *C. williamsii* are 8—12 mm wide with close grooves and short internodes between alternating nodes. This tree up to 4 m high is found in coastal areas from Bay of Plenty to East Cape and on the Poor Knights, Little Barrier and Alderman Islands. Just below natural size.

Fig 2 *C. williamsii* flowers are large, about 25 mm long, borne as one to five-flowered racemes. Half natural size.

Fig 3 *C. arborea* forms a tree up to 5 m high with ascending branches and compressed, straight branchlets. Found in the South Island, mainly west of the main divide, along streamsides and forest margins and in alluvial boggy scrubland.

Fig 4 Close view of a *C. arborea* branchlet with flower clusters. Twice natural size.

Fig 5 *C. odorata* grows to 2 m high, usually as a much-branched shrub but sometimes as a tree with long fan-like branches rising from a short central trunk. These flowers and flower buds are from a plant in my garden at Waikanae, February 1979. *C. odorata* occurs in the North Island along streamsides and forest margins, from sea level to 750 m, from about Tolaga Bay southwards. The flowers occur as five to fifteen-flowered racemes.

Fig 6 *C. odorata* is usually in leaf in spring and summer. The branchlets, which tend to droop, are flattened, striated to deeply grooved and 1—3 mm wide. Natural size.

Fig 7 *C. odorata* leaves are five to seven-foliolate; the leaflets are often emarginate, and both they and the branchlets are hairy. Six times natural size.

Fig 8 Seed pods of *C. aligera* after the valves have fallen off, showing the red seeds left attached. Natural size.

Fig 9 *C. aligera* grows to 10 m with thick, hairless, flattened branchlets 6—7 mm wide, finely grooved, branching freely at the nodes. Natural size.

1

2

3

4

Family *Papilionaceae*

Genus *Carmichaelia:* A genus of thirty-nine species of mostly leafless shrubs or small trees found throughout New Zealand and also on Lord Howe Island. The thirty-eight New Zealand species are endemic; they are now classified under several subgenera, one of which is the subgenus *Carmichaelia* which includes six species that can grow into small trees. These are *C. aligera, C. angustata, C. arborea, C. odorata, C. silvatica* and *C. williamsii.*

5

6 7

8

9 10

11

12

13

Fig 10 Finely grooved *C. aligera* branchlet, closer view. Twice natural size. The tree is found in North Auckland and south to Taranaki along coastal to lowland forest margins and in scrubland.

Fig 11 *C. angustata* forms a shrub or a small tree which reaches 2 m in height with many slightly flattened branches. The branchlets arise almost at right angles to the branches and are more rounded than flat, usually drooping. About natural size.

Fig 12 Unlike most other tree broom species *C. angustata* nearly always has a few leaves, the young branchlets and leaves quite hairy. The leaflets are about 4 mm long by 2 mm wide on short stalks, here at twice natural size. The whole leaf is up to 3 cm long and may be three or four to seven-foliolate. The species is found in the South Island along streamsides and forest margins from Karamea to just below Hokitika and between the Clarence and Hurunui Rivers on the east coast.

Fig 13 A branchlet of *C. angustata.* This photograph shows the hairs, hairy young leaves towards the tip and older leaves nearer the base that have lost their hairs. About natural size.

I have been unable to find the native tree broom *C. silvatica.* It is reputed to grow along the Waipoua River and to be 10 m high with flattened, grooved branchlets 3 – 5 mm wide. Allan's *Flora* records it as known only from the type specimen.

207

Family Fagaceae
Genus *Nothofagus*

The family Fagaceae is the family of the beeches, a large, world-wide family that includes the Northern Hemisphere genus *Fagus* and the Southern Hemisphere genus *Nothofagus,* most of which are tall forest trees. The family includes eight genera and about 100 species of trees and shrubs distributed throughout the world except for tropical South America and tropical Africa and South Africa. Besides the beeches the family also embraces the oaks, genus *Quercus,* the chestnuts, genus *Castanea,* and the genera *Chrysolepsis* and *Lithocarpus,* important timber trees of the Americas and Asia. The tanoak, *Lithocarpus densiflorus,* is a massive tree of the Pacific coast of North America, while *L. edulis* is a smaller tree found in Japan.

The genus *Nothofagus* consists of thirty-five species of trees and shrubs. The four New Zealand species are endemic evergreen forest trees. All are valuable timber trees.

The beech trees of the Southern Hemisphere are referred to as the southern beeches and in New Zealand they are amongst our most distinctive trees. Although occurring sparingly in the far north they may be found from Kaitaia and Mangonui southwards, particularly along the mountain chains of both islands and on the central plateau of the North Island. The beeches generally grow from sea level to around 1,100 m, but the mountain beech, *N. solandri* var. *cliffortioides,* see illustration below, is found up to 1,200 m. In the South Island beeches form vast tracts of forests composed almost entirely of one or two species. Beeches are absent from Mt Egmont and Stewart Island.

A beech forest has a distinctive appearance. The trees form dense stands of large, straight-trunked specimens among which an undergrowth of smaller trees and shrubs is sparse, sometimes almost absent. This contrasts strongly with the dense undergrowth which is characteristic of our virgin podocarp forests.

The flowers of our beeches occur in inflorescences which arise in the axils of the bud scales and leaves produced in the spring. The staminate or male inflorescence is conspicuous with highly coloured flowers, while the female inflorescence is much smaller and green, and more or less concealed in the leaf axils above the males.

As we saw earlier, the beech trees of New Zealand are very ancient tree species, having a long line of descent reaching back in time for about 135 million years to the great continent of Gondwanaland. The earliest beeches, the *brassi* group, were followed in the New Zealand region by the *menziesii* and *fusca* groups, from which developed our present species.

Nothofagus menziesii
Silver beech/Tawhai

In the forest the silver beech is a tall tree with its spreading branches arranged more or less in tiers (Fig 16); in the open this beech forms a broad, spreading, magnificent dome-shaped tree with its lower branches arching towards the ground (Fig 2).

The silver beech reaches a height of 30 m, with a trunk up to 2 m through. Very old trees tend to form thick, heavy branches spreading outwards and upwards, each with a small crown of foliage and with the trunk often heavily coated with mosses and lichens. The bark is silvery-white on young trees but grey and flakey on old trees. The trunk often develops large buttresses around its base.

The tree is found in forest from sea level to 900 m, from Thames southwards (excluding Mt Egmont). In the high mountains of the South Island trees that are dwarfed, only a metre or two high, can often be found above the normal bush line; the severity of the climate may even reduce them to shrubs.

The branchlets are round and are clothed with brownish hairs, as are the petioles and peduncles. The leaves are from 6 – 15 mm long and 5 – 15 mm wide; they are doubly crennate, thick, leathery, rigid, with petioles up to 3 mm long. The principal veins are not very distinct below, but the midvein is hairy and there are usually one or two domatia, fringed with hairs, in the axils of the two basal veins. New leaves are often yellowish with orange-red margins.

Sexes are together on the same tree. The male inflorescences arise on stalks from the branchlets, one to four per stalk. They each consist of a single flower on a sparsely hairy peduncle about 3 mm long.

Fig 1 A leaf spray of silver beech showing alternate leaves and the hairy branchlets. About natural size.

Fig 2 A magnificent specimen of silver beech growing in the open. This fine tree is in the Eglinton Valley, photographed in January 1976.

Fig 3 New leaves of *N. menziesii* showing their paler colour and tinged margins. From Tararua Forest Park, December 1975.

Female inflorescences occur one to four per stalk, arising between the leaf axils. They are situated beyond the males, further towards the tip of each branchlet; each is two to three-flowered and has a short hairy peduncle. Flowering is very irregular from year to year and occurs during November, December and early January. The fruit is a nut inside a four-segmented cupule covered by four to five rows of processes with swollen glands at their tips.

The red-coloured wood of *N. menziesii* possesses an even, compact and straight grain. In the past it has been used for wharf and bridge construction, for railway sleepers and for house building. Today the wood is used mainly for furniture and decorative work.

4

5

6

7

Fig 4 Three silver beech branchlets showing male flowers on peduncles near the base of the branchlets and a number of tiny green female inflorescences arising from the leaf axils at the tips of the branchlets. These are especially clear on the middle and top branchlets. Tararua Forest Park, November 1975.

Fig 5 Close view of the upper surfaces of two leaves, which are gland dotted, and a hairy branchlet. This specimen three times natural size.

Fig 6 Leaf undersurface showing the vein pattern, thick edges, hairy petiole and two hair-fringed domatia. Three times natural size.

Fig 7 A very old silver beech in the Upper Stillwater. Fiordland, December 1970.

Fig 8 The relatively smooth bark of a young silver beech tree.

Fig 9 Rough flaking bark on an old tree.

Fig 10 Silver beech trees can be attacked by two brownish-yellow looking fungi. This grove near Lake Rotoroa, Nelson, shows witch's broom disease, *Aceria waltheri,* which can be mistaken at a distance for flowers. January 1972.

Fig 11 A close view of the other fungus, *Cyttaria gunnii*. Mt Robert Track, Lake Rotoiti, Nelson, January 1972. About natural size.

8

9

Fig 12 Male flowers of silver beech are not as dense as in some other species of beech. The tiny female inflorescences can be seen in this photograph on the tips of some of the branchlets. From a tree growing in Tararua Forest Park, November 1975.

Fig 13 A close view of the male flowers, which in this photograph are shedding pollen. From the Tararua Forest Park, November 1975. Twice natural size.

Fig 14 A female inflorescence on a tree at Lewis Pass in January 1971. The hairy nature of the branchlet, leaf petioles and midveins can be clearly seen. In the female flower of silver beech the two to three flowers of the inflorescence are enclosed by bracts that become the cupule. This specimen at twice natural size.

Fig 15 Seed cupules of silver beech, also from a tree at Lewis Pass, January 1971. Here at three times natural size. One of the foliaceous bracts that subtend the cupule can be seen under the one at top right and the swollen glands at the tips of each of the processes are also visible.

Fig 16 A fine old specimen of silver beech exposed by the cutting of a forestry access road into the Kaimanawa Forest Park. The photograph was taken in December 1973. The tiered open crown with its massive spreading branches can be clearly seen, as well as new branches lower down which have been produced in response to the light admitted after road construction.

10

11

12 13

14 15

16

Nothofagus truncata
Hard beech/Tawhairaunui

1

This beech is a tree up to 30 m high with a trunk up to 2 m through which is often buttressed. It occurs from sea level to 900 m, from Mangonui southwards to Greymouth on the West Coast and the Wairau River in Marlborough. The tree is partly deciduous in late winter or early spring.

The glossy leaves are 25−35 mm long and about 20 mm wide, without any hairs except when young. They are broadly ovate to elliptic-oblong or rounded in shape, with petioles 2−3 mm long. The leaf margins are coarsely and bluntly serrate with eight to twelve pairs of teeth; the leaves usually have a more or less rounded or truncate apex bearing three teeth.

The male inflorescences occur one to ten per branchlet, each consisting of one to three subsessile flowers on a sparsely pubescent peduncle up to 10 mm long. Each flower has ten to thirteen stamens with anthers 3 mm long. Female inflorescences, which arise one to five per branchlet, are sessile, 2−3 mm long, ovoid in shape and three-flowered.

The wood of hard beech is red when freshly cut but dries to a light brown colour. As its name indicates, it is harder than the wood of other beech species and it has been used for bridge building, railway sleepers, posts and poles. The bark of this tree is so full of tannin that it has been used in leather tanning.

3

Fig 1 The fresh young leaves of hard beech are a lighter green colour than older leaves. As this photograph shows they are slightly hairy, as are the young branchlets. The serrations are shallow and the rounded toothed apex shows here clearly. Domatia rarely occur in the leaves of *N. truncata*. About natural size.

Fig 2 The undersides of the old leaves are yellow-green, paler in colour than the upper surface (illustrated in Fig 4). Also about natural size.

Fig 3 A splendid specimen of this very tall tree rises above the surrounding forest on the hills behind the Hutt Valley. It was photographed in October 1970. The common name "hard" beech originates from the density of the tree's timber; all the New Zealand beeches have wood of a medium density, but the wood of *N. truncata* is the strongest and most dense. Unlike other beeches there is little difference in density between the wood of northern and southern hard beech trees.

Fig 4 Male flowers of hard beech occur in attractive red or orange forms and in full flower the tree can be as spectacular as *N. solandri*, which is one of the most profuse flowering of the native beeches. Photograph also shows the distinctive dark-green glossy upper surfaces of typical old leaves as well as the flowering habit towards the tips of the branches. Near Linton, September 1962. Natural size.

Fig 5 A close view of male flowers which are of the more orange-coloured form. From a tree on the Rimutaka Hill, November 1970. Twice natural size.

Fig 6 Male flowers more red in colour. Those pictured here are just beginning to shed pollen. Kaitoke Gorge, October 1974.

2

4

5
9

7
6

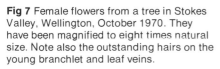

Fig 7 Female flowers from a tree in Stokes Valley, Wellington, October 1970. They have been magnified to eight times natural size. Note also the outstanding hairs on the young branchlet and leaf veins.

Fig 8 Flange buttresses such as these are typical of older hard beech trees and often extend up the trunk for 2 m or more. This tree in the Kaimanawa Forest Park had four such buttresses around the base of the trunk. January 1975.

Fig 9 The massive straight trunk of the tree shown in Fig 8 rises towards the light in the forest canopy.

Fig 10 The bark of hard beech.

8

10

Nothofagus fusca
Red beech/Tawhairaunui

This is probably the most handsome of our beech trees. Like the other *Nothofagus* species, red beech is a very tall tree, reaching a height of 30 m with a trunk up to 2−3 m through. The foliage of young red beech trees is usually a deep but bright red colour during winter, a character that is retained for many years and is often seen where beech seedlings line a road or forest clearing. A mature red beech tree drops its old leaves as the new leaves open during the spring.

N. fusca occurs from sea level to 1,050 m, in lowland and mountain forests from near Te Aroha and Rotorua southwards to Fiordland and Southland.

Like the other beeches it is absent from Mt Egmont. Some particularly fine stands of red beech can be seen in the Kaimanawa Mountains and in the Eglinton Valley in Fiordland.

The leaves are thin but leathery, 2−4 cm long and 1.5−2.5 cm wide. Their margins are deeply cut with prominent teeth and their undersides have domatia in the axils of the basal lateral veins. The venation is distinct on both leaf surfaces. The sharp teeth and domatia distinguish *N. fusca* leaves from those of *N. truncata*. The bark of young trees is smooth and whitish, that of the old trees grey, deeply furrowed. The wood is the most durable of our beeches.

1

Fig 1 This fine red beech specimen growing in the Kaimanawa Mountains shows clearly the straight trunk and spreading to ascending branches characteristic of the tree. December 1973.

Fig 2 Red beech foliage in sunlight is bright and fresh looking. These trees were growing in the Eglinton Valley, December 1975.

Fig 3 The alternate leaves of *N. fusca* are broadly ovate or ovate-oblong. These are at natural size.

2

Fig 4 An ovate leaf underside with three domatia. One and a half times natural size.

Fig 5 An ovate-oblong leaf underside showing venation and one domatium. Also at one and a half times natural size.

Fig 6 Bark of a mature tree. From Kaimanawa Forest Park, January 1975.

Fig 7 The bark of a very old tree. Eglinton Valley, December 1975.

Fig 8 Male inflorescences arise one to eight per branchlet, each on a peduncle 4 mm long. They usually consist of one to three flowers, occasionally five, with anthers 3 mm long. From a tree at Renata Ridge, Tararua Range, November 1970.

Fig 9 Male flowers shedding pollen. Also at Renata Ridge, November 1970. Twice natural size.

Fig 10 Fully coloured male anthers just splitting to shed pollen. Renata Ridge, November 1975. Six times natural size.

Fig 11 The female inflorescence is axillary, sessile, ovoid, three-flowered and about 3 mm long. Lewis Pass, January 1971. This is magnified to eleven times natural size.

Nothofagus solandri
Black beech/Tawhairauriki

Another tall forest tree up to 25 m high with a trunk up to 1 m through. Black beech is found in lowland and mountain forest from a line joining southern Waikato and East Cape southwards, from sea level to 750 m, throughout the North and South Island. *N. solandri* frequently forms the dominant species in extensive tracts of forests clothing mountain slopes and rolling hill country, imposing a sombre green mantle upon the whole landscape.

The bark of young trees is pale and smooth while that of old trees is dark, furrowed and flaky. Old trees are often covered on their trunks and lower branches with a thick, black, velvety fungus that drips a sweet, sticky liquid.

The branchlets, leaf petioles and flower peduncles are densely pubescent with short golden hairs. The dark-green shining leaves have their margins rolled downwards towards the undersurfaces, which are covered by greyish-white hairs. The leaves are normally narrow-oblong to elliptic-oblong; they are rounded apically, sometimes apiculate, and obliquely cuneate to the petioles, which are 1−2 mm long. Domatia are not present on the leaves.

The male inflorescences arise one to four per stalk. They consist of one or two flowers, each with six to seventeen bright-red stamens that arise from within brownish-green, bell-shaped perianths.

Female inflorescences, which consist of one to three flowers, are tiny and arise in the leaf axils beyond the male inflorescences. Black beech flowers more profusely than the other beeches. The pale yellow-red or red wood is streaked with black but is not durable unless cut from very old trees.

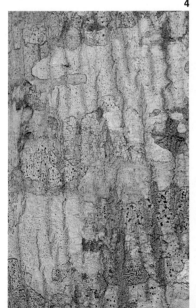

6

7

8

Fig 1 Leaf spray showing alternate leaf arrangement. Black beech leaves are 10 – 15 mm long by 5 – 10 mm wide. About one and a half times natural size.

Fig 2 A small grove of black beech trees in the Pahaoa Valley, East Wairarapa. Two tall trees on the right display the typical broad, spreading crown of mature black beech; the younger trees at left foreground show the typical bright-green, drooping spring foliage. November 1970.

Fig 3 The spring leaves are always fresh in appearance, especially when lit by bright sunlight. Pahaoa Valley, November 1964.

Fig 4 The bark of a young black beech tree is smooth, whitish and faintly furrowed.

Fig 5 The rough, furrowed and flaky bark of an old tree.

Fig 6 Leaf spray showing the hairy lower surfaces with rolled down edges and densely pubescent branchlet and leaf petioles. One and a half times natural size.

Fig 7 New season's spring buds and shoots are sparsely hairy. The upper branchlet in this photograph also shows some narrower elliptic-oblong leaves.

Fig 8 Leaf undersurface showing the whitish hairs, especially along the mid and prominent side veins; this is not as dense as in the variety *cliffortioides*. Five times natural size.

9

Fig 9 The black beech seed cupule takes about twelve months to ripen and mature. The mature cupule here is from a tree growing in the Pahaoa Valley, November 1970. Four and a half times natural size. The cupules contain two or three seeds.

Fig 10 Branch of black beech with a profusion of male flowers just ready to shed their pollen. The tiny female flowers are hidden nearer the tips of the branchlets. Black beech flowers more profusely in some years than others. The tree's brilliant red stamens impart a red glow to a tree that is heavy with flower, making it quite noticeable some distance away. Rimutaka Hill, October 1965.

10

Nothofagus solandri
var. cliffortioides
Mountain beech/Tawhairauriki

1

A smaller tree than black beech, growing to only 15 m with a trunk up to 1 m through; its branches spread outwards in tiers. The leaves are distinct from black beech, being thick, leathery, ovate to ovate-oblong, with acute tips and rounded bases, sparsely hairy above. The branchlets are pubescent. It grows in mountain and subalpine forest, from sea level to 1,200 m, from the Volcanic Plateau to Southland.

2

3   4   5   6

Fig 1 Leaf spray. Otari, March 1970.

Figs 2, 3 Leaf upper and lower surfaces showing the distinctive rolled down margins, hairy petiole, densely pubescent lower surface and occasional hairs on the upper surface. Three times natural size.

Fig 4 Mature mountain beech, Mt Ruapehu, January 1975. The wood is similar to that of *N. solandri* but is not at all durable.

Fig 5 A spray of male flowers from a tree on the Volcanic Plateau. December 1970.

Fig 6 The seed cupules are 6 – 7 mm long. Volcanic Plateau, January 1974. Four times natural size.

Family *Moraceae:* A family of seventy-five genera and 3,000 species of trees and shrubs found in tropical, subtropical and some temperate regions from the Americas through Africa, India, Asia, Malaysia, and Australia to New Zealand and Polynesia. It includes the mulberries, *Morus* sp., found in the subtropical and temperate parts of the Northern Hemisphere, the edible fig, *Ficus carica,* and many other famous species: *F. sycomorus,* the "sycomore" of the Bible; the Cape fig, *F. capensiae,* the Natal fig, *F. natalensis,* and the wonderbroom, *F. pretoriae,* all of South Africa; the banyan tree, *F. benghalensis,* of India, and its related large-leaved banyan, *F. wightiana,* of southern China, Japan and Taiwan; the rubber tree, *Castilla* sp., originally of Central America; the upas tree, *Antiaris toxicaria,* a poisonous tree of south China, India and Malaysia; the breadfruits, *Artocarpus incisus,* of the Polynesian Islands; and the jack fruit, *A. heterophylla,* of India and Asia, that produces the largest fruits known, reaching almost 1 m long.

Genus *Paratrophis:* Contains ten species; seven occur in Polynesia and three are endemic to New Zealand.

Paratrophis smithii
Smith's milkwood

A shrub or small tree up to 5 m high which occurs naturally only on the Three Kings Islands. The photographs on this page were taken from a plant grown at the Mt Albert Research Station, Auckland.

P. smithii has slender zigzagging branchlets and simple, shining, leathery, stipulate leaves 10 – 20 cm long and up to 12 cm wide, on stout petioles up to 15 mm long. The stipules are lanceolate and the leaves ovate to elliptic-oblong, either obtuse or rounded apically. The venation on the leaves of this tree is distinct. The older stems and bark are rough and corky. Like that of other *Paratrophis* species, the bark exudes a thick white sap when cut.

Flowers are on spikes up to 12 cm long, males with spreading segments, females minute with appressed segments. Drupes are red and 8 – 9 mm across.

1

2

4

3

5

Fig 1 Upper surface of a typically shining *P. smithii* leaf. About half natural size.

Fig 2 Leaf lower surface. Half natural size.

Fig 3 The plant of *P. smithii* growing at the Mt Albert Research Station is more a shrub than a tree. January 1977.

Fig 4 The leaves are alternately arranged; the stipules are not shown because they fall off at an early stage.

Fig 5 Spikes of *P. smithii* female flowers showing how flowers are arranged in two dense, appressed rows, one on each side of the flattened axis. The flowers occur throughout most of the year.

Paratrophis banksii
Towai/Large-leaved milk tree

A spreading canopy tree growing up to 12 m high with a short, stout trunk up to 60 cm through which when injured exudes the milky sap of trees of this genus. Towai is found in lowland forests, from sea level to 450 m, growing from Mangonui south to the Marlborough Sounds.

The leaves of both juvenile and adult trees have crenate margins and are on petioles up to 1 cm long. Juvenile leaves are elliptic-oblong in shape and often deeply lobed; they are 2 – 6 cm long and 1 – 3 cm wide. The adult leaves are ovate to ovate-elliptic in shape with rounded to subacute apices. Their bases have margins abruptly narrowed to the petiole. They are 3.5 – 8.5 cm long and 2 – 3.5 cm wide.

The flowers are borne on spikes, usually from the axils of the leaves, either singly or paired but sometimes in threes. The male spikes are up to 3 cm long, the females up to 2.5 cm. The flower spikes of *P. banksii* are often attacked by a disease, possibly a fungus; when thus affected these spikes change into densely bunched panicles of overlapping bracts.

1

2

3

4

5

Fig 1 Seen against the light the membranous leaves of towai show a delicate pattern of vein reticulation and brilliant margins. This leaf is ovate with a subacute apex. One and a third times natural size.

Fig 2 A broad-ovate leaf of towai. This leaf has a rounded apex and shows a pale underside and a young pubescent branchlet. The leaf bases have margins abruptly narrowed to the petiole or even faintly cordate. One and a third times natural size. Juvenile leaves remain on the tree for some years after these adult leaves have appeared.

6

Fig 3 Spikes of male flowers arising axillarilly and terminally, the latter being fairly rare. Waiorongomai, November 1968. Also reproduced at one and a third times natural size.

Fig 4 A pubescent branchlet with alternate leaves and three male flower spikes. Also from Waiorongomai, November 1968.

Fig 5 Towai's bark is smooth and usually marked by faint horizontal rings. A white latex-like sap flows freely when it is cut, hence the common name of milkwood. The bark shown here is from the base of a low branch.

Fig 6 A fine mature towai tree showing the short, stout trunk, stout spreading branches and leafy branchlets which together give this tree its characteristic spreading and rounded canopy. Waiorongomai, November 1973.

Fig 7 A close view of a male flower spike. Clearly visible in this photograph are the flower buds and an opened flower with its four stamens and their anthers just beginning to shed pollen. From a tree at Waiorongomai, November 1973. At about three times natural size.
    The female flower of *P. banksii* (not shown here) is similar in general appearance to the flower of *P. microphylla*.

Fig 8 The fruit of towai is an ovoid red drupe about 6.5 cm long. Those here are from a tree at Waiorongomai, February 1962. At about three-quarters natural size.

Fig 9 A flower spike of *P. banksii* which has been attacked by a disease, possibly a fungus. This photograph illustrates clearly how flower spikes affected in this way change shape, becoming closely bunched panicles of overlapping bracts. This specimen was on a tree at Waiorongomai, photographed in November 1968.

7

8

9

Paratrophis microphylla
Turepo/Small-leaved milk tree

A small forest tree which is similar to *P. banksii* but which differs in having smaller leaves. The tree grows up to 12 m high with a trunk up to 60 cm through. It is found in moist areas or along creeks and river banks in lowland forests and forest margins, from sea level to 450 m. It is found throughout the North and South Islands.

When the bark of the small-leaved milk tree is cut it exudes a thick, milky sap which like that of *P. banksii* was often used in tea in place of milk by early settlers. The bark itself is rough and ridged, with raised lenticels.

The tree's leaves are ovate to obovate-oblong or elliptic, up to 25 mm long by 12 mm wide, on petioles up to 5 mm long; their margins are crenately serrate. Juvenile leaves are borne on slender zigzag branchlets of the young tree and are 5 – 10 mm long by 3 – 10 mm wide, obovate in shape with crenate margins. They often have large terminal and smaller lateral lobes.

The flowers arise on spikes which are either single or paired; the male spikes are up to 2.5 cm long and the female up to 1.5 cm. Male flowers are thickly covered with flowers but the females are sparsely so; the stalks of both are hairy. The fruit of *P. microphylla* is a round red drupe about 5 mm in diameter.

1

2

Fig 1 A typical leaf. Notice the hairy bud, petiole, branchlet and mid and lateral veins of the young leaf below. Twice natural size.

Fig 2 The pale underside of a turepo leaf with its prominent vein network. Notice the occasional hairs on the mid and lateral veins. Twice natural size.

Fig 3 A juvenile leaf showing two typical lateral lobes. Eight times natural size.

Fig 4 The bark of a young turepo tree.

Fig 5 A very old turepo tree growing at Waiorongomai, March 1975.

Fig 6 A spike of female flowers. They have a more sparse and open arrangement than the male flowers in Fig 9. Waiorongomai, November 1968. Five times natural size.

Fig 7 The tip of a female flower spike magnified fifteen times to show the hairy spike axis, hairy buds, perianth and stigmas of the female flower. Waiorongomai, November 1968.

Fig 8 Turepo drupes. Notice varying leaf shapes. Waiorongomai, February 1962.

Fig 9 A male flower spike with more crowded buds and flowers, at varying stages of opening and shedding pollen. The leaves in this photograph are more obovate-oblong than that shown in Fig 1. Waiorongomai, November 1973. About two and a half times natural size.

Fig 10 Close view of a male flower showing the four stamens with anthers and the four-partite nature of the hairy perianth and abortive ovary. Waiorongomai, November 1973. Twelve times natural size.

Fig 11 Turepo flower spikes which have been affected by a disease, possibly a fungus. Waiorongomai, November 1968.

3

4

Urtica ferox
Ongaonga/Tree nettle

Family *Urticaceae:* A widespread family found in tropical and temperate parts of the world, comprising forty-five genera and about 1,000 species of mainly herbs and subshrubs. A few are soft-wooded trees. Five genera occur in New Zealand.

Genus *Urtica:* A mainly north temperate zone genus with a few species in the south temperate zone and the tropics. There are some fifty species, mostly herbs with stinging hairs; six occur in New Zealand of which one forms a shrub or small tree.

The tree nettle or ongaonga as it is also known is a shrub or small soft-wooded tree which grows up to 3 m high with a trunk 12 cm across. It is much branched, the branches of both juvenile and mature forms tending to be intertwined.

The leaves, branchlets and branches all bear stout stinging hairs which can inflict a painful sting. The stinging hair is silicified; the head breaks off on contact and the poison is injected into the puncture. Trampers attempting to penetrate a thicket of ongaonga can be seriously affected by the many stings they receive and one or two cases of fatal effects have been recorded. As recently as 1961 a young tramper in Hawke's Bay died from the effects of stings from ongaonga in the bush. Bad stinging causes a lack of co-ordination of movement and a groggy condition which can last for about three days. It is extremely painful. The nature of the toxin is not completely known, although an acetylcholine derivative is suspected. Horses and dogs are often affected; three Home Guard horses died from stings in the Hutt Valley in 1944.

Ongaonga occurs throughout the North Island and west of the main divide in the South Island, between sea level and 600 m. It is found in scrubland and along forest margins, where it often forms thickets. The tree's paler green leaves are thin and membranous, ovate-triangular in shape with a truncate or semicordate base. They are pointed at the tips, with serrate margins and rows of stinging hairs. The marginal teeth are up to 1 cm long.

The flowers of this unusual tree arise from the leaf axils, on spikes up to 8 cm long, the sexes appearing on separate trees. Like other parts of the tree, the flower spikes bear stinging hairs. Ongaonga's seed is ovoid, about 1.5 mm long and brown coloured.

1

2

Fig 1 Upper leaf surface showing stinging hairs along the midvein, at the tip of each serration and around the petiole. The leaves of ongaonga are 8 – 12 cm long by 3 – 5 cm wide and the petioles are up to 5 cm long. The leaves of juvenile plants may be up to 15 cm long. This specimen at three-quarters natural size.

Fig 2 A foliage spray of ongaonga showing opposite leaves with stipules almost like miniature leaves. The flower spikes pictured here are male. Trentham, by the Hutt River, November 1965.

Fig 3 Male flower spikes arising at the leaf axils. Pohau Valley, November 1970. Reproduced here at about a quarter natural size.

Fig 4 A close view of the male flower buds shortly before opening. Hinakura, November 1970. Five times natural size.

Fig 5 An ongaonga branchlet containing female flower spikes. In this photograph the tips of the stinging hairs that break off are clearly visible on the petioles of the two central leaves. Pohau Valley, November 1970. About a quarter natural size.

3

4

5

6

7

8

Fig 6 The paler underside of a *U. ferox* leaf, showing soft pubescent hairs which occur especially along the veins. Also clearly visible in this picture are the usual stinging hairs along the leaf's midvein, margins and petiole. This specimen at almost natural size.

Fig 7 A close view of ongaonga's female flowers, magnified three and a half times. The tiny green ovoid structures are the ovaries and the brush-like white structures on top of them are the hairy tipped stigmas. Notice that the axes of the flower spikes are hairy, as are the flower pedicels. This specimen from a tree at Hinakura, November 1970.

Fig 8 A shrubby form of ongaonga showing the many branches and their typical interlacing habit. This tree was photographod at Gladstone, Wairarapa, in November 1972.

Fig 9 A tree nettle branchlet. Visible in this photograph are tiny basal soft hairs characteristic of the tree. Notice their pungent tips. From a tree at Hinakura, November 1970. Magnified to three and a half times natural size.

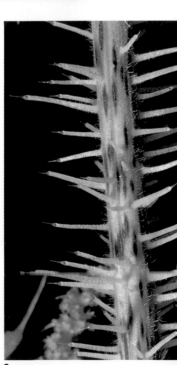

9

225

Family *Urticaceae*

Genus *Boehmeria:* **A** genus of 100 species of trees occuring in tropical and northern subtropical regions with a few in southern regions. The latter include the New Zealand species *B. australis* var. *dealbata,* which is endemic to the Kermadec Islands.

Boehmeria australis var. dealbata

1

Of very limited distribution, *B. australis* var. *dealbata* is found only on Raoul Island in the Kermadecs group north of New Zealand. There is a plant at Mt Albert Research Station in Auckland. In its juvenile stage *B. australis* var. *dealbata* is a shrub, but it grows to a small tree up to 8 m high. The leaves are large, up to 15 cm long and 4 cm wide; they are ovate to ovate-lanceolate in shape with a pointed apex and serrate margins. The petioles are up to 2.5 cm long with the undersurfaces velvety. The branchlets, petioles and leaf veins are pubescent with fine, silky hairs. Flowers are sessile, in dense axillary clusters, male and female occurring on the same or separate trees. It will flower for most of the year.

Fig 1 *Boehmeria australis* var. *dealbata* foliage showing mainly alternate leaves, large stipules and axillary clusters of flowers.

Fig 2 Leaf upper surface; the leaves are soft, somewhat rugulose. Half natural size.

Fig 3 The leaf lower surface is covered with white pubescence and has a soft, velvety texture. The petiole and branchlet are also pubescent. Half natural size.

Fig 4 The plant at the Mt Albert Research Station from which all these photographs were taken in April 1979. Now eight years old, it is still in the shrubby stage.

Fig 5 Mixed male and female inflorescences between pubescent petioles and the branchlet. Each male has three to five extended stamens; females have long, slender, withering stigmas. Two and a half times natural size.

Fig 6 A group of female inflorescences. The white stigmas are receptive; the brown are withering after pollination. Two and a half times natural size.

2

3

4

5

6

Family *Corynocarpaceae:* A small family of one genus with five species of trees confined to New Guinea, New Hebrides, New Caledonia, Queensland and New Zealand.

Genus *Corynocarpus:* This genus has the same distribution as the family. One species, *C. laevigatus,* occurs in New Zealand.

Corynocarpus laevigatus
Karaka

Karaka is a handsome, leafy, canopy tree which grows up to 15 m high with a trunk up to 60 cm through and stout, spreading branches. The thick, leathery, glossy leaves are large, generally 10—15 cm long but sometimes 20 cm long, and 5—7 cm wide. The leaves are elliptic to obovate-oblong in shape, on stout petioles 10—15 mm long. Their margins are usually recurved. The perfect flowers arise on stiff, stout terminal panicles up to 20 cm long; each flower is 4—5 mm in diameter.

The karaka occurs in coastal regions, often as groves, in the Kermadec Islands, both the North and South Islands and the Chatham Islands. It is, however, less common in the South Island than elsewhere. It produces large numbers of its fruit annually and the seeds germinate so freely that groves of karakas often have seedlings growing underneath.

The fruit of karaka is an orange drupe 2.5—4 cm long, known as kopi by the Maori people who used it for food. The outer fleshy layer of the kopi is edible, but the kernel contains a very deadly poison, a nitro-compound called karakin, which is the only one of its kind so far isolated in nature. To remove this poison the Maoris steamed the drupes in their stone ovens for several hours and then washed them in flax kits immersed in the water of a running stream or a pond for one or two days. This removed the poison and husks. The remaining kernels were dried and stored until required.

1

Maori children were often affected by eating karaka kernels that had not been properly prepared. The poison karakin causes convulsions and a twisting of the limbs which can become permanent. The kohekohe was used in some way as an antidote to karaka poisoning. Karaka leaves are said to heal if their upper surfaces are applied to wounds.

Maori legend maintains that the karaka tree was brought to New Zealand by the early Maoris from their homeland, the legendary Hawaiki, but the known distribution of the genus *Corynocarpus* appears to contradict this. It seems more probable that they confused the karaka with a very similar tree growing in their Hawaiki. It is certain, however, that the Maoris cultivated the karaka as a source of food.

2

Fig 1 Karaka's distinctive orange, fleshy drupes are heavy. Although the tree's flowers are erect (see Fig 5) the drupes invariably hang downwards. The fleshy outer part is edible but it is the kernel, the hard seed inside the fruit, which possesses poisonous properties. The karaka was actually one of the few native trees raised artificially by the Maori people. This specimen from a tree at Karaka Bay, February 1969. Slightly less than natural size.

Fig 2 Karaka trees normally bear drupes each year. Usually they occur in profusion, as on this tree photographed at Coromandel, December 1965. Masses of the orange drupes during late summer and autumn give the trees a striking appearance. It is unfortunate, and rather paradoxical, that the fallen fruits rotting on the ground create an unpleasant smell around the base of karaka trees during this period.

Fig 3 A fine karaka tree growing in the open. A tree growing in forest will develop a broad canopy, but when the surrounding growth is removed the tree will often then develop a secondary layer of branches, as on this tree at Ngunguru, near Whangarei, January 1970.

Fig 4 A panicle of karaka flowers on a tree growing at Karaka Bay, October 1968. About natural size.

Fig 5 The terminal portion of a flower panicle showing the perfect bisexual flowers. They have been magnified here to four times natural size. Also from Karaka Bay, October 1968.

Fig 6 Upper surface of a typically large, thick, glossy karaka leaf. At about natural size.

Fig 7 The lower surface of a karaka leaf showing the paler surface and prominent midvein. The recurved leaf margins are also clear on this specimen, which is at about half natural size.

Family *Icacinaceae:* A widespread tropical and subtropical family containing fifty-eight genera and about 400 species of trees and shrubs and a few lianes. One genus, *Pennantia,* has two endemic species in New Zealand.

Genus *Pennantia:* A genus of five species, two in New Zealand and the others in Australia and Norfolk Island.

Pennantia baylisiana

This is a tree with a very limited distribution. *P. baylisiana* is a tree which grows up to 5 m high and is found on Great King Island of the Three Kings Islands. It is actually known there from only a single tree. A specimen has been grown at the Mt Albert Research Station in Auckland.

The branchlets of *P. baylisiana* have conspicuous lenticels and swollen, flattened leaf nodes. The leaves are wavy, leathery and glossy, up to 25 cm long and 15 cm wide; they are obovate in shape with a rounded or almost truncate apex and a rounded or cuneate base. Domatia occur where the lower surface mid and lateral veins meet. The flowers occur in panicles arising below the leaves or terminally.

1

Fig 1 A spray of *P. baylisiana* foliage. This attractive specimen shows lenticels on the branchlet, the alternate leaves arising from swollen nodes and the stout petioles, which are 25 – 30 mm long. There are varying leaf shapes pictured here. All the photographs on this page were taken in December 1977 from the tree growing at the Mt Albert Research Station.

2

3

4

5

Fig 2 A typical glossy leaf with its wavy form, stout petiole and distinct veins. At one third natural size.

Fig 3 Leaf underside showing raised veins, domatia and truncate apex. Also one third natural size.

Fig 4 The specimen growing at the Mt Albert Research Station shows the typical habit of this tree, with its leaves occurring in clusters towards the tip of the branchlets. The leaves fall as the branchlets grow, leaving conspicuous leaf scars on the branches.

Fig 5 The bark of *P. baylisiana.*

229

Pennantia corymbosa
Kaikomako

A slender canopy tree up to 12 m high. Kaikomako passes through a juvenile stage when it is a straggling, twiggy plant with interlacing branches carrying a few small, wedge-shaped and lobed leaves far apart on the branches. The stage may last for many years until finally the main stem of the adult tree grows upwards from the tangled branches, which slowly atrophy and fall away. Kaikomako is found throughout both North and South Islands from Mangonui southwards in lowland forests, from sea level to 600 m.

In both juveniles and adults the leaf petioles, branchlets and inflorescences are pubescent. The leaves of juveniles are 7 – 15 mm long by 5 – 10 mm wide, obovate, cuneate at the base and lobed or toothed around the apex; they occur on slender petioles 2 – 3 mm long. The adult leaves are thick, leathery, 5 – 10 cm long by 1 – 4 cm wide; they are oblong to obovate-oblong, coarsely crenate-dentate or lobed, growing on slender petioles about 1 cm long.

The flowers of kaikomako are delightfully fragrant and occur in panicles 4 – 8 cm long. There are male,

1

female and sometimes bisexual flowers, occurring on separate trees. In full flower the tree is so smothered with creamy-white panicles of flowers that the foliage is almost obscured.

The fruit of this tree is a black drupe, ovoid in shape. It is the favourite food of the bellbird, korimako, from which the tree's Maori name is derived. In the forest the tree is sometimes attacked by the black, velvety fungus that often occurs on beech trees.

Fig 1 A spray of kaikomako foliage showing alternate to sub-opposite obovate leaves, branchlets with lenticels (at left) and thick leaf margins. At about half natural size.

Fig 2 Kaikomako drupes are shining black when ripe. Woodside Gorge, March 1969. About natural size. The leaves pictured here are obovate-oblong.

Fig 3 Flower panicles in bud and with male flowers. Lake Pounui, December 1968.

FIRE LIGHTER

Kaikomako wood was used by the Maori people to make fire. A sharp pointed kaikomako stick was rubbed up and down a piece of mahoe, Melicytus ramiflorus, or pate, Schefflera digitata, until a groove formed and filled with fine dust, which would gather towards one end of the groove. If it was rubbed vigorously it would smoke and could be fanned into a flame.

2

3

4

6

7

5

Fig 4 Female flowers and rounded female buds. They have been magnified four times to show the large, three-lobed stigma and short, abortive stamens. From a tree at Makara, December 1973.

Fig 5 Male flowers and elongated male buds magnified three times to show the long, filamentous stamens with their large anthers, just starting to split open to shed pollen, and the tiny, abortive ovary. Lake Pounui, December 1968.

Fig 6 The bark of kaikomako.

Fig 7 A small kaikomako tree in flower near Lake Pounui, December 1972.

Fig 8 Juvenile leaves with their short, slender, lightly pubescent petioles and pubescent branchlets. Opepe Bush, April 1965. About natural size.

Fig 9 A juvenile kaikomako plant. The tree illustrated here is just beginning to produce its adult stem. At Opepe Bush, September 1978.

8

9

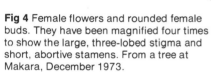

Family *Santalaceae:* A tropical and temperate region family of thirty-five genera and about 400 species of trees, herbs and semi-parasitic shrubs. Two genera have species occurring in New Zealand; one of these, *Mida salicifolia*, is a tree.

Genus *Mida:* A genus containing two species, one of which occurs in Juan Fernandez and the other in New Zealand, where it is endemic.

Mida salicifolia
Maire

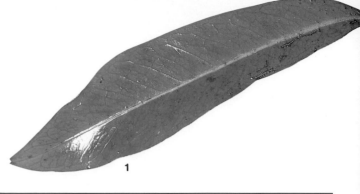

1

A slender tree up to 6 m high with a trunk up to 20 cm in diameter, found rather locally in lowland to lower montane forest from near North Cape southwards (more common in the north), from sea level to 450 m.

The leaves of *M. salicifolia* are alternate or in subopposite pairs, on short, slender petioles. The leaf blade is narrow-lanceolate, 5—12 cm long and 3—10 mm wide; the leaves are mostly acute, membraneous to thinly leathery and somewhat glossy above. They have a paler, less shining lower surface. The inflorescences of *M. salicifolia* are axillary, the flowers bisexual or functionally unisexual and 4—6 mm across. The narrow, bright-red fruit is about 12 mm long and takes twelve months to mature.

2

3

4

5

Fig 1 Upper surface of a typical maire leaf. Natural size.

Fig 2 Spray with alternative leaves and flower buds. Rewa Reserve, East Wairarapa, October 1973.

Fig 3 Spray of very narrow maire leaves. Also from Rewa Reserve.

Fig 4 Leaves of plants in the more northern regions tend to be much broader than those further south. This spray shows opposite, sub-opposite and alternate leaves.

Fig 5 The paler leaf lower surface. About natural size.

Fig 6 Two *M. salicifolia* trees growing in the Rewa Reserve, October 1973.

Fig 7 The rough bark of *M. salicifolia*.

Fig 8 The fruit is bright red when ripe and the rim of the receptacle persists on top of it. Rewa Reserve, late October 1973. About natural size.

6

7

8

9

10

11

12

Fig 9 Functionally male flowers. From a tree at Mt Meredith, October 1973. Five times natural size.

Fig 10 A spray with alternate leaves and inflorescences arising from the leaf axils. Rewa Reserve, late October 1973.

Fig 11 Perfect flowers, here magnified to five times their natural size. Also from a tree growing at Rewa Reserve, late October 1973.

Fig 12 A functionally female maire flower, surrounded by developing fruits. From a tree at Mt Meredith, October 1973. Six times natural size. Compare this with the functionally male flower in Fig 9.

233

Discaria toumatou
Matagouri/Wild Irishman

Family *Rhamnaceae:* A cosmopolitan family of fifty-eight genera containing some 900 species of trees and shrubs. Many of the shrubs are climbers with twining stems or tendrils; some have thorns. The familiar garden shrubs of the genus *Ceanothus* are probably the best-known members of this family. Two genera have species in New Zealand.

Genus *Discaria:* A genus of shrubs or trees with rigid branches and opposite leaves. Ten species are known from the southern Andes, Brazil, Australia and New Zealand. The single New Zealand species is endemic.

A branching, thorny shrub or a small tree up to 6 m high. Matagouri, or wild Irishman as it is also known, is found in open tussock, dune country and rocky places, from sea level to 900 m. It grows abundantly down the east coast of the South Island, rarely on the west coast of the North Island and less commonly along the west coast of the South Island. In high country the tree is deciduous. The leaves occur abundantly on plants growing in shade and on those in the open in spring, arising either singly, in bundles from below the axils of the thorns, or opposite on short shoots.

The flowers, which are 3−5 mm across, arise singly or in fascicles on short, hairy pedicels from below the axils of the thorns. The globose fruit of wild Irishman is three-lobed and about 5 mm in diameter.

1 2

3

Fig 1 A tree growing near Lake Pukaki in December 1964.

Fig 2 Wild Irishman in full flower. Thomas River, December 1959. The thorns are so hard that they were used by Maori people as tattooing needles.

Fig 3 The fruit, here full-sized but not yet ripe. Jordan Creek, January 1971. Three times natural size.

Fig 4 A branchlet showing fascicles of both leaves and flowers. From a tree at Otari, October 1970.

Fig 5 Close view of a single wild Irishman flower. The perianth consists of sepals; the flowers are sweet-scented and bisexual. From a tree at Otari, October 1970. Nine times natural size.

Fig 6 The leaves are very thick, leathery and glossy. They are 5−20 mm long by 2−5 mm wide, narrow obovate to obovate-oblong in shape; the apex bears a blunt apiculus or spine. Otari, October 1970. Six times natural size.

Fig 7 The bark of wild Irishman.

4   **5**   **6 7**

Family *Rhamnaceae*

Genus *Pomaderris:* An Australian and New Zealand genus of forty-five species of shrubs or small trees. Seven species are found in New Zealand and three of these can grow into small trees.

Pomaderris apetala
Tainui

1

An erect-growing, much-branching shrub or small tree found in New Zealand and Australia. In New Zealand it occurs naturally only in a few coastal localities from Kawhia Harbour to the Mokau River, but it has been widely grown as an ornamental plant.

The tainui is easily recognised by its distinctive upright growing habit. It grows to a height of about 5 m, with ascending branches and with the branchlets, petioles, veins and lower leaf surfaces covered by a soft, thick, velvety tomentum of starlike hairs. The leaves of *P. apetala* are 5−7 cm long by 2−3 cm wide, the margins recurved and minutely crenulate; the upper surfaces of these leaves are quite wrinkled and bear scattered star-like hairs when young.

Fig 1 A tainui tree growing at Otari showing the typical erect growing habit. Flowering branches of another tree appear at the left. November 1970.

Fig 2 The spectacular flower head is about 10 cm long. From a tree at Otari, November 1965.

Fig 3 A close view of tainui flower buds and a single flower, which is without petals. Otari, November 1970. Seven times natural size.

Fig 4 Section of an inflorescence showing starlike hairs on the main stem and the pedicels. Otari, November 1970. Three and a half times natural size.

Fig 5 A branchlet with growing shoot and young leaves clothed with tomentum. The new alternate leaves have starlike hairs on the upper surfaces and petioles 1 cm long.

Fig 6 The hairy tainui leaf lower surface with its distinctive raised veins. Natural size.

2

3

4

5

6

Pomaderris kumeraho

Kumarahou/Golden tainui
P. hamiltonii

1

Normally regarded as shrubs reaching 2—3 m high, these two species can grow into small, slender-trunked trees 3—4 m high when growing in the shade or in sheltered positions. They are found mostly on clay soils in scrubland from about North Cape south to the Bay of Plenty, *P. hamiltonii* being more common in southern parts from Warkworth to Thames.

The leaves of *P. kumeraho* are about 6 cm long by 3 cm wide; those of *P. hamiltonii* are narrower, about 2 cm wide, and elliptic in shape with often acute apices, whereas *P. kumeraho* leaves are oval with obtuse apices. Both species have distinct venation above and below with a white-to-buff tomentum of star-like hairs on the lower surfaces.

The inflorescence in *P. kumeraho* is a much-branched, tight, round-headed corymb, about 10 cm across, produced in profusion all over the plant at the tips of the branches and containing many small flowers each about 8 mm across. In *P. hamiltonii* the flowers arise in more open-branched, conical-headed corymbs, and the flowers are a paler yellow. The seeds of both are smooth and dark-brown to black.

P. kumeraho inflorescence buds begin to form as soon as the flowers for the current season are spent. They appear at the ends of the branchlets, first arising below this season's flowering branchlets as small, dark-brown buds. These buds slowly grow over the next twelve months until they burst into flower.

Fig 1 A small tree of *P. kumeraho* in full flower at Otari, October 1969.

Fig 2 A spray of *P. hamiltonii* with some developing flower buds on the much more open corymb typical of this species. Notice also the tomentose branchlets and acute and obtuse-tipped leaves.

Fig 3 Lower leaf surfaces of *P. hamiltonii* showing the fine tomentum.

Fig 4 The soft leaf of *P. kumeraho* showing depressed venation on the upper surface. Natural size.

Fig 5 A tight, conical-headed corymb of flowers of *P. kumeraho*. They are terminal on a branchlet. Waikanae, September 1976.

Fig 6 "Tufted" tomentum on a leaf petiole of *P. kumeraho,* magnified four times. This tomentum, which consists of long, star-like hairs overlying a lower layer of short, sessile, star-like hairs, also extends on to the veins of the leaf lower surfaces.

2

3

5

4

6

Family *Rutaceae:* A widespread family containing 150 genera and 900 species of small trees and shrubs, mostly the latter. The most notable member is the genus *Citrus,* the lemons, oranges, grapefruits and limes. All have oil glands in their leaves that are aromatic smelling when crushed. The Amur cork tree *Phellodendron amurense,* of northern China, also belongs here, as do many well-known garden shrubs such as *Boronia, Diosma* and *Eriostemon.*

Genus *Melicope:* A genus of seventy species found in Indomalaysia, Australia, some Pacific Islands and New Zealand. The two New Zealand species are endemic.

Melicope simplex
Poataniwha

A small tree up to 8 m high or a low shrub with slender, divaricating branches. Poataniwha is found along the margins of coastal and lowland forests from North Cape southwards throughout both the North and South Islands.

Poataniwha's slender branchlets bear unifoliolate, crenate-margined leaves dotted with glands. They are rhomboid to sub-orbicular in shape, 5—20 mm long on slender, flattened petioles about 5 mm long. There is a juvenile stage, the plants of which have trifoliolate leaves with slender petioles up to 2 cm long and leaflets up to 10 mm long. Inflorescences each bear one to four greenish flowers which are mostly functionally unisexual and on peduncles about 5 mm long. The seeds are black and shining.

1

Fig 1 A small tree. Opotiki, December 1974.

Fig 2 Upper surface of the thick, leathery leaf. Twice natural size.

Fig 3 Leaf underside dotted with aromatic glands. Twice natural size.

Fig 4 Fruits. Trentham, December 1968.

Fig 5 Female flowers. Trentham, November 1968. Eight times natural size.

Fig 6 A male flower. Trentham, November 1968. Ten times natural size.

Fig 7 Opening seed capsules. Waipunga Gorge, April 1974.

2

3

4

5

6

7

237

Melicope ternata
Wharangi

A stiff branched small tree up to 7 m in height. In the forest wharangi reaches up to the light before branching; in the open it is more bushy and spreading. An example of regenerating wharangi trees growing thickly in the bush is illustrated in **Fig 1,** taken in the Wiparata Reserve, Waikanae, in February 1979. The tree is found from sea level to 300 m, mainly along the margin of coastal and lowland forests, in scrub and in rocky places, on the Kermadec and Three Kings Islands and from North Cape to Nelson.

The slender green branchlets bear opposite, trifoliolate, bright yellow-green leaves on petioles up to 5 cm long. The leaflets are thin, slightly leathery and 7—10 cm long by 3—4 cm wide; they vary in shape from obovate-cuneate to obovate-elliptic or ovate-oblong, with their petiolules up to 5 mm long. Leaves near flowers are sometimes only one or two-foliolate.

Wharangi's inflorescences arise usually as paired, axillary, three-branched cymes on peduncles about 2 cm long. The fruit of this tree is a dry, four-lobed, wrinkled capsule and the seeds are black and glossy.

2

3

4

Fig 2 The bark of wharangi.

Fig 3 A wharangi tree 7 m high left leaning after surrounding trees had fallen. The tree had grown tall towards the light. Photographed in the Wiparata Reserve, Waikanae, February 1979.

Fig 4 *M. ternata* and *M. simplex* trees often hybridise; this photograph has been taken from such a tree. It shows how as the fruit opens the seeds are left hanging each by a thread attached to its valve. Otari, March 1961.

Fig 5 A wharangi spray showing leaves and the typical paired cymes with buds and flowers. From a tree growing at Karaka Bay, September 1968.

Fig 6 The flower magnified three times. Also from a tree at Karaka Bay, September 1968.

Fig 7 A leaf showing the pale lower surface of the leaflets and the prominent veins. About half natural size.

Fig 8 Branchlet showing the upper surfaces of trifoliolate leaves. These are at natural size.

5

6

7   8

Dysoxylum spectabile
Kohekohe

Family *Meliaceae:* A family of fifty genera and about 550 species of trees and shrubs found mainly in tropical America and tropical Asia. The family includes cedars such as the West Indian cedar, *Cedrela odorata,* and the Chinese cedar, *C. chinensis.* There is also the genus *Melia,* with *M. azedarach,* the Pride of India tree, also called Persian lilac. The family also includes the true mahoganies, which embrace such famous trees as the West Indian mahogany, *Swietenia mahogani,* and the broad-leaved mahogany, *S. macrophylla,* of Honduras. One species of the genus *Dysoxylum* occurs in New Zealand.

Genus *Dysoxylum:* An Indomalaysian genus of 200 species with one endemic species in New Zealand.

With its long, drooping panicles of greenish-white, waxy flowers sprouting from the trunk and branches during early winter the kohekohe is one of New Zealand's most spectacular trees. Quite young trees less than 5 m high can flower profusely. The three to four-celled fruit capsule which ripens about fifteen months later is equally spectacular when it opens to reveal two seeds enclosed by a fleshy, scarlet aril sitting in each cell. Individual trees flower in alternate years, there being no flowers in the season the tree is maturing its fruit capsules.

Kohekohe used to form extensive tracts of coastal and lowland forest in damp situations, from North Cape south to Nelson, but these have now mostly disappeared in the face of settlement and damage by opossums. Groups of the tree can now be found only in a few reserves and in straggling remains such as those in the Waikanae-Paraparaumu area.

With its columnar trunk, stout, spreading branches and large, glossy leaves, the kohekohe is always a handsome tree. The pinnately compound leaves have petioles about 4 cm long; the opposite or subopposite leaflets have petiolules about 1.5 cm long and leaf blades which are undulate, slightly leathery and obliquely ovate- to obovate-oblong in shape. The inflorescences are up to 30 cm long, with individual flowers up to 3 cm across on short pedicels. Seed capsules, several to a stalk, are up to 2.5 cm across.

1

Fig 1 This fine old kohekohe growing at Waikanae shows the typical columnar trunk and stout canopy-forming branches of the tree. June 1973.

Fig 2 The smooth bark on a kohekohe trunk is often covered with lichens. The tough red wood has been used for furniture and fence posts.

Fig 3 A habit characteristic of this tree: the main lateral roots spread on the surface and form small buttresses. Waikanae, August 1968.

Fig 4 Clusters of panicles of flowers sprout from the trunk of a tree at Huntleigh Park, Wellington, May 1970.

Fig 5 The individual flowers of kohekohe are delicate with waxy, quite thick petals and darker-green hairy sepals. Waikanae, August 1968. About twice natural size.

Fig 6 This flower bud in the process of opening shows the way the petals fold over one another. Also clearly illustrated is the cylindrical, toothed, staminal column to which the anthers are attached. From a tree at Waikanae, August 1968. About twice natural size.

Fig 7 A short panicle of mature kohekohe seed capsules, some opening. Waikanae, May 1972. Reproduced at about natural size.

Fig 8 The fleshy nature of the capsule and the red arils that hold the seeds is clearly shown in this photograph. Waikanae, May 1972. Twice natural size.

Fig 9 The upperside of some of the leaflets which make up the large, pinnately-compound kohekohe leaf. The leaf lower surface is a paler yellow-green. At about half natural size.

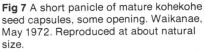

Family *Sapindaceae:* A tropical and subtropical family comprising 150 genera and about 2,000 species of trees, shrubs and lianes. It includes the attractive lychee (or litchi) tree, *Nephelium litchi,* of China, with its delicious edible fruits, and a number of timber trees. Two genera, *Alectryon* and *Dodonaea,* have species in New Zealand.

Genus *Alectryon:* A genus of fifteen species found in Malaysia, tropical Australia, New Guinea, Hawaii, some Polynesian islands and New Zealand. The two New Zealand species are endemic.

Alectryon excelsus/Titoki
A. grandis

1

Titoki is found in lowland forests from sea level to 600 m, from North Cape to Banks Peninsula in the east and to about Bruce Bay in the west. It favours river flats. With its short, stout trunk about 60 cm through and spreading branches with attractive pinnate leaves it forms a handsome tree growing up to 10 m high.

The imparipinnate leaves of titoki are 10—40 cm long on petioles about 8 cm long. Each leaf consists of four to six pairs of alternate to subopposite leaflets which have petiolules about 5 mm long. The leaflets are 5—10 cm long by 2—5 cm wide, ovate-oblong to ovate-lanceolate in shape, more or less sinuate, with margins serrate, dentate or simple.

The tiny flowers occur in axillary panicles up to 30 cm long and are pleasantly fragrant. The flowers are usually functionally unisexual (although the female often looks bisexual); they are 3—4 mm in diameter with five basally fused hairy sepals and no petals. The slender pedicels, 5 mm long, are hairy, as are the panicle axes. The anthers are the main visible part of each flower, splitting longitudinally down their sides to release the pollen. The style is densely hairy, the stamens sparsely so, giving the open flower a hairy appearance. The seed capsule is somewhat woody and opens to reveal a glossy black seed partly embedded in a scarlet, fleshy aril.

2

3

Fig 1 Close view of several of the leaflets making up the large leaf. Here at natural size.

Fig 2 A spray showing pale-coloured young titoki leaves, flower panicle arising from the leaf axils, and hairy branchlets and petioles.

Fig 3 A panicle of seed capsules, some of which have opened. Trentham, December 1968. About natural size.

ALECTRYON GRANDIS

The species A. grandis is found only on the Three Kings Islands and differs from A. excelsus in having longer leaves from 30 to 45 cm long and its leaflets in two to three pairs instead of four to six. It is also a smaller tree, growing only up to 5 m high.

4

5

6

7

Fig 4 Titoki bark is often covered with growths of lichens.

Fig 5 Typical form of titoki's imparipinnate leaf, upperside. The leaf lower surface is paler in colour. In some conditions these leaves will grow up to 40 cm long. About one-eighth natural size.

Fig 6 The wide spreading form of titoki is shown by this tree growing at Hinakura, November 1964.

Fig 7 The terminal portion of the titoki flower panicle. Clearly illustrated here are the hairy axis, pedicels and sepals and the circlet of six to eight anthers. From a tree growing in the Pahaoa Valley, November 1970. Reproduced here at five times natural size.

Fig 8 An open male flower with the anthers splitting and shedding pollen. Also clearly illustrated are the flower's lack of petals, and the hairy stamens and hairy abortive ovary. Trentham, November 1968. Nine and a half times natural size.

Fig 9 Titoki male flowers. The flower in the foreground in this photograph has shed its pollen, but those above and behind have yet to do so. From a tree growing in the Pahaoa Valley, November 1970. Nine times natural size.

Fig 10 Close view of the seed capsules, some of which have opened. Notice the brownish hairy clothing on the unopened capsules. Titoki seed capsules take about one year to mature; when they ripen they open to reveal the large, black, glossy seeds and striking scarlet aril. Trentham, December 1968. At about one and a half times natural size.

8

9

10

Dodonaea viscosa
Akeake

Family *Sapindaceae*

Genus *Dodonaea:* A genus of about sixty species of trees and shrubs found mainly in Australia with a few species in other tropical and subtropical regions. The New Zealand representative is not endemic, being widespread in most warm regions of the world, with many variant forms.

Akeake is an erect shrub or small tree up to 7 m high with spreading, gently ascending branches and sticky branchlets. It is found in New Zealand in coastal and lowland scrub and forests, from sea level to 550 m, from North Cape to Banks Peninsula in the east and just south of Greymouth in the west. It also grows on the Chatham Islands. Akeake's hardy properties make it useful as a shelter plant, particularly in exposed conditions.

The leaves are alternate to subopposite, 4—10 cm long by 1—3 cm wide. The flowers are without petals and arise in terminal, densely flowered panicles up to 4 cm long; each flower is on a pubescent pedicel 4 mm long. The flowers are predominantly unisexual on the common form, with males and females mostly on separate plants; the coloured form 'Purpurea' bears many bisexual flowers. Male flowers have eight to ten anthers on very short filaments; the females have an elongated two-pronged style and no stamens, not even aborted ones. The fruit is a compressed capsule about 15 mm across, with two to three thin, veined, broad, lobed wings.

Akeake wood is black, variegated with streaks of white and very hard. It was used by the Maori people for making clubs.

Metcalf records that the coloured form, 'Purpurea', was discovered growing on the banks of the Wairau River in Marlborough in the early 1890s. It is now widely cultivated in parks and gardens. This form of *D. viscosa* is more sticky than the common form.

1

2

3

Fig 1 A typical akeake tree, photographed growing in the East Takaka Valley in January 1971.

Fig 2 Upper surface of an akeake leaf. The leaves are narrow-obovate to narrow-elliptic in shape, obtuse and gradually narrowed to a petiole about 1 cm long. This specimen reproduced here at a little less than natural size.

Fig 3 Undersurface of a leaf, showing the prominent midvein and vein network. About natural size.

Fig 4 A beautiful specimen of the form 'Purpurea', clearly showing the attractive purplish-red leaves of this cultivar. This tree was growing at Taupo, April 1965. The form 'Purpurea' can be easily raised from seed.

Fig 5 Male flower of the cultivar 'Purpurea'. Its distinctive colour is markedly different from that of the flower of the common form, illustrated in Fig 10. Here at nine times natural size.

244

4   5   6

7   8   9

Fig 6 The striking bright purplish-red seed capsules of the form 'Purpurea'. Clearly illustrated in this photograph are their broad, thin wings. From a tree at Taupo, December 1969.

Fig 7 The reddish bark of akeake peels from the trunk in thin flakes.

Fig 8 A single female flower of the common form of akeake. In this photograph it has been magnified nine times to show the two-pronged style and the four narrow sepals that make up the flower. From a tree at Otari, October 1973.

Fig 9 Seed capsules from the common form. These were from a tree growing on the Upper Waima Ure River bed in March 1969. The yellowish-red seed capsules make an attractive sight when a tree is heavily laden.

Fig 10 Male flowers. Notice the closely packed anthers and in the centre the aborted ovary. From a tree at Otari, October 1970. Nine times natural size.

Fig 11 A typical densely flowered panicle of *D. viscosa* flowers, arising terminally from the branchlet. Those pictured here are male flowers, which usually grow on separate trees from the female. This specimen photographed on a tree growing at Otari, October 1965.

10   11

Family Araliaceae
Genus *Meryta*
Genus *Schefflera*
Genus *Pseudopanax*

The family Araliaceae is mainly a tropical family but with some genera in temperate regions. It includes fifty-five genera with about 700 species of trees, shrubs, herbs and lianes, including the rice paper tree, *Tetrapanax papyrifera,* of China and Formosa, and the Japanese angelica tree, *Aralia elata,* as well as the well-known European ivy. Five genera occur in New Zealand and three of these, *Meryta, Schefflera* and *Pseudopanax,* include trees.

Pseudopanax is a genus known from South America, Tasmania, New Caledonia, China and New Zealand. In this country it now includes the seven species previously classified in the genus *Neopanax,* giving a total of twenty-two known species of trees and shrubs. All the fifteen New Zealand species are endemic; they include our five-fingers and lancewoods, many of which have striking juvenile stages. Two remaining species are found in temperate South America, one in Tasmania, one in New Caledonia, and three in China.

Some of the species belonging to *Pseudopanax* are remarkable for the extraordinary metamorphosis they pass through during growth from a seedling to the juvenile and adult stages. In fact the juvenile and adult forms differ so remarkably that the famous botanist J. D. Hooker in his *Handbook of the New Zealand Flora* (1867) described these two stages as quite different species (under the generic name of *Panax*): *P. longissimum* for the juvenile plant and *P. crassifolium* for the adult. Considering how they appear in the forest this error is not surprising.

T. Kirk first described the seedling forms of *P. crassifolius* in 1889; they were later enlarged upon by L. Cockayne in 1899. The various stages passed through by the growing *P. crassifolius* (two are illustrated here) are:

(1) The two cotyledons have prominent midribs and recurved margins; they persist for a long time.

(2) The first leaf is linear-oblong, rather leathery, 2.5–5 cm long, green blotched with brown and ir-regularly coarsely toothed. There is a long, four-angled leaf stalk about one-third the length of the leaf blade.

(3) Subsequent leaves become longer and more linear-lanceolate, with more even widths and small distant teeth. The second and third leaves are dark black-green with pale-brownish or yellowish spots and raised midveins. Their lower surfaces are paler.

(4) The fourth and several succeeding leaves are linear in shape, spreading and pointing slightly up-wards. There are several stout distant teeth entirely different from the serrations or "teeth" of the first leaf. The upper surface is black tinged with green, often with pale-brown blotches, yellowish towards the tip. The leaves at this stage have no stalks.

(5) From now on, for about fifteen to twenty years, the leaves are rigid, and extremely long and nar-row. They are arranged in deflex fashion to surround the top of the stem like the ribs of a partially opened umbrella. They reach 18–100 cm in length but are not more than 1–1.25 cm wide and are very thick and leathery with distant mar-ginal teeth and sharp tips. The mid-vein, broad and yellowish in colour, makes up about one-third of the leaf upper surface, which is black faintly tinged with underlying green and adjacent to the teeth. The stem forms a slender, straight, un-branched trunk 4.5–6 m high.

(6) After a period of growth the stem begins to branch at the top. The linear leaves are now replaced by upright broader and shorter leaves; they may be all unifoliolate, or three to five-foliolate or mixed.

(7) In the mature stage only unifoliolate leaves are produced. They are thick and leathery, 10–20 cm long by 2–3 cm wide and lanceolate to narrow ellip-tic-cuneate or linear-obovate in shape. There are acute or obtuse apices; the margins are entire to sinuate or coarsely serrate. The prominent midvein is raised and the petiole short and stout. The tree becomes round-headed with spreading branches and a tall, straight trunk as it assumes its adult form.

Family *Araliaceae*

Genus Meryta: This is a genus of twenty-five small, resinous trees found in New Caledonia, New Guinea, the Solomon Islands, some Polynesian islands, Queensland and New Zealand.

Meryta sinclairii
Puka

Reaching up to 8 m high with a rounded head of huge, flat leaves set on a trunk up to 50 cm through, puka is a most unusual looking tree, one of the most handsome of our native species. It grows naturally on the Three Kings Islands and also on the Hen and Chickens Islands, but is now widely grown as a garden specimen in warmer parts of New Zealand.

Puka's leaves are amongst the largest of any dicotyledonous native plant. They can grow as long as 50 cm and as wide as 20 cm, on petioles up to 35 cm long. The leaves are very thick and leathery with a glossy upper surface. Puka's flowers and fruits arise on erect terminal panicles up to 50 cm long.

1

2

3

4

5

6

Fig 1 A fine example of a mature puka tree growing at Mt Eden, Auckland, December 1970. It shows the spreading, rounded crown typical of this species.

Fig 2 A terminal flower panicle. As the flowers open the whole panicle becomes crowded with insects such as native wasps, ichneumon flies, bees, small diptera, aphids and even ants. Waikanae, May 1979.

Fig 3 Leaf spray showing the way in which puka leaves crowd towards the tips of the branchlets.

Fig 4 Underside of a leaf showing the distinct venation. One-sixth natural size.

Fig 5 The flowers are normally functionally unisexual, with male and female on separate trees, occasionally bisexual flowers occur. These male flowers are shedding their pollen as they open. Waikanae, May 1979. About four and a half times natural size

Fig 6 A panicle of ripening fruits; they become black when ripe. From a tree at Lake Pounui, February 1962.

Family *Araliaceae*

Genus *Schefflera:* A genus of some 200 species of small trees and shrubs found commonly in tropical and subtropical regions of both the Northern and Southern Hemispheres. One endemic species occurs in New Zealand.

Schefflera digitata
Pate

Pate grows throughout the North, South and Stewart Islands, from sea level to 1,200 m. It is usually found in damp parts of the forest and along stream banks. Pate forms a small, spreading, low-growing tree up to 8 m high with stout branches. It is often commonly found as a shrub growing along shady roadsides through bush.

The large compound leaves of *S. digitata* are three to nine-foliolate on long petioles up to 25 cm long. The leaflets are rather thin and somewhat soft to touch. They are obovate-cuneate in shape with sharply serrate margins and petiolules about 2 cm long. In the northern North Island a juvenile stage of *S. digitata* occurs in which the leaves are irregularly lobed or pinnatifid.

Pate's inflorescence is large and drooping, and up to 35 cm across, formed of umbels of small, greenish flowers arising irregularly along the branches of a panicle. Each umbel contains up to ten flowers, each flower being about 7 mm in diameter.

Pate is one of the commonest plants parasitised by *Dactylanthus taylori,* an extraordinary and unique plant known to the Maori people as Pua-o-te-reinga, meaning the flower of Hades. It is a root parasite belonging to the family Balanophoraceae and grows on the roots of possibly a dozen trees and shrubs in the forests of the North Island. Collectors boil and sell this plant as the curio known as wooden rose.

1

2

3

4

5

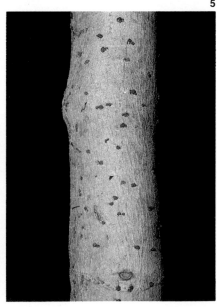

7

6

8

Fig 1 A central leaflet of one of pate's large compound leaves showing the sharply serrated leaflet margin and the reddish petiolule. The thin, membraneous nature of the leaflet blade is also clearly shown. About natural size.

Fig 2 A wide view of pate's distinctive three to nine-foliolate leaf showing the petiolules and sharply serrate margins of the leaflets. The larger central leaflet is up to 20 cm long.

Fig 3 An inflorescence of pate. From a tree growing at Akatarawa, February 1969. The inflorescences arise towards the ends of the branches just below or among the leaves.

Fig 4 An individual flower and flower buds. Akatarawa Saddle, February 1969. Six times natural size.

Fig 5 The bark of a *S. digitata* tree. The sap of this tree has medicinal uses; it has been used to treat ringworm and also scrofulous sores.

Fig 6 A branch of pate photographed from underneath to show the paler undersides of the leaflets. Also clearly shown are the prominent leaflet midveins and venation as well as the long, stout petioles of the compound leaves.

Fig 7 Clusters of ripening pate fruits; they are as large and spectacular as the inflorescences from which they developed. The fruits are fleshy and more or less round but grooved when dry; they are each about 3.5 mm in diameter. The fruit will follow the flowers within two to three months; in this respect *S. digitata* is unlike so many other of our native plants in which the fruits take a year or more to ripen.

Fig 8 A leaf with five leaflets from the juvenile stage. This specimen shows the upper surface of the lobed leaflets, which have sparse, short hairs. About half natural size.

Fig 9 The lower surface of a leaf from a juvenile plant showing part of the long hairy petiole, the hairy leaf blades and the prominent raised midveins of the leaflets. About one-third natural size.

Fig 10 A tree from the Rahu Saddle showing the typical spreading form with the leaves borne towards the ends of the branchlets. January 1973. Pate was one of the woods used by the Maori people to rub with kaikomako to make fire.

9

10

Family *Araliaceae*

Genus *Pseudopanax:* A genus of twenty-two species of small trees and shrubs found in South America, Tasmania, New Caledonia, China and New Zealand. All fifteen New Zealand species are endemic and thirteen of these grow into small trees.

Pseudopanax arboreus
Five-finger/Puahou

1

Previously classified in the genus *Nothopanax,* then *Neopanax, P. arboreus* is a small, much-branched, round-headed tree with thick, brittle, spreading branches. The five-finger is one of our commonest native trees; reaching to 8 m high, it is found from sea level to 760 m in forests and open scrub from North Cape to Southland. It can be epiphytic on tree fern trunks, with its roots descending to the ground.

The leaves are compound, consisting of five to seven leaflets on a petiole 15 – 20 cm long; the petiolules of the central leaflets are each 1 – 3.5 cm long and the leaflets 10 – 20 cm long by 4 – 7 cm wide. They are obovate-oblong to oblong-cuneate in shape, rather thick but still leathery, with coarsely serrate or dentate margins.

The flowers occur in terminal compound umbels with each small umbellule consisting of ten to fifteen flowers. The sweet-scented flowers are borne in great profusion from June to August or September.

Fig 1 A fine old specimen of five-finger. It was growing in the Waipahihi Reserve, Taupo, May 1973.

Fig 2 The rough, corky bark of the tree in Fig 1. The bark of a young five-finger is relatively smooth with dark streaks and shows transverse leaf scars.

Fig 3 The typical rounded form of young five-fingers can be often seen on the edges of forest and in scrub. Those here were growing at Mission Bay, Lake Taupo, January 1965.

Fig 4 Female flowers are borne in large compound umbels like the males; but whereas male flowers are about 7 – 8 mm

across, the female is only about 3 mm across. Females open to reveal five abortive anthers on short stamens with five small petals which surround two styles. Within a day or so the petals fold outwards and backwards; they and the anthers drop off, leaving the styles exposed on top of the ovary. At this time the styles are yellowish-white and become surrounded by a sticky nectar which attracts insects in large numbers, especially bees. After pollination the styles darken; the ovary swells slightly to form the fruit (as in Fig 11). The fruits should not be confused with flower buds, which have a different terminal structure (Fig 9). Taupo, August 1979. Five times natural size.

2

3

4

Fig 5 Male flower and bud clusters will smother the tree's foliage. From Waipahihi Reserve, August 1969.

Fig 6 Upper surface of a typical leaf. This specimen has seven leaflets. One-third natural size.

Fig 7 Umbels of male flowers. Karaka Bay, July 1970.

Fig 8 The male flower, 7–8 mm across, is identified by its long radiating stamens with non-functional or abortive style. Karaka Bay, June 1968. About five times natural size.

Fig 9 Male flower buds, almost ready to open. Karaka Bay, April 1969. Three and a half times natural size.

Fig 10 Umbels of fruits at an early stage. When ripe they are purplish-black. Karaka Bay, September 1968.

Fig 11 Ripening fruits, each 5–8 mm across. Karaka Bay, September 1968. About twice natural size.

Pseudopanax laetus
P. colensoi/Orihou
P. macintyrei

Pseudopanax laetus grows as an attractive shrub or small tree up to 5 m tall. Its distinctive, shining, five to seven-foliolate leaves arise on characteristic purplish-red petioles up to 25 cm long. It grows naturally in forests and forest margins or in open scrub from the Coromandel Peninsula southwards to Taranaki and is readily recognised by its reddish-coloured leaf petioles and red-coloured midveins on the leaflets. These are 12 – 25 cm long and 5 – 10 cm wide, obovate-oblong to cuneate-oblong in shape with the upper half of the margins serrate to dentate.

The flowers of *P. laetus* occur in compound umbels on the branchlets; both flowers and fruits are similar to those of *P. arboreus.* The flowers are unisexual with male and female on separate trees.

P. colensoi grows as a shrub or small canopy tree 5 – 6 m tall with stout, spreading branches. When cut, the stems exude a thick sap. Orihou is found throughout the North, South and Stewart Islands, from sea level to 1,200 m, in forest and open scrub. It is common above the bushline in subalpine scrub.

P. colensoi leaves are three to seven-foliolate with a petiole 5 – 20 cm long. The leaflets are either sessile or shortly petiolulate, a feature which distinguishes this species from *P. arboreus,* which has longer petiolules. The green, heavy-scented flowers occur in compound umbels; male flowers are 7 – 8 mm across, similar to those of *P. arboreus.*

According to the number of leaflets, *P. colensoi* is divided into three varieties (see below). They are var. *colensoi,* var. *ternatus* and var. *fiordense.* Of the three varieties only var. *colensoi* is illustrated here.

Fig 1 *P. laetus* as a young shrub, showing the typical five to seven-foliolate leaves. Both leaves and leaflets have purplish-red petioles and petiolules. Also shown is the distinct venation on the dark-green upper surfaces. Lower leaf surfaces are paler in colour. Otari, March 1973.

Fig 2 Bark of a young plant of *P. laetus* showing leaf scars and typical yellowish furrowing running down the stem.

PSEUDOPANAX COLENSOI

The three varieties of P. colensoi *differ in leaflet number: var.* colensoi *(five-foliolate leaves) grows in higher areas of the North Island; var.* ternatus *(three-foliolate leaves) grows at higher levels in Marlborough-Nelson and around sea level in the west and south of the South Island; var.* fiordense *(five-foliolate leaves) is found in Fiordland and Stewart Island.*

4

3

5

6

Fig 3 A small tree of *P. colensoi* growing at about 850 m above the Kauaeranga Valley in the Coromandel Peninsula, December 1970.

Fig 4 Upper surface of a *P. colensoi* leaf showing the thick, leathery, subsessile leaflets with their coarsely serrate to dentate margins along the distal halves. The leaflets are 5–17 cm long by 2–11 cm wide. About natural size.

Fig 5 The paler underside of a *P. colensoi* leaf showing the distinct midvein but rather obscure lateral veins. Also about natural size.

Fig 6 Fruit is produced in profusion and becomes black when ripe. From a tree at Mt Egmont, December 1973.

Fig 7 Close view of some ripening fruits, also from Mt Egmont, December 1973. About three times natural size.

Fig 8 A complete leaf on its petiole but with sessile leaflets. About half natural size.

PSEUDOPANAX MACINTYREI

The species P. macintyrei (not illustrated) is found in the Nelson province and in Westland northwards from Greymouth, growing on limestone and calcareous soils. It is a much-branched shrub or small tree growing up to 5 m high. The three-foliolate, petiolate leaves have subsessile leaflets 3.5–7.5 cm long, leathery with sharply serrate margins.

7

8

Pseudopanax crassifolius
Lancewood/Horoeka

The adult lancewood is a round-headed tree up to 15 m high with a straight, clean trunk up to 50 cm through. The tree is found throughout the North, South and Stewart Islands, from sea level to about 760 m in forest and shrubland.

The juvenile forms are described on page 246. The longlasting juvenile form from which the name of the tree is derived has long, narrow leaves up to 1 m in length that form a deflexed cone surrounding the apex of the main stem. As the young tree changes to the adult form the main stem branches near the top and shorter upright leaves appear. At this stage the tree may start to flower. Lancewood flowers are in irregular compound terminal umbels that form large clusters; the male flowers have a calyx and petals while the females are rather similar to those of *P. arboreus*.

The wood is one of the toughest of native timbers.

2

1

3

Fig 1 Juvenile forms left in foreground and at right, with a young adult in the centre and a juvenile changing into an adult behind it. Pelorus Bridge, January 1972.

Fig 2 An adult tree showing the straight trunk and spreading branches forming the round head. Hinakura, November 1970.

Fig 3 The subglobose fruits are 4 – 5 mm in diameter. Lake Pounui, March 1961.

Fig 4 The thick, leathery, stiff adult leaves are 10 – 20 cm long and 2 – 3 cm wide. Upper surface. Two-thirds natural size.

Fig 5 The paler lower leaf surfaces. Two-thirds natural size.

Fig 6 The umbrella-like form of a young tree. Donnelly's Flat, January 1968.

Fig 7 The apical portion of a juvenile leaf. About natural size.

Fig 8 A cluster of male flowers. Waikanae, February 1979. The flower buds have style and stamens folded downwards inside them. As the flower opens the petals fold out. The style and stamens straighten, the anthers quickly release their pollen and the petals then quickly reflex back — all in the space of one day.

Fig 9 An unusual lancewood specimen in the Pohangina Valley, August 1970.

Fig 10 Lancewood bark varies from brown to grey and is often covered by lichens.

4

5

6

7

8

9

10

255

Pseudopanax chathamicus
P. ferox/Toothed lancewood

Both these members of *Pseudopanax* are fairly rare.

P. chathamicus grows as a tree up to 7 m tall with stout, ascending branches which create a bushy-topped tree on a slender, straight trunk. It is found only in forest on the Chatham Islands but has been grown elsewhere as an ornamental tree. Juvenile forms have shorter, broader leaves than those of *P. crassifolius;* they are ascending, never deflexed as in *P. crassifolius*. The adult leaves of *P. chathamicus* are 10—20 cm long by 2.5—4 cm wide; they are thick and leathery, obovate-oblong, narrowing to a petiole 1— 2 cm long.

P. ferox forms a bushy-topped tree with a tall, slender trunk branching at the top with short, stout branches having the leaves crowded towards their tips. It reaches 6 m high and is found from sea level to 900 m in forest. It is fairly rare, being found in scattered local groups from Mangonui south to Otago.The juvenile form of *P. ferox* is a particularly striking plant, having narrow deflexed leaves down its main stem rather like cross-cut saws. *P. ferox* passes through several juvenile stages similar to those of *P. crassifolius,* but its leaves are always simple unifoliolate, never multifoliolate. The flowers and fruits of this tree occur in compound terminal umbels as in other species of the *Pseudopanax* genus.

1

2

3

4

Fig 1 The adult leaves of *P. chathamicus* are spreading to upright, alternately arranged with the margins toothed along the distal halves and the venation distinct. Photographs on this page from a plant grown by Mrs Audrey Cameron at Hinakura.

Fig 2 Flowers occur in February. The fruits, shown here in July, are rounded, about 6 mm in diameter and occur in terminal umbels. When they ripen after eight to ten months they are almost black.

Fig 3 Upper surfaces of *P. chathamicus* leaves showing, at left, an acute tipped leaf and, at right, a leaf with an obtuse tip. About half natural size.

Fig 4 The paler *P. chathamicus* lower leaf surface showing the prominently raised midvein, indistinct venation and stout petiole. About half natural size.
Juvenile plants have leaves at first 5—15 cm long; later these become 15—30 cm long and 3—5.5 cm wide before changing to the adult form.

5
6
7

8
9
10

Fig 5 Two juvenile forms of *P. ferox* growing as branches from the base of a mature tree at Otari, April 1973.

Fig 6 A group of *P. ferox* trees growing at Otari, April 1973. The tree in the centre is changing from the juvenile to the adult stage.

Fig 7 Two *P. ferox* trees showing the bushy tops changing from juvenile leaves around the tops of the trunks to adult leaves on the stout, short branches that form the heads. Otari, April 1973.

Fig 8 Close view of the rounded, swollen ridges that traverse the trunk from ground to branches. This can also be seen on the trunks of the trees in Fig 7.

Fig 9 A close view of *P. ferox* juvenile leaves showing clearly the saw-toothed margins and very distinct midveins. They are dark-green or bronze-coloured above with silvery-grey coloured lower surfaces. The leaves are rigid, very thick and leathery; the tips of the teeth and lobes along the margins bear almost spinous hooks. Juvenile leaves are up to 50 cm long, the adults 9 — 15 cm long and 1 — 2 cm wide.

Fig 10 Almost ripe fruits; the bluish-green bloom disappears as the fruit dries and wrinkles. Otari, April 1973. About three times natural size.

Fig 11 A terminal umbel of fruits which are not yet fully ripe. Otari, April 1973.

11

257

Pseudopanax gilliesii
P. discolor
P. lessonii/Houpara

These species all grow either as shrubs or as small trees up to 5—6 m high. All have thick, leathery leaves; those of *P. gilliesii* are usually unifoliolate but sometimes trifoliolate, those of *P. discolor* and *P. lessonii* three to five-foliolate. All have long petioles: *P. gilliesii* slender, up to 8.5 or even 11 cm; *P. discolor* slender, 2—8 cm long; *P. lessonii* stout, 5—15 cm long. *P. gilliesii* is found in coastal forest and scrub from North Cape to Whangaroa and on Little Barrier Island; *P. discolor* grows in lowland forest and scrubland from Mangonui to about Thames; *P. lessonii* is found in coastal forest and scrub, growing from the Three Kings Islands south to Poverty Bay.

Fig 1 Leaves of *P. gilliesii* showing both unifoliolate and trifoliolate leaves. The former are 4—8 cm long; leaflets of the latter are 7—8 cm long. The leaflets are ovate or lanceolate-cuneate in shape.

Fig 2 A foliage spray of *P. gilliesii* showing older leaves lower down the stem with very much longer petioles.

Fig 3 A trifoliolate leaf of *P. discolor* with its long petiole and flower racemes. The terminal leaflet is 4—8 cm long by 1.5—2.5 cm wide. About half natural size.

Fig 4 The bark of *P. discolor*

Fig 5 A five-foliolate leaf of *P. discolor*. Natural size.

Fig 6 Undersurface of the leaf in Fig 3.

Fig 7 A tree of *P. lessonii* growing above the Kauaeranga Valley, December 1970. The leaves are typically crowded towards the tips of the branchlets. Terminal compound umbels of fruits can also be seen here.

Fig 8 Upper surface of the thick, leathery leaf of *P. lessonii* showing the raised midvein, clear venation, bluntly serrate distal half, sessile leaflets and part of the long petiole. The terminal leaflet is 5 – 10 cm long by 2 – 4 cm wide. About half natural size.

Fig 9 The paler underside of a *P. lessonii* leaf with its raised midvein. This leaf has more sinuate-crenate distal margins on the leaflets than that in Fig 7. About half natural size.

Fig 10 *P. lessonii* bark is finely wrinkled and usually carries growths of lichens.

Fig 11 Close view of a *P. lessonii* flower. From a tree growing in Hukutaia Domain, January 1974. Four and a half times natural size.

Fig 12 A spray of *P. lessonii* foliage. Coromandel, December 1969.

7

8

9

10

11

12

Pseudopanax simplex
Haumakaroa

Formerly known as *Neopanax simplex,* this species grows as a much-branched shrub or small tree up to 8 m high and is found from just north of Thames south to Stewart Island in forest from sea level to 1,200 m. There are juvenile stages with three to five-foliolate leaves; these are either (1) mostly elliptic to linear-oblong, deeply lobed to pinnatifid, 4—15 cm long on petioles 10 cm long; or (2) more obovate to lanceolate, with serrate margins, 5—8 cm long on petioles up to 6 cm long.

Adult *P. simplex* leaves are usually unifoliolate with occasional trifoliolate ones appearing, although in the variety *sinclairii* they are still trifoliolate.

1

2

3

Fig 1 Adult leaves are glossy and vary in shape from lanceolate to broad-lanceolate, elliptic to ovate-elliptic, or obovate-oblong (as shown here), with acute, acuminate or obtuse apices. They are somewhat leathery, 5—10 cm long with a raised midvein and sharply serrate margins. About natural size.

Fig 2 The much-branching habit of a small tree of *P. simplex*. Taurewa Intake, January 1975.

Fig 3 A foliage spray showing alternate leaves on very long petioles 3— 8 cm long.

Fig 4 The underside of an elliptic leaf with its paler, duller surface and distinct vein pattern. About natural size.

4

6

5

7

8

Fig 5 Male flower and bud. The folding back of the petals is typical and occurs as soon as the flower opens. Taurewa Intake, January 1975. Four times natural size.

Fig 6 The flowers occur in axillary or terminal umbels which branch into a terminal cluster of female flowers and two or more lateral clusters consisting partly or wholly of male flowers. The flowers here are opening. Taurewa Intake, January 1975.

Fig 7 Ripening flattened *P. simplex* fruits. Akatarawa, April 1974. Four times natural size.

Fig 8 The rather blistery bark of the tree in Fig 2, clothed with moss and lichens.

Fig 9 A foliage spray of *P. simplex*. Clearly illustrated here are adult unifoliolate leaves and juvenile trifoliolate leaves together on the same branchlet.

Fig 10 The upper surface of an elliptic adult leaf and petiole. Compare this leaf shape with that of the adult leaf in Fig 1. This specimen is at about half natural size.

Fig 11 A glossy trifoliolate juvenile leaf on a petiole about 6 cm long. It consists of elliptic to lanceolate leaflets with serrated margins, the leaflets 5—8 cm long. About natural size. A specimen of *P. simplex* with leaves at this stage may actually begin to flower.

9

10

11

Pseudopanax edgerleyi
Raukawa
P. kermadecense

A tree up to 10 m high with a trunk up to 40 cm through; it is found from sea level to 600 m, from Mangonui to Stewart Island. The aromatic adult unifoliolate or bifoliolate leaves are a deep glossy green above with entire to sinuate margins, yellowish midvein and distinct lateral veins; they are paler olive green below with a prominent midvein. Young juvenile plants have three to five-foliolate leaves, the leaflets 5—15 cm long by 1.5—3.5 cm wide, linear-oblong in shape and deeply lobed with acute to acuminate apices. The older juvenile plants of *P. edgerleyi* have three-foliolate leaves which have leaflets 10—15 cm long by 2.5—3 cm wide. Most adults are unifoliate.

1

2

3

4

Fig 1 Upper surface of a typical raukawa adult leaf. The leaves can vary in size from elliptic-oblong to obovate-cuneate, with obtuse to acuminate apices. Adult leaves are 7—15 cm long by 3—5 cm wide. This leaf at about natural size.

Fig 2 A spray of semi-adult foliage with uni- and tri-foliolate leaves. From Mt Kaitarakihi, Coromandel Ranges, April 1974.

Fig 3 A stem with leaf petioles and an apical bud showing the tree's hairless nature. Four and a half times natural size.

Fig 4 The rather pimply rough bark.

Fig 5 Underside of a typical adult leaf, elliptic-oblong in shape with an acuminate apex. At about natural size. All leaves have slender petioles up to 5 cm long.

Fig 6 A bifoliolate semi-adult leaf form with acute and obtuse apices. This is the lower surface. About natural size.

Fig 7 The upper surface of a bifoliolate semi-adult leaf, with acuminate apices. About natural size.

Fig 8 A further variation in leaf shape. This is a trifoliolate lobed leaf from a juvenile plant. Notice that the terminal leaflet is longer than the lateral ones and that all three have short stalks (they are sometimes subsessile). *P. edgerleyi* leaflets may be entire and the apices are always acuminate to obtuse. About half natural size.

Fig 9 Flower umbels are small and occur on slender branched stalks up to 5 cm long. The terminal umbel of each stalk consists of female flowers (developing into fruits here) while those below consist mainly of male flowers. *P. edgerleyi* flowers from November to March. From Mt Kaitarakihi, Coromandel, January 1974.

5

6 7

Fig 10 The flowers on this tree are very small, measuring only 3—4 mm across. This photograph is of a male flower along with a newly formed fruit on an adjacent umbel (of the same stalk). Also from a tree growing at Mt Kaitarakihi, Coromandel Ranges. Six times natural size.

Fig 11 Typical leaf from a young juvenile *P. edgerleyi* plant. Such leaves are somewhat thick and leathery, glossy above with a distinct midvein. The linear-oblong leaflets are 5—15 cm long, either subsessile or with short stalks. The undersides of these leaves vary in colour from pale green through ocherous to reddish-brown. About half natural size.

Fig 12 *P. kermadecense* grows as a round-headed tree up to 10 m high in damp forest at the tops of the hills on Raoul (Sunday) Island of the Kermadecs. The six to seven-foliolate leaf is thin and membraneous. The leaflets are elliptic to elliptic-obovate, 5—14 cm long by 2.5—6 cm wide. Otari, July 1979. One-third natural size.

8

9

10

11 12

Family *Cornaceae*

Genus *Griselinia:* A genus containing six species, of which four are endemic to Chile and south-east Brazil and the remaining two to New Zealand.

Griselinia littoralis
Papauma/Broadleaf
G. lucida/Puka

1

G. littoralis grows as a tree up to 15 m high and is seldom epiphytic, unlike *G. lucida,* which starts life as an epiphyte. *G. littoralis* is found in forest from sea level to 900 m, from Mangonui south to Stewart Island. Its thick, shining, yellow-green leaves are 5—10 cm long by 2—5 cm wide, broad-ovate to ovate-oblong with a rounded apex; they are usually equal-sided at the base, unlike those of *G. lucida.*

G. lucida, puka, begins life as an epiphyte perched high in kahikatea, rimu, hinau, kohekohe, puriri or cabbage trees. As the young puka seedling grows, its white, pliable roots covered with root hairs extend towards the ground down the trunk of the host tree.

As they extend they become corky and ridged and give off many girdling roots that extend around the branches and trunk of the host, securely anchoring the epiphyte. The main roots finally reach the ground and establish the plant as an independent tree. *G. lucida* can grow directly from the ground in stony and rocky places. It occurs throughout the North and South Islands, being more common in the north.

The flowers of both species occur in panicles, although *G. littoralis* sometimes has only simple racemes. They are unisexual on separate trees and are generally about 4—6 mm in diameter; the female flowers of *G. lucida* are smaller and lack petals.

Fig 1 The leaves of *G. littoralis* showing upper surfaces, distinct venation, stout petioles 1—2 cm long and slightly unequal to equal sides at the bases. About natural size.

Fig 2 In the open *G. littoralis* forms a tight, bushy tree; in the forest it is more open. Caanan, Abel Tasman National Park, April 1965.

Fig 3 The paler, duller underside of the leaf of *G. littoralis* showing the slender raised midvein and obscure venation. About natural size.

Fig 4 Clusters of flowers of *G. littoralis* arise in panicles from the leaf axils towards the tip of a branchlet. Caanan, April 1965.

Fig 5 Part of an inflorescence of male flowers of *G. littoralis,* close view. It shows the greenish petals of the flowers and the pubescent panicle axes and pedicels. Renata Track, Tararua Range, November 1970. This specimen four times natural size.

2

3

4

5

7

6 8

9

10

Fig 6 An epiphytic *G. lucida* perched on a cabbage tree, *Cordyline australis,* near Waikanae, August 1979.

Fig 7 Leaves of *G. lucida* showing upper and lower surfaces, unequal margins at the bases and stout petioles 2—3 cm long. The large leaves of puka are broad-ovate to oblong in shape with rounded apices; they are glossy above with a distinct venation that becomes obscure on the lower surfaces. The leaves are very thick and leathery, and are up to 18 cm long and 3.5—12 cm wide. About half natural size.

Fig 8 The unequal basal margins of two puka leaves as they pass into the petiole. About half natural size. This provides one of the easiest ways to distinguish between *G. lucida* and *G. littoralis.*

Fig 9 A section of the furrowed aerial root of an epiphytic puka plant growing at Totaranui, February 1974.

Fig 10 The blistery and furrowed bark of *G. littoralis.*

Fig 11 Puka male flower panicles clustered at a branchlet tip. Abel Tasman National Park, November 1965.

Fig 12 Immature fruits, 5—10 mm long, of *G. lucida;* they become blue-black when ripe. Each contains one seed and numerous oil canals. Lake Pounui, March 1974. Two and a half times natural size.

Fig 13 Ripening fruits of *G. littoralis* are 6—7 mm long. From a tree at Karaka Bay, March 1961.

11

12 13

Family *Cornaceae:* Mainly woody plants comprising twelve genera and about 100 species in the north temperate regions, Central and South America, Africa, Madagascar, Indomalaysia and New Zealand. Two genera occur in New Zealand, although there is uncertainty over whether they belong to this family.

Genus *Corokia:* A genus of three shrubs and small trees endemic to New Zealand.

Corokia macrocarpa
Chatham Island korokio

A shrub or small tree up to 6 m high found in forest and along forest margins in the Chatham Islands. It forms a dense, spreading head of stout branches with deep-green leaves; they have a silvery or ochraceous-coloured tomentum on their lower surfaces which tends to give the foliage an attractive silvery or greenish-grey appearance, depending on the orientation of the leaves. The leaves are 4 – 8 cm long by 1.5 – 3.5 cm wide on stout petioles up to 1 cm long. The yellow flowers are borne on crowded racemes about 3 cm long arising from the axils of the leaves; each flower is about 1 cm across. The fruit, about 1 cm long, is an orange to red-coloured drupe.

1

2

3

4

5

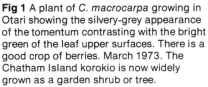

Fig 1 A plant of *C. macrocarpa* growing in Otari showing the silvery-grey appearance of the tomentum contrasting with the bright green of the leaf upper surfaces. There is a good crop of berries. March 1973. The Chatham Island korokio is now widely grown as a garden shrub or tree.

Fig 2 Underside of a leaf with its raised midvein and lateral veins and ochraceous tomentum. Leaves vary from elliptic-oblong to obovate-cuneate or broad-oblanceolate in shape. The young leaves have a silvery-white tomentum below, which darkens as the leaf ages, as well as thick, hairy margins and scattered hairs on the upper surfaces. About natural size.

Fig 3 The attractive yellow flowers occur round the tips of the branchlets. The tomentose lower surfaces and thick, hairy margins of young leaves are shown clearly here. Otari, November 1964. Natural size.

Fig 4 A branchlet of drupes which also shows the upper surfaces and alternate arrangement of the rather thick, leathery leaves. Otari, May 1979. About half natural size.

Fig 5 The hairy clothing on a branchlet of *C. macrocarpa* and on the margins, upper and lower surfaces, buds and petioles of new leaves is clearly shown. Otari, March 1979. Twice natural size.

Family *Epacridaceae:* Thirty genera and 400 species in South America, Hawaii, Indochina, Borneo, Celebes, New Guinea, Australia, Tasmania, some Pacific Islands and New Zealand. Six genera occur in New Zealand, two containing tree species.

Genus *Leucopogon:* A genus of some 100 species found in Australia, Malaysia, New Caledonia and New Zealand. Of the five New Zealand species only one grows as a small tree.

Leucopogon fasciculata
Mingimingi

Mingimingi is a rather openly branched shrub or a small tree growing up to 5–6 m tall depending on the conditions. Mingimingi grows from sea level to around 1,150 m and is found in coastal and lowland scrub or forest and in rocky places. It occurs from the Three Kings Islands and North Cape to Canterbury.

The leaves are linear to narrow-lanceolate or linear-oblong in shape. They are spreading and sharp pointed, 12–25 mm long by 2–4 mm wide.

Mingimingi flowers occur in axillary or terminal drooping racemes or spikes containing six to twelve flowers each. The oblong fruit is 2–4 mm long; it is usually red-coloured, although white fruits do occur.

2

3

Fig 1 A rather bent mingimingi tree growing near Taupo, May 1973.

Fig 2 Mingimingi leaves. Clearly visible are upper and lower surfaces, venation, finely denticulate-ciliolate margins, pungent tips and pubescent branchlet. Volcanic Plateau, October 1973. Twice natural size.

Fig 3 The tiny flowers, here magnified six times, are only 3–4 mm long and have quite exquisite detail. They have hairy petals and stalks and are sweetly fragrant. From a tree growing on the Volcanic Plateau, October 1973. Six times natural size.

Fig 4 The drooping racemes of mingimingi flowers are themselves only 1–3 cm long. Taupo, October 1968. Twice natural size.

Fig 5 When fully ripe, mingimingi fruits are a deeper red than those pictured here, or white. Taupo, April 1974. Three and a half times natural size.

Fig 6 The flaky bark peels off in thin strips.

4

5

6

Family Epacridaceae
Genus *Dracophyllum*

The genus *Dracophyllum* consists of plants which are dicotyledons with a monocotyledonous appearance resulting from their narrow leaves with parallel veins. Some forty-seven species are known from Australia, Tasmania, New Caledonia, Lord Howe Island and New Zealand. They are mostly shrubs or small trees; twelve of the thirty-five New Zealand species grow into small trees.

The New Zealand dracophyllums confront one almost everywhere in scrub or forest. Almost extraterrestrial in appearance, they are among the most unusual of our native plants.

The tree species of *Dracophyllum* vary in leaf form from long, relatively wide leaves not unlike those of a cabbage tree to shorter, grass-like leaves or needle-like leaves. In most species the leaves tend to be crowded towards the tips of the branchlets in spiral fashion.

The base of the leaf is prolonged onto a sheath which leaves a broad scar on the branchlet when the leaf falls. The sheath of the leaf may pass gradually into the blade (below left, *D. traversii*) or it may have a shoulder where the blade begins (centre and right, *D. lessonianum*). This shoulder may be smooth or hairy, rounded or auricled, and the leaf margins may be simple to finely serrulate-crenulate and/or ciliate. The blade tapers, often very gradually, from the base to the tip, which is usually brownish, and may be acute or acicular and with three faces.

Six of the *Dracophyllum* species form a group distinguished by having paniculate inflorescences and rather broad leaves in which the sheath gradually tapers to the blade. The other six tree species form another group having racemose inflorescences and narrow to very narrow grass-like to needle-like leaves which generally have a shoulder where the sheath passes into the blade; their leaf margins are usually finely serrulate or ciliated. In species with needle-like leaves the blades are 6–16 cm long and not more than 1.5 mm wide.

The flowers of *Dracophyllum* are heath-like and are borne in panicles or racemes. The panicles range in length from 5–30 cm (occasionally reaching 45 cm in one species), while racemes range in length from 2–5 cm. The flowers are usually crowded on the racemes or panicles; the fruits that follow consist of crowded capsules which are sometimes hidden by persistent sepals.

The tree dracophyllums are found in coastal scrub and in lowland, coastal and upland forests and scrub, from sea level to about 1,000 m. They grow from North Cape south throughout both the North and South Islands and Stewart Island, as well as the Auckland Islands and also the Chatham Islands.

Fig 1 *D. traversii* forest, Mt Arthur. ▶

Dracophyllum traversii
Mountain neinei

The mountain neinei is one of the finest and most imposing of the New Zealand grass trees. It has candelabra-like branches and tufts of foliage which give it a most distinctive appearance.

In form it is a stoutly branching tree growing as high as 10—13 m, with a trunk 60 cm through. It is found in montane and subalpine regions from Nelson to about Arthurs Pass, growing between 760 and 1,400 m. A spectacular pure stand grows on the main ridge leading from the Flora Hut to the summit of Mt Arthur (Fig 1, previous page).

The leaf blades are 30—60 cm long and 4—5 cm wide with smooth margins. The sheath is 3 cm long.

3

4

5

Fig 1 (previous page) In the *D. traversii* forest on Mt Arthur the fallen leaves off the tree turn red-brown and persist on the forest floor for a long time. This area on Mt Arthur is a fascinating area of forest, being one of the few pure stands of mountain neinei known. The photograph was taken in January 1972.

Fig 2 Young plants of *D. traversii* growing on the forest floor at Mt Arthur. January 1972.

Fig 3 Fine specimens of mountain neinei in the Mt Arthur stand. The figure of the boy in this photograph gives an indication of the size of this imposing tree. January 1973.

Fig 4 A trunk of *D. traversii* showing the peeling bark typical of this species. Mt Arthur, January 1972.

Fig 5 An immature seed head of *D. traversii*. From a plant at Otari, photographed in January 1979. The flower panicle is terminal and densely branched.

Dracophyllum latifolium
Neinei/Spiderwood

Like *D. traversii,* to which it is closely related, *D. latifolium* is a striking and unusual tree. It is open branched in form, with its leaves in dense clusters towards the ends of the upturned branches, giving the tree a candelabra-like appearance similar to that of *D. traversii.*

The distribution of neinei is different, however. It is found in the forests of the North Island from Mangonui southwards to North Taranaki and the Mahia Peninsula, growing from sea level to 1,100 m.

Leaf blades of *D. latifolium* are 25–60 cm long and 2.5–3.5 cm wide, tapering to a long, fine, pointed tip. The margins of the leaves are finely serrated.

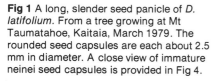

1 **2**

Fig 1 A long, slender seed panicle of *D. latifolium*. From a tree growing at Mt Taumatahoe, Kaitaia, March 1979. The rounded seed capsules are each about 2.5 mm in diameter. A close view of immature neinei seed capsules is provided in Fig 4.

Fig 2 A beautiful specimen of neinei growing in the forest at Mt Kaitarakihi, Coromandel Ranges. It was photographed in February 1974. The bark of this tree flakes in small chips and is transversed by a series of longitudinal parallel grooves similar to those of *D. pyramidale.*

Fig 3 The serrulate edge of a leaf of *D. latifolium*. The sheath is 4 cm long. Six times natural size.

Fig 4 A portion of a *D. latifolium* flower panicle with immature seed capsules. The flower panicle is terminal on the branches, up to 30 cm and sometimes 45 cm long, more or less erect but becoming drooping at the fruiting stage. The reddish flowers are crowded on small pedicels.

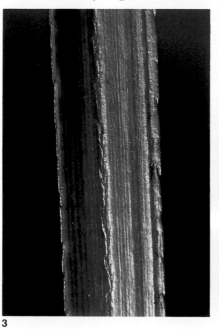

3 **4**

Dracophyllum fiordense
D. townsonii
D. pyramidale
D. mathewsii

D. fiordense is a rather small tree up to 3 m high, generally with only one trunk and one or two branches. These carry at their tips a dense cluster of thick, leathery leaves, the blades of which are 60—70 cm long and 4—5 cm wide with smooth margins. The flower panicles arise just below the leaf clusters. This species is found only in scrub, open tussock country and forest in an area covering western Otago and Fiordland, from sea level to about 1,050 m.

D. townsonii is a species rather like neinei in general appearance. It grows to a tree 6 m tall with stout branches and leaf blades 15—30 cm long by 8—15 mm wide. The leaf margins of this species are minutely serrulate-crenate, and the drooping flower panicles arise below the leaves.

D. pyramidale grows as a slender, upright tree up to 10 m tall with ascending branches bearing candelabra-like clusters of thick, leathery leaves towards their tips. The leaf blades are 50-60 cm long and 2.5-3 cm wide, with smooth margins. The flower panicle is stout, erect and terminal. The tree has striped, dark-grey bark. *D. pyramidale* is found in forest and scrubland from sea level to 900 m. Its distribution is restricted to an area from Great Barrier Island to the northern Kaimai Ranges.

D. mathewsii grows as a rather open tree of slender habit and is similar to *D. pyramidale.* It too has a limited distribution, being restricted to an area from Kaitaia south to Hokianga, where it is found growing on dry ridges in forests. The leaf blades of *D. mathewsii* are 20—30 cm long by 1—2.5 cm wide; they have acute leaf tips and smooth margins.

1

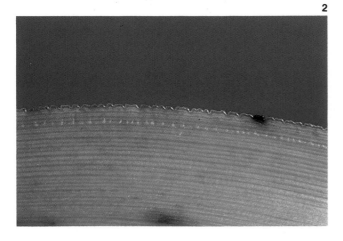

2

3

Fig 1 Two fine specimens of *D. fiordense*. They were growing in subalpine tussock in the Upper Stillwater Basin, Fiordland, December 1970.

Fig 2 The edge of a leaf of *D. townsonii*. The leaf crenulations are clearly shown. Six times natural size.

Fig 3 The flowers of *D. fiordense*, from one of the plants in Fig 1. Fiordland, December 1970.

Fig 4 A tree of *D. pyramidale* showing its upright form and clustered leaves. From Mt Ngamoto, Lake Waikaremoana. April 1974.

Fig 5 A branchlet tip of *D. pyramidale* showing part of the leaf blades and the clasping sheath 5 cm long of the outermost leaf. Also clearly illustrated in this photograph are the scars left on the branchlet by the fallen leaves.

Fig 6 The characteristic striped bark of *D. pyramidale*.

Fig 7 A plant of *D. mathewsii* growing in dense forest on a hill near Kaitaia. March 1979.

4

6

7

5

273

Dracophyllum viride
D. sinclairii

D. viride is a small tree up to 5 m tall with slender, ascending, leafy branchlets. It is found in scrub and forest only from North Cape south to Kaitaia. The thin, grass-like leaves tend to be spreading; their blades are 5—7 cm long by 5—6.5 mm wide, with a distinct ciliated shoulder at the top of the sheath. The slender, five to six-flowered, rather open racemes arise just below the tufts of the leaves on the branchlets.

D. viride appears to have a juvenile form with longer, wider leaves than the adult. I found both forms growing on the Herekino Saddle near Kaitaia, where these photographs were taken in March 1979.

D. sinclairii is a slender, much-branched tree very similar to *D. viride,* although more leafy with closer-set leaves, growing to 3—6 m tall. It has leaf blades 3.5—12.5 cm long and 4—8 mm wide with finely serrulate margins, passing into long, acuminate apices. The flowers are in four to eight-flowered racemes up to 5 cm long, arising either terminally or subterminally on lateral branchlets.

This rather leafy dracophyllum used to be found in lowland scrub and forest from North Cape to about Kaipara and Kawhia Harbours and Rotorua. Nowadays, as scrubland everywhere is converted to farmland, *D. sinclairii* is becoming much harder to find.

2 3 4 5

Fig 1 A spray of the juvenile form of *D. viride* with adult foliage sprouting on lateral shoots low down.

Fig 2 Shoulder of the leaf in the juvenile form of *D. viride*. Allan's *Flora* records the sheath as narrowed to the lamina, but all the plants I have seen in the field and at the National Herbarium have a ciliated shoulder, as shown here and in Figs 3 and 5. Reproduced here at four and a half times natural size.

Fig 3 The shoulder on the adult leaves of *D. viride*, with the finely serrulate margins showing on several leaves. Two and a half times natural size.

Fig 4 The plant which appears to be a juvenile form of *D. viride,* growing on the Herekino Saddle near Kaitaia, March 1979. Because of the darkness of the forest interior where this plant was growing it was necessary to use a flashlight here.

Fig 5 The shoulder of the sheath of *D. sinclairii,* magnified here twice. The comments in the caption to Fig 2 concerning the shoulder of *D. viride* also apply to *D. sinclairii.* Notice also the finely serrulate leaf margins in this specimen.

Fig 6 Flowers, opening flower buds and the closer-set leaves of *D. sinclairii*. Kaitaia, May 1979. Five times natural size.

6

Dracophyllum lessonianum

This is a small tree growing up to 10 m high with needle-like leaves and erect or ascending branches with the leaves crowded towards the ends of the branchlets. This species is found in scrub from North Cape south to about Kawhia and is very common in manuka scrub north of Kaitaia.

The leaf blades are 6–10 cm long and 1–1.5 mm wide, canaliculate along their lower halves. The shoulder, which is distinct on the sheath, is ciliolate and auricled; the margins are finely serrulate with occasional cilia and the apex is acute.

A juvenile form of *D. lessonianum* with large leaves occurs on seedlings growing under manuka scrub.

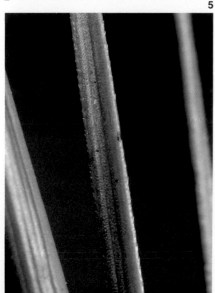

Fig 1 A tree of *D. lessonianum* amongst manuka scrub. All the photographs on this page were taken near Kaitaia in April 1979.

Figs 2, 3, 4 Different leaf forms. Left: Seedling stem showing the larger juvenile leaf form which occurs on seedlings growing under the short manuka scrub. Centre: Stem showing both juvenile and smaller adult leaves, which appear when the growing tree reaches the brighter light. Right: Fully adult foliage, here with racemes of seed capsules.

Fig 5 *D. lessonianum* leaf showing the serrulate edges. Six times natural size.

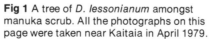

Fig 6 The six to eight-flowered racemes are about 3 cm long and arise singly or in clusters terminally on the short lateral branchlets. Two and a half times natural size.

275

Dracophyllum longifolium/Inanga
D. arboreum
D. filifolium

D. longifolium is the most widespread member of the *Dracophyllum* genus. It is found in coastal, lowland and subalpine scrub and forest from East Cape southwards in the North, South and Stewart Islands, the Auckland Islands and the Chatham Islands. *D. longifolium* is a tree growing up to 12 m high with slender erect or spreading branches and branchlets. The rigid, leathery leaves of this species are stiff and usually crowded towards the tips of the branchlets; they have a ciliated shoulder on the sheath. The leaf blades are 10—25 cm long by 3—5 mm wide, tapering to a long acuminate tip. Their margins are usually smooth but are sometimes minutely serrulate. The drooping, six to fifteen-flowered raceme is terminal on the short lateral branchlets.

D. arboreum, a species of *Dracophyllum* which can grow up to 10 m high, is found only in the Chatham Islands, where it grows in bogs and forest and occasionally as an epiphyte on other plants. It has narrow, rigid, leathery leaves with blades 5—8 cm long by 1.5—2 mm wide, clustered towards the ends of the branchlets. The pubescent leaves have minutely serrulate-crenulate margins which are densely ciliolate.

D. filifolium is a small tree growing only up to 2 m high with slender, erect branches and thin, flexible branchlets. This species is found in montane to subalpine rocky places, fellfields and scrub in the North Island from the Huirau Range southwards. The leaf blades are 10—16 cm long by 0.5—1 mm wide with a three-faced, finely serrulate apex; the shoulder is deeply auricled, with the margins of the leaves finely serrulate. Small flowers, about 5 mm long, occur in racemes of four to nine flowers each.

1

2

3

Fig 1 The attractive flower racemes of *D. longifolium* arise from the short lateral branches. The flower buds on the right are not yet opened. The six to fifteen-flowered raceme of *D. longifolium* is up to 5 cm long; the tiny flowers are white. From a tree growing at Mt Dobson, Lake Tekapo, December 1972.

Fig 2 The leaf shoulder of *D. longifolium.* The sheath is 15 mm long by 10 mm wide, passing, by a ciliated shoulder, into the leaf lamina. The shoulder of this species is normally rounded but may be sometimes auricled. Magnified here at five times natural size.

Fig 3 *D. longifolium* stem and typically rigid leaves. This photograph illustrates the rounded outer surfaces, shoulders and leaf tips of the species.

Fig 4 Leaf tuft of *D. longifolium* showing the typical tapering tips. The apical portion of the leaf is normally brown, not green. From a tree growing at Otari, photographed in April 1979.

4

5

6

Fig 5 The densely ciliated leaf margins of *D. arboreum*, magnified five times. This is the only dracophyllum with ciliated leaf edges, as this photograph shows.

Fig 6 A leaf cluster of *D. arboreum*. The new leaves are stiff, drooping as they mature.

Fig 7 A branch of *D. filifolium* showing its leaves and thin, flexible branchlets.

Fig 8 The shoulder of the sheath of *D. filifolium* showing clearly its prominent auricle. Five times natural size.

Fig 9 *D. filifolium* leaves. This specimen has been magnified to seven and a half times natural size to show the typically serrulate leaf margins of this species.

Fig 10 The leaf tip of *D. filifolium* is triangular in cross-section (triquetrous) and finely serrulate. The actual leaf tip of *D. filifolium* is normally brown. In *D. longifolium* (Fig 4) the whole apical portion is normally brown.

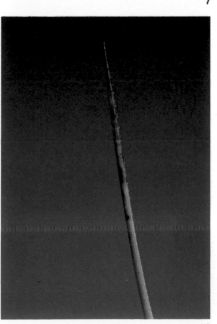

7

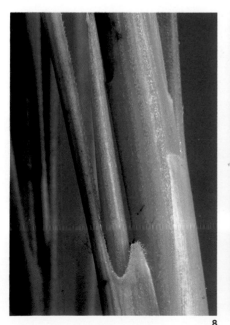

8

9

10

Planchonella costata
Tawapou

Family *Sapotaceae:* A pantropical family of trees and a few shrubs of seventy-five genera and about 800 species. Sapotaceae form a large component of the rain forests of Malaysia and Borneo; they include the gutta-percha tree, *Palaquium gutta,* of Malaya, Sumatra, Java and Borneo, the latex of which produces gutta-percha. The tree *Achras zapota* yields chicle or sapodilla plum, used for making earlier chewing gums; the *Calocarpum* species yield fruits known as sapote.

Genus *Planchonella:* A genus of about 100 species found in the Seychelles, South America, Indochina, Malaysia, tropical Australia, New Zealand and some Pacific Islands. The single New Zealand species is probably endemic, although it is closely related to species occurring on Norfolk Island and in Fiji.

Tawapou is a handsome, closely branched tree reaching 15 m high with a trunk up to 1 m across. It is found sporadically growing on islands and headlands from North Cape south to Tolaga Bay in the east and Manukau Harbour in the west. It does not grow to the south of this area. Tawapou can be found from sea level to about 450 m, always close to the sea.

The branchlets and petioles are clothed with appressed hairs and both bleed a milky latex when cut. The thick, leathery, shining leaves of *P. costata* are 5–10 cm (sometimes growing up to 15 cm) long by 2–5 cm wide, mostly elliptic to obovate-oblong in shape. The leaves are obtuse at the tip and cuneately narrowed at the base. The midvein and lateral veins of the leaves are distinct both above and below.

The flowers, generally perfect but sometimes unisexual, arise singly, or occasionally in pairs, on stout peduncles about 12 mm long, mostly from the leaf axils but also directly from the branchlets.

The fruit, a distinctive feature of the tree, is a large berry up to 2.5 cm long which passes through successive stages of colouring from green to deep red. The berries take from twelve to fifteen months to mature and ripen, and a tree with a heavy crop of ripe berries is a spectacular sight. The Maori people used the hard polished seeds to make necklaces.

The white-coloured wood is hard and durable.

1

2   3

4

5

6

7

8

Fig 1 Tawapou trees are relatively hardy but become gnarled and ragged when growing in exposed situations like this one on the shore of Houhora Harbour. Photographed in January 1970. The tree is found only on headlands and in coastal areas.

Fig 2 Tawapou foliage showing the shining, dark-green, mature leaves and the pubescent young foliage which is a more bronze-green. The varying shapes of the leaves are shown here.

Fig 3 The bark of *P. costata* is rough and varies in colour from grey to brownish-grey.

Fig 4 Leaf upper surface. About natural size.

Fig 5 Lower leaf surface, showing raised midvein and lateral veins. Natural size.

Fig 6 A shapely tree of tawapou growing in relatively sheltered conditions above Martins Bay, near Warkworth. December 1971.

Fig 7 Foliage from a tree at Piha. In this photograph the flowers are just opening and a green fully grown berry from last year's flowering can be seen. The berry is not yet ripe. Also illustrated here are the alternate arrangement of the leaves and the hairy clothing of the branchlet. January 1971.

Fig 8 Branchlet with two leaf petioles and two flower buds. Auckland, December 1970. Four times natural size.

Fig 9 The tiny, delicate flowers are only 4—6 mm in diameter. They arise on hairy peduncles usually in the leaf axils. Piha, January 1971. Reproduced here at five times natural size.

Fig 10 The tawapou's distinctive berries. This branchlet from a tree at Kaitaia shows berries at varying stages of ripening, from the orange-green of the three lower berries to the dark red of that at the top. Each berry contains up to four hard, curved, smooth, almost polished seeds, almost as long as the berry. April 1979.

Fig 11 The large berries are very heavy and will fall from the tree if only lightly disturbed. From a tree growing at Kaitaia, April 1979.

9

10

11

279

Myrsine australis
Mapou/Mapau/Red matipo
M. chathamica
M. kermadecensis

Family *Myrsinaceae:* A family of about thirty-two genera and 1,000 species of trees and shrubs found throughout tropical and warm temperate regions of Africa, South and Central America, Mexico, Florida, India, South-east Asia, Japan, Australia, Malaysia, Indonesia, the Philippines and New Zealand. Some species are used for medicinal purposes in Malaya, Indonesia and the Philippines, and some are grown as ornamental trees.

Genus *Myrsine:* This genus was established by Linnaeus for the species *M. africana,* which is found from Africa through India to China. The original concept covered about 200 species, but the genus has been divided by some botanists into *Suttonia* and *Rapanea.* Both of these names have been applied to the nine endemic New Zealand species at times. Six of the New Zealand species are trees, but three of these are found only on outlying islands.

Mapou is a shrub or small tree up to 6 m high. A feature of this tree is that while the bark on the mature trunk is grey, the young branches and branchlets are distinctly reddish in colour. Mapou is found from sea level to 900 m along forest margins and in scrubland, sometimes inside forests, throughout the North, South and Stewart Islands.

The smooth, leathery leaves are 3– 6 cm long by 1.5– 2.5 cm wide, on red petioles up to 5 mm long. The leaf margins are usually strongly undulate, sometimes flat; the leaves vary from obovate-oblong to broadly elliptic in shape.

The unisexual flowers, which are up to 2.5 mm across, have short pedicels and occur in crowded clusters along the bare branches usually below the leaves. The smaller female flowers have a large fringed stigma. The fruits of mapou are drupes, about 3 mm in diameter, clustered around the branchlets.

Fig 1 A spray of mapou foliage showing the alternate leaf arrangement, red branchlet and reddish petiole. Notice the hairy midveins.

Fig 2 The bark of a mapou trunk.

Fig 3 An unusual forked tree growing at Hinakura in November 1964. The trees are rather openly branched with the leaves occurring towards the branch tips.

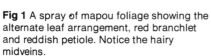

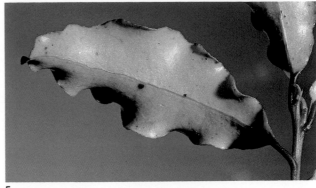

4

5

6

7

8

Fig 4 Upperside of a mapou leaf showing the characteristic undulate margins and hairy midvein. Natural size.

Fig 5 Underside of a leaf, also at natural size. The midvein here is smooth.

Fig 6 A cluster of male flowers with their anthers shedding pollen, which can be seen here sprinkled on the branchlet in the upper part of the photograph. Karaka Bay, December 1969. Seven and a half times natural size.

Fig 7 Close view of the male flowers showing the flower parts arranged in groups of four. Pollen grains have been scattered all over them. Karaka Bay, December 1969. Twelve times natural size.

Fig 8 Clusters of female flowers showing their large, fringed, sessile stigmas. Female flowers have sterile anthers. Whangarei, January 1970. Six times natural size.

Fig 9 Fully grown but at this stage still unripe drupes. Most of those pictured here show the remains of the corolla underneath and the withered stigma still on top. From a tree growing at Otari, photographed in March 1970. Here about twice natural size.

Fig 10 Branchlets clustered with mature mapou drupes, which turn black when ripe. From a tree at Otari, April 1971.

M. CHATHAMICA
M. KERMADECENSIS

Myrsine *species not illustrated here are* M. chathamica, *up to 6 m tall with hairy branchlets, found only in swampy forest in the Chathams, and* M. kermadecensis, *5 m high with wavy margined leaves, growing only on Raoul (Sunday) Island of the Kermadecs.*

9

10

Myrsine salicina/Toro
M. oliveri

Toro forms an attractive, rather fresh-looking, open-branched tree growing up to 8 m high. It has thick, furrowed bark and thick, leathery, smooth leaves about 7—18 cm long and 2—3 cm wide; they are narrow-elliptic to narrow-oblong or sometimes linear in shape. Toro occurs from sea level to 850 m in forests from North Cape to about Greymouth; it is more common in the North Island than in the South, where it is absent in the east.

The flowers occur in long dense clusters along the branchlets below the leaves. They are usually perfect and about 3 mm in diameter; the calyx is finely ciliated. Toro fruits are ovoid drupes up to 9 mm long.

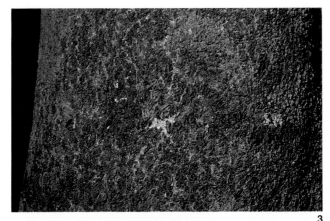

Fig 1 Upper surface of a toro leaf showing the elongated oil tubes resembling veins, rounded apex and gradually narrowing base. About natural size.

Fig 2 Lower surface, showing the oil tubes more clearly and the base narrowing to the petiole, which is normally about 10 mm long. About natural size.

Fig 3 The dark, furrowed bark.

Fig 4 Close view of flower buds and opening flowers releasing pollen. Tararua Forest Park, November 1975. About nine times natural size.

M. OLIVERI

This grows as a small tree up to 6 m high with leathery obovate to elliptic leaves 5—10 cm long by 3→4 cm wide. Found only on Great Island of the Three Kings group.

7

8

9

Fig 5 Toro branchlets with flower buds and flowers. Tararua Forest Park, November 1975. As the bark ages it turns black or sometimes a dark red-brown.

Fig 6 Toro drupes; the red ones are ripe. Here the branchlet is more brown. Each drupe contains one seed, or rarely two. Mt Holdsworth, December 1965.

Fig 7 A fine specimen of toro in flower. Tararua Forest Park, November 1975.

Fig 8 A spray of toro foliage showing the alternate arrangement of the leaves and a young terminal shoot.

Fig 9 The attractive yellow-green shoots are characteristic of this species, as is the reddish-coloured young branchlet. From a tree at Kaitoke, October 1970.

Myrsine divaricata
Weeping matipo

The weeping matipo is a shrub or small tree up to 4 m high with rigid, spreading branches and stiff, drooping branchlets that are hairy when first formed. The alternate leaves are small, about 5—15 mm long and 5—10 mm wide, on short petioles. The leaves are gland-dotted and leathery; they are broad-obovate to obcordate in shape, usually emarginate or two-lobed at the apex with their margins often recurved and ciliolate when young. The small flowers arise either singly or in small clusters below the leaves.

Weeping matipo occurs throughout the North, South and Stewart Islands and on the Auckland and Campbell Islands. It grows from sea level to 1,200 m on forest edges, in scrubland or along river banks.

Fig 1 The thick, gland-dotted leaves, upper surfaces. Twice natural size.

Fig 2 Leaf lower surfaces showing recurved margins, strong midvein and faint lateral venation. Twice natural size.

Fig 3 A close view of a male flower and opening flower buds showing the hairy margins of the petals. The flowers are only 3 mm across. Otari, September 1969. Twelve times natural size.

Fig 4 The typical drooping, twiggy form of a tree of M. divaricata, growing at Lewis Pass, January 1973.

Fig 5 Two clusters of male flowers on a branchlet. Otari, August 1970. Five times natural size.

Fig 6 Branchlets with ripe drupes and leaf undersides. Travers Valley, April 1966. Each drupe is about 5 mm across.

Fig 7 The bark of a weeping matipo is often clothed with lichens.

Family *Myrsinaceae*

Genus *Elingamita:* A genus of one species of tree that grows only on West Island of the Three Kings Islands. The name commemorates the wreck of the passenger steamer *Elingamite,* which came to grief on the rocks beneath the cliffs of West Island where the tree grows. The tree is named after Major M. E. Johnson, who discovered it on the island in 1950.

Elingamita johnsonii

A small tree up to 3 m tall with a spreading canopy reaching 5 m across. The large, smooth, satiny leaves are 10—18 cm long and 4—9 cm wide, on short, stout petioles 1 cm long. These photographs are of plants grown at the Mt Albert Research Station in Auckland. Allan's *Flora* gives the flowers as hermaphrodite, but only one of the two plants at Mt Albert bore fruits; it flowered only sparingly while the other plant flowered profusely and shed pollen. It behaved as a male while the other, which did not shed pollen, behaved as a female. The fruit took twelve months to develop and was only partially ripe after fifteen months, It was growing in shade, however; in full sun the fruits would probably be ripe.

1

Fig 1 The tree at the research station which bore fruit. December 1977.

Fig 2 A flower panicle of opened female or perfect flowers, some flower buds and possibly some fertilised ovules. Early February 1978. The panicles are up to 5 cm across, the flowers about 2.5 mm across.

Fig 3 Close view of the female or perfect flowers in Fig 2. Four times natural size.

Fig 4 The male flower panicle is longer than the female and has many more flowers. There are also more panicles on the male tree. Early February 1978. Four times natural size.

Fig 5 Close view of the male flowers with the anthers shedding pollen. Early February 1978. Four times natural size.

Fig 6 Two of the fruits, which are drupes, and which formed on the tree in Fig 1. They are about 17 mm across. Mid-April 1969. About half natural size.

Fig 7 Leaf upper surface with the apical bud of a branchlet. Half natural size.

Fig 8 Leaf lower surface. Half natural size.

2

3

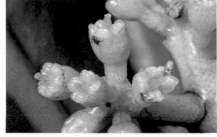

4

5

6

7

8

Nestegis cunninghamii
Maire/Black maire

Family *Oleaceae:* This is the family of ashes, olives and lilacs. Its twenty-nine genera and 600 species of trees and shrubs are almost cosmopolitan, though they are more common in Southeast Asia and Australasia. The family includes such well-known trees as the European ash, *Fraxinus excelsior,* the American white ash, *F. americana,* and the Chinese flowering ash, *F. mariesii.* The olive, *Olea europaea,* the common jasmine, *Jasminium officinale,* the common European privet, *Ligustrum vulgare,* and the garden species of *Forsythia* all belong here.

Genus *Nestegis:* A Pacific region genus with species in New Zealand, Norfolk Island and possibly the Hawaiian Islands. Three of the four New Zealand species are endemic; the fourth is also found on Norfolk Island.

This is a tall, handsome canopy tree growing up to 20 m high with a stout, straight trunk up to 1.5 m through. Maire was once found commonly throughout the forests of the North Island, from sea level to 760 m; the species was also known to occur sparingly in Nelson and Marlborough. It is now found only in isolated districts, largely because its heavy wood is the best firewood available amongst our native timbers. From my boyhood in Palmerston North I can recall the rail truckloads of maire logs obtained each year by my parents for firewood; in our fireplace maire burned slowly with great heat and without sparking.

The tree passes through a juvenile stage, when the leaves are leathery, narrow-linear and acute, 15—25 cm long and 8—16 cm wide. The smaller adult leaves are also leathery, from 7.5 to 15 cm long and 1.5 to 4.5 cm wide; they are lanceolate to ovate-lanceolate in shape, obtuse or sub-acute, on stout petioles about 10 mm long. The inflorescence is an eight to twelve-flowered raceme 1—2.5 cm long arising from a leaf axil. The raceme axis and flower pedicels are densely hairy. Individual maire flowers are very small.

The heavy, dark-brown wood, often streaked with black, is very hard and can be given a fine finish.

1

2

Fig 1 A large black maire tree raises its huge crown on its stout, straight trunk above surrounding scrub. Mt Ruapehu, May 1972.

Fig 2 A group of maire leaves showing the dark-green upper surface and paler lower surface with prominent midvein and distinct lateral veins. The centre leaf is elliptic-lanceolate in shape and has a sub-acute tip.

Fig 3 The rough, corky bark.

Fig 4 A foliage spray showing opposite leaves and leaf upper surfaces as well as terminal and lateral buds for the next season's growth.

3

4

5

6

Fig 5 A growing raceme of male flowers clearly showing their two large exserted anthers and hairy stalk. The male flowers possess a vestigial ovary. Hinakura, September 1972. Twice natural size. Flowers are perfect or unisexual, male flowers being very short-lived.

Fig 6 The male flower anther at right is just splitting to release pollen. The hairy pedicel is clearly visible. Hinakura, September 1972. Four times natural size.

Fig 7 Racemes of female flowers arising from leaf axils. Hinakura, September 1972. The flowers are usually borne in great abundance.

Fig 8 A female flower showing its large two-lobed stigma, rather like a parasol. The female flowers possess two empty, non-functional, sessile anthers. Hinakura, September 1972. Four times natural size.

Fig 9 Fruits are borne in great profusion along the branchlets, giving the tree a bright glow of colour. They take twelve months to ripen. Hinakura, October 1965.

Fig 10 A group of ripe drupes from last season with this season's new drupes just forming on the racemes from female flowers on the branchlets above them. Hinakura, October 1965.

Fig 11 Some black maire trees form drupes that are yellow when ripe. These are from Mt Ruapehu, November 1963. About natural size.

7

8

9

10

11

1

2

Nestegis apetala/Coastal maire

Coastal maire is a small tree up to 6 m high, sometimes a shrub, with spreading and often tortuous branches and a furrowed bark. It is found usually growing on rocky headlands around Whangarei Heads, on the Hen and Chickens, Great and Little Barrier, Fanal, Cuvier and Poor Knights Islands and around the Bay of Islands.

The leaves are leathery and glossy, elliptic to broadly elliptic in shape, occasionally slightly ovate or lanceolate, or even rotund when young. Juvenile leaves are up to 14 cm long by 8.5 cm wide, adults 4.5—12.5 cm long by 1.5—6 cm wide. They are often wavy and very dark green, with prominent raised mid-veins on both upper and lower surfaces. The petioles are about 10 mm long.

Racemes of up to twenty-one flowers each arise from the leaf axils or direct from the branchlets. The individual flowers, which can be unisexual or bisexual, are about 2.5 mm across and lack petals. In unisexual flowers the male has two stamens, each with a large bilobed anther; the female has two abortive anthers and an ovary with a two-lobed stigma. The fruit is a drupe 9 mm long, richly purple-coloured when ripe and spotted with white.

The photographs of coastal maire on these pages are from trees growing at Oke Bay, Bay of Islands.

3

Fig 1 The paler and duller lower surface. Natural size.

Fig 2 The glossy upper surface of a broadly elliptic leaf. Also natural size.

Fig 3 A small tree of coastal maire growing above Oke Bay, January 1978.

Fig 4 The tree can grow on steep rock faces such as this at Oke Bay, January 1978.

Fig 5 The rough, furrowed and flaky bark.

Fig 6 A spray of foliage showing the dark-green opposite leaves with their wavy margins and prominent midveins.

Fig 7 A raceme of male flowers arising from a leaf axil. The anthers here are greatly distended with pollen and although the bilobed stigma can be seen the ovary is not fully developed and is presumably non-functional. January 1978.

Fig 8 Male flowers, some possibly bisexual, with their anthers splitting to release pollen. Late January, 1978. Three and a half times natural size.

Fig 9 A cluster of female racemes arising both from leaf axils and direct from the branchlet. Late January 1978. Natural size.

Fig 10 A female flower showing the bilobed stigma, the non-functional anthers devoid of any pollen, the reduced calyx and the hairless pedicel. Late January 1978. Four times natural size.

Fig 11 A rather unusual female flower with a three-lobed stigma, which has darkened after receiving pollen.

Fig 12 These drupes have taken about twelve months to mature. Two are still green and the others are only partly ripe. December 1977. One and a half times natural size.

Nestegis lanceolata/White maire
N. montana/Oro-oro/Narrow-leaved maire

White maire is a canopy tree rather similar in appearance to black maire. It is a smaller tree, however, reaching 15 m high (black maire grows to 20 m) with a trunk up to 1 m through. White maire is found in lowland forests, from sea level to 600 m throughout the North Island and around Nelson. The tree is restricted in distribution nowadays and is found only in isolated localities.

The smooth, leathery leaves of *N. lanceolata* are glossy above. They are narrow-lanceolate to ovate-lanceolate or narrow-elliptic in shape, with a midvein flush above and prominently raised below. The leaves are 5—12 cm long by 1—3.5 cm wide, on petioles about 10 mm long. Racemes of flowers arise from the leaf axils or directly from the branchlets; they are 1—2 cm long and usually have five to ten flowers, each about 2 mm across. The sexes are either together or on separate trees. The fruit of *N. lanceolata* is a drupe 10—12 mm long, slightly attenuated from its middle to the apex, not ovoid as in black

maire. The wood of white maire is tough and durable, like that of black maire.

N. montana is a smaller, much-branched, round-headed tree 10—15 m high with slender branches. The trunk, which is up to 60 cm through, is usually short. The branchlets are pubescent near their tips when they are young. Oro-oro is found from sea level to 600 m in forests from Mangonui in the north to Nelson and Marlborough in the south.

The opposite, leathery, shining leaves of *N. montana* are on very short petioles only 2—3 mm long with the midvein slightly raised both above and below. The adult leaves are 3.5—9 cm long and 6—9 mm wide. They are linear to very narrow-lanceolate in shape, with acute or obtuse apices.

N. montana flower racemes are about 3—4 cm long, each having five to seventeen individual flowers on slender pedicels 2—3 mm long. The drupe is shorter and narrower than in the other species, only 6—9 mm long. The drupe is reddish when ripe.

1

Fig 1 A foliage spray of *N. lanceolata* showing opposite narrow-lanceolate leaves and a developing shoot.

Fig 2 A long narrow-elliptic leaf of *N. lanceolata* with acute apex and distinct midvein and petiole. The upper surface has a rough though shiny texture. Natural size.

Fig 3 The paler lower leaf surface with its raised midvein shows the venation more clearly. Also about natural size.

Fig 4 A white maire spray with both opposite and alternate ovate-lanceolate leaves. Also shown are female flower racemes and drupes maturing from the previous season. Waipunga Gorge, December 1973.

Fig 5 Both *N. lanceolata* and *N. montana* are illustrated in this photograph taken in the Waipunga Gorge, December 1973. The tall tree at the left is a fine specimen of white maire. The shorter tree growing alongside on the right is a specimen of *N. montana*, showing the slender, upright, spreading branches and broad leafy canopy.

Fig 6 White maire's rough, furrowed bark.

Fig 7 A raceme of male or possibly bisexual white maire flowers from a tree growing in the Waipunga Gorge, December 1973. The male flowers have two to six exserted anthers similar to those of *N. cunninghamii*. Twice natural size.

2

3

4

5

6

7

8

Fig 8 Close view of some ripening drupes of *N. lanceolata*. Clearly illustrated is their slightly attenuated shape. Waipunga Gorge, late December 1973. Twice natural size.

Fig 9 A spray of *N. montana* foliage showing the dark-green upper surfaces of the leaves, their very long, narrow shape, the short petioles and the opposite arrangement. The leaves of juvenile plants of *N. montana* are similar to the adult leaves, although they can be longer — up to 13 cm. The lower leaf surfaces are rougher and duller with indistinct venation.

Fig 10 The older bark of *N. montana* is rough, deeply furrowed and grey-brown.

Fig 11 Racemes of the tiny *N. montana* male flowers arising from the axils of the leaves. Those pictured here are shedding pollen, which covers the lower leaf. Also illustrated here is the reddish-brown bark of the young branchlets. From a tree growing at Otari, October 1972. This specimen is reproduced here at about two-thirds natural size.

Fig 12 A close view of *N. montana* male flowers. Some anthers are splitting, while others have completely released their pollen. Notice the dusting of yellow pollen on the lower leaves. The pistil of male flowers is abortive in all four species of *Nestigis*. Also from a tree at Otari, October 1972. Five times natural size.

9

10

11

12

291

Geniostoma rupestre
Hangehange

Family *Loganiaceae:* A widespread family of trees, shrubs and lianes found throughout the tropical and temperate regions of the world. A number of species yield extremely poisonous substances, such as strychnine from the tree *Strychnos nux-vomica,* from India and Ceylon, and aucubin from *Buddleia* species. The genus *Fagraea* from Indo-Malaysia, north Australia and some Pacific Islands contains some fine timber trees. Three genera occur in New Zealand, one of which includes a small tree.

Genus *Geniostoma:* A genus of about sixty species found from Madagascar through Mauritius, Malaya, New Guinea, Polynesia and Australia to New Zealand. The single New Zealand species is endemic.

A hairless, bushy, much-branching shrub or small tree up to 4 m tall found abundantly amongst larger trees in coastal and lowland forests, from the Three Kings Islands south to Golden Bay and the Marlborough Sounds. Hangehange has rather brittle branches and pale-green, shining, opposite leaves 5—7 or even 9 cm long and 2—3 or even 4 cm wide. The leaves are ovate to broad or elliptic-ovate, abruptly narrowing to an acuminate apex. Hangehange's pubescent flowers are each 6 mm across.

1

Fig 1 A foliage spray of hangehange showing the green branchlet and the upper surfaces of the oppositely arranged leaves. The indistinct venation and the brittle nature of the branchlet are clearly apparent. The slender petioles of hangehange are 5—10 mm long. About half natural size.

Fig 2 Clusters of hangehange flower cymes. The greenish-white to white flowers are bisexual and faintly lemon-scented.

Hairs on the upper surface cf the corolla show clearly here. Otari, October 1969. Twice natural size.

Fig 3 The paler and duller undersurfaces of the leaves, with prominent raised veins. About half natural size.

Fig 4 A rather small tree growing in shade deep in the forest. In these situations the tree can be very plentiful, although it is often not easily seen. Otari, October 1969.

Fig 5 The fruit of hangehange is a capsule 5—7 mm or even 10 mm long and about 5 mm in diameter. The seed capsules follow the flowers, hanging in profusion on drooping stalks around the branchlets. The capsules are green when immature, black when ripe. Akatarawa Saddle, February 1969.

Fig 6 The rather rough bark. In older trees the bark is often clothed with mosses and lichens.

2

3

4

5

6

Family Rubiaceae
Genus *Coprosma*

Rubiaceae is one of the largest families of plants, containing about 500 genera with about 7,000 species of trees, shrubs and herbs. They are found mainly in the tropical and subtropical regions of the world, with some species in temperate and cold regions. The family includes *Coffee arabica* and *C. robusta,* the two most important producers of coffee. Species of *Cinchona* yield the drug quinine, and amongst the many ornamental garden plants that belong here are the *Gardenia* species.

The genus *Coprosma* contains some ninety species of small trees and shrubs found in New Zealand, Hawaii, Borneo, Java, New Guinea, Malaysia, some Polynesian islands, Australia and Tasmania. Except for one species, the forty-five New Zealand *Coprosma* species are all endemic; fifteen of them grow into small trees.

In New Zealand coprosmas are found from the coast to the high mountains. They grow in rocky places, in forest, along forest margins, along streamsides and in scrubland. Those New Zealand species that grow into small trees fall naturally into two groups, one with big leaves and the other with small leaves.

Most coprosmas have male and female flowers on separate plants. The male flower is often pendulous, consisting of a cup-like structure from which long anthers hang on long, thread-like filaments. The clusters of male flowers of *C. lucida* at left below are typical coprosma male flowers, with the spindle-shape anthers clearly visible. The coprosma female flower is normally erect, consisting of a similar cup-like structure from which protrude two long slender styles; these are stigmatic for most of their length.

This is shown in the photograph of the female flowers of *C. lucida* at right below.

The leaves of coprosmas may be large, as in taupata, small or very small. Most species have peculiar small pits (domatia) between the midvein and one or more of the lateral veins of the undersurface; these are a useful diagnostic feature for identifying *Coprosma* species. In most species the venation is distinct.

All species produce many fruits, which are drupes. These colour up in autumn, ranging from translucent whites to blues, and through yellow to oranges and reds. Most species flower in the spring, some in winter; flowering may occur out of season.

Coprosma species may be variable; but although hybridization between some related species does occur, recent studies indicate that it is not as common as was originally thought.

The family Rubiaceae have opposite stipulate leaves; in some genera, including *Coprosma,* the stipules are interpetiolar and usually tipped by a denticle. This denticle is provided with glands which secrete a mucous that protects developing buds. The stipules of each species are distinctive in structure and are therefore very useful in identifying *Coprosma* species. They reach their fullest development at an early stage of stem growth and are therefore best seen on younger shoots. As the leaves mature the stipules in some species tend to dry out and wither away. Stipules occur at every node; they are associated with a collar that surrounds each node on the stems, and the thin tissue in this collar that joins the two stipules together is called the sheath. Some stipules are hairy; the denticles are single or multiple.

Coprosma lucida
Karamu

Karamu is a small tree or shrub 3—6 m tall found in forests, along forest margins and in scrub all over the North, South and Stewart Islands. It grows from sea level to 1,060 m, and is one of the best known of the larger-leaved *Coprosma* species. It is readily recognised by its pale bark and glossy, leathery, dark-green leaves which are paler below with distinct domatia. In season, karamu is covered with clusters of orange-red drupes which take almost eighteen months to mature after flowering. These drupes are much sought after for food by native birds, as are the drupes of all coprosmas. The female flowers of karamu are borne on a three-branched inflorescence with three to four flowers at the end of each branch.

1

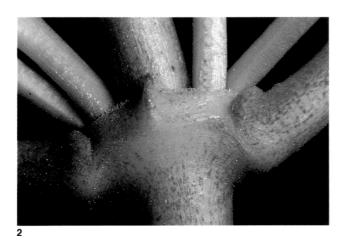

2

3

5

Fig 1 A karamu foliage spray with male flower clusters and reddish flower buds.

Fig 2 A stipule of *C. lucida*. The main stem continues above in the centre, the lower lateral axes are leaf petioles and the thinner stems between these two are branchlets and inflorescence stems.

4

Fig 5 A small tree of *C. lucida* growing out from the wall of the Woodside Gorge in March 1973. It displays the stout branches and branchlets of the species. This specimen is bearing many clusters of largely ripe drupes.

Fig 6 With its scattered pustules, the finely furrowed bark of *C. lucida* is typical of many of the coprosmas. Most coprosmas emit an unpleasant odour when they are burned.

Fig 7 The underside of a karamu leaf. In this photograph the domatia (which appear to be swollen as a result of infection in this specimen) show very clearly. Domatia are seen as swellings on the leaf upper surface. About natural size.

Fig 3 *C. lucida* can be smothered with drupes in a good season. The drupes are oblong, 8—12 mm long, prized by native birds for food. Mt Ruapehu, April 1963.

Fig 4 The leaves are thick and leathery, glossy above, 12—19 cm long by 3—4 cm wide, obovate to narrow-obovate or broad-elliptic. They have a raised midvein and a stout petiole 10—30 mm long. Natural size.

Fig 8 Close view of the male flowers of *C. lucida*. These specimens show how the anthers split lengthwise in a manner characteristic of the coprosmas to release their pollen which is then borne away by the wind. The long filaments are so delicate that they allow the slightest air movement to carry the pollen away. From a tree growing at Karaka Bay, October 1969. Four and a half times natural size.

Fig 9 A close view of the female flowers showing the hairy stigmatic surface of the styles and the recurved lobes of the corollas. Karaka Bay, October 1969. Two and a half times natural size. The female flowers are borne in great numbers.

Fig 10 Karamu drupes. A fine stipule shows at the second branching from the left. Opepe Bush, April 1963.

295

Coprosma arborea/Mamangi
C. macrocarpa
C. chathamica

All three of these coprosmas are limited in their distribution. *C. macrocarpa* is found only on the Three Kings Islands and in Northland from North Cape to about Kaipara Harbour. *C. arborea* extends further south, growing from North Cape down to about Kawhia and Tokomaru Bay. *C. chathamica* occurs only in forest on the Chatham Islands.

C. macrocarpa grows as a shrub or small tree 5—10 m high; this species has stout branches and branchlets. *C. arborea* is more common, growing up to 10 m high in forest and on forest margins; it has close-set branches and slender, pubescent branchlets. *C. chathamica* forms a tree up to 15 m tall and has rather stout branches and branchlets.

1

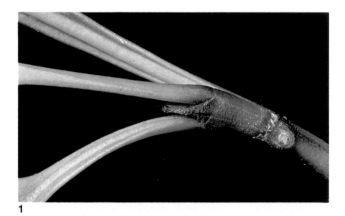

2

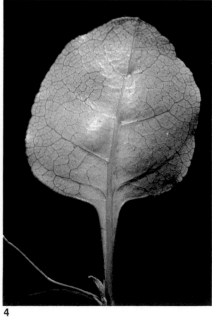

3

4

5

6

7

8

Fig 1 The stipule of *C. arborea*. Five times natural size.

Fig 2 A specimen of *C. arborea* growing in Hukutaia Domain, January 1977.

Fig 3 Leaves of *C. arborea* are thin with distinct venation and domatia. They are ovate to broad-elliptic or suborbicular, cuneately or abruptly narrowed to the petiole. The leaves have thickened margins that are slightly wavy or crenulate, and are 5– 6 cm long by 3.5– 4 cm wide. Here about natural size. The winged petiole about 12 mm long is a distinctive feature.

Fig 4 Pale undersurface of a *C. arborea* leaf showing venation. Natural size.

Fig 5 A spray of foliage of *C. arborea* showing the broad, winged petioles. They are about 12 mm long, sometimes up to 20 mm long. Coromandel, December 1969.

Fig 6 *C. arborea* bark is furrowed and flaky.

Fig 7 Leaves of *C. macrocarpa* are somewhat leathery, not as thick as those of *C. lucida*, and a little wavy. They are broad-ovate to elliptic-ovate, obtuse to subacute, 9– 13 cm long by 4– 8 cm wide, with prominent midvein. Half natural size.

Fig 8 Undersurface of a *C. macrocarpa* leaf showing veins and domatia. The petiole is 12– 25 mm long. Half natural size.

Fig 9 A spray of foliage of *C. macrocarpa* with drupes. These are 10– 25 mm long. Warkworth, December 1977.

Fig 10 The stipule of *C. macrocarpa* with its long denticle. The stipule becomes dry and papery at an early stage. Five times natural size.

Fig 11 A spray of foliage of *C. chathamica*. The somewhat leathery leaves are variable, ovate to ovate-oblong, obtuse or sometimes mucronulate. They are 3.5– 7.5 cm long and 2– 3.5 cm wide. The triangular hairy stipule shows in the centre. Auckland, December 1977.

Fig 12 The underside of a *C. chathamica* leaf. Domatia, although present, are not very distinct. About natural size.

9

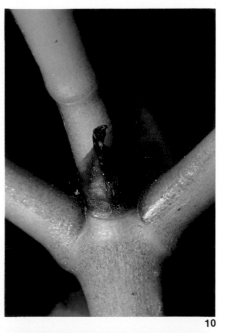

10

11

12

297

Coprosma repens/Taupata
C. robusta/Karamu
C. grandifolia/Kanono

1

C. repens is a small tree or shrub up to 8 m high, found in coastal situations from North Cape to Marlborough and Greymouth. It can often be seen growing straight out of a crevice in rock. This is an extremely tough and hardy plant that can withstand gales and salt spray. In very exposed coastal situations it often becomes prostrate or assumes strangely grotesque, gnarled and twisted shapes. Because of its hardiness it is often used for hedges in coastal areas. Variegated varieties are grown.

Both *C. robusta* and *C. grandifolia* can be shrubs or small trees up to 6 m high with stout, hairless branches and branchlets; those of *C. robusta* are more spreading than those of *C. grandifolia*. Both are found from the Three Kings Islands throughout the North and South Islands, with *C. robusta* also growing on the Chatham Islands. Both occur in forest and scrubland, with *C. robusta* favouring forest margins and hillsides and *C. grandifolia* being more common on alluvial soils and in moist sheltered places. As trees, both have slender trunks and bear drupes in great profusion, making a wonderful display.

3

Fig 1 *C. repens* leaves are thick, somewhat fleshy and glossy, with wavy, recurved or inrolled margins. They have a prominent midvein and distinct venation. Taupata leaves are broad-oblong to broadly ovate-oblong, rounded to truncate or retuse at the apex. They are 2 — 3 or 6 — 8 cm long by 1.5 — 2 or 4 — 5 cm wide; the larger leaves occur in shady situations, the smaller in full sun. This is the leaf upper surface. Natural size.

Fig 2 Underside of a taupata leaf showing the distinct venation, domatia and stout petiole. The petioles vary from 8 — 16 mm in length. Natural size.

Fig 3 A taupata with fruit growing along the shore of Wellington Harbour. January 1971.

Fig 4 A young taupata beginning life in tough fashion from a rocky crevice. This tree was growing in Karaka Bay, Wellington Harbour, November 1964.

Fig 5 Seen against the light the drupes of *C. repens,* like those of most coprosmas, are beautifully translucent. Karaka Bay, January 1971.

4

5

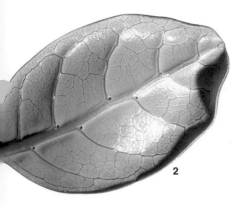

Fig 6 The stipule of *C. repens*. Clearly visible are the terminal and accessory denticles.

Fig 7 A taupata branchlet showing, besides the clusters of male flowers, the pairs of stipules at each node. There are four in all, the top ones being in side view in this photograph. From a tree at Karaka Bay, October 1969.

Fig 8 *C. repens* drupes. They are borne in such profusion that they smother the branches. Karaka Bay, January 1971.

Fig 9 The stipule of *C. robusta* on a main stem, with two on a secondary stem one to each side. Three times natural size.

Fig 10 The ripe drupes of *C. robusta*. They are 8 – 9 mm long and 4 – 5 mm wide, oblong or narrow-ovoid in shape. Waipunga Gorge, April 1974. Twice natural size.

Fig 11 *C. robusta* drupes. From a tree at Taupo, April 1965.

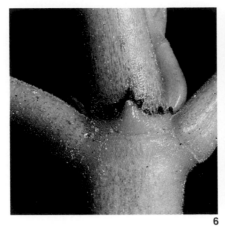

Fig 12 Leaves of *C. robusta* are leathery, elliptic to elliptic-oblong or broad-ovate. They are acute or obtuse apically on a petiole 1 – 2 cm long. The leaf is up to 12 cm long and commonly up to 5 cm wide.

Fig 13 Lower surface of a *C. robusta* leaf showing the stout prominent midvein and the vein pattern. About natural size.

Fig 14 Spray of *C. robusta* showing the wavy nature of the leaves, the opposite leaves typical of *Coprosma* and the stipules. Stokes Valley, October 1970.

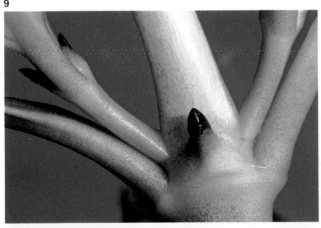

15

16

17

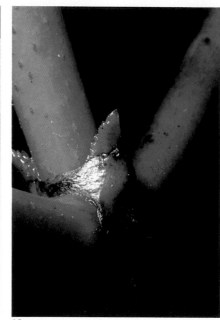

18

Fig 15 The leaves of *C. grandifolia* are 15-20 cm long and 7-10 cm wide, rather membraneous, often mottled and not very glossy. They are broadly elliptic to obovate in shape with a subacute or apiculate apex and a stout petiole 2-5 cm long. Swellings mark the positions of domatia. About natural size.

Fig 16 The undersurface of a *C. grandifolia* leaf has a prominent midvein and lateral veins, domatia and distinct vein pattern. About natural size.

Fig 17 A branchlet of *C. grandifolia* showing stipules. They are provided with glandular denticles toward the apex, clearly seen in the lower pair. About natural size.

Fig 18 Close view of the stipules of *C. grandiflora*. Magnified five times.

Fig 19 Trees of *C. grandifolia* with their typical long, slender trunks growing in scrub near Taupo, January 1974.

Fig 20 The rather flattened, oblong drupes of *C. grandifolia*. Opepe Bush, May 1963.

19

20

Coprosma rotundifolia/Round-leaved coprosma
C. areolata/Thin-leaved coprosma
C. crassifolia
C. acutifolia
C. petiolata

C. rotundifolia occurs throughout the North, South and Stewart Islands in damp forest and along stream and river banks from sea level to 600 m. In the open it forms a rather stunted shrub, but in the forest it grows as a shrub or small tree up to 5 m high. The branches are spreading to divaricating, the branchlets hairy, sometimes pubescent. Flowers arise in axillary clusters of two or four flowers each.

C. areolata grows as a shrub or as a small tree up to 5 m tall. It is found from Spirits Bay southwards in forest from sea level to 960 m, in the North, South and Stewart Islands. The flowers are solitary or in groups of two to four, occuring at the apices of the branchlets.

C. crassifolia grows as a shrub or at times as a small tree, with spreading, interlacing, stiff branches. It is found from Mangonui south in both islands, from sea level to 400 m on rocky places on coasts and river terraces and in tussock lands and forests. The male flowers occur in groups of one to four; the female flowers are solitary. Both flowers of *C. crassifolia* occur terminally on very short branchlets.

Fig 1 A small tree of *C. rotundifolia* growing near Pelorus Bridge, January 1972.

Fig 2 *C. rotundifolia* bark is furrowed and flaky.

Fig 3 The drupes of *C. rotundifolia* occur singly on very short stalks amongst the leaves. Pelorus Bridge, January 1972.

4

5

6

7

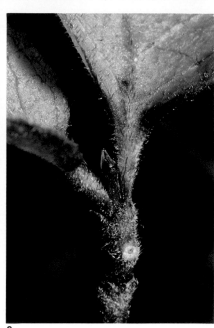

8

9

Fig 4 The leaves of *C. rotundifolia* are only 20−25 mm long by 14−20 mm wide. They are obtuse, sometimes apiculate, and have rounded to truncate bases on hairy petioles 4−6 mm long. Twice natural size.

Fig 5 The paler leaf lower surface. Also twice natural size.

Fig 6 A group of two *C. rotundifolia* male flowers. Hutt Valley, October 1973. Five times natural size.

Fig 7 The rather flattened but rounded drupes of *C. rotundifolia*. Pelorus Bridge, January 1972. Four times natural size.

Fig 8 *C. rotundifolia* stipule. Five and a half times natural size.

Fig 9 A tree of *C. areolata* growing near Kaitaia, April 1979.

Fig 10 *C. areolata* leaf upper surfaces. The leaves are thin and membraneous, broad-elliptic to obovate in shape. They are acute apically, usually 9−10 mm long by 7−10 mm wide. The petioles are slender and winged, and finely hairy or pubescent; they are about 7 mm long.

C. ACUTIFOLIA AND C. PETIOLATA

The two species C. acutifolia and C. petiolata are not illustrated here. Both these Coprosma species belong to the group of plants in this genus having very small leaves and both are found only in the Kermadec Islands.

C. acutifolia grows as a tree up to 10 m high and has ovate to ovate-elliptic or lanceolate leaves 60 mm long and 20 mm wide. Its drupe is orange-red and 7−8 mm long.

C. petiolata forms a shrub or a small tree up to 6 m high, usually with larger leaves on the female plant than on the male; the female leaves are up to 69 mm by 29 mm and male leaves up to 41 mm by 23 mm. The larger drupes of this species are usually two-lobed.

Fig 11 *C. areolata* leaf, lower surface. Eight times natural size.

Fig 12 The hairy stipule of *C. areolata*. Six times natural size.

Fig 13 The hairy petioles and stipules of *C. crassifolia*. Nine times natural size.

Fig 14 Clusters of *C. crassifolia* ripe and unripe berries. Twice natural size.

Fig 15 Upper surfaces of *C. crassifolia* rounded to oval or broad-oblong leaves; they are 6 — 15 mm long by 5 — 10 mm wide on narrow-winged pubescent petioles 1 — 2 mm long. Three times natural size.

Fig 16 Lower surfaces of the thick and leathery leaves. Three times natural size.

Coprosma tenuifolia
Wavy-leaved coprosma
C. foetidissima
Stinkwood/Hupiro

C. tenuifolia is a rather slender shrub or small tree up to 5 m high with rather stout, ascending branches. It is found from about Thames southwards to the Rua-hine Ranges inside forests or along forest margins. The flowers of *C. tenuifolia* occur in clusters; the flower buds and also the young stems and leaf peti-oles are often purple-tinged.

C. foetidissima grows in forest, along forest mar-gins, in scrub and in grasslands from sea level to 1,360 m. It grows from Moehau at the tip of the Coro-mandel peninsula southwards through the rest of the North Island and in the South Island and Stewart and the Auckland Islands. *C. foetidissima* is easily recog-nised by the odour of rotten eggs given off when a piece of the tree is bruised, crushed or broken. It forms an open branched shrub or small tree about 3 – 4 m high, and unlike the previous coprosmas its flowers occur singly at the tips of the branchlets.

Fig 1 Branchlet of *C. tenuifolia* showing male flower clusters, upper and lower leaf surfaces and the dry, papery stipule. Two and a half times natural size.

Fig 2 Foliage spray of *C. tenuifolia*. It shows leaf upper surfaces and flower buds at the tips of some of the branchlets. The leaves are ovate-oblong, usually apiculate but sometimes acute, 7 – 10 cm long and 3 – 4.5 cm wide, with slightly wavy margins.

Fig 3 Lower surfaces of the spray in Fig 2. The leaves are on pubescent petioles 1 – 2.5 cm long. Domatia are present.

Fig 4 Stipules of *C. tenuifolia* have denticles surrounded by hairs and have hairy shoulders to the sheath. The purple tinge of the young stem and petioles is evident. Four times natural size.

Fig 5 A young plant of *C. tenuifolia* in Opepe Bush, February 1977.

6 7

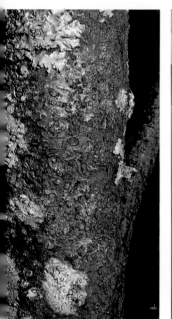

8   **9**   **10 11**

Fig 6 The ovoid drupes of *C. tenuifolia* are 7— 8 mm long and are borne in great abundance on short branchlets. Opepe Bush, May 1969.

Fig 7 A fine specimen of *C. foetidissima* growing on the forest margin on Mt Ruapehu, March 1974.

Fig 8 The bark of stinkwood is glossy and blistered and is unlike the bark of most other coprosmas.

Fig 9 The foliage of *C. foetidissima*. The leaves, which are fairly uniform here, can vary from obovate to oblong to broadly ovate, with obtuse, apiculate or mucronulate apices. They have winged petioles. The leaf blades themselves are 30— 50 mm long by 14— 20 mm wide; they are dull, membraneous to somewhat leathery, with conspicuous domatia underneath.

Fig 10 The undersurface of an unusual ovate-apiculate leaf of *C. foetidissima* showing the venation and the winged petiole, which is 8— 15 mm long.

Stinkwood stipules are truncate with a long denticle and sometimes some subsidiary denticles. About natural size.

Fig 11 A solitary female flower among the leaves at the tip of a stinkwood branchlet. Dun Mountain, Nelson, November 1969. Twice natural size.

Fig 12 Another solitary flower, this one male, arising from the apex of a branchlet of *C. foetidissima*. Also shown are the pubescent petiole and shorter stamens. Dun Mountain, November 1969. One and a half times natural size.

Fig 13 The oblong drupe of *C. foetidissima*, 7— 10 mm long, is borne rather sparsely. Taurewa, March 1970. Twice natural size.

12

13

Coprosma propinqua
Mingimingi

Mingimingi is a small-leaved shrub or small tree 3— 6 m high rather similar in appearance to *C. parviflora*. It has divaricating branches and more or less interlacing branchlets, and sometimes takes a more or less prostrate form. Mingimingi is common in swampy forests, in scrub, along creek and stream banks and in stoney places. The tree is found from Mangonui southwards throughout the North, South and Stewart Islands, growing from sea level to 460 m.

The male flowers of *C. propinqua* occur in axillary clusters of one to four on very short branchlets; the females are solitary at the tips of short branchlets. Drupes, pale when immature, become flecked with dark blue or turn completely dark blue when mature.

C. propinqua will hybridize freely with *C. robusta*.

1

2

3

4

5

Fig 1 Leaves of *C. propinqua*, mainly the upper surfaces. They arise in opposite pairs or in opposite fascicles and are only 10 — 14 mm long by 2 — 3 mm wide, growing on slender petioles clothed by very short hairs. Mingimingi leaves are thick and leathery, and mostly linear-oblong to broad-oblong in shape; they have obtuse or subacute apices. Three and a half times natural size.

Fig 2 The lower surface of *C. propinqua* leaves showing the distinct midvein.

Fig 3 Two small mingimingi trees growing together on a stream bank in the Upper Waipunga Valley, December 1966.

Fig 4 The shining, lightly furrowed green bark of a young mingimingi.

Fig 5 As a *C. propinqua* tree ages, the bark becomes deeply furrowed and flaking.

Fig 6 Stipule of *C. propinqua*. The stipules are pubescent, with a short sheath and a solitary denticle. Six times natural size.

Fig 7 Clusters of mingimingi male flowers arising in typical fashion on very short branchlets. The male flowers are smaller and more erect than in the large-leaved coprosmas. Waipunga Gorge, October 1966.

Fig 8 Mingimingi's solitary female flower arises, like the male, terminally on very short branchlets. Notice the long, rather hairy styles. Woodside Gorge, November 1969. Five and half times natural size.

Fig 9 Berries from a form of *C. propinqua* from the Waima Ure River Gorge, March 1969. This could possibly prove to be a distinct species; these berries look mature (although they may have turned blue by April or May).

Fig 10 Ripe mingimingi drupes. Upper Waipunga Valley, March 1967. Just below natural size.

Fig 11 Leaf undersides from a *C. propinqua* x *robusta* hybrid. Waipunga Gorge, December 1973. Three times natural size. Hybridizing between these two species occurs freely. Recent studies indicate that hybridism in the genus *Coprosma* is generally not as rampant as was thought to be the case. Most of the known hybrids appear to be of rare occurrence.

Fig 12 The stipule of the *C. propinqua* x *robusta* hybrid. Five times natural size.

Fig 13 A *C. propinqua* x *robusta* hybrid growing in the Waipunga Gorge, April 1974.

Coprosma linariifolia/Mikimiki/Yellow-wood
C. parviflora/Leafy coprosma
C. rigida/Stiff karamu

C. linariifolia is a small-leaved coprosma that grows as a shrub or as a small tree up to 6 m high. It is found from about Thames southwards to Southland, growing from sea level to about 900 m in forest and scrub. The male flowers of *C. linariifolia* are in terminal clusters of two to five flowers, while the females are solitary and terminal on the branchlets.

C. parviflora grows as a shrub or as a small tree up to 5 m high. It is found from sea level to 1,200 m, from North Cape southwards to Southland, and also occurs on Stewart Island and the subantarctic islands. According to Kelly (1969) the typical form of this species may be confined to the northern parts of the North Island; the southern forms may therefore be varieties. *C. parviflora* is a small-leaved species; the male flowers are solitary or in twos or threes and the females are always solitary, both occuring along the branchlets.

C. rigida grows as a shrub or a small tree 2 – 5 m tall and is found in forest and along forest margins from Mangonui southwards in the North Island and in the South Island. It has characteristic stiff, spreading and intertwining branches with a shining reddish-coloured bark. The flowers of this coprosma are solitary at the tips of their own short branchlets; the oblong drupe is orange-yellow or white and translucent.

1

2

3

4

Fig 1 A branchlet of *C. linariifolia* clad typically in soft hairs and showing the long stipules joined into a tubular sheath. The long, narrow leaves of mikimiki arise in opposite pairs.

Fig 2 Upper surface of a typical leaf of *C. linariifolia*. Leaves of this species are thick and leathery, 20 – 30 mm long by 2 – 4 mm wide. The midvein is sunk in and the margins are purplish tinged. Leaves vary in shape from linear to linear-lanceolate; they are acute and usually slightly curved. Twice natural size.

Fig 3 Lower surface of a typically thick, leathery *C. linariifolia* leaf. Also at twice natural size.

Fig 4 Close view of the hairy stipules of *C. linariifolia;* there are two denticles, one in front of the other. The union of the two stipules to form a single tubular sheath is clear here; it has the effect of making the branchlets appear as if they were jointed. Two and a half times natural size.

Fig 5 A small tree of *C. parviflora* growing near Kaitaia. Note the flat spreads of branchlets more or less in tiers.

Fig 6 The bark of *C. parviflora.*

Fig 7 *C. parviflora* stipules are obscured by hairs, and the young stem, petioles and midvein below are very hairy. Seven and a half times natural size.

5

6

7

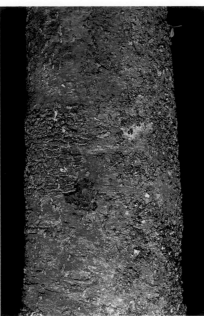

Fig 8 The upper surfaces of the leaves of *C. parviflora*. The leathery leaves are 7 – 12 mm long by 4 – 6 mm wide, mostly in fascicles and arising on slender, pubescent petioles not more than 1 mm long. They vary in shape from oblong to obovate, being obtuse tipped and cuneate at base. Two and a half times natural size. Figs 5 – 10 all from Kaitaia, photographed in January 1980.

Fig 9 Leaf undersurface of *C. parviflora* showing vein reticulation, pubescent young stem and petioles, and hairy midveins of leaves. Four times natural size.

Fig 10 A branch of *C. parviflora* with spreading branchlets and fascicles of leaves. Young branchlets of this species are generally hairy, while the older ones are smooth.

Fig 11 Branchlets of *C. rigida* showing the reddish bark and sparse, thick, leathery leaves. These are 10 – 20 mm long and 3 – 9 mm wide, on petioles 2 – 3 mm long. The leaves vary in shape from obovate to oblong, rounded or almost truncate at their tips and cuneate at the base. They are paler below with evident venation.

Fig 12 Stipules of *C. rigida* are usually hairy and denticles may be present or absent. Seven times natural size.

Fig 13 The rounded, slightly elongate drupe is 4 – 6 mm long. Here the red, shining bark and the truncate, almost emarginate leaves show clearly. Waipunga Gorge, April 1974. Three times natural size.

8

9 10

11

12 13

Family Compositae
Genus *Olearia*

Comprising about 1,100 genera and some 25,000 species, the Compositae is possibly the largest family of the flowering plants. Compositae are found all over the world, except on the Antarctic continent. They are recognised by their daisy-like flowers as in the familiar dandelion, sunflower, dahlia, chrysanthemum and the New Zealand mountain *Celmisia* or mountain daisy. The lettuce and artichoke also belong here. Most Compositae are shrubs or perennial and annual herbs; trees are not common amongst them. It is interesting, therefore, that in the twenty-nine genera of Compositae we have in New Zealand, three include plants that grow into small trees.

The flower is an inflorescence and is known as the *capitulum,* commonly referred to as the flower head. It consists of many small, bisexual *disk florets* that form the centre or disk of the flower, which is surrounded by a circle of larger *ray florets,* which are usually female or sterile. The flower head is surrounded near its base by an involucre of bracts.

Most of the tree species of Compositae found in New Zealand belong to the genus *Olearia,* which contains about 130 species of shrubs and trees found in New Guinea, Australia, Lord Howe Island and New Zealand. All the thirty-two species occurring in New Zealand are endemic, and nineteen of these are small trees.

There is considerable diversity in the arrangement, size and form of flower heads among our tree olearias, including: (1) solitary large flower head up to 5 cm across, consisting of a ring of ray florets around a centre of disk florets (*O. angustifolia,* illustrated in both photographs here from plants from Stewart Island grown by Mrs S. Natusch); (2) racemes of flower heads each 2—3 cm across and containing numerous disk florets but not ray florets (*O. colensoi*); (3) corymbs of smaller flower heads with both disk and ray florets, the latter irregularly arranged (*O. ilicifolia*); (4) corymbs of tiny flower heads, each with a single disk floret (*O. paniculata*).

Olearia townsonii/Coromandel tree daisy
O. thomsonii
O. angustifolia/Tete a weka

These three *Olearia* species are quite limited in their distribution.

O. townsonii grows as a shrub or small tree up to 5 m high only in rocky places above the Kauaeranga Valley near Thames. Its branchlets are four-angled, somewhat grooved and along with the petioles and leaf undersides are clad in a distinctive dense, shining, yellowish tomentum. The leaves are 5—10 cm long and 2—3.5 cm wide, thick and leathery and elliptic-oblong in shape. The flower heads are 1—1.2 cm across and occur in large corymbs.

O. thomsonii is also a shrub or small tree up to 5 m high and is found in the Ohura Basin and east of Taumarunui at the head of the Wanganui River. The leaves, including the petiole up to 5 cm long, are 7—16 cm long by 3—5 cm wide, somewhat leathery in texture. The flower heads are in large corymbs on slender pedicels 1.5 cm long.

O. angustifolia grows as a shrub or small tree up to 6 m high along coastal areas of Southland and Foveaux Strait and on coastal headlands of Stewart Island. Its large and scented flower heads 3.5—5 cm across are particularly beautiful with violet disk florets and white ray florets. With calloused teeth on their crenate or dentate margins and thick, white undersurface tomentum, the leaves are also distinctive.

1

2

3

Fig 1 A branchlet of *O. townsonii*. Clearly illustrated are the distinctive four-angled shape, the shallow grooving and the rather unusual dense, shining tomentum which is a feature of this species. At about twice natural size.

Fig 2 A spray of *O. townsonii* with its long-stalked corymbs of white flower heads. This photograph shows the alternate leaf arrangement as well as the distinctive tomentum on the branchlet and petioles. From a tree growing in the Kauaeranga Valley at 600 m, November 1970. With their pale violet disk forets and long white ray florets the flower heads of *O. townsonii* make the tree a very attractive specimen when it is in full flower.

5

4

6

Fig 3 Close view of some of the attractive flower heads of *O. townsonii*. From a tree growing in the Kauaeranga Valley, 600 m, November 1970. At four and a half times natural size.

Fig 4 Upper surface of a thick, leathery leaf of *O. townsonii*. Here at about natural size. The leaf margins are slightly sinuate or undulate.

Fig 5 The lower surface of a leaf of *O. townsonii*. It shows the characteristic yellow tomentum and the raised midvein with its prominent lateral veins. Also at about natural size.

Fig 6 A small tree of *O. townsonii*. This specimen, which had recently completed flowering, was growing in typical fashion from a rocky cleft in the Kauaeranga Valley at 600 m. January 1974.

Fig 7 The branchlets of *O. thomsonii* are stout and angular, becoming rounded as they age. They are distinctly reddish when they are young.

7

Fig 8 A foliage spray of *O. thomsonii* showing the alternate arrangement of the somewhat leathery leaves with their long petioles. *O. thomsonii* leaves are oblong to elliptic-ovate in shape with cuneate bases. The tree's reddish angular branchlet is also evident here.

8

Fig 9 A foliage spray of *O. thomsonii* showing the leaf undersurfaces. Notice the prominent midvein.

Fig 10 Spray of *O. angustifolia* showing the beautiful flower head and the leaf form. Clearly illustrated in this picture are the distinctive calloused teeth on the leaf margins and the soft, white tomentum on the leaf lower surfaces, branchlets and peduncles. This photograph and those of *O. angustifolia* on pages 310 and 311 are from a plant from Stewart Island grown by Mrs S. Natusch in Wellington, November 1964. The leaves of *O. angustifolia* are thick and leathery, narrow-lanceolate in shape; they are 7—15 cm long and 1—2 cm wide.

9

10

Olearia rani
Heketara

1

This is one of the commonest olearias throughout the North Island, growing also in Nelson and Marlborough. It grows from sea level to 800 m in forest, along forest margins, in clearings, on river or stream banks and in second-growth forest or scrub. Along with *O. angustifolia, O. rani* is the most beautiful of the New Zealand tree daisies.

When growing in the open, heketara forms a spreading tree up to 7.5 m high with a short trunk and thin, greyish-brown bark. Enclosed in forest or scrub it grows as a shrub 2– 3 m tall or as a tree with a slender trunk reaching up to the light, where it forms a crown that becomes smothered with flowers.

The branchlets, petioles, leaf undersides and flower branchlets are all densely covered with a soft, white or pale-fawn tomentum. The leaves are broad elliptic-ovate to oblong in shape, 5 – 15 cm long and 5 – 6.5 cm wide. They are thin but leathery in texture with prominent venation on the lower surfaces; the margins are irregularly or coarsely toothed.

The flower heads of this outstanding tree daisy are white with yellow centres; they are about 1 cm across and occur in large, much-branched panicles. In spring and early summer these panicles brighten hillsides, river banks and scrub, their eye-catching masses of flowers being visible some distance away.

2

3

Fig 1 A leaf spray of *O. rani* with elliptic shaped leaves.

Fig 2 A superb specimen in full flower in the Otaki River Gorge, October 1976.

Fig 3 Flower heads of heketara. Kaitoke Hill, Upper Hutt Valley, November 1968. Four times natural size.

Fig 4 Flowering crowns of heketara show through second-growth forest on a hillside in the Otaki Gorge, October 1976.

Fig 5 The bark of heketara, like that of most *Olearia* species, is thin and furrowed, peeling in narrow flakes. The leaves here belong to a fern growing on the trunk.

Fig 6 The upper surface of the leaf of heketara. About natural size. The stout petiole is up to 4 cm long.

Fig 7 The lower surface of the leaf in Fig 6 showing the dense tomentum, which is fawn on the raised mid and lateral veins and on the petiole, and white between the veins. Also about natural size.

Fig 8 Panicles of flower heads from Kaitoke Hill, November 1968.

Fig 9 A further leaf spray in which the leaves are broader in shape than those in Fig 1. The tomentose branchlet can also be seen, as well as the mainly alternate leaf arrangement.

Olearia arborescens
Common tree daisy
O. cheesemanii
Streamside tree daisy

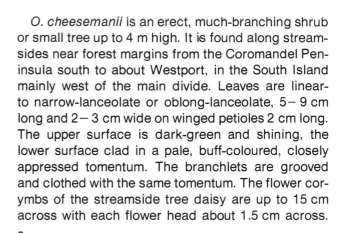

5

O. arborescens forms a shrub or small tree up to 4 m tall, found from sea level to 1,200 m in forest and scrub from the Bay of Plenty south through the North, South and Stewart Islands. The branchlets are angular and the leaves are 2–6 cm long by 2–4 cm wide, broad- to elliptic-ovate in shape with an acute apex; they have sinuate-dentate margins. The leaves are thin but leathery, shining above but with a thin, appressed, satiny tomentum below. The white flower heads are in large, rounded corymbs, the slender pedicels pubescent; the individual flower heads are up to 1.5 cm across, each with fifteen to twenty florets, there being seven to ten ray florets.

O. cheesemanii is an erect, much-branching shrub or small tree up to 4 m high. It is found along streamsides near forest margins from the Coromandel Peninsula south to about Westport, in the South Island mainly west of the main divide. Leaves are linear- to narrow-lanceolate or oblong-lanceolate, 5–9 cm long and 2–3 cm wide on winged petioles 2 cm long. The upper surface is dark-green and shining, the lower surface clad in a pale, buff-coloured, closely appressed tomentum. The branchlets are grooved and clothed with the same tomentum. The flower corymbs of the streamside tree daisy are up to 15 cm across with each flower head about 1.5 cm across.

1

2

3

Fig 1 A small tree of *O. arborescens* among shrubs on the Whangamoa Saddle, December 1979.

Fig 2 Flower spray of *O. arborescens*. Note also the characteristic square stem with its tomentum. From a tree growing on the Whangamoa Saddle, December 1979.

Fig 3 The bark of *O. arborescens* is thin and somewhat papery and peels in long, thin flakes.

Fig 4 A leaf spray of *O. arborescens*. It shows the stem structure, tomentum and leaf arrangement. The leaf petiole is up to 2 cm long.

4

6

7

8

9

10

Fig 5 The upper surface of a leaf of *O. arborescens*. About natural size.

Fig 6 Lower surface of an *O. arborescens* leaf showing the appressed, satiny tomentum and prominent midvein. About natural size.

Fig 7 Foliage spray of *O. arborescens* showing the alternate leaf arrangement.

Fig 8 A tree of *O. cheesemanii* in full flower is sometimes so smothered in bloom that the leaves almost disappear from sight. Otari, October 1967.

Fig 9 A close view of some flower heads of *O. cheesemanii* showing the small number of disk florets, about seven, and the nine to twelve ray florets. Pappus hairs show clearly on several of the disk florets; these are modifications of the calyx. Otari, October 1968. Four times natural size.

Fig 10 The grooved and tomentose branchlet typical of *O. cheesemanii*. The tomentose petioles of two leaves also show clearly. About twice natural size.

Fig 11 The bark of *O. cheesemanii* is rough and furrowed and continually flaking off in thin strips.

Fig 12 Lower surface of an *O. cheesemanii* leaf showing the very prominent midvein and distinct lateral veins. Natural size.

Fig 13 *O. cheesemanii* leaf upper surface. Also about natural size.

11

12

13

Olearia albida
Tanguru

This olearia grows as a shrub or a small tree up to 5 m high with rough, furrowed, paper-like bark that peels in narrow strips. It is found from North Cape south to about Tokomaru Bay in coastal forest, being rather local in occurrence.

The branchlets of *O. albida* are grooved and angular and clothed with a fluffy white tomentum. The leathery leaves, on tomentose petioles up to 2 cm long, are 7—10 cm long by 2.5—3.5 cm wide; they are oblong to ovate-oblong in shape with the margins flat or slightly wavy and the undersurfaces clad in soft, white, appressed tomentum. Flower heads occur in large rounded panicles on long tomentose stalks arising from the leaf axils towards the branchlet tips.

1

2

3

4

5

Fig 1 Panicles of flower heads of *O. albida*. There are three to ten florets to each flower head, the one to five ray florets being irregularly arranged. From a tree growing in Wellington, April 1969.

Fig 2 *O. albida* forms a most attractive round-headed small tree or a shrub with many spreading branches. This specimen from near Coromandel, January 1965.

Fig 3 The upper leaf surface showing the tiny star-like hairs as well as a young leaf. About natural size.

Fig 4 The lower surface of the same leaf showing the characteristic tomentum and prominent veins. About natural size.

Fig 5 A section of a branchlet. It shows the grooving and the dense, fluffy tomentum covering the leaf petiole and the new bud. At about three and a half times natural size.

Fig 6 The rough, furrowed bark of *O. albida*. It peels in long narrow strips.

Fig 7 This close view into a panicle of *O. albida* flower heads shows the white female ray florets and the yellow bisexual disk florets. At about twice natural size. Wellington, April 1969.

Fig 8 An isolated flower head. Illustrated are the tubular form with the phyllaries (bracts) below. There are two open white ray florets (and others yet to open) and one open yellow disk floret. All of these parts of the *O. albida* flower head bear pappus hairs. About four and a half times natural size. Wellington, April 1973.

Fig 9 An *O. albida* branchlet. Illustrated here are the alternate leaf arrangement and the dense, white tomentum.

6

7

8

9

Olearia pachyphylla
Thick-leaved tree daisy
O. furfuracea
Akepiro/Tanguru

O. pachyphylla grows mostly as a shrub but sometimes as a small tree up to 3 m high. It is limited in its distribution, being found only in coastal regions of the Bay of Plenty, usually in scrub. The branches are stout, and the young branchlets are clad in thick, woolly, buff-coloured, appressed tomentum. The thick, leathery, wavy-margined leaves are 7—13 cm long by 5—6.5 cm wide. They are glossy above, but are clad with a dense, appressed, silvery or buff-coloured tomentum below, which extends on to the stout petiole. The leaves vary in shape from somewhat obliquely ovate to ovate-oblong. The flower heads are in large, flat corymbs; each flower head of *O. pachyphylla* has seven to ten florets, up to five being ray florets.

O. furfuracea grows as a shrub or a small tree up to 5 m tall. It is found from sea level to 600 m along forest margins and streamsides and in scrub, growing from North Cape to the Southern Ruahine range. The angled branchlets are grooved and pubescent. The elliptic-oblong or ovate-elliptic leaves are thick and leathery, 5—10 cm long by 3—6 cm wide on petioles about 2.5 cm long. The leaves are dark green and shining above but with a buff-coloured satiny tomentum below. The flowers occur in large, flat corymbs around the ends of the branchlets. Each flower head is 8—10 mm across and has eight to ten florets, of which up to five can be ray florets.

2

3

4

Fig 6 A branchlet of *O. furfuracea*. It shows the tomentum and the alternate leaf arrangement.

Fig 7 An angled branchlet of *O. furfuracea* with a leaf petiole showing the appressed tomentum. About three and a half·times natural size.

Fig 8 The bark of *O. furfuracea* peels off in small flakes.

Fig 1 The glossy, thick and leathery upper surfaces of an *O. pachyphylla* leaf showing a stout pubescent petiole. At about natural size.

Fig 2 The end of an *O. pachyphylla* branchlet with the corymbs of flower buds on their long stalks. From a tree near Opotiki, January 1974.

Fig 3 *O. pachyphylla* leaf undersurface showing the tomentum, raised midvein and wavy margins. Also at about natural size.

Fig 4 The dark brownish-grey bark of *O. pachyphylla* is furrowed and peels in short, narrow flakes.

Fig 5 The lower surface of a leaf of *O. furfuracea*. This clearly illustrates the satiny appressed tomentum characteristic of both *O. furfuracea* and *O. pachyphylla*. Also shown here are the raised midvein and petiole. This specimen at about natural size.

Fig 9 Large flat corymbs of *O. furfuracea* flower heads. Taupo, December 1965.

Fig 10 The shining dark-green upper surface of a leaf of *O. furfuracea*. Tomentum on the petiole and the branchlet is clearly visible.

Olearia lacunosa/Rough-leaved tree daisy
O. avicenniaefolia/Akeake

O. lacunosa grows as a shrub or a small tree up to 5 m tall with thick, twisted, sometimes gnarled branches. It is found between 600 and 900 m in mountain forests and scrub from the Tararua Range southwards to about the Franz Josef Glacier. The branchlets, petioles, leaf lower surfaces and flower cluster stalks are all clothed with a dense brown to reddish-brown tomentum. The distinctive leaves are 7.5–17 cm long by 8 mm–2.5 cm wide, linear to linear-oblong in shape with acute or acuminate apices. They are very thick and leathery with the upper surfaces rugose. The midvein is very prominent and the lateral veins are almost at right angles to it, giving the leaf lower surface a rather broadly pitted appearance. The flower heads are in corymbs on long stalks around the ends of the branchlets. Each flower head is about 1 cm across with eight to twelve florets, of which four to five are ray florets.

O. avicenniaefolia forms a shrub or small tree up to 6 m tall and is found from sea level to 900 m in scrubland throughout the South Island and Stewart Island. The branchlets are angular and are densely clothed with a white tomentum. The leaves are elliptic to oblong-lanceolate in shape, 5–10 cm long by 3–5 cm wide; they are shining above with a soft, white or buff-coloured appressed tomentum below. The margins are entire and usually slightly wavy. The flower heads occur in much-branched corymbs on very long stalks. Each flower head has only two to three florets; ray florets are absent or in twos or threes.

Fig 1 A group of *O. lacunosa* trees. They are growing here on the edge of a sinkhole on the slopes of Mt Arthur, Nelson, February 1973.

Fig 2 The thin, papery bark of *O. lacunosa* peels in long, narrow strips; the bark is several layers thick.

Fig 3 A spray of *O. lacunosa* foliage. It shows both upper and lower surfaces of the distinctive leaves, which are very thick and leathery. From a tree growing at Moor Park, Abel Tasman National Park, November 1965.

1

2

3

4

5

6

7

9

10

Fig 4 Corymbs of *O. lacunosa* flower heads; they are on long stalks around the end of a branchlet. Mt Arthur, January 1973.

Fig 5 Close view of *O. lacunosa* flower heads. Mt Arthur, January 1973. About three and a half times natural size.

Fig 6 The upper surface of a leaf of *O. avicenniaefolia;* it shows the grooved petiole. At about three-quarters natural size.

Fig 7 *O. avicenniaefolia* leaf underside showing the white tomentum and distinct venation. Also three-quarters natural size.

Fig 8 A typical *O. avicenniaefolia* tree growing in Lewis Pass, January 1966.

Fig 9 A spray of *O. avicenniaefolia* foliage showing the leaf arrangement and the distinctive buff-coloured tomentum. The tomentum covers the branchlet and petioles and the stalks of the corymbs of flower heads. Lewis Pass, January 1971.

Fig 10 The bark of *O. avicenniaefolia* is light-coloured, thin and papery, peeling off in long, narrow strips.

8

Olearia ilicifolia/Hakeke/Hakekeke
O. macrodonta

O. ilicifolia is a shrub or small tree up to 5 m high with a musky scent. It is found from East Cape southwards to Stewart Island, mainly in the mountains, from sea level to 1,200 m. The stout branchlets of hakeke are pubescent only when young. The sharply dentate-serrate leaves are broad in South Island and Stewart Island plants and narrow in North Island plants, 5—10 cm long and 1—2 cm wide. The leaves are stiff and leathery, lanceolate to linear-oblong in shape with acute to acuminate apices and truncate bases; the margins are wavy and the lower surface is clad with a thin, yellowish-white to deep-ochraceous, satiny tomentum. The petioles are 2 cm long. Hakeke flower heads occur in large corymbs on long stalks around the ends of the branchlets; each flower head is about 8 mm across with ten to fifteen florets, of which six to eight are ray florets.

O. macrodonta is found from about Thames southwards to Southland, from sea level to 1,200 m in forest. This tree is very similar to *O. ilicifolia,* but it has branchlets clad with a soft, white tomentum as well as the leaf undersides. The foliage has a strong musky odour. *O. macrodonta* is in fact a doubtful species; it is now suspected of being simply a hybrid between *O. ilicifolia* and *O. arborescens*. The leaves of this plant are 5—10 cm long by 2.5—4 cm wide.

1

2

3

4

5

6

7

8

9

Fig 1 A typical leaf of *O. ilicifolia* from the South Island. Note the deeply grooved petiole. About natural size.

Fig 2 Lower surface of a South Island leaf showing its yellowish, satiny tomentum and prominent midvein. About natural size.

Fig 3 The narrow form of a North island *O. ilicifolia* leaf. The petiole is deeply grooved and the marginal teeth are almost spines, a condition common on both North and South Island forms of hakeke. About natural size.

Fig 4 Corymbs of *O. ilicifolia* flower heads on their long, stout stalks. From Ruahine Mountains, December 1966.

Fig 5 Flower heads with their ray florets (which open before the disk florets) at different stages. West Taupo, December 1973. Four and a half times natural size.

Fig 6 A fine specimen of hakeke growing in the Hollyford Valley, December 1975.

Fig 7 Underside of *O. ilicifolia* leaves from a tree at Taupo. The tomentum here is a much richer ochraceous colour. At three-quarters natural size.

Fig 8 A piece of a young *O. ilicifolia* branchlet with groove and soft pubescence. About four times natural size.

Fig 9 Hakeke bark is thin and papery, peeling in long, thin, narrow strips.

Fig 10 A spray of *O. macrodonta* foliage showing the alternate leaf arrangement. The leaves are ovate-oblong to oblong in shape with acute to acuminate apices and rounded to truncate bases; the wavy margins are closely and coarsely serrate-dentate.

Fig 11 Undersides of *O. macrodonta* leaves. About half natural size.

10

11

Olearia traversii
Akeake

This olearia grows as an erect, small tree up to 10 m high with ascending branches. It is found naturally only on the Chatham Islands, but it has been planted in many places elsewhere as shelter belts.

The branchlets of *O. traversii* are four-sided. Along with the panicle branchlets and leaf undersides they are clad in a white, appressed, silky tomentum. The leaves are flat and leathery, oblong to ovate-oblong in shape; they are 4–6.5 cm long and 2.5–3 cm wide, on very short petioles. Each flower head of *O. traversii* is about 6.5 mm across with from five to fifteen disk florets. Flower heads occur in axillary panicles.

1

2

3

4

Fig 1 Two *O. traversii* specimens growing at Otari. They show the erect form with ascending branches. April 1973.

Fig 2 The upper surface of a new leaf has scattered hairs which are lost as the leaf ages. About natural size.

Fig 3 Leaf underside, showing the tomentum and raised midvein. About natural size.

Fig 4 A branchlet of *O. traversii* showing silky tomentum and opposite leaves glossy above and tomentose below.

Fig 5 A section of a four-angled branchlet showing the clothing of silky tomentum on the branchlet and the leaf petiole. Three and a half times natural size.

Fig 6 A panicle of *O. traversii* flower heads showing the silky-haired peduncles and axis and the narrow, urn-like flower heads with tubular florets. Levin, December 1979.

5

6

Olearia paniculata
Akiraho

Akiraho grows to a small tree up to 6 m high or as a shrub, along forest margins and in scrub from East Cape and Raglan Harbour south to about Greymouth and Oamaru. It has angular, grooved, tomentose branchlets. Akiraho leaves are elliptic to ovate-oblong, 3–10 cm long by 2–4 cm wide. They are leathery with thin, appressed, white to buff-coloured tomentum on the undersurfaces; the margins are entire and either flat or strongly wavy. The flower heads are sweet scented and arise in fascicles on small, slender, branched corymbs. Arikaho is used as a hedge, although galls often form on the flower heads.

1

2

3

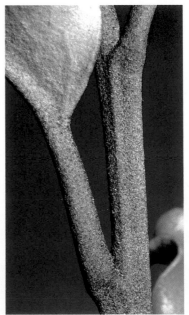

4

5

Fig 1 A fine specimen of akiraho in full flower. Worser Bay, March 1973.

Fig 2 Leaf upper surface. The pubescent petiole is about 5 mm long. About three-quarters natural size.

Fig 3 A foliage spray of akiraho showing the white tomentum on the lower surfaces.

Fig 4 Close view of the angled tomentose branchlet with a petiole. Four and a half times natural size.

Fig 5 Corymbs of numerous small flower heads. Karaka Bay, March 1968.

Fig 6 Each flower head contains a single tubular floret; ray florets are absent. Each floret is bisexual. Some here show anthers producing pollen while some have the style exserted and the two style arms parted. Four and a half times natural size.

Fig 7 The rough, deeply furrowed bark.

6

7

327

Olearia solandri/Coastal tree daisy
O. fragrantissima/Fragrant tree daisy
O. hectori/Deciduous tree daisy
O. virgata/Twiggy tree daisy

These four *Olearia* species all have small flower heads with both ray and disk florets. All except *O. virgata*, which is twiggy with divaricating branches, have an erect habit with ascending branches.

O. solandri commonly grows in coastal places from North Cape to about Westport and the Clarence River, either as a shrub or as a small tree up to 4 m high. It has stiff, angled, spreading, sticky branchlets covered with a yellowish tomentum. The leaves of young plants are up to 1.5 cm long and linear-spathulate in shape. Adult leaves are 5 — 10 mm long and linear-obovate in shape; they are somewhat leathery on petioles 1 mm long with revolute margins and the lower surface clad with yellow tomentum. The flower heads, which occur singly on short branchlets, are each about 10 mm across; there are eighteen to twenty florets, of which there may be up to fourteen ray florets.

O. fragrantissima forms an erect, much-branched shrub or tree up to 5 m high with rather stiff, zigzagging branchlets and a delicious scent reminiscent of peach fruit. It is found in scrub and along forest margins from Banks Peninsula south on the east of the Alps to Southland, from sea level to about 450 m. The leaves are very variable in shape, from elliptic-oblong to elliptic-ovate, broad-ovate or obovate, with obtuse or acute apices. They are 7 mm — 3 cm long by 5 — 10 mm wide, on petioles about 3 mm long; the leaves fall during winter. Flower heads occur in dense clusters up to 2 cm across of up to twelve sessile flower heads, each of which has four to eight fragrant florets.

O. hectori grows as an erect-branching shrub or small tree up to 5 m high with slender, rounded, somewhat grooved, smooth branchlets. It is found from sea level to 900 m in scrubland near Taihape and from about the Clarence River south to Southland, but it is not common. It is deciduous, but in season its pale-green, narrow-obovate to oblong-ovate or broad-obovate leaves with their thin, silvery tomentum below make it a distinctive tree. The flower heads occur in fascicles of two to five; each flower head is 5 mm across and has twenty to twenty-five florets, of which up to fifteen are narrow ray florets.

O. virgata is commonly a shrub or a small tree up to 3 m high. The branches tend to be straight, slender, elongate, and pliant, the branchlets four-angled, more or less divaricate, grooved and hairy only when young. This species is found from sea level to 1,050 m in scrub and boggy ground from near Thames to Stewart Island. The obovate to narrow-obovate, rather leathery leaves are 5 — 10 mm long by 3 — 5 mm wide, occasionally longer. They have a soft, white or buff-coloured tomentum on the lower surfaces. *O. virgata* flower heads are 9 mm across with four to eight disk florets and five to eight ray florets.

Fig 1 *O. solandri* foliage and flower heads. Karaka Bay, April 1970.

Fig 2 An angled branchlet of *O. solandri* showing leaves and some developing seeds. Karaka Bay, June 1970.

Fig 3 A small tree of *O. fragrantissima* growing at Otari, April 1973.

Fig 4 A spray of *O. fragrantissima* showing leaves and clustered flower heads. Otari, November 1969.

Fig 5 The undersides of the leaves of *O. fragrantissima* showing the soft, white tomentum. About natural size.

Fig 6 Flower heads of *O. fragrantissima* in dense clusters. Otari, November 1969.

Fig 7 A branchlet of *O. hectori* with an opposite pair of short, arrested branchlets bearing leaves. About natural size.

Fig 8 *O. hectori* flower heads with young leaves. Four times natural size.

1

2

3

4

5

6

7

8

Fig 9 Various leaf shapes of *O. hectori*. The leaves occur in opposite fascicles of two to four; there are short branchlets, which bear most of the leaves, and long, slender branchlets, which bear the short branchlets. The leaves are 2 – 5 cm long by 5 mm – 2 cm wide.

Fig 10 Branchlet of *O. hectori* showing the reddish-brown bark and clusters of flower heads. From a tree at Otari, September 1965.

Fig 11 The leaves of *O. virgata* occur in widely separated opposite fascicles of two to four. Shown here are the upper surfaces and the grooved, four-angled branchlets. At about two and a half times natural size. *O. virgata* includes several varieties; one of these, var. *lineata,* has narrow linear leaves up to 4 cm long, much longer than those of the main species.

Fig 12 Branchlet of *O. virgata* with leaves showing the thick tomentum on their lower surfaces. At two and a half times natural size.

Fig 13 Branchlets of *O. virgata* showing the widely spaced leaf fascicles and the fascicles of flower heads which arise in association with the leaves. Otari, November 1970. The flowers occur in opposite or paired fascicles.

Fig 14 A close view of fascicles of flower heads of *O. virgata.* From a tree growing at Otari, November 1970. Four times natural size.

9

10

11

12

13

14

Family *Compositae*

Genus *Senecio:* **A** cosmopolitan genus of herbs, lianes, shrubs and trees containing 2-3,000 species. Of the 10 species in New Zealand all except one are endemic and one can grow as a small tree.

Senecio huntii
Rautini

1

This distinctive member of the *Senecio* genus comes from the Chatham Islands, in particular from Pitt Island. In its natural habitat it grows in forest and along the edges of bogs where the ground is becoming dry. Rautini is now grown by gardeners in many parts of the country as a hardy ornamental tree which provides a fine display of yellow flowers and is able to withstand prolonged dry conditions.

S. huntii forms a shrub or a small, round-headed tree up to 6 m or more tall with ascending branches, the lower ones being rather candelabra-like. All the branchlets are marked by persistent leaf bases. The tree is an impressive sight when in full flower between December and February. The flower heads are borne in large terminal panicles 12—18 cm high on almost every branchlet, virtually covering the crown of the tree. Individual flower heads are about 2 cm across. *S. huntii* fruit is a tiny achene, about 1.5 mm long.

Fig 1 The crown of a rautini tree is a spectacular sight when the tree is in full flower. The fifteen to twenty ray florets in each flower tend to be rolled back at their tips. From a tree growing at Otari, December 1964.

Fig 2 The end of a branchlet with a panicle of flower heads also showing the crowded leaves with their distinctive shape; both upper and lower surfaces can be seen. The leaves of *S. huntii* are lanceolate-oblong to elliptic-oblong, subacute at the tips, 5 — 10 cm long by 2 — 3 cm wide. They are pale and shinning green above, and are clad with a fulvous tomentum on both surfaces when young. The margins are entire or slightly rolled back. Otari. December 1964.

Fig 3 The impressive sight of a rautini tree in full flower. This specimen was growing at Otari, photographed in January 1965.

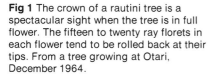

2

3

Family *Compositae*

Genus *Brachyglottis*: An endemic New Zealand genus containing five species and two varieties that grow as small trees.

Brachyglottis repanda
Rangiora

Rangiora is a very handsome shrub or small tree growing up to 7 m high, common from North Cape south to Greymouth and Kaikoura. It is found from sea level to 750 m in scrub and forest and along forest margins.

It has stout, brittle, spreading branches densely covered with a soft, white or buff-coloured tomentum. The characteristic large, membraneous leaves are somewhat leathery, dull or slightly shining above, with a white, close, appressed tomentum below. The petiole is stout, grooved and up to 10 cm long. The leaf blade is 5– 25 cm long by 5– 20 cm wide; it is broad to ovate-oblong in shape with an obtuse to subacute apex and a truncate to cordate base.

The fragrant flower heads are borne in great numbers on large, much-branched panicles, each flower head about 5 mm across. The panicles are erect near the top of the tree but often drooping lower down.

Fig 1 Upper surface of a broad rangiora leaf. About half natural size.

Fig 2 A tree in full flower showing erect panicles near the top and drooping panicles lower down. Karaka Bay, September 1965.

Fig 3 A flower panicle with buds ready to open. Note the tomentose stem. Karaka Bay, September 1969.

Fig 4 A large flowering panicle in full bloom. Kaitoke, December 1968.

6

7

5

Fig 5 Lower surface of a rangiora leaf showing the prominent raised veins and white tomentum. About half natural size.

Fig 6 Flower head with female and bisexual florets and some opening buds. Note the woolly tomentum covering the peduncles and flower head stalks. Each phyllary is about 3 mm long. Otari, October 1970. Five times natural size.

Fig 7 A single flower head showing, from the outside inwards: the thin, translucent, linear phyllaries; the female ray florets with small, recurved corollas and bifid style arms; the bisexual disk florets with orange anther tubes and emerging styles. Otari, October 1970. Nine times natural size.

Fig 8 The bark from a young rangiora tree 6.5 m high.

Fig 9 The rougher bark of the variety *arborescens*.

Fig 10 *B. repanda* var. *arborescens* has more glossy leaves and a rough, corky bark. This variety of rangiora is found on Great Island of the Three Kings Islands. From a tree growing in Hukutaia Domain, November 1968.

8

9

10

Brachyglottis elaeagnifolius
B. rotundifolia
Muttonbird scrub

1

B. elaeagnifolius is a shrub or small tree up to 3 m high found from about 800 to 950 m in the North Island from Te Aroha Mountain southwards. The rather similar *B. rotundifolia* grows to 6 m tall and is found in coastal South Island south of Jackson's Bay and on Stewart Island and Solander Island.

The branches of *B. elaeagnifolius* are grooved and the branchlets, petioles and inflorescence axes are clad in a white to buff-coloured woolly tomentum which is appressed on the leaf undersides. The thick, leathery leaves are obovate to lanceolate-oblong with obtuse to subacute apices; they are 6 – 9 cm long by 3 – 5 cm wide, glossy above. The flower heads are borne on stout panicles up to 15 cm long.

B. rotundifolia leaves are more broadly oblong to suborbicular; they are glossy above with a dense white to buff-coloured tomentum below. The flowering panicle of *B. rotundifolia* is up to 20 cm long.

2

Fig 1 Foliage spray of *B. rotundifolia*. It shows the leaf upper surfaces and the long petioles, which are grooved and up to 5 cm long. Leaves are 4-10 cm long by 4-9 cm wide.

Fig 2 Leaf of *B. rotundifolia* showing the lower surface with prominent raised mid-vein and lateral veins. About natural size.

Fig 3 *B. elaeagnifolius* flowering panicle on its woolly branchlet. Each flower head is 1 cm across. Phyllaries and peduncles of the flowers are very woolly.

Fig 4 Foliage spray of *B. elaeagnifolius* from Mt Holdsworth showing the alternate leaf arrangement.

Fig 5 Glossy upper surface of a leaf of *B. elaeagnifolius* showing the distinct venation and the grooved petioles up to 5 cm long. About natural size. The margin is sometimes minutely toothed.

Fig 6 Undersurface of the leaf in Fig 5 showing the yellowish-buff tomentum. Also about natural size.

3

4

5

6

Brachyglottis hectori
B. stewartiae

Family *Compositae*

Genus *Urostemon:* A genus containing one endemic species of small tree.

Urostemon kirkii
Kohurangi/Kohuhurangi

B. hectori grows as a shrub or when in forest sometimes as a small tree up to 4 m high. It has stout, brittle, tomentose branches and leaves closely set towards the tips of the branchlets. It is found in the South Island only from about 100 m to 1,050 m along streamsides and forest margins from north-west Nelson to north of Greymouth.

The soft, membraneous leaves of *B. hectori* are broadly oblanceolate with coarsely dentate or serrate margins, pinnate or pinnatifid towards the base. They are 10–25 cm long by 4–12 cm wide, on a petiole about 4 cm long. The leaves have a sparse cottony-white tomentum below when young. The flower heads are in large, somewhat lax terminal corymbs, each flower head being up to 5 cm across with many yellow disc florets and eight to twelve ray florets.

Urostemon kirkii, kohurangi, is an epiphytic or ground-dwelling shrub or sometimes a small tree up to 3 m high. It grows throughout the North Island from sea level to 780 m in forest. I have found it growing as a small tree in Waipoua and Omahatu Forests and the Coromandel Ranges. (See also page 6.)

The branches of kohurangi are brittle. The soft, rather fleshy, variable shaped leaves are elliptic-lanceolate to broad-oblanceolate or obovate-cuneate. They are 4–10 cm long by 2–4 cm wide on petioles 1 cm long; the margins are often coarsely and irregularly sinuate-dentate to entire. Flower heads occur in corymbs up to 30 cm across.

Fig 1 A small tree of kohurangi, var. *angustior* (see Fig 5), in flower in Waipoua Forest, January 1970.

Fig 2 Kohurangi leaves cluster towards the ends of the branchlets. These show both young and older leaves.

Fig 3 Upper surfaces of leaves of kohurangi from the Coromandel Ranges. About one and a half times natural size.

Fig 4 The leaf undersides. Also at one and a half times natural size.

1

2

3

4

B. STEWARTIAE

B. stewartiae (not illustrated) is a shrub or a small tree reaching 6 m high with stout, spreading branches. It has ovate-lanceolate to elliptic-lanceolate leaves up to 18 cm long and is found on a number of islands in Foveaux Strait.

5

6

Fig 5 These are the more narrow leaves of a special form of kohurangi, *U. kirkii* var. *angustior.* A full specimen in flower of this variety appears in Fig 1. Var. *angustior* has lanceolate to narrow-oblong leaves which are 5– 12 cm long and 1– 2 cm wide, and is found growing in Northland and around the Auckland district. This specimen is from a tree growing in the Waitakere Ranges, Auckland, April 1966.

Fig 6 A pair of kohurangi flower heads, close view. Each flower head has numerous yellow disk florets and six to eight white ray florets. From a tree growing in the Mangamuka Gorge, January 1970. Natural size.

Fig 7 A corymb of kohurangi flower heads with some unopened buds. Mangamuka Gorge, January 1970.

7

Fig 8 A shrub of *B. hectori* in flower near the summit of the Takaka Hill, January 1972.

Fig 9 Leaves of *B. hectori* around the tip of a branchlet.

Fig 10 The single daisy-like flower head of *B. hectori* is attractive at close quarters. Mt Arthur Track, Nelson, January 1972. Natural size.

8

9

10

Family *Scrophulariaceae:* This is the foxglove family, consisting of herbs, lianes, a few shrubs and two genera, *Paulownia* and *Hebe,* containing three species. The foxglove tree, *Paulownia tomentosa,* from China, is the best known of the former; it is grown in many temperate places as an ornamental. The family is cosmopolitan, with some 220 genera and about 3,000 species. It includes some poisonous plants such as *Digitalis.* The family is represented in New Zealand by the genus *Hebe.*

Genus *Hebe:* A genus of possibly around 100 species found mainly in New Zealand. Two of our species also occur in South America and one extends to the Falkland Islands. There are also a few species scattered through Tasmania, south-east Australia and New Guinea. There are seventy-nine species in New Zealand, all except one of which are shrubs; the odd one includes a small tree.

Hebe parviflora var. arborea/Koromiko-taranga

The main species of *H. parviflora* is a shrub, like all other members of the genus *Hebe,* but the variety *arborea* grows as a small dome-shaped tree up to 7.5 m high. It is found in coastal locations from Whangarei south through the Hen and Chicken and Great Barrier Islands to about Cape Runaway and the central North Island high country in the vicinity of Wellington, and in Marlborough.

The Wellington plant on which the description of the variety was based is still found on the Rimutaka Hill. It bears leaves in characteristic fascicles near the ends of the branchlets; the leaves are linear-lanceolate and acute tipped, 2.5 – 7 cm long and 4 mm wide. The flowers of *H. parviflora* var. *arborea* occur in dense racemes about 3 cm long, each flower about 4 mm in diameter.

Some idea of the size to which this unusual variety of hebe will grow is given by the figure standing beside the tree in **Fig 1** on this page. This fine specimen of the variety used to grow at Otari; it shows clearly the long narrow leaves grouped towards the ends of the branchlets. Photographed in March 1973.

1

Hebe parviflora var. *arborea*

Fig 2 The bark of koromiko-taranga is a distinctive grey colour.

Fig 3 Lower surfaces of several leaves. About natural size.

Fig 4 A foliage spray of the linear-lanceolate, acute-tipped leaves of *H. parviflora* var. *arborea*.

Fig 5 Several leaves showing the upper surfaces. This specimen at about natural size.

Fig 6 The dense-flowered inflorescence. From a tree growing on the Rimutaka Hill, February 1966.

Fig 7 The best grove of *H. parviflora* var. *arborea* I know of occurs on the northern side of the Rimutaka Hill, about halfway down. Photographed there, these trees show how when growing in exposed places the variety becomes taller and more open branched than the tree in Fig 1. *H. parviflora* var. *arborea* can also be seen on some steep hillsides around Wellington city. February 1966.

2

3

4

5

6

7

Family *Solanaceae:* This is the potato family of some ninety genera and about 3,000 species found almost all over the world but with centres of concentration in Central and South America and Australia. Besides the potato and its relatives, the family includes the tobacco plant, *Nicotiana tabacum,* and *Capsicum frutescens,* from which paprika, chillies and green and cayenne peppers are obtained. There is also the tomato, *Lycopersicon esculentum,* the cape gooseberry, *Physalis peruviana,* and a number of poisonous or medical plants, such as the deadly nightshade, *Atropa belladona,* the mandrake, *Mandragora officinarum,* and black henbane, *Hyoscyamus niger.* Tree species belong to the genera *Solanum, Cyphomandra* and *Dunalia.*

Genus *Solanum:* A genus containing about 1,700 species of herbs, lianes, shrubs and trees found mainly in tropical and temperate regions. The potato, *S. tuberosum,* the aubergine, *S. melongena,* and several tropical American food plants such as pepino, *S. muricatum,* belong here.

Solanum aviculare
S. laciniatum
Poroporo

The poroporos are shining, soft-wooded, openly branching shrubs or small trees. *S. aviculare* can be distinguished from *S. laciniatum* chiefly by its green to purplish stems; *S. laciniatum* always has purplish stems.

The rather soft, membraneous leaves are 15–30 or even 40 cm long, linear-lanceolate or lanceolate in shape. They are either entire or irregularly pinnatifid, with one to three lanceolate lobes; the petioles at their base extend down and are fused to the branchlet. Flowers occur most of the year in one to three, several or many-flowered cymes.

Both species are found in scrub and along coastal and lowland forest margins. *S. aviculare* occurs on the Kermadec and Poor Knights Islands, around Auckland and south to about Banks Peninsula and the Karamea River. *S. laciniatum* can be found from near Auckland through both islands to near Dunedin.

1

Fig 1 A shrub of *S. laciniatum* in flower. Otari, December 1965.

Fig 2 Berries of *S. aviculare*. From Lake Pounui, April 1961.

Fig 3 A spray of *S. laciniatum* foliage showing upper surfaces and purple stems.

Fig 4 Bark from a young *S. laciniatum* tree.

Fig 5 Flowers of *S. laciniatum,* Karaka Bay, October 1966. About natural size. These are dark blue-purple, up to 5 cm across, with the corolla lobes notched at the tip. *S. aviculare* flowers are lavendar or white, up to 3.5 cm across with the corolla lobes acute.

PLANT HAS VARIED USES

The Maori people used the juice from poroporo leaves mixed with soot to rub into wounds made by tattooing instruments. Decoctions of the leaves and of the inner bark were used to treat ulcers, scabies and itch. The pith of dry stems was used to treat bruises. Today some alkaloids extracted from the plant have been used in the commercial manufacture of hormones.

2

3

4

5

Myoporum laetum
Ngaio

Family *Myoporaceae:* A small family of trees and shrubs made up of four genera and 150 species found mainly in Australia but also in New Guinea, some Pacific Islands, eastern Asia, Hawaii, Mauritius, South Africa, the West Indies and New Zealand.

Genus *Myoporum:* A genus of about thirty-two species of shrubs and trees found in east Asia, New Guinea, Australia, Pacific Islands, China, Japan, Mauritius and New Zealand. Two species occur in New Zealand, one of which is a tree endemic to this country.

Ngaio is a tree up to 10 m high with a trunk up to 30 cm through, although in coastal places it is often low growing and dome-shaped. It is found along coastal or lowland forest margins and often isolated in exposed coastal places. Ngaio occurs from the Three Kings Islands throughout the North Island, the South Island to about Otago, where it becomes rare, and on the Chatham Islands.

It forms a particularly fresh-looking, bright-green tree with stout, spreading branches; the tips of the branchlets and leaf buds are sticky. The glossy, somewhat fleshy leaves are lanceolate to oblong-lanceolate or oblong to ovate, with acute to acuminate apices. The leaves are 4 – 10 cm long and 1 – 3 cm wide. Their margins are crenulate-serrulate along the upper halves but sinuate in the lower halves; or they may be sinuate only. The bisexual flowers of *M. laetum* arise in clusters of two to six on leaf axils all along the upper parts of the branchlets, on peduncles up to 15 mm long. Each flower is 1 – 1.5 cm across.

1

Fig 1 A fine old ngaio growing on the Kaikoura coast, February 1973.

Fig 2 Branchlets with flowers; they also display the undersides of mature leaves. The corolla tube fills with nectar, as in the flower at right centre. Karaka Bay, December 1968.

Fig 3 A single ngaio flower magnified two and a half times. It shows the purple-spotted corolla lobes and minutely hairy style. Karaka Bay, December 1968. Three times natural size.

Fig 4 Branchlets with ripening drupes, which are up to 9 mm long and pale to dark purple when ripe. Some leaves here have serrated margins. Karaka Bay, March 1968. Half natural size.

Fig 5 A beautiful dome-shaped ngaio on the Kaikoura coast. December 1964.

Fig 6 The rough, wrinkled, corky bark of an old ngaio tree.

Fig 7 A spray of ngaio foliage showing the alternate, rather fleshy, gland-dotted leaves on their flattened petioles up to 3 cm long. Flowers and flower buds arise in reduced axillary cymes.

Vitex lucens
Puriri

Family *Verbenaceae:* A tropical and subtropical family of about seventy-five genera and at least 3,000 species of herbs, shrubs, lianes and trees. The best known tree species is teak, *Tectona grandis,* of Burma, Thailand, Java and the Philippines. Zither wood comes from the *Citharexylum* species of Mexico and South America and is used to make musical instruments. New Zealand has one representative in the giant puriri tree.

Genus *Vitex:* A tropical, subtropical and temperate region genus of about 250 species of mainly timber trees, such as *V. celebica* of Sulawesi (formerly Celebes).

Puriri is a massive, handsome tree up to 20 m tall with a trunk up to 1.5 m through. It bears stout, spreading branches with four-angled branchlets. The distinctive leaves of puriri are digitately compound, opposite, on long, stout petioles 3.5 – 12.5 cm long. Each leaf consists of three to five leaflets; the upper three are 5 – 12.5 cm long by 3 – 5 cm wide, shining, rather leathery and undulate. The leaflets are elliptic-oblong to obovate in shape, with acute to almost acuminate apices and entire margins. Domatia occur on the lower surfaces in the axils of the midvein and the lateral veins.

Puriri's attractive flowers are produced almost the whole year round, often in great abundance. They occur on four to fifteen-flowered axillary cymes, each flower being 2.5 – 3.5 cm in diameter. The fruit is a bright-red drupe about 2 cm across; like the flowers, the drupes of puriri are present almost throughout the year and are much sought after for food by native birds.

The wood of puriri is one of our most valuable hardwoods. Dark reddish-brown in colour, it is very heavy and dense in texture, and is of great strength and durability. The grain is irregular and uneven, however, making the wood difficult to work. It is also often spoiled by the puriri moth, *Hepialis virescens.*

1

3

Fig 1 Paler lower surface of the attractive compound leaf of puriri showing the clear venation, domatia, petiolules and the top of the petiole. About one-third natural size.

Fig 2 Shining upper surfaces and distinct venation of the five leaflets of a puriri leaf. The three upper leaflets are always the largest. About two-thirds natural size.

Fig 3 Clusters of puriri's distinctive pinkish-red flowers occuring at the tip of a branchlet. From a tree in Wellington, September 1968. Puriri trees carry flowers throughout most of the year.

2

4

Fig 4 A fine spreading puriri tree growing on the Coromandel Peninsula; it shows the broad, dome-like shape. January 1965.

Fig 5 The delicate beauty of two puriri flowers, with anthers shedding pollen. Wellington, April 1966. Natural size.

Fig 6 A cluster of ripening drupes. From a tree in Wellington, February 1969.

Fig 7 The peeling bark of an old tree.

Fig 8 The trunk of an enormous puriri tree growing at Brooklands, New Plymouth. It is estimated that this specimen is about 2,000 years old. May 1966.

Fig 9 The enormous trunk and branches of Taki Takerau, the huge sacred puriri tree growing in Hukutaia Domain, Opotiki. This tree is sacred to the Maori people because the large hollows within its roots are believed to be the repository for the mortal remains of important people. Puriri trees were sometimes used in this way. November 1968.

5

6

9

7

8

Avicennia marina var. resinifera
Manawa/Mangrove

Family *Avicenniaceae:* A small family containing one genus and fifteen species of trees and shrubs found in coastal areas of tropical and subtropical regions, generally referred to as mangroves.

Genus *Avicennia:* This genus contains fifteen species found in mangrove swamps, all being characterised by having aerial roots that project upwards out of the mud. The New Zealand variety is endemic.

The mangrove, manawa, is a small tree up to 15 m tall, or a shrub, which grows in tidal waters around estuaries and shallow, sheltered harbours and inlets. The main roots spread wide around the tree, producing thousands of upright aerial roots resembling asparagus shoots. Called pneumatophores or breathing roots, these can be seen extending out of the mud at low tide. They allow the tree's root system to obtain oxygen which it cannot obtain from the sour, sticky mud in which it grows. As the outgoing tide ebbs away from a mangrove swamp the countless numbers of aerial roots are revealed, as the photographs on these pages show.

These aerial roots perform a valuable ecological function, trapping more mud, as well as decaying vegetation, around their parent tree. In this way the land around the tree is slowly built up until it is above the tide. It can then be inhabited by other terrestrial plants less tolerant of saltwater than the mangrove.

This becomes a continual process. As the land behind the mangroves becomes dry, the mangrove trees advance further seawards, ever maintaining their rich and productive ecosystems until calamity intervenes, in the form of interference by man or climatic change.

Mangrove swamps comprise some of the world's most biologically productive areas, forming nurseries of high fertility and habitats for wildlife.

Manawa is found only in the north of the North Island from North Cape south to about Kawhia Harbour on the west and Ohiwa Harbour on the east. Only in the warmer far north does it reach a height of 15 m. Around Whangarei it reaches only 5 m; at Whangamata it grows to 3 m, and at Kawhia and Ohiwa it attains a height of only 30—50 cm. It is here little more than a small shrub.

Manawa forms a tree with a broad, flat, leafy crown on a stout but short trunk giving off stout, spreading

branches; lower down these tend to grow horizontally over the water surface at high tide. The branchlets are pubescent. The thick, leathery leaves are 5–10 cm long by 2–4 cm wide, elliptic-oblong to ovate in shape. They have more or less acute apices and are occasionally mucronate; they occur on narrow, winged petioles up to 1 cm long and have lower surfaces clad in a white or buff-coloured tomentum.

The flowers occur in small four to eight-flowered clusters on erect, four-angled pubescent peduncles up to 2 cm long. Each flower is 6–7 mm in diameter. The fruit is a flattened ovoid capsule about 2 cm across. The flowers are borne from February to April, and the fruit takes until the following January to ripen. Each capsule contains four ovules, one of which grows into a large embryo with its roots projecting outside the capsule. At this stage the embryo plant is well developed. When the capsule falls it floats on the water until it is deposited on the mud by the outgoing tide. The plantlet immediately anchors itself with its root before the incoming tide can sweep it away. Mangrove capsules may float considerable distances, unharmed, before being deposited in a suitable place for growth. In this way the tree secures wide and rapid dispersion.

The wood of the mangrove tree is brown and heavy and rather strikingly grained. Being non-splitting and durable, it has been found to be fairly easy to work.

2

3

Fig 1 A typical mangrove swamp near Paihia, photographed in January 1970. As the tide ebbs, the receding water exposes the characteristic aerial roots of the manawa trees. The swamps are immensely fertile areas, supporting hundreds of species of terrestrial, marine and amphibian forms of life. These swamps of mangroves protect the shoreline against the effects of long-term erosion.

Fig 2 A tall manawa tree in a swamp near Paihia; only in the far north do the trees attain this height. The lower branches are nearly horizontal just above the water at full tide. February 1965. The destruction of such areas overseas, for example in Florida, has had serious effects; one has been a major decline in the quantity and quality of fish caught in surrounding waters.

Fig 3 A spray of manawa leaves showing the opposite arrangement with the somewhat swollen nodes where the petiole joins the branchlet. Some leaves here are ovate, one obovate (at top right) and others elliptic.

Fig 4 Upper surface of a manawa leaf at about natural size. The winged petiole is clearly evident.

Fig 5 Angled pubescent stem of a manawa branchlet. Leaves and flower clusters are also shown in this photograph. Hokianga Harbour, April 1970.

4

5

Fig 6 The mature manawa flower, which occurs in small four to eight-flowered clusters. From a tree growing at Hokianga Harbour, April 1970. At seven times natural size.

Fig 7 Flower bud and flowers magnified here five times to show the anthers discharging pollen. From a tree growing at Whangaparoa, April 1979. Pollen can be forcibly ejected from the anthers of manawa flowers if they are only lightly touched. Under the heat of a photographic spotlight the anthers will spontaneously eject pollen. Presumably they do it in sunlight, but I have not observed this.

Fig 8 Flowers and flower buds. Although the flowers are bisexual, flowers appear on certain plants with anthers that seem to be non-functional, as shown here. Also from a tree at Whangaparoa, April 1979.

Fig 9 The bark of a mangrove tree is grey and furrowed. From the tree in Fig 10.

Fig 10 An interesting large specimen of manawa growing at Tapotupota Bay near Cape Reinga in January 1970. The tree has been photographed at low tide to show the trunk and the aerial roots emerging from the mud.

Fig 11 Manawa fruit capsules. From a tree growing at Russell, December 1977. One quarter natural size.

Fig 12 A small group of the aerial roots of the tree in Fig 10.

6   7

8   10

9   11

12

2. Monocotyledones
Family Agavaceae
Genus *Cordyline*

The family Agavaceae consists of twenty genera and some 700 species of rhizomatous, woody plants that are found mainly in arid regions of tropical and subtropical parts of the world. Most are erect, but some are climbers and others are succulent. The family includes the hemp plants, *Agave sisalana* and *A. fourcroydes,* and other fibre-producing species such as the New Zealand flax, *Phormium tenax.* The best-known genera are *Agave, Yucca, Sanseverinia, Dracaena, Furcraea, Cordyline* and *Phormium,* the latter two being represented in New Zealand. Dragon's blood, a red resin, is obtained from *Dracaena cinnabari* and *D. draco;* the Mexican drinks pulque and mescal are made from the sap of *Agave americana.*

Cordyline is a genus of fifteen species of slender to stout-trunked, tufted trees found in warm to temperate regions from India through Queensland and some Pacific Islands to New Zealand and South America. Five endemic species occur in New Zealand, collectively known as cabbage trees. They range from the tall, imposing *Cordyline australis,* which grows as high as 20 m, to the dwarf *C. pumilio,* which reaches barely a metre tall.

With their unusual and distinctive shape, cabbage trees are a feature of the New Zealand landscape. Almost everywhere one moves there are cabbage trees — along the edges of forests and swamps or on riverbanks, or standing alone in fields or on hillsides. The fine stand of ti kouka, *Cordyline australis,* on this page was photographed on the edge of a swamp at Waiorongomai in November 1964.

The flowers of all species are fragrant, some more so than others. Cabbage trees are often very heavy with flowers in late spring; according to Maori legend a heavy flowering is a sign for a good summer to follow. *Cordyline* species are widely grown overseas as ornamental trees, but it is a pity that they are not especially popular in New Zealand, their native land.

Cordyline australis
Ti kouka/Cabbage tree

This is the most common of our cabbage trees, growing throughout the North, South and Stewart Islands along forest margins, in clearings and around swamps. In distribution ti kouka ranges from sea level to 600 m. With its tall, straight trunk or trunks and dense, rounded heads it is a characteristic feature of the New Zealand landscape.

Ti kouka grows to 12—20 m high. When young it is a slender, unbranched stem with tufted leaves at the top and often with leaves covering the upper half.

Older trees develop a massive caudex or trunk up to 1.5 m through; this branches in the upper half, with tufted leaves towards the end of the branches.

The long, narrow leaves are 30—100 cm long by 3—6 cm wide; they may droop slightly at their tips and bend down from their bases when old. They are thick with the midrib indistinct. The fine nerves or longitudinal strands are more or less equal and parallel. The upper and lower leaf surfaces are similar. Ti kouka bears many strongly scented flowers.

1   2

3

LARGEST LILY NOW LARGEST AGAVE?

C. australis has in the past been called the largest lily in the world, but although this tree remains closely related to the lilies, this claim can no longer be made. The New Zealand cabbage trees were formerly classified in the family Liliaceae, but in recent years that family has been sub-divided and Cordyline is now included among the Agavaceae. These changes in the classification have centred around the flower structure of the genus. However, C. australis may remain notable for another reason; it may not be the largest lily in the world, but it may be among the largest agaves.

4

5

6

Fig 1 The distinctive top of a cabbage tree in flower. This specimen was growing at West Taupo, November 1973. It shows the older leaves bending down from their bases, as well as the long, narrow leaf shapes. The heavy flower panicles with their branches at right angles with the main axis of the panicle can also be seen. The trees produce large flower panicles 60 cm to 1.5 m long and 30-60 cm wide; they bear strongly scented white or creamy-white flowers which appear on the tree in late spring or early summer. Insects are attracted to the flowers in enormous numbers by their nectar.

Fig 2 A very old ti kouka. This specimen is so heavy with flower panicles that the leaves are almost obscured. It was growing on the hills above Hinakura, November 1970.

WIDELY USED IN EARLY TIMES

Parts of the cabbage tree were used by both Maori people and early European settlers. The pith and inner roots of young trees were known to the Maori people as ti; they were taken from the trees, dried in the sun and used to make a kind of porridge. Early European settlers used the hollowed out trunks of cabbage trees for chimneys for their huts, having discovered that the trunks would not catch fire. On the other hand, the dead leaves of cabbage trees burn readily, giving off an intense heat.

Fig 3 The panicles of a cabbage tree in bud before the flowers have opened have a distinct pink tinge. This tree was growing in the Pahaoa Valley, photographed in November 1970.

Fig 4 The bark is very thick, corky and rough.

Fig 5 The flowers are crowded along the ultimate branches of the panicles. They do not have true petals but rather tepals, which tend to fold back. Lake Pounui, in December 1968. At about twice natural size.

Fig 6 A single flower magnified four and a half times to show the style tipped by a shortly trifid stigma; there are also anthers with pollen, and nectar around the base of the ovary.

Cordyline indivisa
Toii/Broad-leaved or mountain cabbage tree

This cabbage tree grows to 8 m tall with a massive caudex or trunk that seldom branches and has a huge tuft of sword-shaped leaves at its top. Toii is found from the Hunua and Coromandel Ranges south to Fiordland; it occurs in regions with a wet climate, between 450 and 1,350 m above sea level, growing in open places in forest where there is plenty of light.

The leaves are 1—2 m long by 10—15 cm wide, drooping only when old. They form a curtain of dead leaves around the trunk that remain for a considerable time before falling. The conspicuous midrib is broad and often reddish in colour; the leaves are unequal, the nerves angled to the midrib and often also reddish in colour. The leaves become narrow near their expanded bases to short petioles about one-third as wide as the widest part of the leaf blade.

Flowers are borne in large, tightly compact, many-branched panicles that arise from the trunk below the tufts of leaves and hang down. Panicles are 60 cm to 1.6 cm long and 30 cm wide; the flowers, each about 1 cm across, are so densely packed that they obscure the axes of the panicle branches.

1

2

Fig 1 A toii growing on Mt Ruapehu showing the sword-shaped leaves with their coloured midrib and angled nerves. December 1972.

Fig 2 A fine specimen on Mt Egmont in December 1965. The figure of my son Guy beside the trunk gives some idea of the size of this tree, while the curtain of dead leaves round the trunk below the leafy crown with the pendulous flower panicle shows clearly.

Fig 3 A flower panicle hanging below the leafy crown showing its branching structure and tightly packed flowers. Some unopened purplish-brown buds show towards the tip. Mt Egmont, December 1965.

Fig 4 Flowers tightly packed along some branches of a flower panicle. Mt Egmont, December 1973.

3

4

5

Fig 5 Flowers with greenish-white tepals and anthers shedding pollen. The tepals of these flowers vary in colour from whitish-cream to reddish, purplish-brown or greenish-white.

Fig 6 Flowers with purplish-white, reflexed tepals and anthers which have shed their pollen. Note the green ovary with its slender style ending in a minutely three-lobed stigma. Mt Egmont, December 1973. About four times natural size.

Figs 7, 8 The bark of toii is rough, thick and flaky; after the flakes have fallen, however, it is smooth and pustulate, or blistered, as in Fig 8.

Fig 9 A fruiting panicle with toii's dark bluish-black ripe berries. From Mt Egmont, January 1963. Each berry is about 6 mm in diameter and contains many black seeds. The fruits take about twelve months to mature, and the fruit panicle may remain hanging on the tree for many months after the berries have ripened, even after they have fallen.

6

AERIAL SHOOTS ON SOME TREES

Cabbage trees are sometimes found with downward-growing shoots projecting from the undersides of horizontal branches or at the bases of trunks or branches that have been cut or broken. Known as aerial rhizomes, these are usually quite short and appear to be more common on trees growing in or near swamps. New plants can be grown successfully from cuttings taken from these shoots. Cabbage trees can also be propagated from seed.

7

8

9

Cordyline kaspar/Three Kings cabbage tree
C. pumilio/Dwarf or pigmy cabbage tree/Ti koraha

C. kaspar is a short, stout-trunked, widely branching cabbage tree reaching 4 m high. It has stout, spreading branches clothed with dense clusters of stiff leaves that are tufted at the branch tips. *C. kaspar* is found only on the Great, South-west and North-east Islands of the Three Kings group. The name *kaspar* comes from the names Kaspar, Melchior and Balthazar given to these islands by Abel Tasman in 1643.

The leaves are 60−65 cm long by 5.5−7 wide, drooping as they age. They narrow towards their bases to short, faintly channelled petioles about 2.5−3.5 cm wide; the nerves are fine and more or less parallel, but are angled to the midrib which is distinct above but more prominent below.

The flowers of *C. kaspar* are borne in many large, open-branched panicles that arise amongst the leaves. Each panicle is up to 80 cm long, with its branches arising at a narrow angle and its flowers not crowded along the ultimate branches or racemes. Each raceme is 10−20 cm long and each flower about 1 cm across; the flowers are very strongly scented, almost overpowering. The fruit is a blue and white-streaked berry about 4 mm in diameter.

C. pumilio, the dwarf or pigmy cabbage tree, is found in light forest or scrub north of Kawhia and Opotiki. It may easily be mistaken for a grass or sedge. Often leafy to the ground without any appreciable stem, ti koraha can flower at this stage of growth. Older plants have a bare stem rarely exceeding 100 cm high and 1.5 cm thick; there are tufted leaves at the top which are 30−100 cm long and 1−2 cm wide. The strongly scented flowers occur on open, slender-branched panicles up to 60 cm long.

1

2

3

Fig 1 This young specimen of *C. kaspar* grows in the garden of Dr W. M. Hamilton at Warkworth. When photographed in December 1977 it was seven years old; it was grown from an aerial rhizome cutting. This specimen shows well the great density of leaves characteristic of this species.

Fig 2 A flower panicle from Dr Hamilton's tree showing the narrow-angled branches of the panicle and also the widely spaced flowers. The upper leaf surface, indistinct midrib and the more prominent midrib below also show clearly here.

Fig 3 A group of *C. kaspar* flowers. They have been magnified three and a half times to show the long style with its trifid stigma, anthers with pollen and reflexed tepals. Warkworth, December 1977.

Fig 4 The bark of *C. kaspar*.

Fig 5 This fine specimen of *C. kaspar* was transplanted from the Three Kings Islands to the DSIR Plant Diseases Division garden at Mt Albert, Auckland in 1956 as a seedling plant probably then about five to six years old. When photographed in December 1977 it was then about twenty-six to twenty-seven years old. It is here heavy with panicles of flowers and fruits.

Fig 6 Portion of a panicle of fruits from the tree at Mt Albert, December 1977.

Fig 7 A plant of *C. pumilio* with flower panicles, Otari, December 1963. The small, widely spaced flowers are 5 mm across with reflexed tepals and a trifid stigma.

4

5

6   7

Cordyline banksii
Ti ngahere/Ti parae
Forest cabbage tree

1

This cabbage tree grows up to 4 m high, usually with several stems or branches which arise near the ground and bear tufted leaves at their tops. It is found from sea level to 1,050 m along forest margins or in rocky places in wet regions from North Cape south to about Westport. The leaves are 1—2 m long by 4—8 cm wide, broadest at the middle and usually drooping from there; they are narrowed basally into a channelled petiole that is from one quarter to one fifth the length of the leaf. The leaf nerves are angled, unequal, often yellowish. The openly branched flower panicle of *C. banksii* is 1—2 m long with the flowers rather more distantly spaced than in *C. australis*.

2

3

4   **5**   **6**

Fig 1 A fine specimen in flower growing in the Buller Gorge, November 1979.

Fig 2 A young plant of *C. banksii* showing the narrow angled, open branching of the flower panicle and also the long-petioled leaves. Kauaeranga Valley, 600 m, early December 1970.

Fig 3 A section of a flower panicle. It shows buds and open flowers as well as the more or less narrow angle of the panicle branches. From Lake Pounui, November 1961.

Fig 4 Two of the very sweet-scented flowers magnified five times showing the tepals, anthers and nectar. From a tree growing at 700 m in the Kauaeranga Valley, December 1970.

Fig 5 The fruit of *C. banksii* is a white or bluish berry 4—5 mm in diameter. This spray from a tree growing at Hinakura, in March 1974.

Fig 6 The bark of *C. banksii*.

Family *Palmae*

Genus *Rhopalostylis:* A genus of three species, one of which is endemic to New Zealand, one to the Kermadec Islands, and one to Norfolk Island.

Rhopalostylis sapida/Nikau
R. baueri var. cheesemanii/Kermadec nikau

Nikau is a palm reaching 10 m or more high with a trunk 25 cm through. It is found throughout the North Island in lowland forests and in the South Island as far south as Banks Peninsula in the east and Greymouth in the west. It also grows on the Chatham Islands and has the distinction of being the most southern naturally growing palm in the world. Small patches of pure stands occur in both islands; the pure stand at Morere Springs illustrated in Fig 2 is possibly the finest in existence.

The nikau trunk is ringed by closely spaced leaf scars and when young is green between these. The feather-like leaf is up to 3 m long and 2 m wide. The inflorescences develop within two stout, leaf-like, boat-shaped sheaths called spathes, which arise above the leaf scar just below the oldest leaf; they are up to 30 cm long by 15 cm across and fall away as the inflorescence starts to expand. The inflorescence itself is a much-branched spike up to 30 cm long. The small flowers are tightly packed in groups of two or three. The brilliant-red, hard fruit is 10 mm long by 7 mm wide and contains a single, large, hard seed. It takes about one year to ripen.

R. baueri var. *cheesemanii* is found abundantly only on Raoul (Sunday) Island of the Kermadec group. It has larger fruit and larger inflorescences.

Fig 1 A group of old nikau palms growing near Waikanae, February 1979. The tufted leaves and the large swollen, light-green coloured sheaths at the bases of the leaves show clearly, while the leaf scars still show as rings round the greying bark. The trunk on the edge of the photograph has become lichen-encrusted with age, but the leaf scars are still discernible. Some of the palms shown here bear flowering and fruiting spikes.

Fig 2 A view of a dense portion of the pure nikau stand at Morere Springs. It shows clearly the shining nature of the leaves and the leaf scars on the trunks with green between on young plants. January 1977

1

2

3

4

Fig 3 A nikau in flower with the upper spathe still in position. There is an earlier-flowering inflorescence of the same season (pale green on left) with fruits forming, as well as a late-flowering inflorescence of the year before (darker green on right) with fruits well advanced. The latter should be ripe by the next April. Waikanae, February 1977.

Fig 4 A flower spike in bud with flowers just opening and a fruiting spike from the previous year, now fully ripe. Waikanae, February 1977.

Figs 5, 6 Flowers are arranged in groups of three along the inflorescence branches. Each group comprises a small female flower sitting between two males. Fig 5 shows male flowers with their mauve petals and six stamens. Three times natural size. The female flowers open later, after the males have fallen off. Fig 6 shows a small female flower bud sandwiched between two male flower buds. Three times natural size Hukutaia Domain, December 1974.

5

6

Fig 7 A nikau inflorescence a short while after opening. The lower spathe has fallen but the upper one is still adhering. Note the earlier inflorescence with green fruits below the flowering one. Lake Pounui, February 1961.

Fig 8 Two young nikaus at about thirty years old and ready to start flowering and two small plants at about fifteen to twenty years of age, still without trunks. From a forest at Kaihoka Lake, Westhaven Inlet, February 1974

7

8

Family Cyatheaceae
Genus *Cyathea*

There are about 10,000 species of ferns known throughout the tropical, subtropical and temperate regions of the world. They range in form from tiny filmy ferns to tall tree ferns and are found mainly in damp, sheltered places. In New Zealand we have about 180 species of ferns; our dense forest provides for a variety of fern form and a luxuriance of growth equal to that of any other place where ferns grow. Amongst the New Zealand ferns are ten species of tree ferns, eight of which are endemic to this region.

The family Cyathaceae consists of about 650 species of tree ferns found in tropical to temperate regions, especially in mountain forests of the wet tropics. It is represented in New Zealand by seven species of the genus *Cyathea*. These seven species, five of which are endemic, include our largest and most handsome tree ferns, such as *C. medullaris,* mamaku, below. Members of the genus have both scales and hairs on stipes and rachis.

To identify our tree ferns it is necessary to understand the terminology applied to the various parts of the leaves and trunk. Fern leaves are pinnately compound, consisting of a main stem made up basally of the *stipe* and distally of the *rachis*. The rachis bears on each side the leaflets called *pinnae,* which are divided in turn into smaller leaflets, the *secondary pinnae* or *pinnules*. The axis of a pinna is a *rachide*. The entire fern leaf is referred to as a *frond,* which can be dipinnate or tripinnate.

On the lower surfaces of the pinnules occur structures known as *sori*. Protected by membraneous *indusia,* these contain the *sporangia* that produce the fern spores. Each sporangium produces about sixty-four spores. The stipe, rachis and secondary rachides of the pinnae and pinnules can be variously ornamented with scales, hairs and star-like hairs according to the species. The trunk of a tree fern is called the *caudex* (plural *caudices*).

Ferns reproduce by alternating an asexual spore-bearing generation, the fern plant, with a sexual generation, the *gametophyte*. Spores which settle in a suitable damp place germinate to produce a small, green, heart-shaped structure, the gametophyte, which bears the male and female organs known respectively as *antheridia* and *archegonia*. The antheridia liberate motile sperm that swim in a film of water on the gametophyte to fertilise an egg in an archegonium. This fertilised egg then grows into a new fern, nourishing itself at first from the substance of the gametophyte until its roots penetrate the soil.

Cyathea medullaris
Mamaku/Black tree fern

Mamuku is the tallest of our tree ferns, with a great spreading and graceful crown of twenty to thirty curving fronds and a black trunk 20 m high and 30 cm through. The crown of a mature mamaku may spread over an area of 14 m across, with each lamina up to 6 m long by 2 m wide; the stipes are up to 1 m long and 9 cm through. Older black tree ferns can have their trunks buttressed at the bases with matted aerial roots which can increase the diameter to 2 m.

Mamaku is found from sea level to 600 m from the Three Kings Islands south through the North, South and Stewart Islands and the Chatham Islands, and also occurs in the Pacific from Fiji to Pitcairn Island.

1

2

3

5

6

7

Fig 1 A typical stand of *C. medullaris*. These black tree ferns were growing along the Billy Goat Track in the Kauaeranga Valley, November 1970.

Fig 2 A fine grove of mamaku in Waipoua Forest, April 1979.

Fig 3 A tall mamaku growing in Waipoua Forest. As the tree gets older the trunk develops distinct hexagonal patterns; they are scars left by falling leaves.

Fig 4 The graceful curving crown of a black tree fern growing in the Maungamaku Gorge, April 1979. The mamaku has been described by H. B. Dobbie as one of the handsomest tree ferns in the world.

Fig 5 The stipe of the black tree fern is densely clothed at its base with long brown scales. These show clearly here, as do the young unfurling fronds.

Fig 6 Portion of a rachis with a secondary rachide showing the clothing of brownish hairs typical of mamaku, the arrangement of the pinnae and the form of the pinnules. This is the upper surface.

Fig 7 The lower surface of a portion of a rachis, a secondary rachide and pinnules showing scales.

Fig 8 Pinnules of mamaku with sori. They are positioned away from the pinnule margin. Three times natural size.

8

Cyathea smithii/Katote/Soft tree fern
C. cunninghamii/Punui/Gully fern
C. milnei
C. kermadecensis

C. smithii is a very delicate and beautiful tree fern with a caudex reaching 8 m high and up to 30 cm through. The soft, tender fronds are 1.5 – 2.75 m long and 50 – 100 cm wide. When they wither they often persist as a "skirt" of dead stipes around the caudex beneath the new leaves. This tree fern is found in damp places in forests from near sea level to at least 1,000 m from Mangonui south through the North, South, Stewart, Auckland and Chatham Islands.

C. cunninghamii is a tall, graceful tree fern similar to mamaku but with a more slender trunk, much more slender stipes and fronds that appear like a delicate latticework when viewed from below. The trunk lacks the hexagonal scar pattern of mamaku and does not have the skirt of dead stipes characteristic of *C. smithii*. The species ranges from Mangonui to Fiordland and the Chatham Islands, although it is largely confined to the damper west coast of both main islands. It occurs sparingly and rather locally from sea level to 1,000 m in forest, often in gullies near streams.

C. cunninghamii grows to 20 m high with the caudex 20 cm through at the base and with matted aerial roots. The more or less straight fronds of this attractive tree fern are 2 – 3 m long by 60 – 100 cm wide; they are darker green above and paler below.

Fig 1 The upper surface of a portion of a frond of *C. smithii* showing the finely pointed apex and the fine, pointed pinnae of this species.

Fig 2 Lower surface of a *C. smithii* frond showing the paler colour and scales along the rachides.

Fig 3 The crown of a specimen of *C. cunninghamii* growing in the Waipoua Kauri Forest, April 1979.

Fig 4 The junction of a rachis and a secondary rachide of *C. smithii* showing the matted hairs of the upper surface and the form of the pinnules. Twice natural size.

Fig 5 The lower surface of a junction between a rachis and a secondary rachide showing the large, flat scales on both and on the rachides of the pinnules. Note the distinct venation of the pinnules. Twice natural size. The cup-shaped indusia and red star-like hairs on the undersides of the pinnae are as characteristic of *C. smithii* as the skirt of dead fronds shown in Fig 12.

1

2

3

4

5

6

7

8

9

Fig 6 Looking into the crown of *C. smithii* to show the dense masses of golden-brown scales that clothe the bases of the stipes of this tree fern.

Fig 7 The sori of *C. smithii* on the lower surfaces of the pinnulae. One and a half times natural size.

Fig 8 Portion of the upper surface of a leaf of *C. cunninghamii* showing the scales and hairs on the rachis and secondary rachides and the form of the pinnules.

Fig 9 Lower surface of a *C. cunninghamii* leaf showing the paler colour and matted hairs on the rachis and secondary rachides. This tree fern is easily identified by its hooded indusium and by the presence of white or yellow star-like hairs on the underside of the secondary rachides of the pinnae and pinnules.

Fig 10 Junction between the rachis and a secondary rachide of *C. cunninghamii* showing the scales and matted hairs on these and the hairs along the rachide of each pinnule as well as the scattered hairs on the pinnules. Twice natural size.

Fig 11 The stipes of *C. cunninghamii* are slender, dark coloured at the very base and provided with a number of long scales. One and a half times natural size.

Fig 12 A specimen of *C. smithii* growing at Kaitoke showing the characteristic "skirt" of dead stipes surrounding the trunk, rather like the ribs of a large umbrella. January 1980.

10

11

12

KERMADEC FERNS

Two further Cyathea species are found only growing in forest on Raoul (Sunday) Island of the Kermadecs. C. milnei, 2– 8 m tall, is similar to C. medullaris but with fronds up to 5.5 m long and the caudex much shorter. C. kermadecensis, which grows to 21 m tall with fronds 6 m long, has its rachis and secondary rachides deeply grooved above and clothed with silky brown hairs.

Cyathea dealbata/Ponga/Silver fern
C. colensoi/Creeping tree fern

The outstanding ponga is easily recognised by the silvery-white undersides of the lamina and bases of the stipes. It is common throughout the North, South and Chatham Islands in forest and sometimes in scrub, from sea level to 600 m.

Ponga's trunk or caudex reaches 10 m high with a basal diameter of up to 45 cm. The bases of the stipes persist for a long time below the crown as the fern grows. The upper surfaces of the rachis and the secondary rachides are covered when young with yellowish-brown hairs but become smooth as the frond ages. The fronds spread more or less horizontally; each is 2−4 m long by 60 cm to 1.2 m wide, deep green to yellow-green above and silvery or yellowish-white below. The bases of the stipes are clothed with glossy, dark-brown scales.

This is the native fern of our silver fern emblem.

C. colensoi, the creeping tree fern, is a semi-prostrate tree fern in which the caudex spreads over the ground and becomes erect only at the tip, where it reaches a height of not more than 1 m, occasionally producing short, erect caudices. The caudex roots as it creeps along the ground and is scarred by the fallen stipes. The creeping tree fern is found in forests between 600 and 1,200 m above sea level, from about Mt Hikurangi southwards through the North, South and Stewart Islands.

The fronds of *C. colensoi* are erect, the stipes densely clothed at their bases with pale awl-shaped scales up to 2.5 cm long. The rachis and secondary rachides are clothed with a mixture of reddish-brown hairs and scales, especially on the lower surfaces.

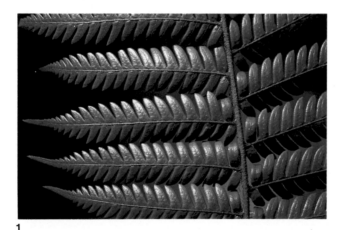

1

2

3

4

Fig 1 The portion of a young frond of a ponga fern showing the dark-green upper surface of the pinnules and the hairy secondary rachides.

Fig 2 Portion of the lower surface of a frond from another, younger fern. This shows the hairy secondary rachide and the rather yellowish-white undersurface bloom on the pinnules. Compare this bloom with the more silvery-white appearance of that in Fig 5.

5

6

7

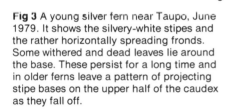

8

Fig 3 A young silver fern near Taupo, June 1979. It shows the silvery-white stipes and the rather horizontally spreading fronds. Some withered and dead leaves lie around the base. These persist for a long time and in older ferns leave a pattern of projecting stipe bases on the upper half of the caudex as they fall off.

Fig 4 Looking at the base of the crown of a ponga showing the dark-brown glossy scales at the bases of the stipes as well as the characteristic silvery-white bloom. Otari, November 1979.

Fig 5 The underside of a portion of the frond of a very silvery-white silver fern showing the hairy rachis and secondary rachide and the dense woolly bloom.

Fig 6 The sori of a silver fern.

Fig 7 A portion of the upper surface of a frond of *C. colensoi* showing the hairy and scaly rachis and secondary rachides and the form of the pinnae. The upper surfaces are clothed with occasional pale scales and matted hairs.

Fig 8 The lower surface of a portion of the rachis and secondary rachides of the creeping tree fern showing the clothing of hairs and scales.

Fig 9 A creeping tree fern growing in bush at Waipahihi, June 1979. This photograph shows how the erect fronds arise direct from the caudex.

9

10

11

12

Fig 10 A view of the crown of a creeping tree fern showing the dense clothing of long, shining scales, each about 3 cm long, around the bases of the stipes. The fronds of *C. colensoi* are 60 cm to 1.5 m long and 22.5 – 60 cm wide.

Fig 11 Pinnules of the creeping tree fern. *C. colensoi* sori are characteristically unprotected by any indusia. Three times natural size.

Fig 12 A portion of a stipe of a creeping tree fern showing some of the long awl-shaped glossy scales. Half natural size.

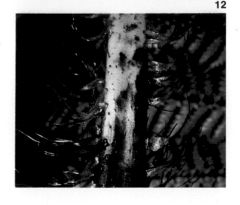

Family *Dicksoniaceae:* A family consisting of about forty-seven species, mostly tree ferns, found in the Southern Hemisphere only through Malaysia, Australia, New Caledonia, tropical America, St Helena and New Zealand.

Genus *Dicksonia:* Three endemic species of this genus occur in New Zealand. Ferns of this genus have hairs but no scales on the stipes and rachis.

Dicksonia squarrosa
Wheki

Wheki is a medium-sized tree fern with a slender caudex or trunk, slender stipes and fronds that spread more or less horizontally. It is easily recognised by the brown colour of the persistent dead fronds and by the bases of the stipes which persist down the caudex after the leaves have broken away. Plants characteristically grow in groves or colonies; they occur abundantly in forest from sea level to 760 m throughout the North, South, Stewart and Chatham Islands.

Wheki fronds are stiff and harsh to the touch. They are 1.2—1.5 m long and 60—75 cm wide, dark green above and pale yellow-green below; they are clothed with long, dark-brown, deciduous hairs up to 4 cm long. The rachis of C. *squarrosa* is rough and hairy when young but becomes smoother and hairless with age. There are no scales on the stipes and rachis.

1

2

3

4

5

Fig 1 The unfurling frond of *D. squarrosa*. The hairs on the stipe bases are typical of this species.

Fig 2 A group of wheki ferns growing at Reikorangi, near Waikanae, August 1977. Wheki is the only tree fern in New Zealand that can multiply by adventitious roots or runners. These spread out from the parent fern and give rise to buds that grow into a new fern. This new plant will grow usually about a metre from the parent fern. Small colonies of wheki can be produced in this way.

Fig 3 The apical section of a wheki frond, upper surface.

Fig 4 Lower side of the apical section of a frond. This specimen displays the typical paler colour and distinct venation of the pinnae.

Fig 5 A typical wheki fern growing in Cascades Kauri Park, Auckland, April 1979. It shows the hanging fronds and persistent stipe bases down the caudex which are characteristic of the plant.

Fig 6 Close view of the junction of the rachis and a secondary rachide of a young specimen of *D. squarrosa* showing the hairs on the upper surface. Twice natural size.

Fig 7 A portion of a rachis from a young frond showing the rachis hairs. These also extend along the lower surfaces of the secondary rachides. Three times natural size.

Fig 8 Wheki has nine to twenty or even more fronds on slender rough stipes that are hairy round their bases, as shown here.

Fig 9 The globular sori of wheki. They develop on the margins of the pinnules, almost completely covering them. Taupo, June 1979. One and a half times natural size.

6

7

8

9

Dicksonia fibrosa
Kuripaka/Wheki-ponga

This is a rather variable fern with a caudex reaching 2—6 m. It is usually densely coated with matted aerial roots that extend the diameter from 10—15 to 60 cm or more at the lower part. The fronds, not so harsh to the touch as those of *D. squarrosa,* are up to thirty or more; they have very short green stipes that are clothed round their bases with reddish-brown hairs, often thick and matted. The rachis and secondary rachides are clad with soft, pale-brown hairs that tend to disappear with age. This species is easily recognised by the "skirt" of persistent whole dead fronds surrounding the trunk below the crown. The matted aerial roots of the caudex were used by the Maori people as building slabs.

It is found from Tauranga and the mid-Waikato southwards through the South Island and the Chatham Islands, in forests from sea level to 950 m.

1

3

2

4

5

Fig 1 A portion of a frond of *D. fibrosa*, upper surface, showing the slender rachis and form of the pinnae and pinnules. The former are rather sharp pointed in this species.

Fig 2 The paler undersurface of the same frond.

Fig 3 A stout specimen of kuripaka showing the typical persistent dead leaves which remain on the trunk below the crown. This tree was growing at Waipahihi Reserve, Taupo, June 1979.

Fig 4 The sori of *D. fibrosa* are round but dense and develop in the margins of the pinnules (as do those of *D. squarrosa*) Taupo, June 1979. Two and a half times natural size.

Fig 5 Each sorus is protected by two indusium flaps which open at maturity to reveal the sporangia. Taupo, June 1979. Three times natural size.

Fig 6 A junction of the rachis and a secondary rachide showing the hairs of the upper surface. Two and a half times natural size.

Fig 7 Junction of the rachis and secondary rachide on the lower surface showing hairs on the rachis and secondary rachides of the pinnae and pinnules. About three times natural size.

Fig 8 Looking into the base of the crown of a kuripaka tree fern. This view shows clearly the short green stipes and the matted, dense, brown hairs around their bases.

6

7

8

Dicksonia lanata

This is a prostrate or erect tree fern with a caudex up to 5 cm in diameter and, when erect, up to 2 m high. The stipes are 20–60 cm long, being about half as long as the frond, which is 30–50 cm long. The stipes around the base are clothed with long, golden-brown hairs. When young the rachis is clad with soft, woolly brown hairs above and below; it becomes hairless with age.

   D. lanata is found from Mangonui to Jacksons Bay and Banks Peninsula, in forests from sea level to about 1,000 m. It is, however, local in its distribution.

1

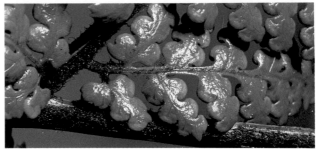

3

2

4

Fig 1 The upper surface of a portion of the frond of *D. lanata* showing the slender rachis and the form of the pinnae and pinnules.

Fig 2 A colony of *D. lanata* growing in the Waipahihi Reserve, Taupo, August 1979.

Fig 3 A junction of the rachis and a secondary rachide showing the fine, woolly hairs, which also extend on to the rachides of the pinnules. Three times natural size.

Fig 4 The sori of *D. lanata* are usually one to each ultimate segment of the pinnule. Here the indusium flaps are opening to reveal the sporangia inside. Taupo, June 1979. Three times natural size.

Fig 5 The paler lower surface of a portion of the frond in Fig 1.

Fig 6 The stipe bases of *D. lanata*. This photograph shows the clothing of hairs which can each be up to 2 cm long.

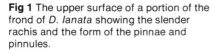

5

6

Maps
Glossary
Bibliography
Index of common names
General index

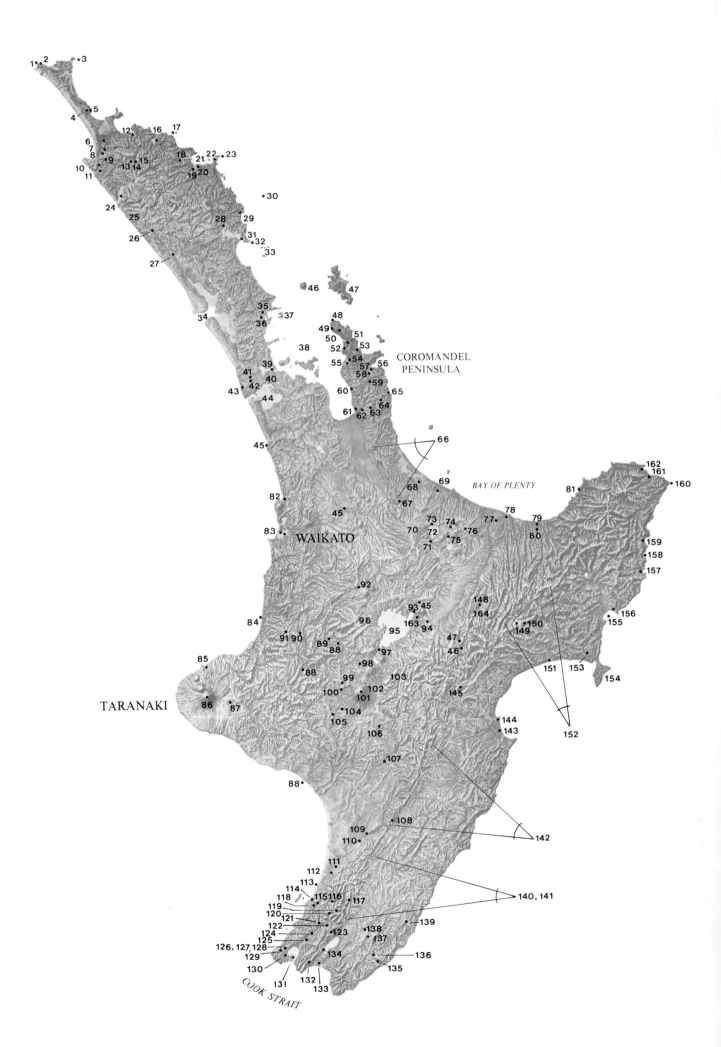

COROMANDEL
PENINSULA

BAY OF PLENTY

WAIKATO

TARANAKI

COOK STRAIT

North Island

NORTH-WEST NELSON

COOK STRAIT

MARLBOROUGH

WESTLAND

SOUTH WESTLAND

NORTH CANTERBURY

Chatham Is. 865km

CANTERBURY

SOUTH CANTERBURY

FIORDLAND

OTAGO

SOUTHLAND

FOVEAUX
STRAIT

STEWART ISLAND

South Island

Glossary

Although technical terms have been kept to a minimum in this book there are many that cannot be avoided. The following glossary explains terms that may be met with.

abortive: imperfectly developed

achene: a small dry fruit that does not split open to release its seed

acicular: with a needle-shaped apex

acuminate: tapering to a fine point

acute: sharply pointed

adventitious: arising irregularly or from an unusual position

alternate: arising singly along an axis

anastomosing: joining up to form networks or loops

androecium: all the stamens together

anterior: occurring on the side away from the axis so as to appear in front

anther: that part of a stamen which bears the pollen

apetalous: without petals

apex: the free end or tip of a leaf or other organ

apiculate: with a short, more or less slender, flexible point

apposite: side by side

appressed: closely and flatly pressed against a surface

arcuate: curved or archlike in shape

aril: an appendage to a seed, often swollen and pulpy

ascending: growing upwards, usually at a narrow angle from the vertical

attenuate: gradually tapering to an apex

auricled: an ear-shaped lobe or appendage

axil: the upper angle between two dissimilar parts

axillary: occurring in the axil

axis: the main stem or central vertical or longitudinal support

barbed: bearing a backwardly directed sharp hook or bristle

beak: a prominent extension of a part or organ

berry: a fleshy fruit containing a number of seeds but not a "stone"

biennial: living two years but flowering only in the second year

bifid: divided into two parts

bifurcate: forked into two sections

bipinnate: leaves that are twice pinnate

bisexual: flowers with both sexes functional

blade: the expanded part of a leaf, petal or sepal

bloom: a white powdery cladding

bract: a modified, often much reduced leaf found especially as scale-like leaves in an inflorescence

bristle: a stout, stiff hair

calyx: the outer, usually greenish-coloured whorl of parts in a flower

campanulate: bellshaped

canaliculate: channelled or grooved along its length

capitulum: the dense head-like inflorescence of Compositae

capsule: a dry fruit that splits open to release its seeds

carinate: having a prominent median rib

carpel: the female unit of a flower consisting of the ovary, style and stigma

carpidium: the cone-scale of the Gymnospermae

catkin: a spike-like inflorescence of usually unisexual flowers on a pendulous axis

caudate: with a tail-like appendage

chlorophyll: the green-colouring material within the leaf cells

ciliolate: with fringing hairs along the margin

cladode: a flattened stem which functions as a leaf

compound: formed of several similar parts

compressed: flattened

cone: the fruiting parts of a conifer

connate: two similar parts joined together

cordate: heart-shaped with the notch at the base

coriaceous: of a leathery texture

corolla: the inner whorl of floral parts, the petals

corymb: a more or less flat-topped raceme

costa: the midvein of a leaf

cotyledon: the seed leaf of an embryo plant

crenate: with shallow, rounded teeth

crenulate: with very small shallow, rounded teeth

cultivar: a horticultural variety or cultivated form of a species

cuneate: wedge-shaped

cupule: a cup-shaped structure

cyme: an inflorescence, usually symmetrical, with the oldest flowers innermost

deciduous: loosing its leaves in the autumn

deflexed: bent sharply downwards

dehiscent: splitting open when ripe to shed seeds

dentate: with sharp teeth at right angles to the margin

denticle: a very small tooth

denticulate: with very small teeth along the margin

depressed: flattened from above

dichotomous: forking into two branches

digitate: spreading from the centre outwards as in the fingers of a hand

dimorphic: occurring in two forms

dioecious: having the male and the female on different plants

disk: the central mass of fertile florets in the capitulum of Compositae

distichous: arranged in two opposite rows but lying in the same plane

divaricating: intertangled stems spreading at a wide angle

divergent: spreading away from one another

domatia: small pits on the lower surface of a leaf or between the mid and lateral veins

dorsal: pertaining to the back in relation to the axis

drupe: a fruit with a "stone" or seed surrounded by a fleshy layer

emarginate: with a shallow notch at the apex

endemic: native to a particular country or region

entire: with a continuous margin without teeth

epimatium: in Podocarpaceae, a scale partly fused with the integument and more or less surrounding the ovule

epiphyte: a plant growing on another but not organically connected to it

excurrent: passing out beyond the apex

exotic: not native; of foreign origin

exstipulate: without stipules

falcate: sickle shaped

fascicled: with a close or tight bundle or cluster

fastigiate: with the branches erect and close to the axis

filiform: thread-like or very slender

fimbriate: fringed

flabelliform: with a fan-like shape

flagelliform: long and very slender

flexuous: with a wavy or zigzag form

floret: a small individual flower in the capitulum of Compositae

foliaceous: leaflike in form

foliate: leaved

foliolate: bearing leaflets

frond: a leaf, especially of ferns

fruit: the ripened ovary containing the seeds

fuscous: of a brown or grey-brown colour

glabrous: without hairs of any kind

glaucous: of a distinctly bluish-green colour

gynoecium: one or more carpels making up the female part of a flower

habit: the general appearance of a tree or plant

habitat: the kind of place in which a tree or plant grows

hyaline: thin and translucent

hypocotyl: the axis of a seedling between the cotyledons and the root

imbricate: overlapping like the tiles on a roof

imparipinnate: a pinnate leaf with a single terminal pinna

indehiscent: not splitting open to release its seeds

indigenous: native to a particular area and not introduced

indusium: a tissue outgrowth covering the sorus of some ferns

inflorescence: a general term for the flowering parts

internode: the part of an axis between two nodes

involucre: one or more whorls of bracts surrounding a cluster of flowers

involute: rolled inwards

keel: a sharp central ridge

lamina: a thin, flat portion especially of a leaf, but may be applied to other organs

lanceolate: lance-shaped

leaflet: one element of a compound leaf

liane: a woody climbing plant

linear: very narrow with parallel margins

micropyle: a minute opening in an ovule through which the pollen tube enters

midrib: the main or central vein of a leaf

monoecious: having unisexual flowers with male and female on the same plant

mucronate: with a short, sharp tip

nectary: a gland near the base of the stamens that exudes the fluid called nectar

nerve: a strand of conducting or strengthening tissue in a leaf

node: the place on a stem marked by the attachment of a leaf or leaves

nut: an indehiscent, single-seeded fruit with woody surrounding layer

oblique: with the sides unequal

obtuse: blunt

ochraceous: ochre-coloured

opposite: (of leaves) with a pair arising at the same level on opposite sides of the stem

ovary: that part of the gynoecium that encloses the ovules

ovate: egg-shaped and attached by the broad end

ovule: the structure that contains the female sex cell or egg

palmate: radially lobed or divided

panicle: an indeterminate branched inflorescence

patent: spreading at right angles to the axis

pedicel: the stalk of an individual flower

perfect: of flowers with both male and female parts present and functional

perianth: the sepals and petals of a flower taken together

petiole: the stalk of a leaf

phyllary: an individual bract in the whorl of bracts surrounding the capitulum of the Compositae

phylloclade: a flattened stem which functions as a leaf

piliferous: bearing hairs

pilose: bearing soft, coarse hairs

pinna: a primary division of a pinnate leaf, as in a fern

pinnate: compound with the parts arranged on either side of the axis

pistil: the female reproductive parts of a flower

pneumatophore: a breathing root

procumbent: flat along the ground without rooting

protogynous: flowers in which the pistils are receptive before the anthers have ripe pollen

pubescent: clad in short, soft hairs

pungent: ending in a sharp, stiff point

pustular: bearing minute blister-like processes

raceme: an unbranched indeterminate inflorescence

rachide: the axis of the pinna or pinnule of a fern leaf

rachis: the axis or main stalk of a fern leaf

ray-florets: the outer ring of florets in the capitulum of Compositae

receptacle: the expanded apical portion of the stalk on which the flower is borne

reniform: kidney-shaped

retuse: with a rounded apex having a small notch

reversion shoot: a branch on an adult plant bearing juvenile-type leaves

revolute: rolled outwards or to the lower side

rhachis: the axis of an inflorescence or of a compound leaf

rhizome: an underground spreading stem

rugose: wrinkled

sagittate: in the form of an arrow head

serrate: sharply toothed

serrulate: with very small, sharp teeth

sessile: without any stalk

sorus: a cluster of sporangia as occurs in ferns

spathulate: spoon-shaped

spike: an unbranched, indeterminate, elongate inflorescence with sessile flowers

spine: a stout, woody, sharp-pointed process

sporangiophore: a stalk bearing a sporangium

sporangium: a sac or similar structure containing spores

spore: a simple asexual reproductive body, usually of one cell as in ferns

sporophyte: a plant which bears asexual spores; in ferns the ordinary plant

stamen: the pollen-bearing organ of flowers

staminode: a stamen that has no pollen usually without an anther

standard: the upper broad adaxial petal of a papilionaceous flower

stellate: star-shaped

stigma: that part of the carpel that is receptive to pollen

stipes: that part of a fern leaf corresponding to the petiole

stipule: a scale-like or leaf-like appendage at the base of a leaf petiole; usually in pairs stoma: a pore in the leaf epidermis through which gases pass

stramineus: straw-coloured

striate: having a longitudinal line or minute ridge

strobilus: a cone-like structure bearing reproductive organs

style: the elongated part of a carpel between the ovary and the stigma

tepal: an individual member of the perianth of a flower

terete: circular in cross section and usually cylindrical and tapering

terminal: borne at the end of a stem and usually limiting its growth

tomentose: having a covering of soft, matted, appressed hairs

tomentum: a dense covering of more or less matted, appressed, soft hairs

trifoliate: having three leaves

trifoliolate: having three leaflets

trifurcate: having three forks or branches

trimorphic: occurring in three forms

triquetrous: triangular in cross section but with the faces more or less concave

truncate: with the apex appearing as cut squarely across

tubercle: a small wart-like swelling

umbel: a more or less umbrella-shaped inflorescence with its pedicels arising from a common centre

uncinate: hooked at the tip

undulate: being wavy in a plane at right angles to the surface

unisexual: having only one sex

vein: a strand of conducting and usually strengthening tissue in a leaf

venation: the arrangement of the veins in a leaf

verticillate: arranged in a whorl around an axis

villous: being clad in long, soft hairs that are not matted together

whorl: an arrangement of three or more parts at the same level around an axis

Bibliography

Allan, H. H., *Flora of New Zealand* Vol. 1. Govt. Printer, Wellington, 1961.

Baylis, G. T. S., *Pennantia baylisiana* (Oliver) Baylis comb. nov. *N.Z. Jour. Bot.* 15 (2) 1977, pp. 511-512.

Brooker, S. G. & Cooper, R. C., *New Zealand Medicinal Plants*. Handbook Akld. War Memorial Museum. Unity Press, Auckland, 1961.

Cheeseman, T. F., *Manual of the New Zealand Flora*. Govt. Printer, Wellington, 1925.

Cockayne, L. & Turner, E. Phillips, *The Trees of New Zealand*. Govt. Printer, Wellington, 1958.

Cockayne, L., *New Zealand Plants and Their Story*. Govt. Printer, Wellington, 1910.

Cockayne, L., *The Vegetation of New Zealand*. "Die Vegetation der Erde XIV", 3rd ed. Engelmann, Weinheim, 1958.

Couper, R. A., Spores and Pollen Grains in Palaeobotanical Research in N.Z. *Bull. Wgtn. Bot. Soc.* No. 25 Oct. 1951, pp. 2-5.

Couper, R. A., The Spore and Pollen Flora of the Cocos-bearing Beds, Mangonui, North Auckland, *Trans. Roy. Soc. N.Z.*, 79 1952, pp. 340-348.

Couper, R. A. and McQueen, D. R., Pliocene and Pleistocene Plant Fossils of New Zealand and their Climatic Interpretation, *N.Z. Jour. Sci. & Tech.* Ser. B. 35 (5) 1954, pp. 399-420.

Couper, R. A., Distribution of Proteaceae, Fagaceae and Podocarpaceae in some Southern Hemisphere Cretaceous and Tertiary Beds. *N.Z. Jour. Sci. & Tech.*, Ser. B. 35 (3) 1953, pp. 247-250.

Couper R. A. and Harris, W. F., Pliocene and Pleistocene Plant Microfossils from Drillholes near Frankton, New Zealand. *N.Z. Jour. Geology and Geophysics*, 3 (1) 1960, pp. 15-22.

Crookes, M. & Dobbie, H. B., *New Zealand Ferns*. Whitcombe and Tombs, Christchurch, 1963.

De Laubenfels, D. J., A taxonomic revision of the genus *Podocarpus*. *Blumel* 30 (2) 1985, pp. 251-278.

Eagle, A., *Eagle's Trees and Shrubs of New Zealand in Colour*. Collins, Auckland and London, 1975. Second series, 1982.

Edgar, E. and Connor, H.E., Nomina Nova III, 1977-1982. *N.Z. Jour. Bot.* 21 1983, pp. 421-441.

Fisher, Muriel E., Satchell, E. and Watkins, Janet M., *Gardening with New Zealand Plants, Shrubs and Trees*. Collins, Auckland and London, 1970.

Fleming, C. A., New Zealand Biogeography. A Paleontologist's Approach, *Tuatara*, 10 (2) 1962, pp. 53-109.

Godley, E. J., Botany of the Southern Zone Exploration, 1847-1891. *Tuatara*, 18 (2) 1970, pp. 41-43.

Heath, E. & Chinnock, R. J., *Ferns and Fern Allies of New Zealand*. Reed, Wellington, 1974.

Heywood, V. H., *Flowering Plants of the World*. Oxford University Press, Oxford, London and Melbourne, 1978.

Johnson, Hugh, *The International Book of Trees*. Mitchell Beazley, London, 1973.

Laing, R. M. and Blackwell, E. W., *Plants of New Zealand*, 4th ed. Whitcombe and Tombs, Christchurch, 1940.

Leathart, Scott, *Trees of the World*. Hamlyn, London, 1977.

McLintock, A. H., *An Encyclopaedia of New Zealand*, 3 vols., Govt. Printer, Wellington, 1966.

McQueen, D. R., Flowering Plants in New Zealand's Fossil Flora. *N.Z. Sci. Rev.* 9 1951, pp. 188-189.

Martin, W., The New Zealand Tree Broom. *Jour. N.Z. Inst. Hort.* 5 (2) 1935, pp. 23-27.

Martin, W., The Vegetation of Marlborough. Reprinted from the *Marlborough Express*, 1932.

Metcalf, L. J., *The Cultivation of New Zealand Trees and Shrubs*. Reed, Wellington, 1972.

Moore, L. B. & Edgar, E., *Flora of New Zealand*, Vol. 2. Govt. Printer, Wellington, 1970.

Moore, L. B. & Irwin, J. B., *The Oxford Book of New Zealand Plants*. Oxford University Press, Wellington, Oxford and New York, 1978.

Nordenstam, B., Taxonomic studies in the tribe Senecioneae (Compositae). *Opera Botanica*, Vol. 44, pp. 1-84, 1978.

Oliver, W. R. B., Botanical Discovery in New Zealand. *Post-Primary School Bulletin*, 5, No. 12 1951. Govt. Printer, Wellington.

Poole, A. L. & Adams, N. M., *Trees and Shrubs of New Zealand*. Govt. Printer, Wellington, 1963.

Reed, A. H., *The New Story of the Kauri*. 4th ed. Reed, Wellington, 1964.

Reichle, E., *Analysis of Temperate Forest Ecosystems*. Springer-Verlag, Berlin and Heidelberg, 1970.

Richards, E. C., *Our New Zealand Trees and Flowers*. Simpson and Williams, Christchurch, 1956.

Salmon, J. T., *New Zealand Flowers and Plants in Colour*. Reed, Wellington, 1963.

Sampson, F. B., Studies on the Monimiaceae II Floral Morphology of *Laurelia novaezelandiae*. *N.Z. Jour. Bot.* 7 1969, pp. 214-240.

St. Barbe Baker, Richard, *Famous Trees of New Zealand*. Reed, Wellington, 1965.

Sykes, W. R., Kermadec Island Flora. An Annotated Checklist. *D.S.I.R. Bulletin* 219, 1977.

Taylor, G. Marie, A Key to the Coprosmas of New Zealand. *Tuatara* 9 1961, pp. 31-63.

Wardle, P., The Taxonomy and Distribution of the Stipulate species of *Pseudopanax* in New Zealand. *N.Z. Jour. Bot.* 6 (2) 1968, pp. 226-236.

Wards, Ian, *New Zealand Atlas*. Govt. Printer, Wellington, 1976.

Willis, J. C., *A Dictionary of the Flowering Plants & Ferns*. 8th ed. revised by H. K. Airey Shaw. Cambridge University Press, Cambridge, 1973.

Index of common names

This special index contains the common names of the New Zealand tree species.

General index

The names in bold italic are those of the native tree species featured in this book.